CREATING THE DYNAMIC CLASSROOM
A HANDBOOK FOR TEACHERS

SUSAN SCHWARTZ   MINDY POLLISHUKE   SECOND EDITION

PEARSON

Toronto

Vice-President, Editorial Director: Gary Bennett
Editor-in-Chief: Michelle Sartor
Editor, Humanities and Social Sciences: Joel Gladstone
Marketing Manager: Kathaleen McCormick
Supervising Developmental Editor: Madhu Ranadive
Developmental Editor: Allison McDonald
Project Manager: Ashley Patterson
Manufacturing Manager: Susan Johnson
Production Editor: Ridhi Mathur (Cenveo Publisher Services)
Copy Editor: Andrew Borkowski
Proofreaders: Jennifer McIntyre, Nancy Carroll
Compositor: Cenveo Publisher Services
Permissions Researcher: Allison McDonald
Art Director: Julia Hall
Cover Designer: Anthony Leung
Cover Image: iStockphoto

10 9 8 7 6 5 4 3 2 1 EB

Library and Archives Canada Cataloguing in Publication

Schwartz, Susan, 1951–
    Creating the dynamic classroom : A handbook for teachers / Susan Schwartz, Mindy Pollishuke. — 2nd ed.

Includes index.
ISBN 978-0-13-284773-5

    1. Teaching—Handbooks, manuals, etc. I. Pollishuke, Mindy, 1951– II. Title.

LB1025.3.S347 2012   371.102   C2011-906905-9

ISBN 978-0-13-284773-5

Contents

Foreword v

Preface to the Revised Edition vii

Acknowledgments xi

About the Authors xii

Introduction 1

1 Classroom Design and Organization 6

Creating the Design and Organization of the Classroom 7

2 Timetabling 17

Creating Timetabling Possibilities 18

3 An Inclusive Classroom Atmosphere 27

Knowing Your Learners 29

Being Proactive 37

Responding to Behaviours 56

Responding to Bullying 62

4 Assessment in a Differentiated Curriculum 69

Understanding How Children Learn and Develop 71

Collecting and Analyzing Assessment Data 75

Strategies and Tools for Assessment 76

Storing Your Assessment Data 103

5 Designing Your Curriculum 104

Creating Long-range Plans 108

Creating Unit Plans 116

Creating Lesson Plans 126

Creating Weekly and Daily Plans 136

Preparing for the Occasional Teacher 139

6 Effective Learning Stations—Small Group Differentiated Learning 143

Creating Effective Learning Stations 144
Managing Learning Stations in Your Classroom 149
Assessing the Learning at Stations 162

7 Out-of-Classroom Excursions—Experiencing the Wider Community 165

Planning Out-of-classroom Excursions 166

8 Literacy and Language Learning 175

The Oral Communication Process 177
The Reading Process 183
The Writing Process 211
Creating a Language-rich Environment 233
Media and Other Literacies 240

9 Technology in a Rapidly Changing World 245

Creating a Technology-rich Classroom 247

10 Evaluating and Reporting Student Progress 259

Determining Student Achievement 261
Preparing Report Cards 264
Reporting Student Progress 265

11 Creating Community—Partnerships with Parents 270

Communicating with Parents 272
Sharing the Learning with Parents 285
Involving Parents in Your Program 291
Homework: A Window into Your Classroom 296

12 "Your Mountain is Waiting"—A Career in Education 310

Preparing Your Application Package 311
Preparing for the Interview Process 318
The Interview Process 323
Landing that Position—You have been hired! 325
Tips for Occasional Teaching 332
A Continuum of Professional Growth 334

References 341

Foreword

Susan Schwartz and Mindy Pollishuke are true professional educators, always tuned in to the changes that confront and sometimes challenge schools and teachers, and, of course, their students, who are growing up in a very different world from even five years ago. New directions and directives in educational policy, guidelines, learning expectations, diversity, equity, and assessment strategies have altered the dynamics of today's classrooms, and these two author/educators have developed their newly revised book to address and support teachers and students in teaching and learning in the 21st century.

This resource package will be a great help to teachers who want to rework and rethink their classroom programs and environments, in light of the changes in our profession, and because we need to constantly examine our practice and refine our teaching. How fortunate we are to have Susan and Mindy mentoring us with new and pertinent information and research for organizing, planning, implementing, and assessing a dynamic classroom that will benefit all our students.

These experienced educators provide a philosophical underpinning for why good teaching requires such a carefully considered approach to the set-up and the running of an effective classroom. An understanding of the "nuts and bolts" of how a classroom works best is exactly what teachers require if they want to focus their teaching time on the children and their different needs. By building a cooperative, collaborative, and safe place called school, we can ensure that we offer a program so professional that parents will recognize, value, and support our contributions to the education of their children. And, of course, the children will want to be there, secure in their knowledge of the way the classroom functions, of the schedule of activities, and of their own responsibilities. They will feel the satisfaction of being in a professional educator's classroom.

Someone just visiting a classroom would not necessarily understand the preplanning and preparation that go into the running of an effective learning environment for 25 or so young people. Fortunately, since Susan and Mindy have read, researched, and reflected on their own educational experiences and observations as teachers, consultants, administrators, and university instructors, they are able to present us with this wide-ranging guide to creating a dynamic classroom, a distillation of the complexities of setting up and maintaining a teaching/learning environment that functions as contemporary educational theories would suggest.

This book offers organizational strategies, teaching techniques, options for helping with management, discipline, and handling bullying. It contains designs and diagrams for classroom set-ups and differentiated support, strategies and tools for diagnostic, formative, and summative assessment, book lists for curriculum connections, and forms or templates for recording and communicating, some of which are available on the Text Enrichment Site. As well, suggestions for incorporating technology and media throughout the curriculum address the concerns of the teachers I meet, and I know that *Creating the Dynamic Classroom: A Handbook for Teachers,* Second Edition, will help them to develop a thoughtful and practical approach to establishing an effective and engaging classroom, with the children at the centre.

Children are, by definition, spontaneous creatures, and for teachers, this reality poses particular challenges. How can we set up school experiences that promote learning while at the same time allowing for the developmental and explorative nature of childhood? One suggestion would be to organize the place of learning so that both our time and strength, and their energies, somehow coalesce. *That is the hallmark of a dynamic classroom,* and this book offers us both careful direction and concrete help in achieving that aim, for experienced teachers, and for those new to our profession. We are fortunate indeed to have Susan Schwartz and Mindy Pollishuke providing us with support in our determination to be true professionals in our classrooms.

David Booth
Professor of Education, Ontario Institute for Studies in Education, University of Toronto

Preface to the Revised Edition

Welcome to the new and updated edition of *Creating the Dynamic Classroom: A Handbook for Teachers,* Second Edition. This revised edition is our attempt to continue to help you develop and refine your practice as you strive to create a dynamic and inclusive environment for your students. This book, along with our previous work, grew out of our profound interest in helping both new and experienced teachers navigate their journeys through the multitude of theories and philosophies about teaching and learning, make sense of the new initiatives that consistently emerge in education today, and understand the many rules, regulations, and guidelines confronting them.

Over two decades have passed since we wrote *Creating the Child-centred Classroom*, and it has been over five years since we wrote *Creating the Dynamic Classroom: A Handbook for Teachers.* Both texts were designed as practical tools to help pre-service and practising teachers create active, holistic, classroom environments and programs. Educators at all levels have repeatedly told us how much they have benefitted from the knowledge and practical understandings our books have given them.

We have continued our pursuits and educational endeavours, continuously striving to bring theory and practice together in a manageable way. Both of us have experienced the joy of working with enthusiastic teacher candidates in pre-service teacher education programs—Mindy previously as course director at the York University Faculty of Education's Concurrent program, and currently as instructor and coordinator with the Bachelor of Education (B.Ed.) program at the Ontario Institute for Studies in Education of the University of Toronto (OISE), and Susan currently as instructor with the Master of Teaching program at OISE and previously as instructor and coordinator with the OISE B.Ed. program. Both of us have also enjoyed working with teachers new to the profession—Mindy worked with new teachers in her role as a literacy consultant with the Toronto District School Board (TDSB). She was also the first Coordinator for Support for Beginning Teachers in the TDSB, initiating and developing an Induction and Mentoring Program that has become a model for programs in other jurisdictions across the country. Susan worked with new teachers in her past roles as consultant, and then as vice-principal and principal in both the elementary and secondary panels. These experiences have helped us realize just how useful such texts as *Creating the Child-centred Classroom* and *Creating the Dynamic Classroom* have been to new teachers and to experienced and seasoned educators and leaders, as well as to course directors and faculty at the university and college levels. This thinking led us, with enthusiasm and with fresh eyes and vision, to revisit *Creating the Dynamic Classroom*, and to bring you a more updated revised edition.

We hope you will find this new book, *Creating the Dynamic Classroom: A Handbook for Teachers,* Second Edition, to be just as useful as our previous resources. Based on positive and constructive feedback from educators who used our earlier books, we use a similar format in this book that highlights important understandings about teaching and learning. We continue to include practical and easy-to-follow classroom-tested strategies and sample tasks. Useful templates for activities, letters, and forms for student and teacher use continue to be found throughout the book, and are also available to you on an accompanying online Text Enrichment Site. These templates on the site can be used as is or revised to meet your needs. Also on the Text Enrichment Site, you will find bibliographies of our favourite children's literature and recommended professional resources, organized in an accessible and reader-friendly way. For easy access, a table of contents that lists all the templates on the website can be found on the Text Enrichment Site, which also contains information that is highlighted in the book, but only fully included on the site.

Similar to our earlier editions, our new book offers a variety of recommended strategies for you to sample and implement. Please look carefully at what works for you, based on your ongoing experiences, readings, and conversations, and feel free to revise accordingly to fit your needs and interests. We ask you to reflect upon your teaching and learning needs and interests, and those of your students, ensuring that these are uppermost in your mind as you go about creating your own dynamic classroom.

Although this book focuses on elementary classroom experiences, secondary educators may find much of value here. Certainly the philosophy presented at the beginning of each chapter addresses the needs of the secondary panel, plus we made a special effort in this edition to include many classroom-tested strategies that will work with older students. University faculty, school principals, mentors, and consultants can use this handbook to facilitate their important work with new and experienced teachers. Seasoned teachers will find many ways to enhance their classroom practice, becoming "cutting-edge" practitioners

and leaders in their schools and beyond. Parents, too, may find this book helpful in providing them with a clearer understanding of the classrooms of today and tomorrow.

Creating the Dynamic Classroom: A Handbook for Teachers, Second Edition, strives to meet today's greater demands for accountability. As we experienced ongoing changes in political initiatives in education, we saw the evolution of clearly delineated learning expectations at each grade level, new units and resources produced to meet the needs of the required curriculum, a heightened awareness of equity, diversity, and social justice issues, a focus on information and content learning, a growing emphasis on standardized testing and evaluation, and a huge increase in usage of different technologies and media in society and in schools. Changes also included budget considerations across all areas of education, a rethinking of special programs, a renewed focus on the role of administration, and continued attention to how we go about the business of education. There was also an increase in parental and community involvement and awareness. We have infused this revised text with our understandings of the current climate and educational environment. We have placed an important emphasis on equity, diversity, and social justice, on a clear understanding of assessment and evaluation coupled with reporting student progress as separate, and equally, essential processes, and placed an important focus on differentiated instruction and meeting the needs, interests, and abilities of all students. In effect, this text reflects current thinking about teaching and learning, yet retains the best of the past texts.

To deal with this new, fast-changing world, either as an emerging or experienced teacher, we encourage you to continue to think about and value your own personal beliefs and understandings about how children learn and how teachers teach. Your philosophy about teaching and learning directly influences what you teach, how you teach, and ultimately, how you assist others in meeting their teaching/learning needs, so it is important that you know yourself and your beliefs. You can then program effectively and appropriately for your class of learners, reflect on your own practice on a continuous basis, and eventually become a leader as you mentor and support others in their pursuit of lifelong learning.

With these underlying beliefs, we write and present this revised book. We provide a variety of effective learning experiences, strategies, and techniques based on these concepts. We explore the learning environment and the design and organization of your classroom as an instructional strategy that plays a major role in what happens in your classroom. We look at establishing routines and an inclusive classroom atmosphere as a way of instilling respect, cooperation, and collaboration, as well as valuing each learner's contributions and backgrounds. We share ideas about designing an integrated, differentiated curriculum based on comprehensive assessment strategies that drive the design of relevant, meaningful and engaging programs. We look at effective learning stations as examples of small group differentiated learning. We highlight the need for relevant out-of-classroom learning experiences to enrich classroom practice. We examine the role of evaluation and reporting in light of the continued focus on reflective practice and accountability today. We share our views on literacy and language learning and introduce ideas for creating a balanced and effective literacy program. We highlight and provide practical strategies for dealing with technology in a fast-changing world as we acknowledge the increased role of computers and media, and the need for technological literacy in today's society. In *Creating the Dynamic Classroom: A Handbook for Teachers,* Second Edition, we share ideas on how to establish strong partnerships with parents and community, realizing that these partnerships benefit both students and the wider educational community. We feature important information on actively involving your parent population in your program, school, and in their children's education, and ensuring clear and consistent communication. We also look at homework as a window into your classroom, and emphasize the importance of different types of homework and of involving parents as active participants in the learning process.

In this revised edition, we have significantly expanded our advice and suggestions for new teachers as they embark on their first years in education, while also offering handy tips and reminders for experienced educators to use when beginning their year in a new school or in a new teaching assignment. In a new chapter, "'Your Mountain is Waiting'—Your Career in Education," we offer valuable insights into securing that sometimes elusive first teaching or leadership position. We provide valuable strategies for your journey through the employment process, including tips for ensuring that you experience a dynamic interview. Information about the use of different types of portfolios and e-portfolios are provided to enhance both the employment process and opportunities for growth and leadership. This revised edition looks at a teaching career as a continuous professional growth process beginning with pre-service teacher education, leading into the induction and mentoring process, and continuing as ongoing professional development and learning, both for teachers entering the profession and for seasoned educators looking for growth and leadership.

We wish you well on your continuing journey to create stimulating teaching and learning environments for your students. As you create a dynamic classroom, we encourage you to continue to work at developing your personal philosophy of teaching and learning. We hope that you will find this text a supportive partner in your quest to bring theory and practice together in meaningful, productive, and exciting ways!

NOTE: For the purposes of this publication the word "parents" is meant to represent parents, guardians, and other essential caregivers.

Supplements

The following supplements are available for this book.

Text Enrichment Site (www.pearsoncanada.ca/schwartz)

The Text Enrichment Site is a password-protected website that includes **Line Masters (LM),** which are indicated with the Text Enrichment Site symbol next to specific figures throughout the text. These figures are reproducible and can be downloaded from the Text Enrichment Site as Word documents, which will allow you to manipulate the content to meet your particular needs and interests. The figures are also available in .pdf format. Some line masters are described in the text only (not given in full), but are available on the website. This site also includes a table of contents that lists the line masters organized by chapter and LM number for easy access. You will also find on the Text Enrichment Site files with Recommended Teacher Resources listing texts you may find helpful, and Favourite Children's Literature, annotated and organized according to themes, such as equity, diversity, culture, names, relationships, bullying, peace, conflict, ageism, science, writing, etc. We hope you will find this website and book easily accessible and practical in your quest to create a dynamic classroom. To enter the Text Enrichment Site, simply go to **www.pearsoncanada.ca/schwartz** and type in the access code. Your access code can be found in the card packaged with this book.

CourseSmart for Instructors (978-0-13-284836-7)

CourseSmart goes beyond traditional expectations—providing instant online access to the textbooks and course materials you need at a lower cost for students. And even as students save money, you can save time and hassle with a digital eTextbook that allows you to search for the most relevant content at the very moment you need it. Whether it is evaluating textbooks or creating lecture notes to help students with difficult concepts, CourseSmart can make life a little easier. See how when you visit **www.coursesmart.com/instructors**.

Pearson Custom Library

For enrolments of at least 25 students, you can create your own textbook by choosing the chapters that best suit your own course needs. To begin building your custom text, visit **www.pearson-customlibrary.com**. You may also work with a dedicated Pearson Custom Editor to create your ideal text—publishing your own original content or mixing and matching Pearson content. Contact your local Pearson representative to get started.

CourseSmart for Students (978-0-13-284836-7)

CourseSmart goes beyond traditional expectations—providing instant online access to the textbooks and course materials you need at an average savings of 60 percent. With instant access from any computer and the ability to search your text, you will find the content you need quickly, no matter where you are, and with online tools like highlighting and note-taking, you can save time and study efficiently. See all the benefits at **www.coursesmart.com/students**.

NOTE: You will only have access to CourseSmart when you are a student, and because this text and website materials on the Text Enrichment Site will also be useful to you when you are in the teacher role, you may want to consider purchasing the hard copy text and adding it to your professional library.

Technology Specialists

Pearson's technology specialists work with faculty and campus course designers to ensure that Pearson technology products, assessment tools, and online course materials are tailored to meet your specific needs. This highly qualified team is dedicated to helping schools take full advantage of a wide range of educational resources, by assisting in the integration of a variety of instructional materials and media formats. Your local Pearson Canada sales representative can provide you with more details on this service program.

Acknowledgments

As we collaborated during many summer and vacation hours to produce this book, we were influenced and supported by so many wonderful people. A great big thank-you to the friends and colleagues who have inspired us with many conversations about teaching and learning.

To David Booth: We thank you for your wonderful sense of humour, your continuous encouragement, and for inspiring us to pursue our professional writing. We are truly honoured to have you write the Foreword to this book and acknowledge our work in such a public and positive way.

To Kimberly Pollishuke-Chernoff: Your contributions have enriched our thinking and have added depth to many of the strategies and suggestions offered throughout this book. We appreciate your ready willingness to share your knowledge and expertise, especially at the intermediate level.

To Carol Rolheiser: Special thanks for your energy, enthusiasm, guidance, and continuous modelling of the teaching/learning process.

To Julia Arnold, Maxine Bone, Bev Freedman, and Kim Gordon: Your positive attitudes and continuing friendships always help to remind us about the importance of collaboration and support.

To Kim MacKinnon: Many thanks for your valuable suggestions about technology which have helped to enrich this text.

Warm thanks to our OISE/University of Toronto "family." Your support and enthusiasm are greatly appreciated.

To the rest of our colleagues across the many boards of education in Ontario with whom we have had the privilege of partnering over the years—our sincere appreciation for your insights, professional dialogue, and ongoing encouragement as we embark on new and exciting initiatives.

Special acknowledgments to the staff, students, and parents of our partnership schools in our role as faculty advisors, and to all the new and experienced teachers and administrators with whom we have worked with over the years. Our interactions with you and your contributions to our learning have helped us to conceptualize and crystallize many of the ideas in this book.

A special thank you to the many teacher candidates with whom we have worked at OISE, University of Toronto, and at York University. Your zest for learning and enthusiasm for the teaching profession have given us the impetus to write this book in order to guide you in your journey into the world of education.

To our partners in life and love, Stephen and Amos, our loving children and grandchildren, our family and extended family, and all our close, personal friends: We appreciate your continuous patience, encouragement, and support of our efforts every step of the way. We are grateful for your love!

About the Authors

SUSAN SCHWARTZ is currently a course instructor in the Master of Teaching program at the Ontario Institute for Studies in Education (OISE), University of Toronto. Along with her 15 years in the classroom, and 9 years as a school administrator in both the elementary and secondary panels, she was and continues to be a curriculum consultant and workshop presenter across North America. Her doctoral work (2005) and research focused on portfolios and leadership. Susan is the 2005 recipient of the *Award for Distinguished Contribution to Teaching* from OISE, University of Toronto, a co-recipient of the *Jennie Mitchell Celebrate Literacy Award* from the International Reading Association and the Ontario Reading Association, and a two times *Writer's Award* winner from the Federation of Women Teachers' Association of Ontario. She is the author of *All Write: A Teacher's Guide to Writing*, co-author with Mindy Pollishuke of *Creating the Child-centred Classroom*, and *Creating the Dynamic Classroom: A Guidebook for Teachers*, and co-author with Maxine Bone of *Retelling, Relating, Reflecting, Beyond the 3 R's*, and *Beyond the 3 R's: Retelling, Relating, Reflecting, 2nd Edition* (in press).

MINDY POLLISHUKE is currently a coordinator and instructor in the pre-service teacher education program at the Ontario Institute for Studies in Education, University of Toronto. In addition to her many years as an elementary classroom teacher, Mindy was also a Generalist and Literacy Consultant for 15 years and the first Project Leader for Support of Beginning Teachers in the Toronto District School Board and continues to share her expertise as a curriculum consultant and workshop presenter across North America. She also spent three years as a Course Director for York University's Faculty of Education pre-service program. Mindy is a recent recipient of the *Friends of the Faculty Award* from York University's Faculty of Education, a co-recipient of the *Jennie Mitchell Celebrate Literacy Award* from the International Reading Association and the Ontario Reading Association, and a *Writer's Award* winner from the Federation of Women Teachers' Association of Ontario. She is the co-author with Susan Schwartz of *Creating the Child-centred Classroom* and *Creating the Dynamic Classroom: A Handbook for Teachers*.

Introduction

Welcome to our vision of the wonderful world of education! Come along with us as we take you on an exciting journey of inquiry and discovery.

As we began to map out this learning journey, we wanted to show you, in a concrete and visual way, our vision of what a dynamic classroom looks like. As educators, we need to have a sound philosophical and theoretical foundation upon which to begin building a dynamic classroom atmosphere, environment, and program. As authors and educators, we often use metaphors to represent our thinking and understandings. As we talked, wrote, drew, and experimented with a number of ideas for possible metaphors for this book, the image of the intricate pieces of a complex puzzle continuously surfaced. A puzzle has many interlocking pieces that fit together. Each piece represents a small part of the whole. We saw these puzzle pieces as the many vital components that teachers need to consider when beginning to translate their vision of a dynamic classroom into practice. As teachers, you need to have a vision of what your classroom will look like, sound like, and feel like, but this vision is often vague, intangible, and hard to put into practical application. There are many parts to teaching and learning that need to be brought together into a cohesive whole, almost like constructing a puzzle. Therefore, in this new edition, we have chosen to represent our understandings through the metaphor of a puzzle. (See Figure 1.)

Figure 1 *Puzzle Metaphor*

Just as puzzle pieces work together to create a picture, so, too, do the important partners in the educational process—the students, educators, parents, and community work together to create a dynamic, collaborative partnership. As a result, in our puzzle metaphor, we have placed these partners around the goal of lifelong learning, which is the centrepiece of our model and the ultimate goal towards which we are all working. (See Figure 2.)

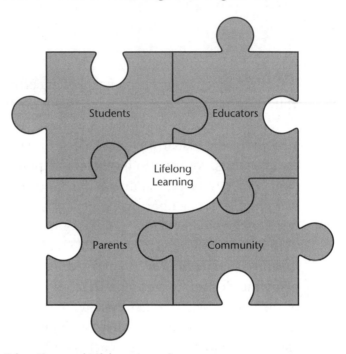

Figure 2 *Puzzle Metaphor: Partners in Education and Lifelong Learning*

All the components that create a dynamic classroom need to come together to make an effective learning environment and program. In our metaphor, the puzzle pieces represent those components of teaching and learning. We see these puzzle pieces as each of the chapters in this book: (1) Design and Organization of the Classroom, (2) Timetabling, (3) An Inclusive Classroom Atmosphere, (4) Assessment in a Differentiated Curriculum, (5) Designing Your Curriculum, (6) Effective Learning Stations—Small Group Differentiated Learning, (7) Out-of-classroom Excursions, (8) Literacy and Language Learning, (9) Technology in a Rapidly Changing World, (10) Evaluating and Reporting Student Progress, (11) Creating Community—Partnerships with Parents, and (12) "Your Mountain is Waiting"—Your Career in Education. (See Figure 3.)

However, as our puzzle pieces form the whole, we see them coming together in a circular pattern that represents to us the shape of a globe reflecting the world in which we live. We believe that creating a dynamic classroom involves more than just putting the pieces together to create a finished product. Rather, we see our puzzle continuously moving and evolving. Just as the world is continuously turning and evolving, so too should our classrooms and programs continuously evolve and change and, as educators, we need to continuously reflect on our practice and grow professionally. (See Figure 4.)

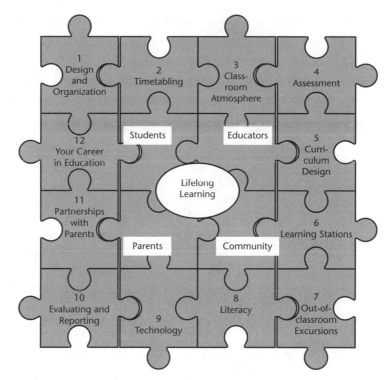

Figure 3 *Puzzle Metaphor—Components of a Dynamic Classroom*

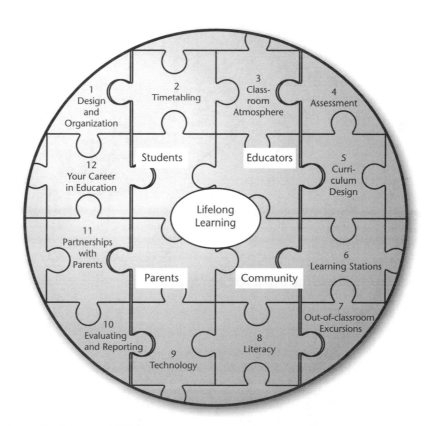

Figure 4 *Circular Puzzle Metaphor—Evolving and Moving*

Lastly, we see our globe encircled with children who are reaching out to each other and to the world through linked arms. This represents to us the ultimate goal of meaningful educational experiences, where all partners work together to create an inclusive, secure, and vibrant atmosphere, where a meaningful, relevant, and differentiated curriculum meets the needs and interests of all learners. (See Figure 5.)

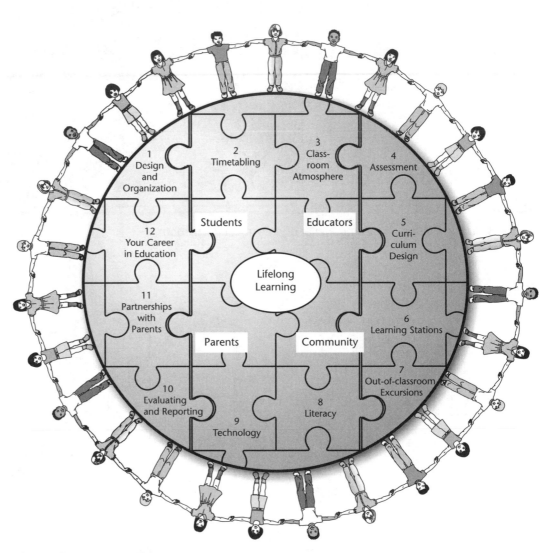

Figure 5 *Puzzle Metaphor—The Dynamic Classroom*

A Vision of a Dynamic Classroom (read with a rap beat)

Used with permission. Written by Jeremy Nusinowitz with contributions from Jeanette Jacobs, William Kearns, Natalie Killick, Gordon Robertson: Graduates of Ontario Institute for Studies in Education (OISE).

This is our dynamic classroom
It's all about respect as you will see soon
Physical set up covers it all
Areas to meet for groups large and small
Furniture, small and tight
Best of all, it's at the right height
We've collected desks in groups
And in the corner is technology soup
Computers, overheads, LCDs
And cubbies to store our resourceeeees
Plants by the window to learn about nature
Books on the shelf about nomenclature
Pillows on the rug to gather 'round
Listen to the stories, don't make a sound
Writing process is on the wall
Appropriate feedback will assist us all
Science, you hypothesize
In grade six we routinize
Hungry—go to cafeteria
Here—we eat "success criteria"
World map up on the wall
So are helping hands both big and small
A globe and aquarium make it hands-on
And the words to that "Oh Canada" song
Aboriginals—Unit One
Native Art on the wall will keep it all fun
Space, Unit Two, Up in the sky
In grade six you'll be soaring high . . .
To Mercury, Venus, even Mars
Open up your mind and reach for the stars
In and out bins to show your stuff
And one for Goose paper when the work is rough
Expectations make it clear
Follow these rules, it'll be a great year
In our class you'll learn dynamically of course
Because we go by the book, by Pollishuke and Schwartz

1 Classroom Design and Organization

The classroom environment that you create has a profound effect on the social, emotional, physical, and intellectual development of the learners you teach. To gain a positive attitude towards school and learning, your students must have visual stimulation, organization, space, and a feeling of inclusion, warmth, and security. Devoting time and energy to the design and organization of your classroom is well worthwhile. In fact, the learning environment can be and should be regarded as **an important teaching or instructional strategy**. How you design and organize the physical environment plays an important role in determining how your students will respond, learn, and relate to one another and to you. An engaging environment is more likely to invite students to become involved and excited about learning. Just a few changes in the physical set-up can bring about major results and can influence the sense of community in the classroom.

We suggest you think carefully about your room arrangement and organization, and how you can make it work for you and your students.

One of the first things to do is to **designate a large group meeting area** where a variety of learning experiences will take place with the whole class. In this area, an essential part of your program will occur, including direct instruction, chanting, singing, presenting, sharing, and discussion. Bringing your students together to an area where they are in close proximity to you and to one another encourages open dialogue, a feeling of inclusion, group interaction, and a relaxed flow of ideas.

Next, it is important to consider how to **organize student desks and tables**. You will want to maximize the amount of space you have, ensure that students can work together in cooperative groups, and create areas for independent reflective work. You may want to set up specific work areas, learning stations or centres in the room where students will share, cooperate, and work together with a variety of materials and resources.

Setting up **areas for materials** that students will use, as well as for **technology equipment**, will help you use the physical characteristics of your room to best advantage. Placing a variety of **storage facilities** around the room or near the work areas provides students with easy access to resources and materials. It also encourages student independence, motivation, and leadership.

A variety of **display areas**, with student work appearing on bulletin boards or walls, hanging from the ceiling, or resting on tables or shelves, enhances the appearance of your classroom and sparks interest in learning. An organized look to your classroom and clearly defined and accessible areas help students feel safe and secure. Motivation to achieve often increases as students see their work on display and feel pride and ownership.

Make sure that **all your students are represented** in the environment you create in your classroom. Accessibility within the set-up of the classroom should ensure ease of access for students who have any physical limitations. The pictures, posters, signs, resources, and materials should reflect the diversity in your classroom as well as in the school, district, and wider global community. By displaying student work samples, you reflect the diverse backgrounds and cultures in the classroom and you encourage all students to feel valued and part of a community of learners.

Creating the Design and Organization of the Classroom

✦ **Survey your classroom** to determine its strengths and limitations. Note the physical layout of the classroom and the availability of equipment, including:

- windows
- doors
- intercom system and/or classroom phone
- lighting
- cupboards
- coat hooks
- cubbies
- bulletin boards
- wall display space

- electrical outlets
- audio-visual equipment
- computer technology
- a teacher's desk
- student desks
- tables
- chairs
- bookshelves
- filing cabinets

- ✦ Establish a **large group meeting area** (preferably carpeted).

- ✦ Include within this large group meeting area a teacher's chair, a chart stand, a chalk or white board, and writing materials within easy reach.

- ✦ Ensure that you have **ample storage areas** for your professional resources and materials so that you have easy access when planning and preparing your lessons. Organization is the key! (See Figure 1.1.)

Figure 1.1 *Organizational Ideas for Teacher Resources and Materials*
Source: Used with permission. Kimberly Pollishuke, York Region District School Board (YRDSB).

- ✦ Collect the **audio-visual equipment and computer technology** that will be housed in your room, such as a CD player, overhead projector and screen, interactive display boards, document camera, computers, etc., and decide where these will be placed to their best advantage and use. Make sure these are close to electrical outlets. If possible, have a bank of computers in one area to facilitate specific teaching of computer skills. (Refer to Chapter 9: Technology in a Rapidly Changing World.)

- ✦ Set up a **work area** (near a sink, if possible) for art, paint, and craft materials and activities. In this area, prepare bins of craft and junk materials, such as paper (construction, tissue, wallpaper, shiny paper), felt, pipe cleaners, tin foil, string, wool, and ribbon. Storing glue, tape, scissors, rulers, and staplers in labelled bins or on the counter permits easy access and cleanup.

✦ Set up any desired permanent **learning stations** that will be used year-long. (Refer to Chapter 6: Effective Learning Stations—Small Group Differentiated Learning.)

✦ Look at the furniture and storage equipment available to see if these are the **appropriate size and height** for your students.

✦ Set up the desks or tables to accommodate **small groupings of students** working together. Figure 1.2 shows some furniture arrangements you can try.

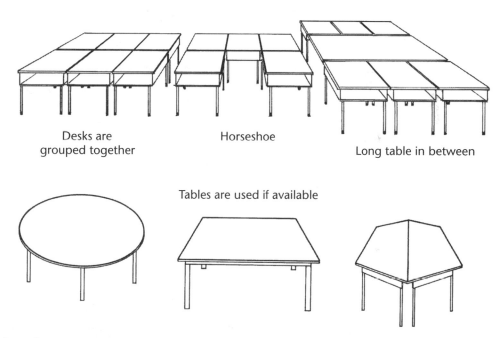

Desks are grouped together   Horseshoe   Long table in between

Tables are used if available

Figure 1.2 *Possible Furniture Arrangements*

✦ Ensure that you have all the necessary **classroom materials**, both non-consumable and consumable, such as pencil sharpeners that work, trash cans, paper towels, and other essentials, such as chalk/whiteboard erasers, pencils, crayons, markers, rulers, paper, tape, and staplers.

✦ Set up shelves or other containers for **storage and display** of materials and resources. These may be placed near the work areas or around the periphery of the room for easy access by all students. Figure 1.3 illustrates some arrangements you can use.

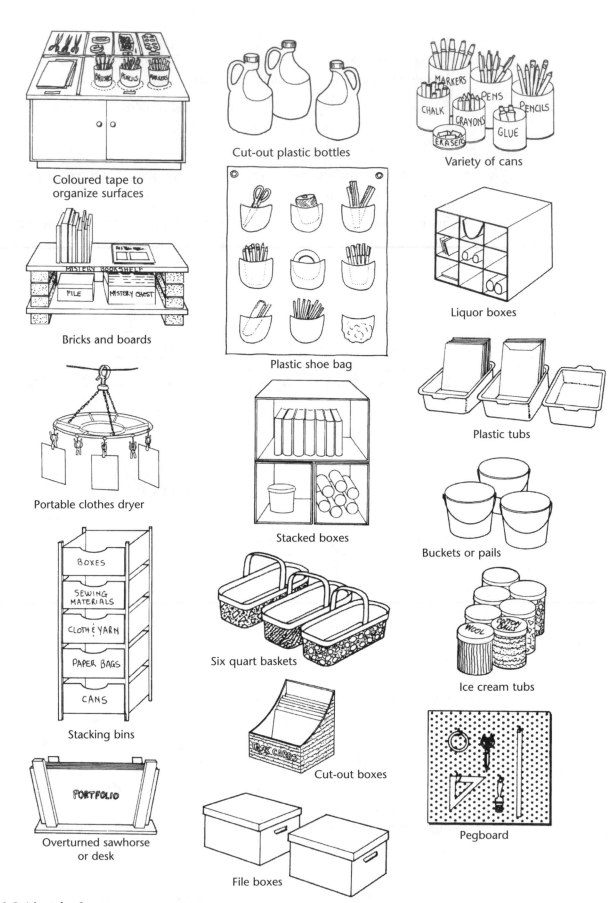

Coloured tape to organize surfaces

Cut-out plastic bottles

Variety of cans

Bricks and boards

Plastic shoe bag

Liquor boxes

Portable clothes dryer

Stacked boxes

Plastic tubs

Buckets or pails

Stacking bins

BOXES
SEWING MATERIALS
CLOTH & YARN
PAPER BAGS
CANS

Six quart baskets

Ice cream tubs

Cut-out boxes

Pegboard

Overturned sawhorse or desk

PORTFOLIO

File boxes

Figure 1.3 *Ideas for Storage*

✦ Determine areas for teacher and student displays. Be creative! Figure 1.4 shows some possibilities.

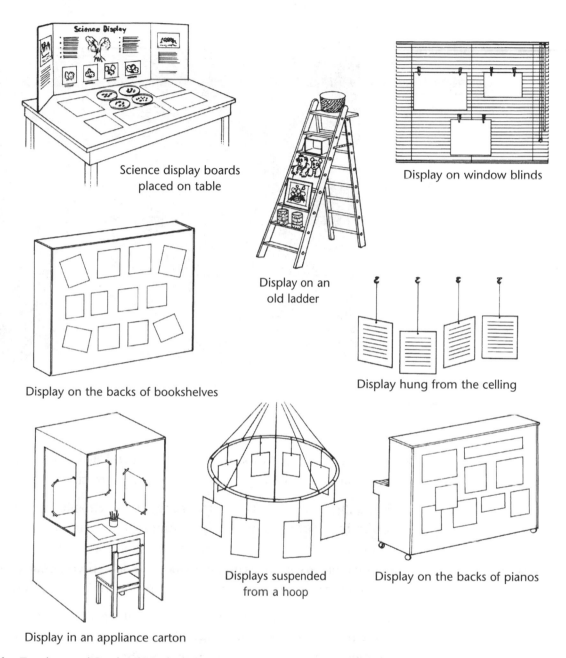

Science display boards placed on table

Display on window blinds

Display on an old ladder

Display on the backs of bookshelves

Display hung from the ceiling

Display in an appliance carton

Displays suspended from a hoop

Display on the backs of pianos

Figure 1.4 *Areas for Teacher and Student Displays*

✦ Consider **health and safety issues** when hanging materials from the ceiling.

✦ Plan the different types of displays you will create on your **bulletin boards**. Remember to consider all the areas available for display, including the hall, your classroom door, or other convenient wall space. (See Figure 1.5.)

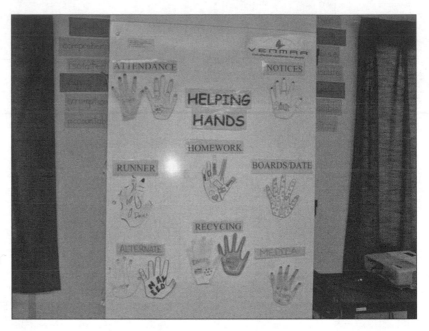

Figure 1.5 *Making Use of All Areas of the Room*
Source: Used with permission. Kimberly Pollishuke, YRDSB.

✦ Consider the needs of **students with special needs** when displaying visuals. Too many visuals may be disturbing and distracting.

✦ Depending on the effect you want to create, **choose backing for your bulletin boards** that is durable, colourful, or neutral. Some ideas for backing include fadeless paper, fabric, paint, or wallpaper. When using wallpaper as your backing, consider the design you choose and the needs of students trying to locate visual information if the walls look too busy.

✦ Ensure that you have provided ample wall space to highlight and **display relevant content-specific materials**, such as charts, rubrics, teacher/ student-developed materials, routines, songs, etc.

✦ Consider where to **post anchor charts** as well as where and how to store them for easy student access when finished with a particular task.

✦ Think about the content presented in each display and ensure that you have a **heading or title** that captures the intended message. Here are a few examples:

Figure 1.6 *Effective Display Headings*

✦ One particular bulletin board, perhaps titled "**Our Best Work**," could present a variety of student work samples across various curriculum areas. Remember to include student work samples of all your students in some way so that they can see themselves represented in the room and feel connected to the classroom program and group.

✦ Ensure that headings or titles are **large enough to read**, and that these and the displays are **visually appealing** and able to attract the attention of students and visitors.

✦ Headings or titles of displays do not need to be centred at the top of the bulletin board, but could be in the middle, at the bottom, or wherever. Be creative!

✦ Keep in mind that displays need not be one-dimensional but, rather, could feature student work or materials that are raised and off the backing, displayed with a ripple effect, off centre, or at different angles. Many possibilities exist. See Figure 1.7 for some ideas for bulletin board displays.

Figure 1.7 *Possibilities for Displays and Headings*

✦ Ensure that you have **clearly defined areas**, and that you can easily organize your learning environment to accommodate specific learning experiences as they arise. You may want to begin one way, and as the year progresses, change the room arrangement to suit the needs and interests of your students and program. **Flexibility** is the key! Figure 1.8 shows a number of examples of classroom set-ups for both younger and older students.

Figure 1.8 *Examples of Classroom Set-ups*

Figure 1.8 *Examples of Classroom Set-ups (continued)*
Source: Used with permission. Kimberly Pollishuke, YRDSB.

As you effectively design the physical layout and organization of your classroom environment, you will see how the overall set-up can and will invite your students to explore, interact, investigate, and learn. It is important that you continuously reflect on the use of space, organization, and accessibility of materials, resources, and equipment in order to assess the overall effectiveness. Flexibility of structure, layout, organization, and design are essential in creating a comfortable, secure, inclusive, and dynamic classroom environment.

2 Timetabling

Finding time for everything and everyone is a continuing challenge in our daily lives and in the dynamic classroom. You will find that no one timetable can accommodate every teacher or student need, every style of teaching or learning, or every programming consideration. Learning takes time, and when preparing a timetable, you should remember to be **flexible**—flexible to adapt to your students' ever-changing needs, to unexpected changes in schedule, and to changes in planning and programming.

Class scheduling involves planning for blocks of time. **Horizontal blocks** of time, which might occur at the same time each day, are often necessary to meet school organizational requirements. You may find that time for physical education, French, or Spanish, which may be taught by someone other than yourself, usually needs to be scheduled first. In addition, scheduling for preparation time affects your timetable. It is ideal if your preparation time can be linked with that of a team partner so that you can engage in team planning during the school day.

Vertical blocks of time are essential in promoting longer and more sustained attention to tasks. These blocks of time accommodate more intensive, active investigations and provide opportunities for you to address specific areas of the curriculum. Larger blocks of time facilitate the differentiation of programming by allowing you to be flexible in the timing of task completion. Some students will have increased opportunities to complete tasks within the time frame while others, who complete tasks quickly, will have more opportunities to expand on their learning and enrich their understanding. Longer blocks of time also allow students to pursue their individual areas of interest or to plan collaboratively with you. When planning for these blocks of time, be sure to balance all curriculum areas, including language arts, mathematics, social studies, science and technology, health and physical education, and the arts. By taking an integrated approach to planning your units of study, you will be better able to accommodate the time needed for all subject areas. In addition, transitions between subject areas are made easier with the integration of curriculum content delivered during a larger time block.

When planning your day, you will want to include **input sessions** that allow time for large-group discussion, direct instruction, demonstration, and explanation. You will also want to provide **daily sharing** times. These times allow students to celebrate what they know, what they have learned, and what they have accomplished. Students' self-concept and confidence levels improve as they share and take pride in their efforts.

Exercising **flexibility** in timetabling is the key to effective scheduling. It allows you to tailor your plans to meet the particular needs and interests of your students on a daily basis.

Creating Timetabling Possibilities

✦ Schedule **horizontal blocks** of time for specific subject areas, such as French, physical education, and other subjects that might involve different teachers. Doing so will assist in the booking of the gym or other facilities, such as the music room or computer lab. Also include your scheduled breaks. Figure 2.1 illustrates horizontal blocks of time.

	Monday	**Tuesday**	**Wednesday**	**Thursday**	**Friday**
8:45					
9:45					
10:15	Recess	Recess	Recess	Recess	Recess
10:30					
12:00	Lunch	Lunch	Lunch	Lunch	Lunch
1:00	Physical Education	Physical Education	Physical Education	Physical Education	Physical Education
1:45	French	French	French	French	French
2:15	Recess	Recess	Recess	Recess	Recess
2:30	Music			Music	
3:30	Dismissal	Dismissal	Dismissal	Dismissal	Dismissal
After-school Activities					

Figure 2.1 *Horizontal Blocks of Time*

- Try to arrange your **preparation time** so that it coincides with that scheduled for your team partner or for a same-grade teacher to facilitate planning and delivery of the program.

- Once your horizontal blocks of time are scheduled, examine your timetable for larger **vertical blocks** of time. Figures presented later in this chapter show examples of vertical blocks of time. Chapter 5: Designing Your Curriculum, both in the text and on the Text Enrichment Site, also includes a number of timetables illustrating vertical blocks of time.

- To begin your year, choose one or more large blocks of time for **language arts**. Allow sufficient time for read-aloud, shared reading, guided reading, independent reading, modeled writing, shared writing, guided writing, and independent writing. Ensure that you integrate oral communication and media literacy into your literacy block(s) and across the curriculum. Refer to Chapter 8: Literacy and Language Learning, for more information about these learning experiences. Refer to figures in this chapter and in Chapter 5: Designing Your Curriculum for some timetables that illustrate literacy blocks.

- Choose a daily block of time for **mathematics** and ensure that you have opportunities for direct instruction, cooperative learning, and independent practice. Remember to address all the components of mathematics, including number and computation, measurement, geometry, data management, probability, and problem solving.

- Choose a large block of time for your **integrated units of study**, which may revolve around social studies, science and technology, and/or health education. These integrated units may also address language, mathematics, and the arts.

- Allocate specific time throughout the week and year to directly focus on all the areas of the **arts**, including visual arts, music, drama, dance, and movement, while continuing to integrate the arts into your units of study. Chapter 5: Designing Your Curriculum offers some guidance in designing integrated units of study.

- Allow time for flexible **input** sessions and for **sharing** when appropriate.

- At the beginning of the year, schedule time when you will introduce lessons to promote **social skills and cooperation** in small-group learning experiences. Chapter 3: An Inclusive Classroom Atmosphere, addresses these issues.

- Create a weekly timetable that meets your timetable and programming needs and allows you to see the week at a glance. See Figure 2.2 for a sample weekly timetable. Chapter 5: Designing Your Curriculum contains other weekly plans, both in the text and on the Text Enrichment Site.

Time	Monday	Tuesday	Wednesday	Thursday	Friday
08:45–9:15	**Writing** Introduce class to cooperative book—Early Settlers	**Writing** Continue	**Writing**	**Writing**	**Computer Lab**
09:15–10:15	**Language** Shared Reading Book bins Guided Reading Red Group	**Language** Guided Reading Blue Group	**Language** Guided Reading Yellow Group	**Language** Guided Reading Red and Blue	**Language** Guided Reading Yellow Group
10:15–10:30	**Recess**	**Recess**	**Recess**	**Recess**	**Recess**
10:30–11:30	**Mathematics** Geometry—3D Shapes	**Mathematics** Number— 3-digit addition with regrouping	**Mathematics** Geometry	**Mathematics** Number	**Mathematics** Geometry
11:30–12:30	Lunch	Lunch	Lunch	Lunch	Lunch
12:30–12:45	Self-selected Independent Reading	Self-selected Independent Reading	Self-selected Independent Reading	Self-selected Independent Reading	Self-selected Independent Reading
12:55–01:30	**Phys. Ed.** Gymnastics	**Health** Nutrition	**Phys. Ed.** Gymnastics	**Music**	**Phys. Ed.** Gymnastics
01:30–02:15	**Social Studies** Integrated Early Settlers unit	**Social Studies** Integrated Early Settlers unit	**Science** Structures	**Visual Arts** Line and design— weaving	**Science** Structures
02:15–02:30	**Recess**	**Recess**	**Recess**	**Recess**	**Recess**
02:30–03:30	**Social Studies** Integrated Early Settlers unit	**Social Studies** Integrated Early Settlers unit	**Science** Structures	**Visual Arts** Line and design— weaving	**Science** Structures

LM 2.1   **Figure 2.2** *Weekly Timetable*

✦ Create a **daily timetable** that meets your programming needs. See Figures 2.3 and 2.4 for sample timetables for older students, including possible rotary timetabling considerations.

Language Block Period 1 9–9:40	
Language Block Period 2 9:40–10:20	
Language Block Period 3 10:20–10:50	
Break 10:50–11:10	
Mathematics Period 4 11:10–11:50	
Mathematics Period 5 11:50–12:30	
Lunch 12:30–1:30	
Period 6 1:30–2:10	

LM 2.2 **Figure 2.3** *Daily Timetable with Large Blocks of Time*

Time	Subject	Activity/Strategy/Interaction
8:55–9:45	7/8A Math	
9:45–10:35	7/8A History/Geography	
10:35–10:55	Break	
10:55–11:45	7/8B History/Geography	
11:45–12:35	PREP	
12:35–1:35	Lunch	
1:35–3:15	7/8A Language	READING/WRITING/ORAL COMMUNICATION/MEDIA LITERACY

LM 2.3 **Figure 2.4** *Daily Rotary Timetable for Older Students*

◆ You might want to use a daily plan timetable that allows you to record specific time slots, curriculum areas, groupings, learning expectations, assessment strategies, tasks, resources needed, and other considerations (See Figure 2.5 below.) Chapter 5: Designing Your Curriculum contains other daily plans, both in the text and on the Text Enrichment Site.

Time	Curriculum Area/ Learning Experience	Grouping	Learning Expectations	Assessment	Task Description	Materials
8:30– 9:15	Language— Writing	Individual	Use adjectives to describe	Work samples— sentences include at least one adjective	In writing folders, create one page of coop book on Global Issues	Large paper, markers, pencils
9:15– 10:15	Language	Whole group Small Groups	Understand main idea Able to infer Use expression in oral reading	Observation— note students who identify main idea in large group Check bins on Friday Guided Reading— observe, anecdotal notes Running Record with. . . .	Read "Global Issues" book—ask questions to elicit main ideas Read together passage from book Blue, Green, Yellow groups continue with Bin work Red: Guided Reading, Discuss main idea, inference	Books on global issues (6 copies for guided reading) Guided Reading Record Sheets Global Issues—books in bins
10:15– 10:30	Recess					
10:30– 11:30	Mathematics: Number— Addition	Whole Group Small groups	Able to add 3-digit num- bers with regrouping	Observation Work samples Self-assessment	Use manipulatives to demonstrate grouping process Exploration activi- ties at stations to reinforce concepts	Multi-links manipulatives Textbook, page 49 for tasks

LM 2.4 **Figure 2.5** *Detailed Daily Plan*

♦ When reviewing your daily plan, decide how you will **begin each day**. Decide whether your students will meet as a large group as they enter, or become involved immediately in small-group or individual tasks.

NOTE: Traditionally, it has been the practice for young students to meet in a large-group area as they enter the classroom. Instead, you might want to have them engage in individual tasks, such as reading or independent writing, doing a math problem, or working independently at learning stations. Doing this means that valuable time is not wasted while students wait for school announcements or for you to begin the day. You are also freed to respond to parents and concerns, take attendance, or collect notes. Time for large-group tasks, such as looking at the calendar and discussing the rest of the day's events, could be scheduled for later in the morning. Similarly, you may want to engage older students in an activity immediately as they come into the classroom so that every minute is used productively. Examples of thought-provoking "bell work" activities might include solving a mathematics question posted on the board or chart, discussing an issue as a table talk activity, responding in some way to a poem or song, independent reading and/or writing, etc.

♦ Use one of the following timetables when implementing learning stations in your program. (See Chapter 6: Effective Learning Stations—Small Group Differentiated Learning.)

Example 1: *A Six-Day Cycle*

A rotation system is one way to begin to implement learning stations. If you set up six stations, students work in one of the six stations each day and then rotate to another station the next day. The rotation cycle will be completed over six days. (See Figure 2.6.)

	Monday	**Tuesday**	**Wednesday**	**Thursday**	**Friday**	**Monday**	**Tuesday**
10:30 – 11:30	1st Rotation	2nd Rotation	3rd Rotation	4th Rotation	5th Rotation	6th Rotation	1st Rotation

Figure 2.6 *Six-Day Cycle Rotation*

Example 2: *A Three-Day Cycle*

Once you and your students are comfortable with rotations, you may want students to visit two stations each day during one or two time blocks. It will take three days for the students in the class to rotate through the six stations. (See Figure 2.7.)

	Monday	**Tuesday**	**Wednesday**	**Thursday**	**Friday**	**Monday**
10:30 – 11:30	1st Rotation	3rd Rotation	5th Rotation	1st Rotation	3rd Rotation	5th Rotation
1:15 – 2:15	2nd Rotation	4th Rotation	6th Rotation	2nd Rotation	4th Rotation	6th Rotation

Figure 2.7 *Three-day Cycle Rotation*

Example 3: *A Two-Day Cycle*

If your students rotate through three stations each day, it will take two days to complete the cycle. (See Figure 2.8.) With this type of schedule, your students spend the majority of their day working at learning stations. You need to be diligent in ensuring that you address major areas of the curriculum at these stations.

	Monday	**Tuesday**	**Wednesday**	**Thursday**	**Friday**
8:45	Writing	Writing	Writing	Writing	Writing
9:15	Physical Ed.	Physical Ed.	Physical Ed.	Physical Ed.	Physical Ed.
9:45	French	French	French	French	French
10:30 – 11:30	1st Rotation	4th Rotation	1st Rotation	4th Rotation	1st Rotation
12:45	*D.E.A.R.	*D.E.A.R.	*D.E.A.R.	*D.E.A.R.	*D.E.A.R.
1:15 – 2:15	2nd Rotation	5th Rotation	2nd Rotation	5th Rotation	2nd Rotation
2:30 – 3:30	3rd Rotation	6th Rotation	3rd Rotation	6th Rotation	3rd Rotation

*D.E.A.R. means **D**rop **E**verything **A**nd **R**ead.

Figure 2.8 *Two-Day Cycle Rotation*

✦ If you monitor student movement among learning stations using a planning board or tracking sheet, the following timetables may prove useful. See Chapter 6: Effective Learning Stations—Small Group Differentiated Learning, for more information on how to implement learning stations, planning boards, and tracking sheets.

Example 1: *Focus on Learning Stations*

In this timetable (Figure 2.9), a separate block of time is designated for mathematics, where there would be several stations with mathematics as the focus. There would also be another block of time for integrated studies in language arts, social studies, science and technology, and the arts.

	Monday	**Tuesday**	**Wednesday**	**Thursday**	**Friday**
8:45	Writing	Writing	Writing	Writing	Writing
9:15	Physical Ed.	Physical Ed.	Physical Ed.	Physical Ed.	Physical Ed.
9:45	French	French	French	French	French
10:30 – 11:30	LEARNING CENTRE TIME (MATHEMATICS)				
12:45	*D.E.A.R.	*D.E.A.R.	*D.E.A.R.	*D.E.A.R.	*D.E.A.R.
1:15 – 3:30	LEARNING CENTRE TIME (INTEGRATED LANGUAGE ARTS/THE ARTS/SOCIAL STUDIES OR SCIENCE)				

*D.E.A.R. means **D**rop **E**verything **A**nd **R**ead.

Figure 2.9 *Focus on Learning Stations*

Example 2: *Focus on Integrated Studies*

This timetable (Figure 2.10) indicates that students are participating in learning experiences at learning stations for the greater part of the day. You must ensure that all curriculum areas are clearly addressed at the stations.

	Monday	**Tuesday**	**Wednesday**	**Thursday**	**Friday**
8:45	Writing	Writing	Writing	Writing	Writing
9:15	Physical Ed.	Physical Ed.	Physical Ed.	Physical Ed.	Physical Ed.
9:45	French	French	French	French	French
10:30 – 3:30	↕	LEARNING CENTRE TIME (INTEGRATED TASKS FOR ALL CURRICULUM AREAS)			↕

Figure 2.10 *Focus on Integrated Studies*

◆ Examine your daily timetable to plan for your students' **transitions** from one learning experience to another. Ensure that these transition times are smooth and well organized so that students always make productive use of their time. Chapter 3: An Inclusive Classroom Atmosphere, provides further information about transitions.

◆ If you are using **homework planners** or agendas, schedule daily time for your students to record information in their planners. Decide when you will check that their planners are up to date and that homework is completed. Chapter 11: Creating Community—Partnerships with Parents, provides further information about homework.

◆ Ensure that you allow time at the end of the day for students to tidy up and for you to distribute any notes going home. Bring **closure** to the day by having your students reflect on what they have accomplished and learned, and what they will do differently tomorrow.

In creating your timetable, remain flexible and open to changes. Expect to make adjustments to your timetable as you plan your program, establish routines, and encourage independence and confidence in your students. You may find that you will begin with one timetable but that you will change it as needs arise and as the year progresses.

An Inclusive Classroom Atmosphere

Creating a warm, caring, non-threatening, and **inclusive** atmosphere in your classroom will not happen without careful thought and planning. Such a desirable atmosphere will help your students learn in exciting and meaningful ways. They will feel represented in your classroom community. They will feel safe to take risks; they will feel free to express their views; and they will be compelled to work cooperatively and collaboratively with others. With your help, guidance, and careful planning, they will become a **community of learners** where mutual respect and self-worth prevail.

In creating a positive, inclusive, and dynamic classroom atmosphere, you need to ensure that **equity** is a fundamental condition and the foundation on which you will build your classroom community. Your equitable classroom will not treat all students in an *identical* way but, rather, it will meet the needs and interests of each and every *individual* student, and provide them with the necessary tools, conditions, and assistance in which they will achieve success and reach their potential. Your inclusive classroom will also provide students with a sense of belonging to a community of learners, where their ability to achieve their full potential is not limited by societal barriers that might stifle growth.

In creating an equitable, inclusive, and dynamic classroom atmosphere, you will immerse your students in a wide variety of active/interactive learning experiences within a diverse and safe environment. As you demonstrate **respect and caring** at all times, provide clear expectations for their learning and behaviour, and encourage approximations and risk taking, you are gradually building a positive, inclusive classroom atmosphere. Your students will realize that people learn from and through their mistakes. They will become risk takers, decision makers, and problem solvers, as they practise their cooperative and collaborative skills, as they value each others' diverse backgrounds and experiences, and learn together in a safe, supportive community environment. When students are given opportunities to help establish and monitor classroom rules and routines, they take **ownership** and begin to realize more and more that the responsibility for their actions and goal setting lies within themselves. Your job as the teacher is to provide feedback and support, encouraging your students to move towards positive goals. You need to ensure that your program planning and authentic assessment practices, including ongoing feedback for learning, encourage your students to believe in themselves and in the value of school and lifelong learning.

Managing the classroom is one of the most important aspects of the "art" of teaching. Good **classroom management** allows you to work with students in a positive and encouraging way. It allows you to use preventative measures to avoid unnecessary interruptions in the flow of your program and to deal with the misbehaviours that will arise no matter how well you have planned your program. Internalizing and using a repertoire of effective classroom management strategies will allow you to get on with the business at hand: teaching your students in an exciting, motivating, and creative way.

You can actively encourage and demonstrate the importance of **cooperation and collaboration** by planning experiences in which students need to cooperate with others in order to learn. Students will find out that cooperation is a life skill and a necessary and fundamental requirement in today's society. Promoting cooperative, heterogeneous groupings in the classroom encourages students to participate in peer teaching and gain important leadership skills. As students work together, they are given many opportunities to clarify their ideas. They develop better problem-solving and decision-making strategies. They gain respect for one another, are better able to appreciate another person's perspective, and become more accepting of other races, genders, cultures, and socio-economic groups. They become more responsible, more independent, and more task oriented, often gaining a more positive attitude towards school.

Although cooperative, heterogeneous **groupings** are usually best for meeting the needs of all your students, you will sometimes need to form homogeneous groupings. Such groupings can address specific academic, social, and emotional needs of individual students in your classroom. Short-term, flexible, and purposeful homogeneous groupings should be the norm rather than the exception. Ideally, homogeneous groupings are temporary and are used as a forum for teaching at the point of need. When you observe that some students need a particular skill or concept, you need to form a small, temporary group. Direct teaching in this small group situation is an effective and meaningful use of your time and provides a forum for differentiating your instruction to meet the diverse needs of all your students.

If you create a classroom that promotes **inclusion**, mutual respect, equitable practices, risk taking, peer teaching, decision making, problem solving, and cooperation, you are better able to serve as a facilitator of student learning.

As your students experience, experiment, and learn together, you are free to circulate, observe, analyze, assess, assist, and differentiate your instruction to meet the needs of individuals and small groups in your community of learners.

Knowing Your Learners

In order to meet your students' needs, interests, and abilities, it is essential that you really know the learners in your class.

✦ Before school begins, collect data from a variety of sources, including student records, previous teachers, principal, resource staff, etc. to find out information that will assist you in knowing the makeup of your classroom.

✦ Once school begins, you may want to send home a form to collect further information about your students. You might ask for information on family structure, languages spoken at home, medical histories, etc. See Chapter 11: Creating Community—Partnerships with Parents for an example of a student information form you might want to use.

✦ At the beginning of the year, involve your students in **"getting to know you" activities** that will help you to find out more about each of your students and identify the diverse makeup of the classroom community.

NOTE: It is important to ensure that you set guidelines or norms with your students before engaging in any of these activities. These guidelines or norms should include showing respect for each other, honouring confidentiality, and an understanding that everyone has a right to pass or not participate.

Identifying Commonalities—Just Like Me (Used with permission. Lipton L. and Wellman B. (2004) Pathways to Understanding: Patterns and Practices in the Learning Focused Classroom. Sherman CT: Mira Via LLC.): Provide a series of statements to the class as a group, and when a particular statement applies to one or more students, these students stand up and call out "Just like me." To engage the students actively and to ensure involvement, you should probably begin the activity with some generic statements which might be representative of all or most of the students in the class, such as "I am in Grade 6," or "I like recess." You can then move towards statements that highlight the diverse makeup of the classroom, such as "I was born outside of Canada." or "I speak more than one language."

Creating a Timeline: On a strip of paper, the students create a timeline that begins with their birth and ends at their current age. Along the timeline, they identify episodes throughout their life that have had significant impact on them; their first day at school, a trip they took, etc. They may need to interview their parents to determine some of the important highlights of their life. They might want to use photos to represent these experiences. With older students, you might also have them identify which experiences reflect their social identity, which might include their race, culture, religion, background, etc.

Using Meaningful Artifacts: In this activity, the students bring in one or more meaningful artifacts that reflect an experience they have had, their background, heritage, culture, etc. They use these artifacts to talk about themselves and their histories, to tell and write stories, and to share with an audience.

Forming an Identity Circle: This activity is aimed at older students who may have a better understanding of their social identity than younger students. Students form a circle with the teacher in the centre. The teacher calls out various statements of social identity, such as: *"I live in Canada"*; *"I was born outside of Canada"*; *"I have a grandparent living with my family"*; *"I visit with my father"*; *"I celebrate Kwanza"*; *"I celebrate the Chinese New Year"*; or *"I celebrate Christmas."* Each time, the teacher asks the students to step into the circle if that statement relates to them, to their social identity. Once students have stepped into the circle, the teacher asks the students to reflect on who is *in* the circle and who is not, and to think about how they feel, and then the teacher asks those students in the centre to step back and again join the remaining students in the circle. Be sure to be inclusive and mention statements that might apply to all cultures/backgrounds in the class. You may want to do a precursor activity asking the students to record onto cards their own questions or answers to a variety of questions such as: "Where do you live?"; "What holidays do you celebrate?"; or "Who lives in your home with you?" You could then refer to these when you call out the various statements.

NOTE: It is extremely important that this activity be processed with the students afterwards to discuss how they felt, how they thought others felt, what assumptions (if any) did they make, and were they aware of any prejudices that surfaced. You could have the students do this processing as a large group, in small groups, or in partners.

Creating an *All About Me* Picture Book (Courtesy of Dr. Carol Rolheiser, Director, Centre for Teaching Support & Innovation, and Professor, Department of Curriculum, Teaching and Learning, University of Toronto): This strategy encourages students to write picture books that celebrate who they are and the diversity of individuals amongst them, allows their creativity to emerge, and provides opportunities to experience the writing process. It is effective for older students, grade 3 to secondary school. The following steps outline a possible process to follow:

- Introduce the concept of social identity. Have your students complete a graphic organizer that identifies the various social identities that make up who they are, including their gender, race, religion, ethnic/cultural background, their geographic origin, etc. This graphic could be in the form of a chart, circle, or flower as in the example in Figure 3.1. (Used with permission. Enid Lee, *Letters to Marcia: A Teacher's Guide to Anti-Racist Education*, Cross Cultural Communication Centre.)

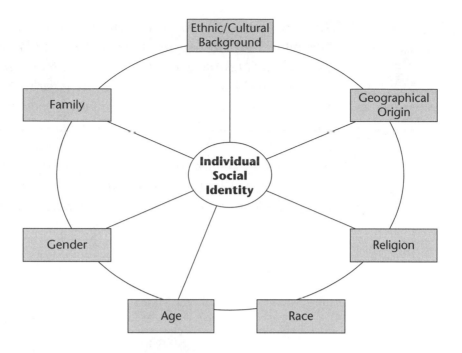

LM 3.1 **Figure 3.1** *Identifying Social Identities*

Source: Used with permission. Enid Lee, *Letters to Marcia: A Teacher's Guide to Anti-racist Education*, Cross Cultural Communication Centre.

- The students discuss their similarities and differences with a partner.

- Introduce the idea of creating a picture book about themselves.

- Show samples of picture books to demonstrate the components of a picture book.

- In order to assist the students in determining a good story to tell about themselves, have them create a timeline of the events of their life from birth to the present. (See Creating a Timeline above.)

- Once their timeline is complete, they can star, or highlight in some way, events in their life that are directly influenced by their social identity.

- They select one of these events as the focus for their picture book.

- Have the students follow the writing phases of drafting, revising and editing, and encourage them to bring their story to completion by publishing it in an interesting way.

- Once their books have been published, they can be shared with other students, other classes, and the home to demonstrate the diversity across the class and the power of story to celebrate who we are! Refer to Chapter 8: Literacy and Language Learning for further information on picture books, the writing process, and publishing ideas.

NOTE: This strategy, first introduced by Dr. Carol Rolheiser, currently Director, Centre for Teaching Support & Innovation, and Professor, Curriculum, Teaching and Learning, University of Toronto, has proven effective when used with pre-service teachers who often share it with their own students year after year as a way to introduce themselves and to engage their students in a similar learning experience. Some teachers attempt and succeed in having their picture book published. For example, the picture book, Violet, *by Tania Duprey Stehlik was originally created when that author was in Mindy Pollishuke's pre-service class. It is a powerful story about multi-racial identity, featuring the main character, Violet, who is teased because her mother is red and her father is blue, and she is a shade of purple. (See Figure 3.2.)*

Figure 3.2 *Picture Book: Violet*

Source: Used with permission. *Violet*, by Tania Duprey Stehlik, Second Story Press.

Meeting the Diverse Needs of Your Students

✦ Ensure that your classroom practices are equitable and designed to meet each student's individual needs. Be aware that each student comes to your classroom with their own unique backgrounds, prior knowledge, experiences, strengths, needs, skills, and attitudes, and therefore your approach to individuals will not always be identical.

✦ Be explicit in demonstrating and explaining that **equity** does not mean that every student is treated in the same way. Be sure that your students are aware that you have high expectations for them and they see and understand your commitment to their individual progress and achievement.

✦ **Reflect on your own personal biases and beliefs** to ensure that you are being consistent in supporting and valuing the individual needs of each student, including their backgrounds, experiences, race, cultures, religions, abilities, gender, sexual orientation, and socio-economic levels.

✦ Be sensitive to the feelings of those **students who are not in the majority**, in terms of religious practices, race, language, backgrounds, culture, family structure, sexual orientation, or class, etc.

✦ When addressing your students, consistently use language that treats all students in a respectful and inclusive way. **Be a role model**.

✦ Use age-appropriate and **culturally-relevant activities and literature**, **visuals**, **or media** to address specific issues and encourage discussion.

✦ Expose your students to the issues of **stereotyping and bias** found in society. You might have your students do as follows:

- Engage in discussions stemming from their personal experiences.
- Dialogue about established definitions for terms such as sexism, racism, classism, ageism, etc. and dispel stereotypical myths.
- Read and discuss picture books or novels that represent different perspectives.
- Present scenarios to encourage discussion about sensitive issues.

✦ Be aware of the impact of your teaching practices on gender differences. Consider the interests, needs, and abilities specific to the boys and girls in your classroom.

- Discuss the issue of "traditional" male and female occupations, such as nurse, doctor, firefighter, tailor, computer specialist, etc., and how they can affect self-image and actions.
- Encourage the girls and boys in your classroom to recognize non-traditional roles and activities. For example, encourage girls to reflect on the "Cinderella/princess" portrayal of girls in media and literature. Encourage boys to think about the positive aspects of engaging in activities that are often seen as "traditionally feminine," such as baking, weaving, dancing, etc.
- Ensure that both girls and boys have opportunities to participate in extracurricular sports activities for their social, emotional, and physical well-being.
- Organize after-school book clubs that specifically target either boys or girls to encourage reading based on books that are of high interest to the group members.

** Excellent resources about gender are *Even Hockey Players Read: Boys, Literacy and Learning,* by David Booth (Pembroke), and *Cinderella Ate My Daughter* by Peggy Orenstein (HarperCollins).

✦ Investigate the supports available within your school and/or district if you are uncomfortable dealing with such sensitive issues with your students. Most districts have **equity resource staff** available to help you. Refer to professional materials/resources available through your district, professional organizations, and unions.

✦ Become familiar with the **culture and religious backgrounds** of your students and the specific customs, traditions, and rituals that they may practise.

✦ Be sure that you address the unique cultural practices and spiritual beliefs of **aboriginal or indigenous groups**. Often, these groups are overlooked in our curriculum content and delivery, and it is important that we address their history and perspective. This can often prove challenging, since resources such as textbooks, have typically been written from a Eurocentric perspective that can distort the history of aboriginal peoples, especially since much of their history was not recorded, but rather based on oral communication passed on from generation to generation.

✦ Ensure that you provide reasonable cultural and religious accommodations as needed. Examples include the following:

- Provide a private area for some students to pray at specific times during the day.
- Do not schedule assignments due, important input, or tests on religious holidays, and provide a plan for students to find out what was covered during these days.
- Make accommodations for those students who might require it during specific times, such as during physical education classes, snack time, out-of-classroom excursions.

✦ Ideas you might consider implementing to address the cultural and religious needs of your students include the following:

- At the beginning of the year, be explicit in your teaching to ensure that your students know that "in our classroom, we respect all cultural and religious practices and value our differences."
- Create your own religious calendar for your classroom that identifies the various religious holidays and events that your students celebrate. You may want to post a large version of this calendar so that your students may become more familiar with the variety of practices within the classroom.

- Infuse cultural and religious diversity into all areas of your curriculum. Include discussion of universal themes in your program that reflect different perspectives that go beyond the traditional Eurocentric point of view. Also highlight a number of religious practices, illustrating the connections and commonalities. For example, you could discuss a Festival of Lights, which may include Christmas, Chanukah, Kwansa, and Divali.

- Ensure that you highlight all cultures and religions and not just the dominant or more visible ones.

✦ For **English Language Learners (ELL) and students new to the country**, be aware of their specific needs and address them accordingly. You might include the following strategies:

- Determine their level of proficiency in their first language. The more proficient students are in their first language, the easier it will be to learn a second language.

- Determine what fluency they have, if any, in the language of instruction.

- Involve outside resource staff if necessary to do language proficiency assessments.

- Orient your English Language Learners who are new to the classroom and school environment by providing bilingual student ambassadors to help them become familiar with their new surroundings.

- Provide English Language Learners with many visuals to help them learn the language of instruction.

- Partner and group your English Language Learners with both native English-speaking students and also with students who speak the same language. The use of peer buddies or tutors is a valuable strategy to use with students learning a new language.

- Encourage students to talk together with others in their first language within the classroom. Research has shown that students who articulate meaning in their first language are better able to process more complex concepts when working in a second language. Encouraging dialogue between English Language Learners in their first language enhances self-esteem and values their culture, background, and the literacy skills that they bring.

- Include dual-language and multi-lingual resources and materials in your classroom library, as well as books that are in English but revolve around stories from different countries.

- You might encourage your students to write in their own language and then have this writing translated into the language of instruction. This writing can then become reading material for these students.

NOTE: Keep in mind that most English Language Learners will go through different phases of language acquisition, including a time when they will often not participate verbally in the language of instruction, but they are usually taking in and processing a great deal of information during this "silent" period. Realize that even though your English Language Learners may become verbally proficient, it may take up to seven years for them to become proficient in the language of instruction in reading and writing.

** Many of these ideas are identified by Dr. Jim Cummins, professor at the Ontario Institute for Studies in Education of the University of Toronto, whose research focus is on second language acquisition, dual language, and bilingual education. (See the References section.)

✦ Ensure that you program accordingly for all **students with exceptional needs**, including those with learning disabilities, behavioural issues, and gifted capabilities. In cases of students with exceptionalities, it is usually necessary to make **accommodations** for their needs, but it is also necessary at times to **modify** their curriculum expectations to help them to attain success. For instructional, environmental, and assessment accommodations that you might put in place for your exceptional students, refer to Chapter 4: Assessment in a Differentiated Curriculum, as well as Chapter 5: Designing Your Curriculum. Also refer to Chapter 9: Technology in a Rapidly Changing World for specific suggestions on using technology to meet the needs of exceptional students.

✦ Ensure that you consult and use the support and guidance of the Special Education and/or English as a Second Language **resource teachers** in your school and/or school district as well as possible outside agencies when needed.

✦ Ensure that your classroom practices are based on the foundation **of inclusion and acceptance** as you demonstrate, in explicit ways, that you value and support the many diverse communities that are represented in your classroom and the broader global community, including all languages, backgrounds, races, cultures, religions, abilities, sexual orientation, and socio-economic levels.

✦ Often teachers who are new to the process of dealing with sensitive issues and a diverse population can find it challenging. Move forward in addressing these issues **at a pace most comfortable for you**.

♦ As you become more comfortable working with sensitive issues and the diverse population in classrooms of today, begin to look at your total curriculum and plan units of study that specifically address issues of equity, diversity, and social justice, and **involve your students in making a difference to the world** around them and in the global community. (Refer to Chapter 5: Designing Your Curriculum.)

Being Proactive

Just as you need to know your learners, you need to know yourself—who you are and what your beliefs are—because this will have an impact on the type of classroom atmosphere you create. You will tend to be more **reactive** and use techniques and strategies that are highly visible if you believe that *all* students should behave *all* the time. On the other hand, you will tend to be more **proactive** and use techniques and strategies that are as low key and invisible as possible if you believe that all students will misbehave *some* of the time. Being proactive will assist you in establishing a positive, inclusive classroom atmosphere.

♦ When interacting with students, always be a **role model** and demonstrate good manners and a positive attitude. Ensure that you say "please" and always thank students for their contributions. Although this is a small point, it has major ramifications to how students regard you as a role model and mentor.

♦ Continue to **build close relationships with your students**. Make sure that you show an interest in them and their home lives by engaging in conversations at the door as they enter, in the hall or schoolyard, and throughout the day. Know when to listen and when to step in. Show them that you are interested in what they have to say. Become sensitive to their needs and interests, and ask carefully-thought-out questions.

♦ As you demonstrate your interest, ensure that you are **culturally and linguistically aware** of the students' social identity. That is, be aware of the norms that are specific to different cultures and religions. For example, some cultures regard eye contact from a child to an adult as an expression of rudeness.

♦ In creating a positive, inclusive learning atmosphere, **use common sense and be alert**.

♦ Continuously survey your classroom, move around the room and circulate among your students as they work and interact with others. Always keep your students in your line of sight. For example, do not stand with your back to your class at the board or in the gym, and project **a sense of "with-it-ness,"** demonstrating that you are aware at all times of what is going on in your classroom. Other proactive measures include the following.

- Remember to consistently stop and wait for all students' attention before you or someone else speaks. **Never talk over your students' voices.**

- Always avoid sarcastic and/or negative comments, which can harm students' self-esteem.

- **Use wait time** effectively. Allow your students the opportunity to think about the questions you ask, and be prepared to wait to ensure that all students have had ample time to reflect and formulate a response. The "art" of teaching is *knowing* how long is too long regarding wait time. You need to know your students well and gauge their responses so that you do not fall into the trap of waiting too long and having classroom management challenges arise.

- **Maximize student involvement** to ensure that as many students as possible are actively engaged. For example, when asking students to respond to questions in a large group situation, ask them first to turn to the person beside them and talk about their responses for 30 seconds (thus, all your students are engaged in the subject at hand), and then ask individual students to respond. This strategy called "think-pair-share" is described later in this chapter.

- Consider the **length of time** you are requiring your students **to sit and listen** for any one period of time. When students are required to sit and listen for a prolonged period of time, they tend to misbehave.

NOTE: *A good barometer is to have them sit and listen for as many minutes as their age in years. For example, a six year old could be required to sit and listen for approximately 6 to 10 minutes and a 10 year old could sit and listen for about 10 to 15 minutes at a time. If you provide opportunities for small group activities, music, or kinesthetic movement in between, the time can be lengthened somewhat.*

✦ When posing questions to students in large or small situations, **vary the types of questions** you use to ensure that you are asking questions at different levels of thinking. (Refer to Chapter 4: Assessment in a Differentiated Curriculum for more information about questioning.)

- ✦ Whenever possible, **link to students' past experiences** in order to scaffold their learning and provide a bridge to connect what they already know to their new learning.

- ✦ **Check for understanding** throughout the learning process to ensure that students are understanding and processing new learning.

Transitions

- ✦ Plan carefully for your students' **transitions** from one learning experience to another. Smooth and quick transitions increase learning time and add an organized and well-managed tone to the classroom program.

- ✦ Ensure that transitions are smooth and well organized by giving clear instructions and directions, having materials and resources ready for use, and thinking carefully about all routines to be followed.

- ✦ When students are required to line up or be dismissed, call them by groups, by the colours they are wearing, by the first letter of their name, by the month of their birthdays, etc.

- ✦ When students are required to retrieve materials, either individually or for their group, stand near the materials to monitor any difficulties that may arise.

- ✦ When you plan to have students work as partners or in groups, *first explain* what they have to do, then *show* them what to do (model), then tell them *how* (as partners or in groups), and then explicitly tell them to begin. Doing this will ensure that they pay full attention to the instructions and will know exactly what to do when you ask them to begin.

- ✦ Time your students as they move through a transitional period. Discuss the length of time they used and set goals to improve the time.

Classroom Procedures and Routines

- ✦ Consider the types of procedures and routines that you would like to establish to assist you in making your classroom efficient, effective, and equitable. Remember that any procedures and routines established need to be clearly outlined and consistent in their application. The following questionnaire, Figure 3.3, is a guide to help you to think about and decide the procedures and routines you will implement.

**Questionnaire for Establishing
Classroom Procedures and Routines**

What procedures will you have for student entry into the classroom?
What will be your procedures for exit and entry for:

- fire drill?
- gym?
- library?
- lunchroom?
- other?

What will the student tasks be upon entry:
- in the morning?
- after each recess?
- after lunch?
- after physical education?

What will your expectations be for your students:

- in large-group situations?
- in small-group situations?
- for individual tasks?
- for transitions from one activity to another—e.g., from carpet to seats, from seats to carpet, etc.?
- for indoor recess?
- for the lunchroom program?
- for the gym?
- for the library/resource centre?
- for the computer lab?
- for learning stations?
- other?

**Questionnaire for Establishing
Classroom Procedures and Routines**

How will you call for your students' attention when they are working individually or in small groups in the classroom? (Examples: STOP and LISTEN! Give me 5! Hands up!)

How will you recognize individual students when they want to contribute in a large-group situation? (Examples: have them raise their hands, pass a talking stick, call out responses.)

What will your students do when they finish their work?

What will your washroom use procedures look like and sound like?

What procedures will you have for storage of:

- students' personal belongings?
- students' completed work?
- students' work to be completed?
- students' materials and resources?
- teacher's resources?
- other?

How will you distribute materials to students during class time?

How will you distribute materials, work, and notices to go home?

How will you collect students' materials?

What cleanup procedures will you have for individuals, groups, and monitors?

What will your procedures be for dismissal?

What will your procedures be for collecting homework?

What other routines and expectations will you establish to encourage appropriate behaviour and actions?

LM 3.2　**Figure 3.3** *Questionnaire for Establishing Classroom Procedures and Routines*

✦ Brainstorm and develop **rules and routines** for your classroom in collaboration *with* your students. You may want to have the students brainstorm individually, in groups, or as the whole class for ideas, while you also include some ideas that you want to see implemented. Remember to keep the rules simple, few, and easy to implement. Examples might include the following:

- We all respect each other.
- We listen when someone is speaking.

- We can pass if we do not know the answer.
- We use our manners when interacting with each other.
- We try our best in everything we do.

✦ You may also want to develop a **code of behaviour** or code of conduct where appropriate consequences are clearly delineated. Use your school's code of behaviour, if available, as a foundation for developing your own classroom code of behaviour. Some of the consequences you can include are as follows:

- discussion/counselling
- contracts
- recording of events and what was learned
- time out or loss of privileges
- staying after school
- written communication with home to be signed and returned
- telephone contact with parent
- a conference with parent and student
- involvement with in-school resource staff or the principal
- payment for repair or replacement of damaged property
- community service
- informal suspension
- formal suspension
- alternative programming
- involvement with outside agencies

NOTE: Always focus on providing **logical consequences** *(vs. punishments), encouraging students to take responsibility for their actions and creating opportunities for growth, learning, and goal setting. Consequences should be directly related to the misbehaviour—a natural extension of the actions. Barbara Colorosa, in* Kids Are Worth It *(Penguin), says it well: "Consequences need to be reasonable, simple, valuable, and practical."*

✦ Include a focus on **character education** and character building as part of your ongoing program planning. Character education helps students focus on specific positive traits and values, such as honesty, kindness, generosity, courage, justice, equality, and respect. It is often a whole school or board initiative.

✦ Continuously **reflect on your program** to ensure that you are meeting the needs, interests, and abilities of all your students through careful planning and the implementation of exciting and dynamic lessons. Doing so will actively engage your students and should prevent misbehaviours due to students becoming frustrated or bored. (Refer to Chapter 5: Designing Your Curriculum.)

✦ Involve your students in a variety of **team-building experiences** where the prime objectives are to promote teamwork, collaboration, cooperation, mutual respect, and a sense of community. Doing so will teach them valuable lessons in developing appropriate classroom behaviour and develop the skills necessary for effective cooperative group learning. The following learning experiences, several adapted from *Tribes: Reaching All by Creating Tribes Learning Communities* (CenterSource Systems) by Jeanne Gibbs, will assist you in building a community of learners. They can be used as stand-alone getting-to-know-you lessons, or as introductions to specific content-based lessons for a topic, theme, or unit of study.

Community Circle (Gibbs): Have your students sit in a large circle. Ask a question or give a sentence prompt, and have everyone in turn give a response. For example: "This morning I feel . . ." or "From this experience, I have learned. . . ." It is important to establish norms before you begin: "You can pass if you wish, but you can't laugh at another's mistakes." At the end, ask questions about how well everyone listened, how everyone felt during the experience, and what was learned about the content or about themselves.

People Hunt (Gibbs): Give your students a list with specific criteria. Have them circulate to find people in the class who fulfill the criteria. They record the person's name in the space provided. This strategy helps the group meet, talk together, and learn about each other in a fun way. (See Figure 3.4.)

People Hunt

Student Name ___Johan___   Date ___25th September___

Find someone who:

1. ___Sally___ has both a sister and a brother.
2. ___Sanje___ was born outside Canada.
3. ___Sudeep___ speaks another language besides English.
4. ___Michael___ has more than two pets.
5. ___Kimberly___ went on a trip recently.
6. ___Matthew___ plays baseball or another sport.
7. ___Yung Hi___ loves to eat pizza.
8. ___Brad___ enjoys reading mysteries.

LM 3.3 **Figure 3.4** *People Hunt*

Source: Used with permission. Jeanne Gibbs, Reaching All by Creating Tribes Learning Communities, CenterSource Systems, LLC. Windsor. California, www.tribes.com, 2006.

People Search Bingo (Bennett, Rolheiser, & Stevahn): Provide each student with a blank card with 16 (or fewer) squares. Ask students to circulate and stop to talk with 16 different people in the room. Each time they stop, they tell the other person a different fact about themselves. This other person records the name and information in one of the blank spaces on his/her card. The game ends when one person completes a card and calls out "Bingo." Debrief this activity with the group by discussing what was learned about different students in the class. It is sometimes difficult for individuals to think of 16 different facts about themselves so you may want them to brainstorm before they begin. Using their names and newly-created game boards, you may also want to play Bingo afterwards as a class activity. (See Figure 3.5.)

People Search Bingo

Robert has one brother.	Lisa went on a trip up north.	Joshua just read an exciting mystery novel.	Sujeep spent the summer at camp.
Tisha recently created a website.	Lovisha attended a skating competition.	Mohammed went to a basketball game.	Marnie went to a movie.

LM 3.4 **Figure 3.5** *People Search Bingo*

Things in Common: Have students fold a piece of paper into four equal parts, and draw a circle in the centre. In groups of four, have them pass the paper so that each student can record information about themselves in one section until the paper contains information about all four students. Or, you might use a large piece of paper so that the students can all write in their section of the paper at the same time. Information might include number of brothers and sisters, place of birth, and hobbies. As they share information within their group, students record all the similarities they notice in the circle in the middle of the rectangle. This activity, also called a "placemat" activity, can be used when dealing with content information: each person is responsible for a different topic or role and records what they know about that topic or role in their section. They then record the similarities (or differences) in the centre circle. (See Figure 3.6.)

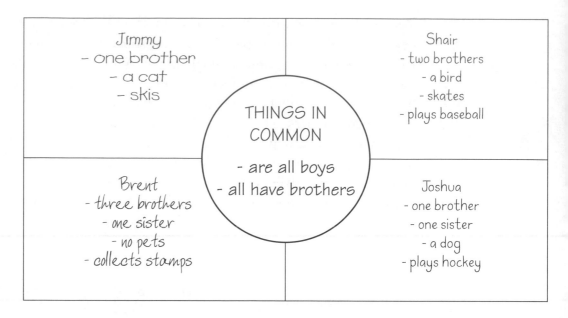

LM 3.5   **Figure 3.6** *Things In Common*

Nametag Art (Gibbs): Make available arts and crafts materials, markers, scissors, and glue, and give each student a card with two holes punched at the top so string or ribbon can be hung to make it into a large nametag. Tell students to write their names in the middle of their cards. Decide on four facts you wish to know about your students and direct them to record the answers in each of the four corners of their nametags. Examples include their place of birth, a highlight in their life, something they do well, and the name of a favourite person, food, book, or movie. Invite the students to decorate their nametags using the craft materials. Afterwards, have them meet in small groups to discuss the words and illustrations they recorded on their nametags.

One variation is to involve the students in deciding what to record in each corner. You could include an added twist where three statements are true and one is false. The students could meet in small groups to discover which statement is not true. (See Figure 3.7.)

NOTE: Using and reinforcing **student names** *in a variety of ways in your classroom enables students to learn the names of their peers as well as creating inclusion, as all individuals feel valued. Along with art ideas using student names, other ideas include: organizing students into different groups using alphabetical order of first or last names or by using the number of letters or syllables in their names; playing word or movement games using their names; creating alphabet books using names; designing an invention, logo, slogan, song, rap, or poem using names; writing acrostic poems using the letters of their first or last names.*

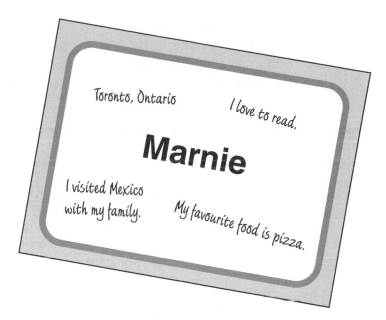

Figure 3.7 *Name Tag Art*

Source: Used with permission. Jeanne Gibbs, Reaching All by Creating Tribes Learning Communities, CenterSource Systems, LLC. Windsor. California, www.tribes.com, 2006.

Coat of Arms: Encourage your students to think about things that are important to them and represent who they are as they begin to create their own personal coat of arms. They can include books that they like to read, places that they like to visit, their family, friends, heritage, etc. (See Figure 3.8.)

LM 3.6 **Figure 3.8** *Coat of Arms*

Lining Up (Used with permission. Jeanne Gibbs, Reaching All by Creating Tribes Learning Communities, CenterSource Systems, LLC. Windsor. California, www.tribes.com, 2006.): Invite your students to form a line in a specific order—for example, by birthdays, age, height, by the first letter of their favourite foods, etc. Consider having them do this without talking and *with* talking. Lining up without talking adds to the challenge.

◆ Consider having your students participate in some **active/interactive learning experiences first *without* talking and then *with* talking** (as in the strategy "Lining Up"). The following learning experiences emphasize the importance of communicating with others while addressing the need for appropriate noise levels in different situations. They can also serve as a baseline to which you can refer later when discussing appropriate noise levels with your students.

Example 1: *Scrambled Sentences*

Have your students write one sentence about themselves on a strip of cardboard and then cut their sentences into individual word cards. They then form into groups of four to six and combine their word cards with the rest of their group's cards. Direct them to shuffle the cards and distribute them evenly to each person in the group. Their goal is to make a complete sentence using the word cards that they have been given. Emphasize *no talking* by displaying the words below on a chart or board.

> Do not talk.
> Do not take a word card from another person unless offered.
> You can give word cards to others in your group.

Scrambling Sentences for Fun

Prompt your students to discuss how they felt about not being able to talk and how they helped in their group. Do the activity again, but this time *with talking*. Afterwards, invite your students to discuss the difference.

Example 2: *Newspaper Scramble*

Using individual pages from the newspaper, cut each page into 8 to 12 puzzle pieces depending on the age of your students. Put each set of puzzle pieces into individual envelopes. Give each group of students one envelope and have them distribute the puzzle pieces evenly among group members. The task is to put the page together again. Emphasize *no talking* by displaying the words below on a chart or board.

> Do not talk.
> Do not take puzzle pieces from others in your group unless offered.
> You can give puzzle pieces to others in your group.

Afterwards, prompt your students to discuss how they felt about being unable to talk. What strategies did they use to accomplish the task? Direct the groups to change envelopes and try the activity again. This time, encourage them to talk. Have them discuss the differences.

Example 3: *Scrambled Poetry*

Find appropriate poems for your students. Record the lines from each poem onto individual strips of paper or cardboard. Mix up the strips for each poem and place them into individual envelopes. Record on the envelope the title, author, and source book of the poem. Have your students work together in small groups to put the scrambled poem back in the right order. Emphasize *no talking* by displaying the words below on a chart or board.

> Do not talk.
> Do not take a card from another person unless offered.
> You can give a card to others in your group.

Prompt your students to discuss how they felt about being unable to talk. Direct the groups to change envelopes and try the activity again. This time, encourage them to talk. Have them discuss the differences.

LM 3.7 **Figure 3.9** *Interactive Learning Experiences*

Teaching Social Skills

✦ Teaching **social skills** is an essential aspect in preparing students to work together cooperatively in pairs or small groups. When social skills are not specifically taught, group work often fails. Model, role-play, and discuss with your students appropriate social skills for working together. Some examples of such social skills include the following:

- listening actively
- taking turns
- sharing materials
- respecting the ideas and rights of others
- not making put-downs
- never laughing at others' mistakes

- making decisions
- solving problems
- praising others
- disagreeing agreeably
- resolving conflict
- reaching consensus

✦ **Use a T-chart** (Bennett, Rolheiser, & Stevahn) to explicitly teach your students the social skills necessary. The T-chart asks students to identify what a social skill sounds like and looks like and focuses the students' attention on concrete examples of appropriate behaviours. (See Figure 3.10.)

Student: _____   Date:_____

T-Chart

Skill:_____

See 👁 What does it sound like?	**Hear** 👂 What does it look like?
"That's a very good idea but I think we might consider…"	smiling
"I can definitely see your point."	head shaking up and down

LM 3.8 **Figure 3.10** *T-Chart*

✦ Use **picture books, poetry, short stories, and media** to stimulate discussion and common understandings about socially acceptable behaviours and human interaction. See Favourite Children's Literature on the Text Enrichment Site for some appropriate titles.

✦ Reinforce the social skills you have taught by encouraging your students to **create related stories, scripts, poems, art, posters, or song lyrics** and have them present their work to the class or school. For example, your students might present a role-play about praising others and receiving compliments, a student-written song about active listening, a play about good manners, or a puppet play or musical performance about respecting differences.

Cooperative Learning Experiences

✦ Once you have begun to build a community of learners through team building activities, have taught and reinforced the necessary social skills, and your students are clear about the expectations of working with others, begin to explicitly introduce the concept of **cooperative learning** (Bennett, Rolheiser & Stevahn).

NOTE: Teachers use cooperative learning structures to instruct, review, clarify, inform, and reinforce, as well as to develop social and interpersonal skills, speaking and listening skills, brainstorming and problem-solving skills, and divergent and higher order thinking skills.

✦ To begin a focus on cooperative learning, **group your students heterogeneously**, using information you know about them. Ensure that each group is heterogeneous, composed of students with varying abilities who are able to help and complement one another. Integrate into these groups any students with special needs, such as those who have an intellectual or physical challenge and English Language Learners.

NOTE: It is a good idea to begin by using partners or triads before you involve larger groups of students. The most effective number for a cooperative group is four to six, but you should view this as a goal towards which you work.

✦ Ensure that each cooperative learning experience incorporates the following elements:

1. *Positive interdependence:* All members of a group work together towards successful completion of a task or achievement of a goal. All members can say, "I cannot succeed unless you succeed."

2. *Individual accountability:* Each member of a group is responsible for completing his or her portion of the task or goal. All need to demonstrate the

learning. All members can say, "We cannot succeed unless I do my share, and I need to be able to demonstrate what we as a group have learned."

3. *Face-to-face interaction:* Group members need to interact and sit in close proximity to one another in order to work together successfully.

4. *Social skills:* Social skills should be taught and in place before cooperative learning experiences will be successful. Students need to learn the skills and techniques on how to work with others and in a group. Cooperative learning experiences often fail, not because the students are unable to work in groups, but because they have not been taught directly how to work in groups.

5. *Processing:* Evaluation of the group process allows students to reflect on what they did individually and as a group in order to set goals for future improvement.

** For a recommended resource on cooperative learning and effective instructional strategies, see *Beyond Monet: The Artful Science of Instructional Integration* by Barrie Bennett and Carol Rolheiser (Bookation Inc.).

✦ Elicit from your students expectations for successful cooperative learning experiences and add these to the rules and routines you and your class generated earlier. Add some of your own ideas to the list. See some possibilities in Figure 3.11.

Expectations for Successful Cooperative Learning

- We respect the rights of others in the class and in our group.
- We never laugh at other people's mistakes.
- We are free to make mistakes, and we learn from and through our mistakes.
- We share resources, materials, and ideas.
- We always help a person in the group if he/she asks for help.
- We listen to what others have to say and ask questions if necessary.
- We praise the efforts and achievements of others.
- We take turns, do our share, and do our best.
- We avoid asking the teacher a question unless we have asked others in our group. ("Ask three before me.")

LM 3.9 Figure 3.11 *Expectations for Successful Cooperative Learning*

✦ Begin to incorporate cooperative learning structures into all areas of the curriculum. Some examples are outlined below.

Jigsaw (Aronson, Blaney, Stephin, Sikes, & Snapp): Assign students to heterogeneous home groups, with each group member having a number from 1 to 4, and being given something to learn or do for the group. Students with the same number (e.g., all the number 1s) join together to form an expert group to learn about types of Australian mammals, for example. Once all groups have completed their work, students rejoin their home groups. They then have the task of teaching their part to the other members of the home group so that everyone learns all the material. This structure works well in science or social studies-based programs where students are responsible for mastering content-related material.

Think-Pair-Share (Bennett, Rolheiser, & Stevahn; Kagan): Students first think individually about an issue, question, or topic, and then partner up with another student to share thoughts, ideas, and feelings. This structure is especially effective when used in large-group situations to ensure that all students are involved and thinking about the topic at hand. It allows rehearsal with a partner before a student participates in a large group, and maximizes student involvement as opposed to the traditional practice of asking a question where five students put up their hands. In this way, the entire class has the opportunity to articulate answers and stay on task.

Roundtable (Bennett, Rolheiser, & Stevahn; Kagan): This structure encourages cooperation as the group shares materials and systematically takes turns contributing. For example, each member of the group generates ideas about a common topic as the paper and pencil are passed from one to the next.

Roundrobin (Bennett, Rolheiser, & Stevahn; Kagan): This structure calls upon each team member to take a turn contributing to the discussion at hand. Group members may pass if they wish to do so.

Corners (Kagan): This structure encourages students to make a particular choice and then verbalize why.

• First, label the corners of the classroom with the words *Agree*, *Strongly Agree*, *Disagree*, and *Strongly Disagree*.

• Next, put a thought-provoking statement up on the overhead, chart, or board, and ask students to decide whether they strongly agree, agree, disagree, or strongly disagree. Be careful that you choose statements that will create controversy and differences in opinion so that all students do not end up in the same corner.

• Direct them to move to the corner that best represents their position. (You might want to also ask students to record on a slip of paper the corner they have chosen before they move so that they do not simply follow their friends.)

- Have them discuss with others in that corner why they made the decision to move there. If students are undecided, they can move to the middle of the classroom.

- Discuss with the whole group why particular decisions were made.

- A variation of the corners structure is to display specific statements on the walls of the classroom and have students move to the statement that best represents their opinion, feelings, or position. Once there, students should articulate why they have taken that position. (See Figure 3.12.)

1. When I first learned to read, I felt like a clown at a circus.

2. When I first learned to read, I felt like a castaway on a deserted island.

3. When I first learned to read, I felt like a mountain climber.

4. When I first learned to read, I felt like an Olympian swimmer at the finish line.

Figure 3.12 *Four Corners Activity*

Graffiti (Used with permission. Jeanne Gibbs, Reaching All by Creating Tribes Learning Communities, CenterSource Systems, LLC. Windsor. California, www.tribes.com, 2006.): This cooperative learning structure helps students to generate ideas or thoughts around particular topics. Each group is given a piece of chart paper and asked to brainstorm words, phrases, or ideas on different topics or on different areas of the same topic. For example: "What words come to our minds when we think of pollution?" Each group will have a different question or topic. The chart paper is then rotated to another group whose members add on to the previous group's contributions. This activity continues until all groups have responded to all questions or topics.

Mindmaps (Bezan; Bennett, Rolheiser & Stevahn): This cooperative learning structure involves students in creating visual images of thoughts, feelings, or ideas around a central topic, theme, or word. Each group is given a piece of chart paper and directions to begin by recording the central image, word, or concept somewhere at the top or side, or most commonly, in the centre of the page. They then begin to make connections for the purposes of brainstorming, summarizing information, and/or presenting key ideas or images. The visual images that they create should demonstrate the relationships between and among all the concepts and ideas recorded. Students use linking graphics such as arrows, bubbles, and chains to show the connections. Using a variety of different colours enhances and emphasizes the points and facilitates the organization of the information shown on the chart paper. The following shows a mindmap that illustrates the feelings and thoughts that a student might have when he/she is new to a country or school.

Figure 3.13 *Sample Mindmap*

Concept Maps (Novak & Musconda; Novak & Cañas; Bennett): This cooperative learning structure involves students in organizing information about different topics or concepts. A concept is anything that has a label, attributes, and can be defined. A concept map is different from a mindmap because it contains only words and lines which show the connections among concepts. Each group is given a piece of chart paper and directions to begin by recording the concept as a word or phrase at the top, side, or centre of the page. As with a mindmap, the students begin to make connections for the purposes of brainstorming, summarizing information, and/or presenting key ideas. Students use lines to show the connections. See Figure 3.14 for a sample student concept map.

NOTE: *Mindmaps and concept maps can also be created by using a variety of software programs. Since they can be created by one student, they can also be considered an individual activity.*

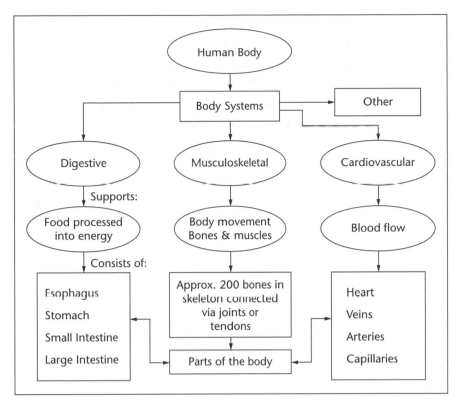

Figure 3.14 *Sample Concept Map*

Inside/Outside Circle (Used with permission. Jeanne Gibbs, Reaching All by Creating Tribes Learning Communities, CenterSource Systems, LLC. Windsor. California, www.tribes.com, 2006.): Students stand in pairs in two concentric circles. The inside circle faces out; the outside circle faces in. Students respond to teacher questions, statements, or issues, and students discuss with the person facing them. As new questions, statements, or issues are posed, students rotate to a new partner. This strategy is useful for checking for understanding, reviewing past material and activating prior knowledge, introducing or processing new material, discussing issues and perspectives, and can even be used as a getting-to-know-you activity at the beginning of the year.

Give and Get (Patterson & Rolheiser): Students are given a GIVE and GET page (see Figure 3.10) and are asked to record five or ten of their own ideas that they can give to a peer. These ideas can be about any topic or subject area. For example: *10 (or 5) things you know about . . . , 10 good ideas about . . . , or 10 pieces of advice about. . . .* When they have recorded their own ideas in the left-hand column, they stand up and meet with other students in the class. When they meet together as a pair, they GIVE their peer one of their good ideas which that person records in the right-hand column of their page, and they GET an idea from this peer and in turn record that in the right-hand column of their page. They continue until they have given and received five or ten good ideas and have completed the page. You may want to give the students a specific period of time to do this (e.g., 10 minutes). You might also want to combine this strategy with a Tribes strategy called Milling to Music, where you play some music and tell the students to "mill" or walk around the classroom until the music stops, at which point they turn to a peer close by and GIVE and GET one idea. When the music starts again, they again "mill" around the room until the music stops and they meet with a different peer to GIVE and GET another idea. They continue to do this until they have given and received five or ten new ideas. This strategy works well in generating ideas from the group in an interactive and personal way. (See Figure 3.15.)

Give	&	Get
1		1
2		2
3		3
4		4
5		5
6		6
7		7
8		8
9		9
10		10

Figure 3.15 *Give and Get*

Note: See LM 3.10b for a variation of this template.

Self- and Peer Assessment

◆ After any cooperative group learning experience, have the students assess their individual contributions to the group, as well as their success in the total group process. Figures 3.16 and 3.17 provide examples of group and self-assessment forms respectively.

WORKING TOGETHER

Did we share?

Did we take turns?

Did we say something nice to each other?

Did we help each other?

3.11 **Figure 3.16** *Group Assessment Form*

Assessing Your Group Work

Group Member's Names: _Rotem_

Avi

Mohammed

My Name: _Jack_   Date: _Mar. 9_

☑ 1. I listened to others while they were speaking.

☑ 2. I offered my own ideas and information.

☑ 3. I asked others for their ideas.

☑ 4. I shared the materials and supplies.

☐ 5. I asked my group for help when I needed it.

☑ 6. I helped someone in my group.

☑ 7. I took my turn and encouraged others to take their turns.

☐ 8. I praised someone in the group.

3.12 **Figure 3.17** *Self-assessment Form*

Providing Genuine Praise, Encouragement, and Positive Reinforcement

✦ Promote appropriate classroom behaviour by providing genuine praise, encouragement, and positive reinforcement whenever possible. Catch someone doing something good, and be specific when you provide praise. Rather than making a general comment, such as "You were great today," point out specific areas that are noteworthy such as, "You participated extremely well in your group. I noticed that you shared and took turns." As well, continue to use specific praise for academic achievements, such as, "Your use of colour for the background in your painting is effective."

Responding to Behaviours

Understand that no matter how proactive you are, students will exhibit behaviours that are inappropriate and/or disruptive, and you will need to have **appropriate strategies** to respond to these misbehaviours. In most classrooms, a large percentage of students will follow established routines and behave in an acceptable manner most of the time. But there will always be a few students who will require extensive support and possible interventions as a result of inappropriate disruptive behaviours. As a teacher, you will find that there is a small proportion of your students who will "straddle the fence" between acceptable and inacceptable behaviours. If these students team up with the small group who need a lot of support regarding behaviour, you will be faced with a much more significant number of students displaying inappropriate behaviours, and it will become increasingly more challenging to manage this class. Your job is to put your primary focus on that small proportion of students who "straddle the fence" to ensure that they join up with the larger group of students who display acceptable behaviours for the majority of the time. In this way, you will be able to then focus on the few who require a great deal of support and intervention.

✦ Think about why students misbehave. It is important to **identify the underlying causes**. Often, students are seeking attention because they lack positive interactions with adults and peers, or a feeling of self-worth. Children need recognition and attention, and if they do not receive them for positive actions, they will seek them in negative and unconventional ways.

Low Key Responses

✦ **Use a repertoire of classroom management strategies** to prevent minor misbehaviours from escalating. Those outlined below depend upon body language, facial expressions, and voice intonation (Bennett & Smilanich).

1. *Proximity:* Move closer to students to indicate to them that you are there, watching and monitoring their behaviour.

2. *The "look":* Communicate to students that what they are doing is inappropriate by looking directly at them for a few seconds and then smiling or nodding and carrying on.

3. *The "pause":* Stop your lesson for a few seconds to wait until the minor misbehaviour ends.

4. *A gesture:* Place your finger on your lips or put your hand up to indicate stop.

5. *Use of a student's name:* Calmly say the student's name to acknowledge that you are aware of the behaviour and expect things to change. If you find yourself using the same name often, consider whether this strategy may be counterproductive. Some students seem to thrive on this attention for negative behaviour.

NOTE: *Practising the five just-outlined strategies in front of a mirror would help you achieve that perfect balance in your body language. Your body should resonate that you are in charge, but should also show that you are inclusive and welcoming. If one message becomes more pronounced than the other, you run the risk of seeming either too wishy-washy or too tough minded. The goal is to be firm and flexible, not too rigid or too loose.*

✦ **Ignore some minor misbehaviours** so that the flow of your lesson is not unduly disrupted. If you stop every time to address misbehaviours, you may be reinforcing them as the students become encouraged by your attention.

Logical Consequences

✦ Ensure that your students know that you will follow through with appropriate consequences when necessary. Be consistent and predictable. Always focus on providing **logical consequences** (vs. punishments), encouraging students to take responsibility for their actions and creating opportunities for growth, learning, and goal setting. Consequences should be directly related to the misbehaviour—a natural extension of the actions. See earlier in this chapter for examples of some possible consequences that could be used.

Resolving Disagreements

✦ To help two or more students **resolve a disagreement**, you may want to consider the following points:

  • Work cooperatively with the particular students to find a viable solution that is fair for all involved.

  • Provide a time and place for the students to calm down before attempting to help resolve the situation.

- Have the students tell their side of the story orally, in writing, or in pictures.

- Actively listen to both perspectives and acknowledge each student's feelings and actions.

- Help the students listen to the other's point of view and to consider feelings.

- Help the students use "I" statements (e.g., *I felt frustrated because . . .*).

- Help the students think of possible solutions to the problem and to assess each one carefully for outcomes and feelings.

- Have the students establish a plan of action and next steps.

- Try to create a win-win situation where each student feels valued, listened to, and able to face their peers.

Self-Monitoring

✦ Teach your students strategies to **monitor and control their own behaviour**. These might include breathing deeply, counting to ten, using steps to problem solving such as STOP, THINK, PLAN, and DO, reflecting on their behaviour in writing, or drawing a picture to express their feelings. See Figure 3.18, as an example of a reflective template you can use with older students, and Figure 3.19, which might be more appropriate for younger students.

Reflecting On My Behaviour
Name: Date:
1.   This is what happened . . .
2.   What could I have done differently?
3.   What is an appropriate consequence for my behaviour?
4.   What have I learned from this experience?

LM 3.13   **Figure 3.18** *Reflecting on My Behaviour*

Reflecting On My Behaviour	
Name:	Date:
Here is a picture of what happened.	
Here is picture of what I could do differently next time.	

LM 3.14 **Figure 3.19** *Reflecting on My Behaviour*

Direct Intervention

✦ Use direct intervention to monitor student noise levels and/or social interactions while working in **group situations**. You may want to try a "**stop and go" strategy** using a red and green circle or square of paper glued back to back. Place one of these circles on the corner of each group's table or desk with the green side up. As you circulate around the classroom, you can turn over the circle to red for any group to indicate that their noise level is too high or their behaviour is not collaborative. Students in this group respond by demonstrating appropriate behaviour so that you can return the circle or square to the green side. This non-verbal intervention allows you to help students regulate their behaviour.

✦ Use more direct intervention with **specific students**, if necessary by using one or more of the following strategies:

  • **Provide a choice** to the student (e.g., "You can choose to sit quietly on the carpet or you can return to your seat until you are ready to attend to the lesson.")

- Have a **discussion or conference** with the student in a location where other students cannot overhear. Avoid centring out the student in front of others, which can possibly spark a power struggle. Be specific by naming the misbehaviour and outlining the logical consequences.
- Follow through with **logical consequences** and ensure that your students know these in advance.
- Develop a verbal or **written contract**, such as the one below. (See Figure 3.20).

Contract

Date: _Dec. 8_

I, _Michael_, agree to _finish my Pioneer research project by Dec. 15._

If I do what I have agreed to, I will _be a hall monitor at recess for one month._

If I do not do what I have agreed to, I will _stay until 4 pm. each day until I finish._

This contract is in effect for _2 weeks._

Michael
Student's Signature

B. Golden
Teacher's Signature

Kate Samson
Parent's Signature

S. Schwartz
Principal's Signature

LM 3.15 **Figure 3.20** *Sample Contract*

◆ In extreme cases, have students monitor their own behaviour throughout the day or week via a **behaviour checklist**. This checklist can be used with individual students, a small group, or a whole class. For example, as shown in Figure 3.21, students could monitor positive behaviours daily, reflect upon their actions, and continue to set goals for improvement. Communicating with parents who also provide support is an important part of this strategy.

Name: *Steve*   Week of *Oct. 3*

DID YOU HAVE A GOOD DAY?

BEHAVIOURS	Mon.	Tues.	Wed.	Thurs.	Fri.
Did you stop, listen, and follow directions well?	✓	✓	✓	✓	✓
Did you listen carefully while others were speaking?	✓	✓	✓	✓	✓
Did you work quietly?	✓	✓	✓	✓	✓
During work periods, did you stay at your centre, desk, or table?	*No*	✓	*No*	✓	*No*
Did you complete the work assigned for the day?	*Math Incomplete*	✓	*Science Incomplete*	✓	*Reading Incomplete*
Did you cooperate with others?	✓	✓	✓	✓	✓

Comments: *Steven has shown some improvement in self-control this week. He continues to need reminders to stay at his table to complete his work. Please discuss with him. He has his reading response to complete for homework.*

Teacher's Signature: *S. Smith*   Parent's Signature: _____

LM 3.16   **Figure 3.21** *Behaviour Checklist*

◆ **Consult educational and resource personnel** when necessary in order to obtain further information, suggestions, strategies, and program accommodations and modifications for specific students.

- Former teachers can provide necessary background information and strategies that have proved successful in previous years.
- Special Education teachers can be asked to share their expertise.
- The school nurse can provide important data, including a medical history or information regarding the home situation. The nurse can also

make home visits to gather pertinent information that may have an effect on a student's progress in school.

- Psychologists can be requested to administer formal assessments to determine cognitive, psychological, social, and/or emotional strengths and difficulties.
- Administrators and other available resource personnel can offer suggestions, strategies, and support.
- Outside agencies can be contacted.

✦ More serious consequences, such as **informal and formal suspension, and/or alternative programming**, need to be considered when the behaviour is extreme.

** Excellent resources are *Classroom Management: A Thinking and Caring Approach* by Barrie Bennett and Peter Smilanich (Bookation) and *Power Struggles in the Classroom, From Start to Finish* by Barrie Bennett and Peter Smilanich (Pearson). They contain classroom-tested strategies for managing student behaviour and will help you with establishing and maintaining an effective classroom atmosphere.

Responding to Bullying

While you are continuously monitoring your students' behaviour inside and outside of the classroom, you may become aware that *bullying* is occurring and is becoming a concern.

Bullying is *repeated* oppression by a more powerful person or group against a less powerful person. It takes the form of **physical** (hitting, kicking, taking or damaging belongings), **verbal** (name-calling, insults, repeated teasing, racist, sexist, or classist remarks, threats, rumours/gossip, hate speech), or **exclusion** when someone is excluded, isolated, or segregated from activities or social groups (e.g., Don't play with her, Don't be her friend.). It can cause physical and emotional consequences and create a negative classroom and school atmosphere. Be aware that bullying is not gender-specific—both boys and girls can be bullies.

** An excellent teacher resource is Barbara Coloroso's *The Bully, the Bullied, and the Bystander: From Pre-school to High School—How Parents and Teachers Can Help Break the Cycle of Violence* (Penguin).

** There are many other good resources specifically about girls and bullying, including *Mean Girls: Creative Strategies and Activities for Working with Relational Aggression*, by Kaye Randall and Allyson Bowen (YouthLight Inc.). For other resources, see Recommended Resources on the Text Enrichment Site.

✦ Watch out for students displaying the characteristics of withdrawal, avoidance, frequent absences, or aggressive reactions. They may be **victims** of a bully. Often, some students who display the characteristics of a bully are victims themselves and are reacting to a bullying situation. In these cases, intervene directly with the students involved or with your whole class. You may also need to involve parents and administrators in discussion with the students and in follow-up actions.

NOTE: Students new to the language of instruction are often targets of bullying because of their language proficiency and different ethnic and cultural practices. Be sensitive to their needs and act accordingly to ensure that they are welcomed and accepted into the classroom community. See the previous section for strategies to build inclusion.

✦ To lessen the number of bullying situations, involve your students in active/ interactive learning experiences about bullying. The following are some examples:

- Involve your students in proactive discussions about bullying.

- Use **children's literature** to engage students in discussions about bullying. One excellent title is *Don't Laugh at Me* by Steve Seskin & Allen Shamblin (Tricycle Press). For other titles to use, see Favourite Children's Literature on the Text Enrichment Site.

- Engage students in **drama, role play**, and/or **Readers' Theatre** in order to dramatize and then discuss bullying scenarios.

- Write **letters to the editor** or to an advice columnist, **create posters** about bullying, and/or **write stories and scripts** having to do with bullying.

- Brainstorm with your students what bullying looks like and sounds like.

- Reinforce with your students that **body language** and **tone of voice** can make a huge difference in how bullying behaviours are perceived.

- Involve your students in **renaming** different types of bullying behaviours as **chargeable offences** or what it can be called if older teens or adults are involved. Knowing how serious these offences are can help students see how severe bullying can be. Here are some examples:
  o Name calling, teasing, insults, or put-downs can be labelled verbal, sexual, or racial harassment, or even discrimination, depending on what was said.
  o Writing mean or hateful notes to someone can be considered hate literature.
  o Inciting gossip can be considered slander.

o Physical punching, kicking, hitting, or tripping is physical abuse or assault.

o Damaging property or pranks can be considered vandalism or gang activity.

o Exclusion, ignoring, isolating, or "freezing someone out" can be called segregation, social isolation, or mental abuse.

✦ Explicitly teach your students that there are different **types of responses** to bullying—passive, aggressive, and assertive.

- **Passive** (where the bullying behaviour is ignored by the one being bullied)

- **Aggressive** (where the bullied individual fights back)

- **Assertive** (where the bullied individual stands up for him/herself, speaks up, and does something when a bullying situation occurs).

NOTE: Assertive responses are the most effective, and students who are silently standing by watching a bullying situation (bystanders) need to know to intervene and/or report to an adult.

✦ Involve your students in specific **role-play** activities to reinforce how to react appropriately and assertively when involved in a bullying situation. This is also a good way to encourage the silent observers or bystanders to intervene in some way. For example, students could be put into groups of three in which one is the bully, one is the bullied, and one is the bystander. The student being bullied could distract the bully by changing the subject (e.g., *That was a cool video we watched in class today.*), asking a question (*Did you see the movie that was mentioned in class today?*), making a joke, naming the behaviour and being assertive (*You are bullying me and that is not allowed.*), walking away, and/or reporting the incident. By engaging in these role-play activities, the bystander would show support for the bullied student. Here is where **body language** and **tone of voice** can be reinforced again.

*NOTE: Students need to know that **reporting** a bullying situation is not "**tattling**." You can clarify this with students by saying: "Tattling is when you want to get someone in trouble, whereas reporting is trying to help someone and improve the situation."*

✦ Involve students in interactive learning experiences with the purpose of **generating feelings and emotions** about how it feels to be bullied, such as the following learning experiences.

Tableaux: The teacher involves the students in drama or tableaux activities, where students are given a role to assume and then instructed to freeze, showing a snapshot of the scene in action. To reinforce bullying situations, the teacher can show a photo or visual, or use a picture book where students are shown involved in a bullying situation. In pairs or small groups, one student plays the bully and the other is the bullied, while others can be bystanders. The teacher directs the students to freeze and hold that pose, encouraging body language and facial expressions showing fear, concern, intimidation, hate, indifference, etc. Afterwards, discussion can centre around how students felt being a bully, the bullied, or the bystanders.

** An effective resource to refer to for effective strategies to teach about bullying is Larry Swartz's *The New Dramathemes: A Practical Guide for Classroom Teachers, 3rd Edition* (Pembroke). In this book, an entire chapter is devoted to anti-bullying strategies, including some of the ones mentioned here.

Explicit Interventions to Address Bullying

As well as involving your students in active/interactive learning experiences about bullying, you can also implement some explicit interventions to address bullying that can make a difference. The following are some examples.

✦ Embed the anti-bullying message in your regular classroom instruction **across all appropriate curriculum areas**, as opposed to a stand-alone unit of study.

✦ Ensure that appropriate **consequences** are in place for bullying behaviours. Consequences should be immediate, predictable, and consistent, and should be escalated if bullying continues. Consistent, ongoing support is important, including monitoring and counselling for the bullies after enforcement of the consequences, and effective support for the victims of the bullying, including protection from repeated bullying.

✦ **Keep records** on bullying incidents in order to look for patterns and have concrete data when talking to parents and administrators. Invite the students involved to write their own versions of what happened and attach these to the bullying incident report. Very young children might illustrate the incident. Figure 3.22 shows a bullying incident report.

Bullying Incident Report

Date of Incident: _____Dec 8_____   Time of Incident: _____2:35 pm_____

Names of Students Involved: _____John Smith, Sudeep Sang, Alison Banks, Dana Crandall_____

Description of Bullying Incident: _____Name calling_____

Reported by: _____Mrs. Taylor_____

Statements: _____See attached_____

Witnesses: _____Mrs. Taylor_____

Intervention: _____discussion with the principal_____

Parent Contact: _____parents were called_____

Signatures: _____S. Schwartz_____

LM 3.17   **Figure 3.22** *Bullying Incident Report*

Involving Your Parents and Community

✦ Inform your parents and community about your classroom and school's **anti-bullying strategies** by inviting them to information sessions, presentations, or plays, or sending home surveys, newsletters, or letters about bullying. The following letter can be used to inform your students' parents about how they can help their children deal with bullying. (See Figure 3.23.)

Whole School Strategies

✦ If bullying appears to be a continuous problem in your classroom or school, you may want to confer with other staff members and/or your principal to determine whether a **whole school approach** is warranted. If this is the case, your administrator(s) may want to include the teaching staff, students, and parent community in developing a plan of action against bullying. Strategies might include the following steps:

- the development of a whole school anti-bullying and safe school policy
- a shared resolve to eliminate bullying

Dear Families,

According to recent research, bullying is an aggressive type of *repeated* behaviour that should be actively discouraged by parents and teachers alike. Without question, bullying inflicts a great deal of pain on its victims.

Here are some tips to help you empower your children when they come face to face with a bully:

* Ask your children how their peers treat them. Children often hide the fact that they are being bullied. Watch, listen, and ask questions.

* Increase social opportunities for your children. Encourage them to invite other children and groups of children over to your house or on outings. Encourage sleepovers. The more socially accepted a child is, the less opportunity there is for bullying to occur.

* See that children in groups have things to do. Bullying flourishes when children are together but have nothing to do.

* Enrol your children in classes or groups that develop strengths in activities that are valued by peers. Even children who do not love sports may like bowling, karate, or chess. The more confident your children feel, the less likely they will be bullied.

* Monitor the TV programs your children watch. Much programming on television reinforces the idea that aggression is the only way to deal with conflicts.

* Do not expect children to work out the problem of bullying on their own. Bullying is not an insignificant disagreement between children; it is aggressive *repeated* behaviour. *Always* intervene. Adults have a crucial role to play in the socialization of children. Consistency is important. Let all children know that bullying is never condoned.

LM 3.18 **Figure 3.23** *Sample Letter to Parents Re: Bullying*

* identification of the bullying problems in the school
* professional development with teachers and parents about bullying and anti-bullying strategies
* the use of a range of interventions to consistently address incidents when they arise
* incorporate/integrate anti-bullying strategies into Character Education initiatives at your school
* the establishing of an atmosphere where students are encouraged to consistently report bullying situations

** Many research studies have been conducted by Dr. Debra Peplar, York University and the Hospital for Sick Children, Toronto, and Dr. Wendy Craig, Queen's University, Kingston, who contend that school-based interventions can significantly reduce bullying.

✦ It is important to continually assess your own actions and program, as well as your school interventions, to determine whether you are implementing the necessary strategies to ensure an effective classroom and school atmosphere. Figure 3.24 provides a checklist that can be used to assess success.

Checklist for Creating an Inclusive, Equitable, and Safe Classroom and School Atmosphere

Check for:

❏ clear and consistent routines

❏ appropriate classroom management strategies to prevent and respond to misbehaviour

❏ effective lesson plans to teach the necessary social skills

❏ relevant, meaningful, and engaging learning experiences that suit the needs, interests, and abilities of students

❏ cooperative learning structures integrated into all aspects of the curriculum

❏ anti-bullying and Character Education strategies incorporated into the classroom and school program

❏ a collaborative approach, involving all school staff including administrators, other professionals, parents and community.

LM 3.19 **Figure 3.24** *Checklist for Creating an Inclusive, Equitable, and Safe Classroom and School Atmosphere*

If you have provided for all of the above considerations, you will be well on your way to establishing and maintaining a classroom and school atmosphere that promotes a safe, secure, and inclusive environment where equity, mutual respect, and self-worth prevail. You will feel more confident and competent in preventing and dealing with all types of behaviour.

4 Assessment in a Differentiated Curriculum

Assessment is the foundation upon which you design your curriculum. It is an integral component of the teaching/learning process. Essentially, assessment is what drives your program, setting the direction and flow of your curriculum and actions. It goes hand in hand with instruction and **should not be confused with evaluation**, which is the application of a value or judgment about student performance and ability at certain end points during the learning process. (See Chapter 10: Evaluating and Reporting Student Progress.)

The initial data you collect on students' needs, interests, and abilities, or **assessing for learning** (Davies; Earl) is the **diagnostic** or baseline assessment that will help you make decisions about what and how to teach. When you assess *for* learning, you will be discovering what your students already know in order to program effectively.

Assessing *for* learning also includes the *ongoing* collection of information you gather about your students as learners during the learning process, and can also be referred to as **formative assessment**. Observation, daily classroom procedures, performance-based tasks, portfolios, and formal and informal testing all provide you with a window into your students' learning process and progress. As you analyze the data that you are collecting, you make decisions about your program, how to differentiate the learning, and about the accommodations and/or modifications necessary to meet the individual needs, interests, and abilities of students in your classroom.

When you **differentiate your program**, you are planning appropriate instructional strategies, curriculum content, and assessment practices that effectively address the needs, interests, and abilities of *all* your students. You will also need to **accommodate** the learning of *some* of the students in your classroom (e.g., English Language Learners, students with special needs, etc.) in order for them to be successful within your program. At times, you will also **modify** your program by changing the actual curriculum expectations for some students who are identified as exceptional (e.g., students who have an Individual Education Plan). In other words, when you apply accommodations and modifications for students in your classroom who are identified as exceptional, you are differentiating your program, but differentiation is not just accommodating and modifying for exceptional students. It is adjusting your program for *all* students.

Your assessment practices must be grounded in what you know and value about education and how children develop and learn. **Knowing your students** as individuals means recognizing and building on their strengths, as well as acknowledging and addressing their needs, interests, abilities, thoughts, and feelings. The knowledge that you gain through your assessment practices provides you with the essential information needed to differentiate your program for all learners—thereby programming effectively and appropriately. Since **assessment** is the gathering and analysis of all the data collected about your students' performance, abilities, and progress, then knowing and understanding where your students have come from helps you to plan where they are going.

As you conduct your assessments, you need to provide your students with ongoing **descriptive feedback for learning** (Black & Wiliam; Chappius; Davies; Stiggins). This feedback needs to be specific, constructive, and focused on strengths as well as on areas that need improvement. It encourages students to monitor their own learning, set goals, and move forward in their learning.

Assessment as learning (Earl) involves students in **self- and peer-assessment** and empowers them towards self-knowledge and self-improvement. When students are involved in **peer-assessment**, they provide their classmates with descriptive feedback and acquire important skills. They gain a deeper understanding of assessment *for* learning and become partners with you and their peers in the learning process, helping to make decisions that influence their success. When students are involved in **self-assessment**, they reflect on and begin to critically analyze their individual learning process, providing themselves with their own feedback for improvement. They think about where they are in relation to where they need to be and what they need to do next. They are encouraged to look for and show evidence of their learning, and they **set achievable goals** to move forward in their learning. Therefore, the more you involve your students in the self-assessment process, the more ownership they will assume for their own learning, the better able they will be to meet with success, and the more they will see assessment *for* and *as* learning.

For **assessment of learning** (Davies; Earl), or **summative assessment**, you need to consider what the students have produced at the end of a unit, term, or year. This cumulative collection of data ultimately forms the basis for evaluative judgments. Assessment *of* learning summarizes the progress made at certain points in time and can be used to move the learning process in different directions, to plan next steps in their learning journeys, or to provide information needed to make judgments and ultimately evaluate the learning.

An important part of assessment *of* learning is designing effective and meaningful **culminating tasks**. These learning tasks, performances, or activities demonstrate evidence of the essential learnings, big ideas, or the most important concepts you expect your students to understand, do, or value in a specific unit of study. Keeping the end in mind helps to guide your planning and the effective design of your program.

In planning what assessment strategies to use, remember to adopt **a variety of alternative assessment strategies** in addition to the more traditional paper/ pencil tasks. The more authentic and performance-based the assessment is, the more students will see the relevancy to their own world, and they will be better able to apply the learning they have gained.

The use of assessment *for, as,* and *of,* or the use of diagnostic, formative, and summative assessment helps to determine where your students are, where they should be going, and how to get them there. These assessment measures increase your confidence and competence in articulating your program to parents, students, colleagues, and administrators, and in programming appropriately and effectively to meet the needs and interests of your students and the curriculum.

NOTE: The use of the terms "assessment for learning," "assessment as learning," and "assessment of learning" have been added to the lexicon of assessment terminology, and are frequently used to supplement and broaden the understanding and use of diagnostic, formative, and summative assessment.

** Excellent resources about assessment include Lorna Earl's work and text *Assessment As Learning: Using Classroom Assessment To Maximize Student Learning* (Corwin Press), and Anne Davies' texts *Making Classroom Assessment Work, 2nd Edition,* and *Leading the Way to Making Classroom Assessment Work* (Connections Publishing). Stiggins' and Chappius' work are also important for a good understanding about assessment.

Understanding How Children Learn and Develop

Having a solid foundation in understanding how children learn and develop is fundamental to designing effective assessment strategies and appropriate programs.

✦ Ensure that you have a solid grasp of the **developmental characteristics** of the various age groups of the children with whom you might work. (See *Developmental Characteristics of Children* in Chapter 11: Creating Community—Partnerships with Parents.)

✦ Involve students in **active, interactive learning** in order for optimum learning to take place. They need to have hands-on concrete experiences prior to being exposed to more abstract concepts. Students need opportunities to communicate, interact, reflect, observe, explore, follow directions, predict, problem-solve, make decisions, manipulate, apply, etc.

NOTE: *Children learn by doing. Constructivism is based on the theory that children must construct their own understandings based on involvement in active, interactive learning experiences and reflection on those experiences (Dewey; Piaget). Once you have a depth of understanding about how children learn and develop, you can then compare your students' assessment data to what you know about child development. Therefore, it is essential that you find out as much as you can about your students and what they know, can do, and feel.*

✦ Recognize that students possess distinct and varied intelligences (Armstrong; Gardner). This knowledge will help you to assess and program for their individual strengths and needs, and will ensure that all types of intelligences are encouraged and enhanced in your programming. (See Figure 11.18: Information for Parents Re: Multiple Intelligences in Chapter 11: Creating Community—Partnerships with Parents.)

NOTE: *By identifying the intelligences in which students excel, you will be better able to plan learning experiences that incorporate those strengths, and use those strengths to learn in areas needing growth. "If we provide students the opportunity to develop the full range of their intellectual capacities and teach them how to use their multiple ways of knowing in the learning task, they will learn the things we are trying to teach them more thoroughly than if we only permit them to learn in the more traditional verbal/linguistic and logical/mathematical ways" (Lazear).*

✦ Understand that students have **different learning styles** and preferred methods of learning. This information will help you to assess and program effectively to meet their needs. (See Figure 11.17: Information for Parents Re: Learning Styles in Chapter 11: Creating Community—Partnerships with Parents.)

✦ Use Bloom's revised taxonomy as a tool to encourage students to move to **higher, more divergent levels of thinking and learning**. When assessing student learning, you need to ensure that you ask questions that elicit the different levels of thinking identified in Bloom's revised taxonomy, and when you design assessment strategies, you need to encourage your students to demonstrate their learning at different levels of thinking. This is useful as a check for **balance** in the thinking and learning experiences teachers provide for their students. (For more information about asking effective questions, see Tests, Quizzes, and Exams and Figure 4.12 in this chapter.)

NOTE: *In the 1950s, Benjamin Bloom theorized about thinking and learning and identified three categories or domains of learning—cognitive (knowledge), psychomotor (skills) and affective (attitudes). His taxonomy of cognitive behaviour is important in assessing student learning and designing an effective curriculum. It was updated in the 1990s by Lorin Anderson, a former student of Benjamin Bloom, and others (Anderson, Krathwohl, Airasian, Cruikshank, Mayer, Pintrich, Raths, & Wittrock; Pohl). (See Figure 4.12 in this chapter for a chart highlighting Bloom's Revised Taxonomy, as well as Figure 5.7 in Chapter 5: Designing Your Curriculum, for an example of how Bloom's Revised Taxonomy can be used during the planning process.)*

✦ Determine what **types of learners** you have in your classroom by observing them or involving them in different learning experiences.

NOTE: *Having a deep understanding of students' developmental characteristics, the theory of constructivism, cognitive behaviours, and the variety of multiple intelligences and learning styles prepares you to differentiate your students' learning. You will take into consideration the different types of learners, and will group and regroup them for both assessment and programming purposes, according to their needs, interests, and abilities.*

✦ **Differentiate your program** for *all* students based on the assessment data that you collect. Your differentiation will *also* include both **accommodations** and **modifications** depending on the needs of specific students in your classroom.

NOTE: *When you **accommodate** for a student or group of students, you are making changes to the instructional process, the environment in which students are learning, or the product expected. Accommodation refers to what you are doing to **support** students in their learning. When you **modify** the program for a student, you are usually instructing and assessing them according to a different set of grade expectations. Modifications are usually reserved for students who are on an individual education plan based on identified learning needs.*

✦ In order to differentiate your program for students with specific special needs, consider the possible **accommodations** following.

Instructional accommodations might include the following:

- Provide an alternative task.
- Decrease a student's workload.
- Increase time allocated for task completion.
- Provide further use of visual aids, models, calculators, manipulatives, real objects, graphic organizers, etc.
- Slow down the rate of delivery to allow more time to process the information and new learning.
- Provide direct teacher assistance one-on-one or in groups.
- Scribe for the student.
- Introduce and explain new vocabulary.
- Use simplified language.
- Adapt teaching materials to make them more easily understood.
- Repeat and reword instructions.
- Check for understanding often.
- Set up peer-tutoring or partner/group situations.
- Use a timer to help with time management.
- Extend learning and provide a challenge.
- Use different forms of technology or media (see Chapter 9: Technology in a Rapidly Changing World).

Assessment accommodations might include the following:

- Scribe for the student.
- Have an interview or conference with the student.
- Provide different modes of response, such as drawing, oral, visual, drama.
- Audio-record or videotape to report knowledge.
- Encourage the use of the computer to record answers.
- Teach the student to use a computer's spell-check.

Environmental accommodations might include the following:

- Change space, seating, or provide a quiet area.
- Change grouping and/or carefully select group members.
- Ensure you have wheelchair access if needed.

- It is also important that you **know yourself**, your own learning style and dominant intelligences—how *you* learn. Your teaching methods can tend to reinforce your own preferred learning styles and intelligences and, therefore, you may not be providing a program that meets the needs of the various learners in your classroom. By knowing yourself well, you can more easily ensure that your assessment and programming strategies are varied and meet the needs, interests, and abilities of all your students.

Collecting and Analyzing Assessment Data

- Examine your **long-range and unit plans** to determine the curriculum expectations that you will be addressing in all curriculum areas (See Chapter 5: Designing Your Curriculum.)

- Look at the expectations you have chosen to address and decide how you will **assess for learning** and which **diagnostic assessment** strategies and tools you will use to collect initial data about what your students already know, can do, and feel in relation to those expectations. These will also help to activate your students' prior knowledge, and will provide data to help you adjust your planning in order to differentiate your program according to your students' needs, interests, and abilities. (See later in this chapter and also Chapter 5: Designing Your Curriculum.)

NOTE: It is important to collect assessment for *learning or diagnostic assessment in advance of the actual implementation of your planned unit of study to allow you to adjust your planning and differentiate for the needs, interests, and abilities identified through the diagnostic assessment.*

- Collect assessment data *during* the learning process. This **assessment** *for* **and** *as* **learning**, or **formative assessment**, is ongoing and continuous while your students are engaged in the learning experiences.

- Ensure that you provide **descriptive feedback** that is immediate, timely, ongoing, constructive, positive, and highly detailed in nature, with the intent to move the students forward in their learning.

** Stiggins, Chappuis, and others (Black & Wiliam; Davies, Rolheiser, Bower & Stevahn), reinforce the use of descriptive feedback *for* learning. Black and Wiliam's 1998 article entitled: "Inside the Black Box: Raising Standards Through Classroom Assessment" (*Phi Delta Kappan*) as well as his follow-up work, reviews the findings of numerous research studies that highlight the benefits of ongoing descriptive feedback for students and concludes that formative assessment and descriptive feedback raise student achievement and especially help to improve the performance of students who are low achievers

- When providing descriptive feedback, whether in writing or orally, it is beneficial to provide students with **concrete examples (samples or exemplars)**

that help them to see what needs to be accomplished. Showing students examples of work at different levels of quality helps them to understand the criteria for success, and to become better at setting achievable goals and next steps for improvement.

✦ Encourage **peer-assessment** as part of the feedback process. The descriptive feedback you provide will serve as a model for your students when they give feedback to their peers in a collaborative, constructive, and positive way, which should help to move the learning forward.

✦ Include **self-assessment** and **goal-setting** as an essential part of your assessment *as* learning. Your students should be provided with adequate time and frequent opportunities and support to self-assess, reflect on their growth, and identify realistic goals, which can assist in determining what next steps they need to take to meet with success.

✦ At the end of a unit, term, or year, collect **assessment** *of* **learning**, or **summative assessment** data, that will help you determine your students' level of progress and achievement.

✦ Strive to make your assessment tasks **as authentic as possible** so that your students will see the relevancy of what they are doing in relationship to real-life situations. For example, if a class is studying water pollution in science and discovers that a pond behind their school has been polluted through the dumping of waste by a nearby company, you might ask your students to write letters to the company president and to the appropriate government agency expressing their concern and their ideas about what should be done about the pollution. Through this letter-writing task, students would demonstrate what they have learned about pollution as well as show growth in citizenship and environmental awareness.

✦ Ensure that you use a variety of the many **alternative assessment strategies** available.

This broad term, popularized by Grant Wiggins, refers to "any type of assessment that deviates from the traditional model exemplified by locally created tests and standardized examinations with their multiple-choice, one-answer format" (Strickland & Strickland).

Strategies and Tools for Assessment

The following are examples of assessment *for, as,* and *of* learning, or diagnostic, formative, and summative assessment strategies and tools. Many of the strategies and tools are **multi-functional** and can be used for all three types of assessment depending on your planning.

It is important to make the distinction between assessment strategies and assessment tools. Assessment **strategies** are the *actions* you will take to collect and analyze data about your learners, whereas assessment **tools** are the forms, charts, templates, graphic organizers, etc. you will use to track student progress and achievement. The data you collect from the assessment strategies and tools you use becomes the "evidence of learning" (Davies) you will use to form the basis for your evaluation. (See Chapter 10: Evaluating and Reporting Student Progress.)

✦ Use many of the following strategies and tools to **activate students' prior knowledge** or **schema**, to set student learning goals, and to document learning achievement over a period of time.

*NOTE: Jean Piaget explained that **activating prior knowledge** is how children bring meaning to their world. They take in new information and try to incorporate it into their current knowledge, and in doing so, they create a **schema**, or visual representation that fit into specific groupings or categories. When they make connections, it allows them to better understand the information using their schema. Thus, it is important to activate students' prior knowledge when you approach any new learning. Students' prior knowledge may contain inaccurate assumptions or biases that need to be explored and brought to the surface to assist in their new learning.*

KWL (Ogle): KWL stands for: What I Think I **K**now and **W**hat I **W**ant to Know, both of which are addressed at the beginning of a learning experience or unit of study. What I Learned is addressed *after* being involved in learning experiences. (See Figure 4.1.)

KNOW	WANT TO KNOW	LEARNED

LM 4.1   **Figure 4.1** *KWL*

NOTE: A variation of the KWL strategy includes adding a fourth column for "How I Learned" which encourages students to engage in metacognition. (See later in this chapter for more information about metacognition.)

Retelling, Relating, Reflecting Similar to the KWL strategy, "retelling, relating, reflecting" includes finding out what students know (when they retell), the experiences they have had (when they relate or make connections), and what their questions are (when they reflect). They retell, relate, and reflect *before* being involved in a learning experience, topic, unit of study, or issue, and then repeat this same strategy again during the learning experience or at the end so as to compare learning and progress. (See Figure 4.2.)

RETELL What do you know about . . .?	RELATE What experiences do you have with . . . ?	REFLECT What questions do you have?

 LM 4.2 **Figure 4.2** *Retell, Relate, Reflect as Diagnostic and Summative Assessment*

Source: Used with permission. Schwartz, Susan, & Maxine Bone. Beyond the 3 R's: Retelling, relating, reflecting, 2nd Edition. Toronto, ON. (pre-publication).

NOTE: The 3 R's framework of retelling, relating, and reflecting (Schwartz & Bone), commonly used as a reading strategy, is also useful in assessment. We have included other uses of this framework throughout this text, including in reading, to encourage effective questioning, and during the interview process. Refer to the recommended text Beyond the 3R's: Retelling, Relating, Reflecting, 2nd Edition *by Susan Schwartz and Maxine Bone.*

An **Anticipation Guide**, originally a pre-reading assessment strategy, can be used in all areas of the curriculum. It acts as assessment *for* learning or diagnostic assessment as it activates and demonstrates prior knowledge while stimulating interest in a topic and engaging students in discussions (Yopp & Yopp). It might have different formats, including agree/disagree, a sliding scale (such as strongly agree, agree, disagree, strongly disagree), anticipation (yes/no *before* the discussion) and reaction (yes/no *after* the discussion), etc. See Figure 4.3 for an example.

ANTICIPATION GUIDE Global Awareness		
STATEMENTS	**AGREE**	**DISAGREE**
The tsunami of December, 2006 was the greatest natural disaster in the history of the world.		
Post-Traumatic Stress Disorder is not really a medical issue.		
A Trip to Haiti today would be the same as a trip to Haiti years ago.		
People who are homeless have many supports available to them.		
A bomb threat in a school in our city is impossible.		
September 11, 2001 is a date that the entire world will never forget.		

Figure 4.3 *Anticipation Guide*

An **"Opinionaire"** (Yopp & Yopp) is a questionnaire that elicits opinions, attitudes, and prior experience about any topic. Through the use of a series of questions, you are able to determine what the students already know and/or feel about a particular topic.

Observation

✦ **Observe** your students at intervals and record objective statements about specific students or groups of students.

✦ Make sure your observations are **objective** and non-judgmental, and record noteworthy behaviours, interactions, performances, challenges, and successes.

✦ Observe your students **at scheduled times and spontaneously**, during each day, in a variety of settings and situations. Observation allows you to hear and see exactly what students are saying and doing.

✦ Implement some of the introductory, community-building, or getting-to-know-you learning experiences as **opportunities for observation**. These serve the dual purpose of providing you with vital diagnostic assessment data while building a community of learners. (See Chapter 3: An Inclusive Classroom Atmosphere.)

✦ You may find the following **student observation chart** (Figure 4.4) helpful in focusing on what to observe. (Although it notes some important aspects related to child development, it is not intended to be an all-inclusive list.)

Student Observation Chart

Physical Development
- ❑ appearance
- ❑ large and small muscle coordination
- ❑ fine-motor skills
- ❑ health and hygiene
- ❑ hearing development
- ❑ sight development
- ❑ speech development
- ❑

Cognitive Development
- ❑ thinking skills
- ❑ decision making
- ❑ problem solving
- ❑ predicting and inferring abilities
- ❑ understanding of cause-and-effect relationships
- ❑ imaginative thinking
- ❑ acquisition of specific skills in all curriculum areas
- ❑ multiple intelligences
- ❑ learning styles
- ❑

Emotional Development
- ❑ self-image
- ❑ self-confidence
- ❑ responsibility
- ❑ independence
- ❑ coping skills
- ❑ organization
- ❑ work habits
- ❑

Social Development
- ❑ interactions with peers and with adults
- ❑ communication skills
- ❑ cooperation
- ❑ problem solving
- ❑ decision making
- ❑ trust of others
- ❑ respect towards others
- ❑

LM 4.3 **Figure 4.4** *Student Observation Chart*

◆ Prepare **at-a-glance observation record sheets** (Figure 4.5) using one square for each student. Write brief and objective comments directly onto a paper divided into squares, or use sticky notes that fit into the squares. If you use sticky notes, you can place them one on top of the other in the squares as you make additional observations throughout the day or week. In this way, an accumulation of observations about many students can be easily stored on one page. With this page, you can also see at a glance if you have missed observing any particular students.

OBSERVATION RECORD SHEET			
Selena	*Karen*	*Salvatori*	*Leeor*
Sept. 12 • Worked with 3 others on cooperative project • Built 3-D tower	Sept. 12 • Keyboarded by herself	Sept. 15 • Wouldn't leave centre until tasks completed the way he wanted	

LM 4.4 **Figure 4.5** *Observation Record Sheet*

◆ Prepare a **summary record sheet** for each student. See Figure 4.6 as a model. At the end of the week or month, sticky notes from the observation record sheets can be transferred to these one-page summaries which make evaluation and report card writing easier.

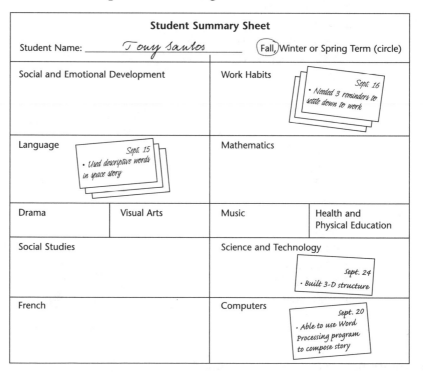

LM 4.5 **Figure 4.6** *Student Summary Sheet*

✦ Based on your observations, write in-depth **anecdotal notes** about each student on a regular basis. These notes for reference could be written in a spiral-bound book, binder, file folders, or on individual file cards.

Interviews, Conferences, Inventories, Surveys, and Questionnaires

✦ Collect further information using **interviews and conferences**, which are face-to-face interactions with students.

*NOTE: It is a good idea to prepare for an interview or conference by having a set list of questions, but you should also be ready to ask questions spontaneously during the conversation. Remember to **use** the information from the interview or conference to program more effectively to meet students' needs. A good idea is to re-interview students later in the year to determine growth over time. The following (see Figure 4.7) is a common form of interview or question and answer (Q & A) to find out first-hand from students how they view the reading process.*

Reading Q & A
Name: Date:
1   Do you like to read? Why or why not?
2   How did you first learn how to read?
3   When do you read at school?
4   How much time do you spend reading at school?
5   What kinds of things do you read at school?
6   When do you read at home?
7   How much time do you spend reading at home?
8   What kinds of things do you read at home?
9   Do you think you are a good reader? Why or why not?
10   What do good readers do when they read?
11   What reading strategies do you use when you are reading?
12   What do you still need to learn about reading?

LM 4.6   **Figure 4.7** *Reading Q & A*

✦ Continue to collect information in all curriculum areas by using **inventories, surveys, and questionnaires**. These sometimes consist of questions, checklists, or sentence completion exercises that elicit information from students, serving as concrete evidence of students' attitudes, interests, perceptions, and learnings. Using them with parents can yield important information about their children's backgrounds and experiences and allow you to develop a more complete picture of your students. (See Chapter 11: Creating Community—Partnerships with Parents). In addition, these tools can be used to elicit parent and student opinions and perceptions about your program and/or school events. (See Figures 4.8 and 4.9.)

Interest Inventory

Name:_____   Date:_____

Grade:_____

1.   What subject do you like best in school?
2.   Why? What is it about this subject that you like?
3.   What subject do you like the least in school?
4.   Why? What is it about this subject that you dislike?
5.   What is your favourite free-time activity in school?
6.   What is your favourite sport?
7.   What kind of music do you like?
8.   What movie have you seen recently that you really liked?
9.   What kind of movies do you like?
10. What is your favourite show on TV?
11. Do you have a pet?
12. If you could have any pet, what would you like?
13. What book have you read recently that you really liked?
14. What did you like about this book?
15. What kind of books do you like?
16. What experience have you had recently with your family that you enjoyed?
17. What was the best time you ever had (in school or at home)?
18. What do you like about yourself?
19. What might you change about yourself if you could?
20. If you had three wishes, what might you wish for?

LM 4.7   **Figure 4.8** *Interest Inventory*

Name: _____   Date: _____
Grade: _____   Interview Setting: _____

Mathematics Attitude Survey

Please circle the appropriate face.

1. Mathematics makes me feel good.   ☺ 😐 ☹

2. When I do Mathematics I feel confident.   ☺ 😐 ☹

3. When I do Mathematics I feel anxious.   ☺ 😐 ☹

LM 4.8   **Figure 4.9** *Mathematics Attitude Survey*

Student Work Samples

✦ Collect and store dated **work samples** of your students' accomplishments in all curriculum areas, either in progress or completed. Work samples might include task sheets, artwork, writing samples, journal entries, reading response logs, science experiments, mathematics worksheets, and maps, graphs, and charts. These often include accompanying descriptive feedback by teachers and peers. Dated work samples provide concrete evidence of growth over time.

✦ File or store these work samples so that you and your students have easy access to them when needed. Types of **individual filing systems** include theme folders, writing folders, art folders, hanging files, a file box, a scrapbook, envelopes, a logbook, a notebook, computer files, a USB stick, a website, and portfolios or e-portfolios.

Checklists

✦ Create **checklists** as needed to record and track your students' progress, completion of tasks, achievement, and/or comments. When used as an assessment *of* learning tool with a group of students or for your entire class, a summary listing achievement levels, grades, or comments can be recorded beside each student's name. Checklists let you see at a glance which students are progressing well and which may still need some intervention. (See Figure 4.10.)

CHECKLIST Re: COMPLETED TASKS				
Names of Students	Learning Experiences			Comments
	Science Experiment # 1	Graph	Create a Structure	
Marie	✓	✓	✓	Very task-oriented
John	✓		✓	Needed support in graphing
Matthew		✓	✓	Absent for science experiment

Figure 4.10 *Checklist Re: Completed Tasks*

✦ You can also create a checklist for **individual** students, as shown in Figure 4.11, **Checklist for Assessing Student Writing**, to check off evidence of specific skills or concepts observed for that student. For other examples of checklists and tracking sheets, see Chapter 6: Effective Learning Stations— Small Group Differentiated Learning.

CHECKLIST FOR ASSESSING STUDENT WRITING

Student: _____ Date: _____

CONTENT	MECHANICS/CONVENTIONS

Form of Writing
- ☐ Narrative story writing
- ☐ Poetry
- ☐ Report
- ☐ Recount/Retelling
- ☐ Procedure
- ☐ Explanation
- ☐ Exposition/Persuasive writing/Point of view
- ☐ Letter
    - ☐ Formal
    - ☐ Informal
- ☐ Other

Grammar and Usage
- ☐ Variety of sentence structure, including:
    - ☐ Complete sentences
    - ☐ Uses short sentences when appropriate
    - ☐ Compound sentences
    - ☐ Complex sentences
    - ☐ Compound-complex sentences
    - ☐ Avoids run-on sentences, sentence fragments
- ☐ Subject-verb agreement
- ☐ Conjunctions
- ☐ Adjectives
- ☐ Adverbs
- ☐ Clauses
- ☐ Adverbial clauses
- ☐ Other

Ideas
- ☐ Beginning/Introduction
- ☐ Middle/Body of text
- ☐ End/Summary/Closure
- ☐ Appropriate features re: the form selected
- ☐ Sufficient information
- ☐ Well developed
- ☐ Unity of thought
- ☐ Smooth flow of ideas
- ☐ Stylistic devices

Capitalization
- ☐ Beginning of sentences
- ☐ Proper names
- ☐ Places
- ☐ Titles
- ☐ Other

Voice
- ☐ Demonstrates passion, excitement, joy, sadness, etc.
- ☐ Awareness of audience
- ☐ Clear purpose

Punctuation
- ☐ Periods
- ☐ Question marks
- ☐ Exclamation marks
- ☐ Quotation marks
- ☐ Commas
- ☐ Colons
- ☐ Semi-colons

Organization
- ☐ Coherent
- ☐ Logical
- ☐ Sequential
- ☐ Suits the purpose of the writing

Spelling
- ☐ Scribble
- ☐ Random letters
- ☐ Initial consonants
- ☐ Phonetic spelling
- ☐ Conventional spelling with few errors
- ☐ Plurals
- ☐ Prefixes
- ☐ Suffixes/Endings (-ed, -ing, -tion)

Vocabulary/Word Choice
- ☐ Appropriate to the writing
- ☐ Descriptive words
- ☐ Conversation/Dialogue
- ☐ Metaphors
- ☐ Similes

Appearance/Presentation
- ☐ Printing
- ☐ Handwriting
- ☐ Computer Font
- ☐ Spacing
- ☐ Margins
- ☐ Headers
- ☐ Graphics

LM 4.10   **Figure 4.11** *Checklist for Assessing Student Writing*

✦ When appropriate, design **tests, quizzes, and exams** that correlate specifically to the curriculum being taught. Paper/pencil tests, the traditional method of assessing students' retention of facts and knowledge, can provide objective assessment data when used for a specific purpose. They measure material taught and are commonly used for pre and post purposes. They can sometimes assist you in finding out what students already know about a topic, theme, or unit of study (assessment *for* learning). Summative tests can help you find out what students have learned at the end of a topic, theme, or unit of study (assessment *of* learning).

✦ When designing tests, quizzes, and exams, be sure to include a **variety of questions** that represent different levels of thinking. Using Bloom's Revised Taxonomy, which classifies cognitive behaviours, will assist in varying the types of questions you ask.

✦ You may want to use the **3R's framework**, as related to **Bloom's Revised Taxonomy**, as a structure for including different types of questions in tests or quizzes. Keep in mind that the 3 *R*'s do not correlate exactly to Bloom's. (See Figure 4.12.)

NOTE: *The **question stems** in Figure 4.12 can be used with older students when they design their own questions or as a tool for discussion. The questions are also effective for you to refer to when engaging your students in large or small group discussions to ensure a balance of different levels of cognitive thinking skills. See Figure 5.7 in Chapter 5: Designing Your Curriculum, as well as Chapter 8: Literacy and Language Learning for more information about using Bloom's Revised Taxonomy and the 3 R's.*

Based on Bloom's Revised Taxonomy		3 R's Framework	Question Stems
Remembering	**Understanding**	**Retelling**	• What is this story/ article/ chapter/ topic about?
• identifying	• defining	• describing	• Tell me about the . . . . .
• labelling	• discussing	• identifying	• Explain. . .
• locates	• describing	• listing	• What might the meaning of . . . . . be?
• listing	• explaining	• noting details	• Who . . . ? When . . . ? Where. . . ?
• naming	• giving main idea	• naming	• Define the word . . .
• observing	• illustrating	• noticing	• Label the following:
• outlining	• paraphrasing	• summarizing	• Identify the . . . . . .
• reciting	• reorganizing	• telling back	• Describe the . . .
• recognizing	• reporting	• telling about one	• What is the order of steps taken in . . . . ?
• recording	• restating	part	• What is the sequence of events that led up to . . . . ?
• repeating	• reviewing	• visualizing	• How would you summarize the story?
• retelling	• summarizing		• Visualize what it might look like?
• sequencing			• What pictures do you have in your mind?
• visualizing			• What did you notice about . . . (gender, age, culture, stereotyping)?
			• What is the author's point of view?
			• What is the message in this . . . ?
Applying	**Analyzing**	**Relate**	• What does this remind you of?
• adapting	• classifying	• applying learning	• What does this make you think of?
• charting	• comparing	to similar	• What connections can you make to personal experiences/texts/stories/
• demonstrating	• contrasting	situations	characters/issues?
• dramatizing	• distinguishing	• comparing	• How does this compare/contrast to . . . ?
• drawing	• deconstructing	• contrasting	• How is this different from . . . . ?
• exploring	• examining	• making connec-	• Differentiate between . . . . and . . . . . .
• graphing	• experimenting	tions to prior	• Categorize/Classify . . . . .
• modeling	• exploring	knowledge,	• Sort the . . . . . .
• relating	• integrating	personal	• What example can you give to illustrate your understanding about . . . ?
• presenting	• investigating	experiences,	• Have you ever seen (felt, experienced) something like this? Explain.
• simulating	• making connections	feelings, stories,	• How does this make you feel and why?
• transferring	• organizing	characters, text,	• How do the characters/authors feel?
• translating	• researching	world issues	
• using	• surveying		
Evaluating	**Creating**	**Reflect**	• What might . . . ?
• appraising	• acting	• evaluating	• How would you . . . ?
• appreciating	• composing	• imagining	• What if . . . ?
• assessing	• constructing	• inferring	• What do you think will happen next?
• checking	• designing	• making insights	• What is your prediction about . . . ?
• critiquing	• developing	-'aha'	• Why do you think that?
• concluding	• devising	• predicting	• What do you infer? (What can you guess based on clues/evidence?)
• deciding	• formulating	• questioning	• What is your opinion about . . . and why?
• debating	• generating	• supposing	• Create . . .
• defending	• imagining	• synthesizing	• Design . . .
• hypothesising	• inventing	• thinking of other	• Why is it valid?
• inferring	• originating	possibilities or	• What are the alternatives?
• judging	• planning	extensions	• What would you do if . . . . happened? Why?
• justifying	• producing	• wondering	• Judge what would be the best way to solve the problem of . . . .
• predicting	• proposing		• Why did you select that solution?
• prioritizing	• supposing		• Think about whether you would . . . . or would not in this situation. Why?
• problem-solving	• synthesizing		• Whose positions/views are not included? Why do you say that?
• questioning	• wondering		• Who might benefit and why?
• rating			• Is it fair? Why or why not?
• recommending			• What would you do and why?
• rejecting			• Why do you think it is written this way?
• respecting			• What goals will you set and why?
• reviewing			• What actions will you take and why?
• validating			
• valuing			

LM 4.11 **Figure 4.12** *Question Stems*

Source: Based on Anderson et al; Used with permission. Schwartz, Susan, & Maxine Bone. Beyond the 3 R's: Retelling, relating, reflecting, 2nd Edition. Toronto, ON. (pre-publication)

Culminating Tasks

✦ Design **culminating tasks** that allow your students to demonstrate their understanding of the most important aspects or concepts in the unit of study. The previous work completed by students during the unit will prepare them for this task.

NOTE: Culminating tasks are assessments of learning (summative assessment), but do not assess everything students might learn during the unit, but rather the most essential learnings that stem from the enduring understandings or big ideas that you have identified during your planning process. A culminating task is an example of a summative assessment, but not all summative assessments are culminating tasks. See Chapter 5: Designing Your Curriculum for more information about culminating tasks.

✦ As you prepare your culminating tasks, select ones that are interesting to ensure student motivation and ownership. You want tasks to represent **real world applications** as much as possible and ones that will demonstrate clearly the most important learnings that students have acquired.

✦ To increase ownership and motivation, involve students in deciding on appropriate culminating tasks or give them some **choice** in the type of task they will do.

✦ Select culminating tasks that encourage students to be involved in **higher level thinking skills** as identified in Bloom's Revised Taxonomy. (See earlier in this chapter.)

✦ The following examples are some of the **possible types of culminating tasks** that students might be asked to prepare:

- Create a commercial, advertisement, newspaper, or website.
- Prepare a PowerPoint, videotape, or multimedia presentation.
- Design a poetry café, mock trial, magazine, or newspaper.
- Design a mask, costume, diorama, pamphlet, brochure, or game board.
- Create a poster or three-dimensional display.
- Prepare a speech or play.
- Devise a gallery of artwork.
- Share highlights of a portfolio or e-portfolio.

NOTE: Ensure that your students are confident, motivated, and knowledgeable about what is expected of them as they prepare for the culminating task. Provide them with the background knowledge needed through the learning experiences and ongoing descriptive and constructive feedback. Developing success criteria and checklists or rubrics with your students, and encouraging peer-assessment, self-assessment, and goal-setting, help to make a culminating task experience more effective.

✦ Identify the **success criteria** that will form the basis for your assessment feedback for specific learning experiences. Success criteria come directly from the learning expectations that you have identified during the planning process, and should be simplified into student language as a way to clarify and make them more accessible. They specifically outline what success will look like/sound like/feel like if the students are demonstrating that they have learned the intended outcomes.

✦ **Involve your students** as much as possible in developing success criteria. As you work together with your students to articulate criteria in student language, learning becomes more explicit, and they are able to see clearly what they need to do in order to achieve success. Developing criteria with students helps to clarify for them what quality looks like, and familiarizes them with the language of assessment (Chappius; Davies; Stiggins). Success criteria should be clearly identified and can be posted for reference as the students engage in the curriculum planned and then revisited during closure activities.

✦ One way to **develop success criteria with your students** is:

- Identify the learning expectations, or learning intentions or goals for the task or performance for which you will need to develop criteria.

- Simplify the language by making it appropriate to students' ages and developmental stages.

- Show the students models or samples of expected products or performances.

- Brainstorm with your students the criteria necessary to create that exemplary product or performance. Add your own ideas to this list. For example, you might ask them: "What makes this piece an exemplary or 'Wow' piece of narrative writing?" or "What might an exemplary or 'Wow' piece of narrative writing look like?"

- Prioritize the criteria you and your students decide are most essential. These become the success criteria to use for assessment and can be posted on a chart as a **checklist** and/or can be developed further into a **rubric**.

- Return to it at the end of the learning experience, and use as self-assessment and/or assessment *of* learning. See Figure 4.13 for some examples.

Learning Goal	Success Criteria
I am learning to . . .	**I will be successful when . . .**
• Analyze the conflicts that took place in Upper and Lower Canada.	• I can explain and discuss the conflicts which occurred in Upper and Lower Canada.
• Explain the significance that these conflicts had in the history of Canada.	• I can discuss the historical significance that these conflicts had on the shaping of Canada as a nation.

Figure 4.13 *Success Criteria Chart*

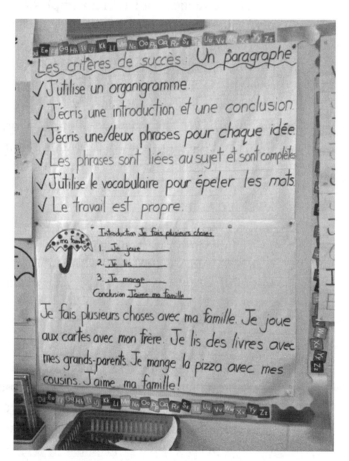

Figure 4.13b *(Continued) Success Criteria Chart*
Source: Used with permission. Michelle Walk, YRDSB.

*NOTE: These success criteria charts (as well as other learning charts developed with your students) are sometimes called **anchor charts** and have a variety of uses, including for assessment, across curriculum areas, or for classroom management. Anchor charts encourage students to make connections, clarify thinking, and/or remember a specific skill, strategy, or concept. They are most effective when they are developed in consultation with your students to make thinking concrete and visible. The charts can be posted around the classroom so that students can see them easily, and they can be reviewed periodically and serve as a daily reminder. When you have created many anchor charts, you may want to think about how to store them so that you and your students can still refer to them easily. For example, hanging them on an easel one on top of the other might work.*

✦ An effective idea for sharing **samples** or **exemplars** of products or performances with your students is to show them four different pieces of work at varying levels. Working in partners or as a group, have them examine these samples and sort them into four levels from the best piece of work (level 4) to the one needing the most improvement (level 1). Ask them to discuss what the level 1 and 2 pieces of work are missing and/or why the Level 4 is a "Wow" piece of work. They then record the criteria they used to determine what level they think each piece represents. In this way, the students are generating the success criteria for an exemplary piece of work, and in the process, they are seeing concrete examples of what each level represents.

NOTE: This is an effective precursor activity to sharing and/or developing a rubric with your students because it actively involves them in looking at different levels with a focus on establishing the success criteria for assessment.

Rubrics

✦ **Involve your students** as much as possible in developing rubrics, usually to prepare them for the assessment of a major learning experience or a culminating task. They will gain ownership and understand what is expected of them and see clearly what they need to do in order to reach a particular level of performance or product.

*NOTE: Rubrics clearly **outline the criteria and levels of achievement** that students are expected to attain. Usually rubrics outline four levels of achievement, but can also use three or five levels, when appropriate. Rubrics can be used to assess a performance task, a unit of study, or achievement throughout the year. Rubrics help to identify the quality and quantity of what is expected of students, making explicit for them what they should know, be able to do, and value. They are often based on the **achievement charts** found in school district documents.*

✦ You may want to involve your students in **using a rubric as a self-assessment and goal-setting tool**, developed at the beginning and used *during* the learning experience and again at the end. As students identify how they are progressing and see what they need to do to improve their performance or increase their knowledge, rubrics help students set achievable goals for their own improvement and progress.

** Heide Andrade, in "Self-assessment Through Rubrics" *(Educational Leadership)*, discusses the difference between using a rubric for self-evaluation (to provide a grade) versus using a rubric as a self-assessment tool. By examining their own works in progress with the help of a rubric, students gain new perspective and can concretely see how to improve.

✦ In order to develop a rubric with your students, you can first develop the success criteria with your students for the task or performance for which you will need a rubric (see above). Once you have the identifiable categories of criteria, look at each category and **write qualifying statements of varying degrees**.

✦ Use the following words as **qualifiers** to help you develop statements for rubrics:

- rarely, sometimes, frequently, consistently
- no variety, some variety, a wide variety
- little use, some use, regular use, excellent use
- not, somewhat, extremely
- none, few, some, many
- many errors, a few errors, hardly any errors, error free
- limited, partial, comprehensive

NOTE: These qualifiers are also useful when combined with report card state-ments. (See sample report card comments (LM 10.1) on the Text Enrichment Site for Chapter 10: Evaluating and Reporting Student Progress.)

✦ When **introducing** rubrics to students, you might do the following:

- Read aloud the picture book *Moira's Birthday* by Robert Munsch (Annick Press) and involve them in creating a rubric about what makes an outstanding "Wow" party, a good party, an average or okay party, and a not-so-good party.

- Develop statements that represent the qualities in each of these par-ties. For example, if food at a party is an essential component or cat-egory, then an outstanding party would have a great amount of pizza, cake, chips, pop, and so on. A good party might have pizza and cake, an average party might have just cake, and a not-so-good party would have cookies and not enough for all the guests.

- Show them visual examples to help them understand and clearly see the quality of each type of party.

- Continue to develop statements that represent the categories for an out-standing party and the descriptive statements for each level. Figure 4.14 illustrates what a completed rubric for a party might look like.

Rubric for a Party				
Category	**Outstanding**	**Good**	**Okay**	**Not-so-good**
Food	Pizza, cake, chips, pop	Pizza, cake	Cake	Cookies
Entertainment	Planned activities Games Performances Active involvement by guests	Games Active involvement by guests	Guests watch a movie	No entertainment
Decorations	Streamers, balloons, posters, flashing lights Theme-based, including napkins, plates, cups, and tablecloths	Theme-based, including napkins, plates, and cups Some balloons Some streamers	Few balloons	No decorations
Loot bags	Filled to the brim with all different toys and candy	Five different items in the loot bags	One or two things in the loot bags	No loot bags

LM 4.12a **Figure 4.14** *Rubric for a Party*

Note: Also see a sample blank rubric template LM 4.12(b) on the Text Enrichment Site.

✦ When involving older students in creating rubrics, you might ask small groups of students to work on **defining the levels of achievement for predetermined categories**. Each group would be responsible for working through one category and then sharing ideas with the whole class for feedback. As students work with and use the rubrics, you might discuss how their created rubrics could be further revised and improved. You could then collate their work and come up with a completed rubric for the class, based on their input.

✦ You might also give older students a **completed rubric in draft and ask them to make suggestions for revisions**. These revisions could be general in nature or you could ask students to fill in a missing column of criteria. For example, you might leave out the words to the third column of a four-column rubric. Again, you could collate their work and come up with a completed rubric for the class. These ideas will encourage them to read the rubric carefully, work together, and become very familiar with the content of the rubric.

NOTE: *Rubrics may not always be appropriate for very young or struggling learners unless the vocabulary and ideas are simple and they are involved in the process of creating the rubric.*

Self-Assessment, Goal-Setting, and Metacognition

✦ Provide many opportunities for your students to engage in assessment *as* learning through **self-assessment** as they begin to take ownership of their own learning, **reflect** on and analyze their progress and performance, and set realistic and attainable **goals** for learning. By involving your students in self-assessment, you increase their motivation to improve and grow.

NOTE: *It is important that **goal-setting** be an integral part of your assessment practices. From the students' perspectives, the goals set must be attainable and able to be accomplished within the time allowed. They must be clearly defined and specific, where students will know what it will look like when they achieve their goal. Students need to feel ownership of their goals; otherwise, they will not be motivated to follow through. Remember that showing them samples at different levels of quality help to make the goals even more attainable.*

✦ Involving students in self-assessment and goal-setting provides them with opportunities to engage in **metacognition**, where they are encouraged to think about how they learn, and pushes them to reflect in a more in-depth way. See Figure 4.15 for a self-assessment tool that encourages metacognition.

What I learned . . .	How I learned it . . .

 **LM 4.13** **Figure 4.15** *Self-assessment*

NOTE: *The first reference to metacognition was found in the work of J. H. Flavell in the mid-1970s, and refers to explicitly reflecting on your own learning processes to understand how you learn. By engaging in metacognition, learners gain more knowledge of and control over their learning. Metacognition heightens the self-assessment process and helps learners set realistic and attainable goals.*

✦ Figures 4.16 and 4.17 are examples of **record sheets** that students can use for self assessment.

3, 2, 1
3 things I feel good about . . .
2 things I found challenging . . .
1 thing I need to work on . . .

 **LM 4.14** **Figure 4.16** *3,2,1 Self-assessment*

Science Experiment #_____

Self Assessment

Student:_____ Date:_____

*Topic of Experiment:*_____

Use the scale below to self-assess your work.

Needs to improve	1
Okay/Satisfactory	2
Good	3
Excellent	4

Self

1. The purpose was clearly stated.   _____
2. The hypothesis was original and thought-provoking.   _____
3. Materials were used effectively.   _____
4. The procedures outlined were sequential and detailed.   _____
5. Observations were objective and thorough.   _____
6. Conclusions were relevant to the hypothesis.   _____
7. Diagram(s) complemented the written portion of the experiment.   _____
8. The write-up was neat and clearly stated.   _____
9. Safety was adhered to throughout.   _____
10. Sharing of work accomplished was well stated.   _____

LM 4.15 **Figure 4.17** *Checklist Re: Self-assessment*

Learning Logs and Response Journals

✦ Involve your students in using **learning logs** to document what they plan to do during the day and what they accomplish. Learning logs can be workbooks, spiral-bound notebooks, binders, folders, or computer files. As another way to foster self-assessment and goal-setting, students can include in their learning logs some of their achievable goals. They can write about how well they are achieving these goals, and they use the learning log as a useful tool to reflect on *how* they are learning (metacognition) and what they need to do to improve.

✦ Involve your students in keeping **personal** or **response journals**. A personal journal can feature a student's recollection of events, personal or imaginative stories and poems, or other personal writings. A response journal can contain student reflections on something experienced, on material read, on movies or videos seen, on music heard, or on a trip taken. See Chapter 8: Literacy and Language Learning for more information.

Peer-assessment

✦ Provide opportunities for your students to engage in assessment *as* learning by participating in **peer-assessment**. They ask questions and/or provide descriptive and constructive feedback to help their peers improve. It is important to provide students with input, structure, and practice, as well as models of effective use.

Figure 4.18 is a peer-assessment form that encourages students to share two positive (stars) and one suggestion for improvement (a wish). This strategy is also effective as self-assessment, where students describe two things they feel good about (stars) and a wish, and the wish then becomes the individual's next steps for improvement.

Assessing My Classmate's Work

Two Stars and a Wish . . .

 A star . . . (something positive) *I really liked your beginning sentence and how you introduced your characters in such a descriptive way.*

 A star . . . (something positive) *When you described the setting, I was able to celarly see the room where your character was working.*

 A wish . . . (an idea for improvement) *You might have included some more detail in your story.*

LM 4.16   **Figure 4.18** *Two Stars and a Wish Peer-assessment*

Figure 4.19 is a peer-assessment form that provides sentence starters for students to provide constructive feedback about a classmate's work (Rolheiser, Bower, & Stevahn).

NOTE: *Peer-assessment should* never *involve students in evaluating and/or grading each other's work. It is important that students know that peer assessment is descriptive, specific, and engages students in providing each other with constructive feedback. It is positive and collaborative and should describe what was accomplished well. It is feedback as learning, which helps move the learning forward in a risk-free atmosphere.*

Providing Peer Feedback

- ❑ I especially like/particularly valued/enjoyed . . .
- ❑ I noticed . . .
- ❑ I was intrigued by . . .
- ❑ What was important to me was . . .
- ❑ You have shown that . . .
- ❑ Something that I relate to is . . .
- ❑ Something you said/wrote that made me think was . . .
- ❑ A connection I made was . . .
- ❑ You reminded me that . . .
- ❑ I agree that . . .
- ❑ I now realize that . . .
- ❑ I learned that you . . .
- ❑ Thanks for reminding me about . . .
- ❑ I infer that . . . . . .
- ❑ Another perspective you might want to think about is . . .
- ❑ A question I now have is . . .
- ❑ I wonder if . . . why . . . how?

LM 4.17   **Figure 4.19** *Sentence Prompts for Peer Feedback*

✦ As you design your integrated, differentiated curriculum, incorporate tasks such as projects, simulations, performances, and audio/video/technological presentations which call for **performance-based assessment**. Keep in mind that performance-based tasks should **have clearly defined criteria** so that students are well aware of what they are expected to produce in order to demonstrate what they have learned.

Portfolios

✦ Another example of a performance-based assessment is creating and using a portfolio. Portfolios are collections of student work maintained for a specific subject area, topic or period of time (e.g., month, term, year) that exemplify, through the inclusion of work samples, products, artifacts and reflections, what students have accomplished, and what they have learned over time.

NOTE: *There are two main types of academic portfolios: growth portfolios and showcase portfolios.* **Growth** *portfolios contain meaningful artifacts and reflections about what students have done and learned over a period of time, and demonstrate how students have grown in their understandings.* **Showcase** *portfolios contain reflections and demonstrations of best work. Both types of portfolios can be used for evaluation purposes.*

✦ Decide on the **type of portfolio** your students will create: growth or showcase or a combination of both.

✦ Decide which **area or areas of the curriculum or topics** the portfolio will represent. For example, decide whether the portfolio will include items from mathematics, writing, or the arts, or if it will contain selections from all curriculum areas. You may also decide to focus on one topic in a curriculum area, such as New France in History, or Geometry in Mathematics.

✦ Decide appropriate **timelines** for using portfolios. For example, will your students use portfolios for a two-week period, a month, a term, or all year?

✦ Determine the **type of container** your students will use for their portfolios. A box, bin, file folder, binder, envelope, or a scrapbook are some options. You may also decide to use technology and have your students contain their portfolio contents on a USB key, or they can create a website as an electronic portfolio (e-portfolio).

NOTE: For an **e-portfolio,** *some school districts will have specific software or online tools you can use, or you may be able to find an appropriate tool on the web with easy-to-follow instructions as well as the ability to password protect the students' work in the online environment. This is especially important for confidentiality reasons. Along with becoming more reflective about their work and learning, students who create e-portfolios will also learn important technology and website design skills. An e-portfolio can also prove to be highly motivating for more reluctant students as it involves technology with which they are usually quite familiar. See Chapter 9: Technology in a Rapidly Changing World for more information about using technology in the classroom.*

✦ Decide how you will introduce portfolios to your students. The following ideas may prove useful:

• Create your own portfolio and share it with your class.

• Invite a photographer, artist, or writer into your class to share his/her portfolio.

• Ask students' parents if they have personal or professional portfolios that they could share with the class.

- Discuss collections of various sorts with your students, and make comparisons to the portfolio as a collection of their work.

- Ask your students to bring in an artifact from home to share with the class. This artifact and an accompanying reflection can then become the first entry for their portfolio.

- Have your students create a finished product, such as a work of art, a report, or a published book. This product and an accompanying reflection can become an entry for their portfolio.

✦ Make decisions about how portfolios will be **organized**. For example, the contents of portfolios can be organized in chronological order, by themes, topics, categories, or according to specific criteria or expectations.

✦ Have your students create a table of contents to clearly identify what is in their portfolios and how it is organized.

✦ Decide who will choose the materials to be featured in the portfolio. Depending on the age of the students and their experience with portfolios, consider **involving students in the selection of portfolio entries**, which promotes a sense of ownership and increases motivation. Students make decisions and solve problems as they choose appropriate artifacts, work samples, and demonstrations of their learning. Usually a good balance is for you to make *some* of the decisions about what to include in the portfolio while allowing your students to also self-select some entries.

✦ You may want to **explicitly teach students how to make decisions about what to include** in their portfolio. For example, at the end of a month or term, have them review a collection of their work on a particular topic, theme, or unit of study. Ask them to choose their best work, the work that shows the most growth, the work that they found the most challenging, the work that they enjoyed the most, etc. Talking or writing about each piece of work encourages students to reflect about their learning.

✦ Invite your students **to reflect** on each artifact included in the portfolio (which represents specific learning experiences). Providing them with questions, sentence starters, or specific formats sparks their thinking and can provide support. Here are a few examples to use:

- Bloom's Revised Taxonomy as a tool (See Figure 4.12.)

- 3 *R*'s framework (Schwartz & Bone) use of sentence prompts or questions: "This is about . . . (retell); This is significant to me because . . . (relate); I learned . . . (reflect)." (See Figure 4.12.)

- Key words or questions that spark thinking, such as *"Who? What? When? Where? Why? and How?"* or for older students: *"What? So what? Now what?"* or *"Successes? Challenges? Changes? Next steps?"*

◆ Continue to **model the process of reflection**. Involving students in reflecting, self-assessing, goal-setting, and sharing helps in metacognition and critical and higher-level thinking, and develops student self-awareness and self-knowledge.

◆ Send a **letter home to parents** explaining the portfolio process. Figure 4.20 provides a sample.

Dear Families,

During this year, our students will use portfolios to assess their learning and achievement. Portfolios allow students to reflect on the work they have done and make thoughtful decisions about goals for future learning. We will introduce the portfolio process by inviting an artist to visit our class to share his portfolio with us. We too have portfolios which we will use to demonstrate the process. If you have a portfolio and are able to join us to share it, please let us know and we will schedule a time for you to visit our class.

At specific intervals throughout the year, students will be required to select pieces of work for inclusion in their portfolios. Work will be collected from all subject areas and will represent best work, most creative work, most improved work, most challenging work, and so on. These collections will enable us to assess and evaluate aspects of your child's growth over time. Students will be required to write about the artifacts they have chosen, why they have selected each one for inclusion, what they have learned, and what goals they need to set for the future. They will share the contents of their portfolios with their peers throughout the year, in addition to using their portfolios at our upcoming parent-teacher conferences to show you what they have learned.

If you have any questions or suggestions, please call us at 416-395-2222.

Sincerely,

S. Schwartz

S. Schwartz

LM 4.18   **Figure 4.20** *Sample Letter to Parents Re: Portfolios*

◆ Provide time at intervals throughout the portfolio process for **sharing** portfolios and portfolio entries with peers and adults. See Figure 4.21 for some questions for students to think about and respond to when they share their portfolios (Rolheiser, Bower & Stevahn).

Sharing your Portfolio:

- What does your portfolio say about you?
- Which entry do you like the best, or are you most proud of? Why?
- Which entry was the hardest for you to do? Why?
- Which entry carries with it your biggest "aha" (learning)?
- Which entry was easy for you to do? Why?
- Which entry took the longest amount of time for you to do?
- What are some goals for your portfolio?
- Describe your process of using your portfolio.
- If an electronic portfolio: What have you learned about computers and technology from your e-portfolio experience?

 **LM 4.19** **Figure 4.21** *Sharing Your Portfolio*

*NOTE: Sharing is a valuable aspect of the portfolio process, as it allows for **peer feedback** and collaboration, helps to push student thinking to higher levels, and celebrates the learning with an authentic audience. Students often gain ideas for their own work and different perspectives when they see their peers' work. They gain constructive and descriptive feedback for their own learning, as well as encouragement and affirmation that they are on the right track.*

✦ Consider how you will assess the portfolio. You might consider creating a checklist with success criteria or a rubric that outlines the categories to be assessed. See Figure 4.22 for a sample rubric that might be useful as a starting point. It can be shared with the students and revised accordingly.

✦ Consider having students share their portfolios with their parents. This might happen during **student-led conferences**. (See Chapter 10: Evaluating and Reporting Student Progress).

*NOTE: You will want to ensure that your students are taught how to show **proof** or evidence of their learning. They should be encouraged to practise talking about their learning when they share their varied work samples and reflections. Ideally, this proof should be in relation to the success criteria established early in the learning process.*

✦ You may want to pass the portfolios on to your students' teachers for the following year, or encourage your students to share their portfolios with their teacher in the next grade.

	Level 1 (Limited)	Level 2 (Adequate)	Level 3 (Proficient)	Level 4 (Outstanding)
Entries	Few entries include an artifact and a reflective writing piece.	Some entries include an artifact and a reflective writing piece.	Most entries include an artifact and a reflective writing piece.	All entries include an artifact and a reflective writing piece.
	Insufficient variety and range of entries showcased.	Adequate variety and range of entries showcased.	Good variety and range of entries showcased.	Excellent variety and range of entries showcased.
Communication and Reflection	Little evidence of growth and understanding of the learning that has occurred.	Some evidence of growth and understanding of the learning that has occurred.	Good evidence of growth and understanding of the learning that has occurred.	Significant evidence of integration and application.
	Little evidence of clarity of thought, organization and coherence.	Some evidence of clarity of thought, organization and coherence.	Good evidence of clarity of thought, organization and coherence.	Strong evidence of clarity of thought, organization and coherence.
	Little or no connections to self, text, or world.	Some connections to self, text, or world. Entries mostly retell events.	Appropriate connections to self, text, and/or world. Use of retell, relate, reflect evident.	In-depth and integrated use of retell, relate, reflect including insightful connections to self, text, and/or world.
	Little presence of author's voice.	Some presence of author's voice.	Clear presence of author's voice.	Strong presence of author's voice.
Organization and Presentation	Entries are sometimes poorly written: many spelling and grammatical errors.	Entries are sometimes adequately written: some spelling and grammatical errors.	Entries are mostly clearly written: few or minor spelling and grammatical errors.	Entries clearly written: free of spelling and grammatical errors.
	Little use of organizational techniques such as title pages, table of contents,	Some use of organizational techniques such as title pages, table	Good use of organizational techniques such as title pages,	Effective use of organizational techniques: title pages, table of contents,

LM 4.20 Figure 4.22 *Sample Rubric for Portfolio*

** Many of the above portfolio activities are adapted from *The Portfolio Organizer: Succeeding with Portfolios in Your Classroom, by Carol Rolheiser, Barbara Bower, and Laurie Stevahn (ASCD), and are being used with pre-service candidates in a number of teacher education programs at the Ontario Institute for Studies in Education of the University of Toronto.*

Storing Your Assessment Data

✦ Consider how you will **store** and keep track of all the essential assessment data you have collected and analyzed about your students (e.g., observations and anecdotal comments, relevant checklists, tracking sheets, photocopies of assessed work samples, surveys, inventories, questionnaires, rubrics, test results, mark sheets, etc.)

✦ You might want to store these in an **assessment binder** or other container, with a section for each student or by subject area or assessment tool. Having all your assessment *of* learning or summative assessment in an organized container will be useful when you begin to prepare for the evaluation and reporting process.

Assessment forms the foundation upon which your differentiated program is built. As you learn about your students, discover what your students know and can do, and base your programming decisions on that knowledge, you will be tailoring your instruction to their unique needs, interests, and abilities. As assessment is interwoven with instruction, your program becomes more meaningful and relevant. Along with using assessment to design your curriculum, the data you collect will ultimately form the basis for the evaluative judgments you will make and share with both your students and their parents. See Chapter 10: Evaluating and Reporting Student Progress for more information about the evaluation process.

5 Designing Your Curriculum

Designing your curriculum with a differentiated approach is one of the biggest challenges that you will encounter as a teacher, but it is what defines you as a skilled and dynamic educator. When you **design** a differentiated curriculum that is effective, integrated, relevant, meaningful, and creative, based on your students' needs, interests, and abilities, it will ultimately provide you with the greatest rewards. "Designing" anything is an art form, whether it is an architect designing a building, an artist designing a masterpiece, or an educator designing a curriculum, there is a creative process in which the designer has a vision of the end product based on knowledge, understandings, and skill.

In *Alice in Wonderland*, Alice asks the Cheshire cat which way she ought to go, and the cat replies, "That depends on where you want to get to" (Lewis Carroll). If you do not have a vision, a goal, or a destination, it does not matter what you do to get there, and you may wander aimlessly. When relating to curriculum design, we begin to see that there are many pathways to success. You can start with curriculum expectations, performance goals, a resource or activity, a required assessment, a big idea, an important skill or process, an existing unit or lesson, or a spark of genius, but however you start, you need to first identify your **desired end results**.

We need to start with the end in mind and have our **end goals** clearly defined (Davies; Wiggins & McTighe). Then we need to understand our learners—*generally* in terms of how children learn and, *specifically*, the children in our classrooms in terms of their needs, interests, and abilities. Once we correlate this information with our goals, we can then design effective learning experiences that steer us in the direction of achieving these goals, while specifically addressing the needs, interests, and abilities of our students through differentiating the instructional process.

As you create plans that meet your school district's requirements in a creative and dynamic way and address your students' needs, interests, and abilities, you will be actively engaging in a **planning process** of thinking and preparing. When planning anything, whether it is an event or trip or program, your advance thinking and prior preparations contribute to its overall success. This process is similar to what you do in your classroom as you prepare the road map to guide your students on their learning journeys. Your responsibility, as a teacher, is to be intentional in the directions in which you lead your students.

An inherent part of the planning process is **assessment**. It is the engine that drives the design of your differentiated curriculum. As you assess your students on an ongoing basis and build on what they know, can do, and value, you will be designing a program that meets your students' specific needs, interests, and abilities and, thus, you will be differentiating your curriculum effectively. (See Chapter 4: Assessment in a Differentiated Curriculum.)

Designing curriculum is a **shared** and articulated planning activity that calls for problem-solving and collaboration. Co-planners include your students, colleagues, other professionals, parents, and the community. Valuing your students as co-planners in the design process helps them to gain a sense of ownership of their learning and of curriculum content. As you work with your colleagues and other professionals, you gain a broader perspective and range of ideas. Parents feel validated and develop a sense of confidence when they, too, are included in the design process—they gain understandings about the responsibilities they share as partners in the process of educating their children. Thoughtful planning as you design your curriculum, when clearly and consistently communicated, becomes the important bridge that allows all participants to believe that our educational process is both effective and accountable.

When you view curriculum design as an important component of your role as a teacher, then what and how you plan take on greater significance. When you look at what you plan, **integration** should become one of your guiding principles. Integration allows you to help your students see relationships and patterns as they make the connections between and among various curriculum areas, topics, and issues. Integration exemplifies the real world as students link their many background experiences and understandings to the various themes, topics, or issues in the curriculum. In a very crowded curriculum, it is virtually impossible to address everything that is required, so an integrated curriculum where expectations are clustered and big ideas are identified also assists you in addressing the multitude of expectations across the curriculum.

Another guiding principle should be to design curriculum that is relevant and meaningful to the lives of your students. As teachers, we need to rethink what we do and begin to move the design of our curriculum from set units of study to issues of **social justice**. Students examine issues and events in the real world and global community, gain multiple perspectives, take ownership of their learning, create action plans to achieve goals, and feel that they are making a difference in their own lives and in the lives of others for the betterment of society. They become active learners, making decisions, solving problems, and taking action. They become more empathetic citizens and learn important life skills.

Once we know what we are teaching, who the students are that we are teaching (what they know, can do, and feel), we can then more effectively and realistically design **an instructional and assessment process** that meets student needs in an active, interactive, and meaningful way. Regardless of the curriculum area, students need to take part in **active/interactive learning experiences**, such as communicating, interacting, reflecting, thinking critically, observing, exploring, following directions, predicting, problem solving, and decision making, to name a few. Active/interactive learning experiences extend curriculum areas and encourage integration and personal connections. Although each curriculum or subject area contains specific knowledge, skills, and attitudes/values that students need to learn, the **process of learning** that occurs in all curriculum areas is similar.

An important component of how to effectively design an integrated and differentiated curriculum is **balance**—a balance among the various curriculum expectations and content areas, among learning expectations (knowledge, skills, attitudes/values), among large-group, small-group, and individual learning opportunities, and among the variety of instructional and assessment strategies and approaches available. Balance helps enable students to learn and grow in any real-life situation. Designing a differentiated curriculum does not mean designing learning experiences for each and every individual student. Rather, it means assessing your students, and then grouping and regrouping them appropriately to engage in varied learning experiences, using different types of groupings that are flexible and change frequently according to students' needs, interests, and abilities.

The processes for instruction and assessment are as wide ranging and different as the students we teach. When you **differentiate** the instructional and assessment practices you use, you need to reflect on what you need to teach (the curriculum expectations, content, topics, issues), the learning experiences in which the students will engage, and what you would expect them to demonstrate as evidence of their learning. You are bridging the gap between what your students already know and what they need to learn. You are differentiating your program effectively to meet each student's diverse and varied needs, interests, and abilities.

As you begin to differentiate effectively, provide frequent choices in alternative activities, and focus more on flexible, small group learning situations, you will find that differentiation will be more easily achieved. There are multiple learning experiences, instructional and assessment strategies, and processes from which to select in order to plan effective programs that are active, relevant, integrated, and differentiated to meet all students' needs. Choosing from cooperative learning structures, learning contracts, or independent study, to name a few, allows you to differentiate your instruction and assessment effectively. (See Chapter 3: An Inclusive Classroom Atmosphere for more information about cooperative learning, learning contracts, etc.)

Involving students in **learning stations or centres** is an effective learning experience and instructional practice in which to engage your students. For young and older students, learning stations provide opportunities for students to work together in small groups, interacting, sharing, and cooperating with one another as they reinforce, practice, apply, and refine previous learnings. (See Chapter 6: Learning Stations—Small Group Differentiated Learning.)

When we design our integrated, differentiated curriculum, we also need to consider **out-of-classroom excursions or field trips** that will extend, enrich, and deepen the learning experiences that occur in the classroom environment. Taking students out of the regular classroom and school environment into the larger wider community generates interest and enthusiasm, helps to motivate students, creates positive attitudes towards learning, and provides students with meaningful and relevant experiences. Effective out-of-classroom excursions encompass all facets of learning. Although field trips can be physically demanding and often require supplementary funding and extra time for preparation, they should be valued and considered as an integral part of your differentiated curriculum. (See Chapter 7: Out-of-classroom Excursions— Experiencing the Wider Community.)

Careful and systematic planning helps to ensure that district and school expectations are met for each grade, division, and course of study. It provides meaningful direction for students and teachers, clarifies program and learning expectations, and maximizes use of time, resources, and materials. When you begin to design your curriculum, you need to consider the various **types of plans** necessary for an effective program.

✦ **Long-range plans** help you to envision your "year-at-a-glance" and the sequential and integrated path you will take over the course of the year.

✦ **Unit plans** are the more short-term, detailed outlines of the themes, topics, issues, or units of study within your yearly long-range plans.

✦ **Lesson plans** provide the details about your planning and delivery of important lessons.

✦ **Mini-lessons** are brief, approximately 5 to 10 minutes of instructional time to teach knowledge, skills, and attitudes/values to large groups, small groups, or individuals.

✦ **Weekly and daily plans** map out your topics, actions, details, etc. and confirm timetabling possibilities.

Be aware that the planning you do becomes even more important when you are absent for a prolonged period of time or even for one day. When an occasional teacher takes over your classroom program and routine, it is critical that plans are in place to fulfill your required responsibilities as a teacher and to ensure consistency for your students. When an administrator or parent asks about your program, detailed plans serve as **a valuable record** of your teaching and learning journey each day and throughout the year.

The process of **curriculum design** is an essential part of creating a differentiated program, and teachers can and will approach it in unique ways. There are many entry points into the curriculum design process. You need to make decisions about how you will begin. As you become more proficient with the design process, you will develop your own style, and it will become a journey of discovery for both you and your students.

** Excellent resources to refer to for more information about differentiated curriculum and planning are: *Understanding by Design, Expanded 2nd Edition* (ASCD), by Grant Wiggins and Jay McTighe, and *Integrating Differentiated Instruction and Understanding by Design: Connecting Content and Kids,* by Carol Ann Tomlinson and Jay McTighe (ASCD).

Creating Long-range Plans

In developing your long-range plans, you need to envision your **year at a glance** and decide on the sequential path you would like to follow. As you begin to organize your long-range plans, consider a number of important elements.

You will want to ensure a **balance** among the main curriculum areas of language arts, mathematics, social studies, science and technology, physical and health education, and the arts, along with their corresponding content strands. By achieving a balance among these curriculum areas and within the strands, you ensure that the knowledge, skills, and attitudes/values in each area will receive the appropriate instructional emphasis throughout the year.

Along with balance, you will want to consider when you will address each of the major themes, topics, issues, or units stemming from each curriculum area. By looking at your year in terms of **blocks of time**, such as terms or semesters, you will be better able to determine when each unit will be addressed and which units can integrate well together. Be sure to look for the links among various curriculum areas in order to facilitate the planning for **integration**. As you decide where these links exist, consider the best time of year to implement certain topics. For example, it would be most fitting to plan an integrated unit on plant growth during warm weather when you and your students could explore the outdoor growth environment in your neighbourhood or city. Remember that the more you plan ahead, the more successful you will find the path chosen.

◆ Examine and become familiar with the **major curriculum areas, content, and student learning expectations** you will need to address for your grade level(s).

◆ Investigate what **school or district-wide plans** exist and how they might influence your own planning. Often, school districts develop far-reaching goals for individual schools and grades based on data collected from classrooms or schools, or based on standardized test results, and these will usually have an impact on your own long-range plans.

◆ When planning your **long-range plans** for the year, keep in mind the following:

- school plans

- division or team plans

- learning expectations for your grade level(s)

- assessment and evaluation practices that might have an impact at a specific time of year such as standardized testing initiated by the province/state, district, or school

- the needs and interests of the students and the community

◆ Consider the availability of **resources and materials**, including teacher resources, student materials, equipment, and technology.

◆ Consider the availability of possible **human resources** such as other teachers, resource staff, parents, volunteers, administrators, and community members. Be flexible when thinking about including human resources in your program **at specific times**. For example, you may know specific volunteers or resource staff who may be available only at certain times of the year. In these cases, you will need to plan around their schedules if you want them to be involved with your class. The same is true of specific physical resources and equipment such as videos, interactive display boards, computer labs, keyboards, or print material where access may be limited to specific time periods.

◆ Consider the school year as divided into distinct **blocks of time**, such as three terms or two semesters. Decide what you hope to accomplish in each major curriculum area in each block of time. By looking at your year in terms of blocks of time, you will be better able to determine which units to address and which units will integrate well together. Be sure to look for the links among various curriculum and subject areas in order to facilitate the planning for integration.

✦ **Choose one curriculum area** with which to begin your planning. Decide which specific topics you need to address at your particular grade level and when you will address each topic depending on the blocks of time available and the estimated length of time required for completion of each unit.

NOTE: Social Studies is a good curriculum area with which to begin your long-range planning. For your first integrated unit of a new school year, you may wish to do one titled "Getting to Know You" or "Looking at Our Roots," which will provide you with valuable information about your students' social identities and the surrounding community. In this opening unit, students are encouraged to research their family histories, heritage, backgrounds, and cultures. You will find this a good way to value the experiences of each student as well as establish baseline literacy skills from which to assess growth in knowledge, skills, and attitudes/values.

✦ **Choose another curriculum area**, decide on the specific topics to address for your grade level, and plan when you will address each.

✦ As you choose subsequent curriculum areas and specific topics, keep in mind **opportunities for links** between and among various topics. For example, a science unit on structures would integrate easily with a social studies unit on the community. The curriculum areas need not be addressed in any specific order as long as all curriculum areas are addressed throughout the year.

✦ Begin to investigate and include in your planning (and familiarize yourself if necessary) topics that represent **issues of social justice** (e.g., poverty, racism, religious persecution, genocide, bias, stereotyping, etc.) that might integrate well with the curriculum expectations you need to address with your students. Consider how these topics might be used to raise and/or heighten your students' awareness of critical issues of equity, diversity and social justice, at the local and global level.

✦ When teaching a **combined grade**, make decisions about how you will meet the expectations for two different grade levels. Continue to differentiate the learning, tasks, and assessment practices for individuals and groups of students at both grade levels. You may decide to do one or more of the following:

- Teach two separate units (perhaps similar in topic or expectations) to each grade group of students at different times in your schedule.

- Teach a whole group lesson on the same topic (e.g., mathematics, reading, writing, media, health, the arts) and have different tasks for each grade, depending on the expectations to be taught for each grade.

- Start with a whole group lesson on the same topic (e.g., mathematics) and have the younger grade students do an independent follow-up task while you continue to work with the older grade to extend the learning as per the expectations to be taught for that grade.

- Teach one grade group one topic while the other group is independently working on a similar or different topic, and then switch groups.

- Combine and align the learning expectations from two different grade levels to create one new integrated unit.

NOTE: There may be many completed units of study for combined grades available from fellow teachers, mentors, or from your school district or ministry of education, which you can adapt for use with your students. Remember that you do not have to reinvent the wheel, but can use available units as a base from which to begin your own planning. When it comes to designing a combined grade unit, it is often advisable to see a sample unit before you begin your own planning.

✦ Keep in mind how you will group your students, ensuring a **balance of groupings** (large group, small group, individuals).

✦ Consider the **time, space, and instructional strategies** that you might use. These will be planned and recorded in more detail in your integrated unit plans. (Refer to the section on unit planning in this chapter.)

✦ **Be flexible** and open to change and possible obstacles to planning and implementation such as the gym being booked for an outside event, resources not being available when you would have liked to use them, etc.

✦ Record your **long-range plans** on a planning template which can be enlarged for easy use. The intent is that you would be able to see the whole year at a glance, on one or more pages. The following figures illustrate different types of templates you might want to adapt for your own use. Templates are also included on the Text Enrichment Site.

Long-Range Plan—by Curriculum Areas GRADE 3					
Language	**Math**	**Science**	**Social Studies**	**Media Literacy**	**Arts**
Reading • Express personal opinions about ideas presented in texts. • Identify and describe the characteristics of a variety of text forms. **Writing** • Generate ideas about a potential topic, using a variety of strategies and resources. • identify and order main ideas and supporting details into units that could be used to develop a short, simple paragraph **Oral Communication** • Distinguish between stated and implied ideas in oral and visual texts • Extend understanding of oral texts by connecting the ideas in them to their own knowledge and experience; to other familiar texts, including print and visual texts; and to the world around them	**Number Sense and Numeration** **Big Idea:** Quantity and Relationships • Represent, compare and order whole numbers to 1000, using a variety of tools • Compose and decompose three-digit numbers into hundreds, tens and ones in a variety of ways, using concrete materials **Patterning and Algebra** **Big Idea:** Patterns and Relationships • Identify, extend, and create a repeating pattern involving two attributes using a variety of tools • Extend repeating, growing, and shrinking number patterns **Data Management and Probability** **Big Idea:** Collection and Organization of Data • Demonstrate an ability to organize objects into categories, by sorting and classifying objects using two or more attributes simultaneously • Collect and organize categorical or discrete primary data and display the data in charts, tables and graphs with appropriate titles and labels and with labels ordered appropriately along horizontal axes, as needed, using many-to-one correspondence keys	**Big Ideas:** Relating Science and Technology to Society and the Environment Developing Investigation and Communication Skills Understanding Basic Concepts **Soils in the Environment** • Assess ways in which plants have an impact on society and the environment • Investigate the characteristics of various plants • Demonstrate an understanding that plants grow and change and have distinct characteristics **Growth and Changes in Plants** • Assess the impact of soils on society and the environment • Investigates and demonstrates understanding of the characteristics of soils and the relationship between soils and other living things	**Early Settlers** • Describe the communities of early settlers and First Nation peoples in Upper Canada around 1800 • Use a variety of resources and tools to gather, process, and communicate information about interactions between new settlers and existing communities • Compare aspects of life in early settler communities and present-day communities. **Urban and Rural Communities** • Identify and compare distinguishing features of urban and rural communities • Use a variety of resources and tools to gather, process, and communicate geographic information about urban and rural communities • Explain how communities interact with each other and the environment to meet human needs	**Big Ideas:** Understanding Media Texts Understanding Media Forms, Conventions and Techniques Creating Media Texts Reflecting on Media Literacy Skills and Strategies • Identify the purpose and intended audience of some media texts • Use overt and implied messages to draw inferences and make meaning in simple media texts • Expresses personal opinions about ideas presented in media texts	**Big Ideas:** Creating and Presenting Reflecting, Responding, and Analysing **Drama and Dance** • Expresses thoughts, feelings, and ideas about a variety of drama experiences and performances **Music** • Sing in tune, unison songs, partner songs and rounds from a wide variety of cultures, styles, and historical periods • Express personal responses to musical performances in a variety of ways **Art** • Create works of art that express personal feelings and ideas inspired by the environment • Use elements of design in art works to communicate ideas, messages, and understandings

LM 5.1 Figure 5.1 *Features a long-range plan—by curriculum areas for a grade 3 class.*

Source: Used with permission. Megan McRae, Toronto District School Board (TDSB).

Long-range Plan—By Term (Fall, Winter, Spring)			
Curriculum and Content Areas	**Fall**	**Winter**	**Spring**
Mathematics — Number, Measurement, Geometry, Pattern & Algebra, Data Management & Probability	• *adding, subtracting, counting, estimation, place value* • *linear – measure "me", – desk, class – our wt. Kg.* • *mass graphing solid shapes structures, pattern blocks, geoboards*		
Language — Oral Communication, Reading, Writing, Media	• *reading friendship books, "me" poems, student published.* • *writing personal narratives, stories, journals, responses* • *storytelling* • *focus on authors, format, publishing media presentations*		
The Arts — Drama, Music, Visual Arts, Dance and Movement	• *role playing "Round Trip" mime mirror group* • *group dynamics* • *songs: "You are My Friend", "Climb Every Mt."* • *rhythm instruments, lummi sticks (chants)* • *name art, silhouettes, paper plate people, line design, puppetry, modelling, colour*		
Social Studies — History, Geography	• *me, family, neighbourhood, community, mapping skills, interviewing skills, community helpers*		
Science — Life Systems, Matter, Energy, Structures, Earth and Space	• *structures expt.-towers, bridges, using different materials: straw, plastic, pins, wood sticks, plastic stirs*		

LM 5.2 Figure 5.2 *Sample Long-range Plan-By Term (Fall, Winter, Spring)*

Long-range Plan for a Specific Curriculum Area				
Curriculum Area(s)	**Topics/Themes/ Issues/Units**	**Timeline**	**Integration Possibilities**	**Consider** • Teacher Resources • Student Materials • Out-of-the Classroom Excursions • Human Resources • Other?
Social Studies	Early Civilizations	6 weeks	Mathematics – cost of living Science – inventions Drama – role playing	Book-Early Civilizations, DVD, Trip to Museum, Artifacts

LM 5.3 **Figure 5.3** *Sample Long-range Plan for a Specific Curriculum Area*

Long-range Year-at-a-glance Plan–By Month	
Curriculum Area(s): *Social Studies/Science* **(Themes, Topics, Issues, Units and Resources/Materials)**	
September *Looking at Our Roots*	October *Structures*
November *Community*	December *Early Civilizations*
January	February

LM 5.4 **Figure 5.4** *Sample Long-range Year-at-a-glance Plan–By Month*

		Year-at-a-Glance Plan				
		Curriculum Area(s)				
		(Themes, Topics, Issues, Units, and Resources/Materials)				
Months	**Language**	**Math**	**Science/ Social Studies**	**Physical/ Health Education**	**The Arts**	**Technology**
Sept–Oct	**Writing** Elements of effective writing Descriptive paragraphs Autobiographies **Reading** Reading/ Spelling strategies Reading/Writing conferences	**Number sense and numeration** Addition, subtraction, multiplication and division **Data Management & Probability** Gathering, Organizing and Analyzing Data	**Canada & World Connections** Provinces and Territories of Canada **Energy & Control** Light and Sound Energy	**Fundamental Movement Skills** Throwing & Catching Ball Skills **Active Participation** Games of low organization	**Visual Arts** Knowledge of Elements Sketching, Colour, Texture **Music** Use music terminology appropriately **Drama/Dance** Understanding of voice and audience	**Research & Inquiry** Class Web Pages describing a specific Province or Territory
Nov–Dec	**Conventions of Writing** Spelling Program Editing Checklists Apostrophes, Quotation Marks **Reading** Book Report: Elements of Story (Plot, Characters, Setting)	**Patterning & Algebra** Identifying Patterns & using them to predict **Measurement Estimating** Calculating the perimeter of regular and irregular shapes	**Matters & Materials** Materials that Transmit, Reflect, Absorb Light or sound **Earth & Space Systems** Rocks, minerals, erosion	**Fundamental Movement Skills** Running Using Implements **Active Participation** Basketball	**Music** Use music terminology appropriately **Visual Arts** Knowledge of Elements Sculpture **Drama/Dance** Elements of movement in environment	**Communication & Collaboration** Email accounts and class conference Spreadsheet Graphs
Jan–Feb	**Structures & Forms of Writing** Purpose + Audience = Form Jot Notes, Summaries, Outlines for Report Writing **Reading** Children's Literature Narratives	**Geometry & Spatial Sense** 2 or 3 Dimensional Shape construction **Number Sense & Numeration** Fractions & Decimals	**Heritage & Citizenship** Medieval Times	**Fundamental Movement Skills** Gymnastics **Active Participation** Volley ball	**Visual Arts** Critical Thinking Comparing works of similar theme from different medieval societies **Dance/Dance** Variety of dance from different cultures	**Issues** Medieval Times Web
Mar–Apr	**Media Literacy** Target Audience, Intended Message, Implied Message Deconstructing TC and Print Ads Creating Advertisements Novel Study	**Measurement** Capacity, Volume, Mass **Data Management & Probability** Predicting Outcomes	**Structures & Mechanisms** Pulleys & Gears	**Healthy Living** Healthy Eating Substance Use and Abuse **Active Participation** Co-operative Games	**Drama/Dance** Enact/create/ rehearse/present drama and dance works based on novel, poem or play **Visual Arts** Creative Work 2 or 3 D works of art	**Communication & Collaboration** Creation of video commercials
May–Jun	**Oral Communication** Class Poetry anthology Scripted Plays Class Speeches	**Geometry & Spatial** Sense Transformations, Angles **Number Sense & Numeration** Review Basic Operations	**Life Systems** Habitats & Communities	**Fundamental Movement Skills** Jumping Track and Field **Active Participation** Soccer Baseball	**Visual Arts** Creative Work Identify strengths & areas for improvement in own work and others **Music** Create an accompaniment for a story, poem	**Productivity & Application** Creation of a class electronic CD Yearbook

LM 5.5 **Figure 5.5** *Sample Long-range Bi-monthly Plan*

Creating Unit Plans

Unit planning is a complex process that involves a number of specific steps to follow. This section will guide you through the unit planning process as you prepare the topics, themes, issues, or units of study that you will address throughout the year.

1. Beginning the Process

✦ Select the **curriculum area(s)** and the specific **topic, theme, issue, or unit of study** you will be addressing, as identified in your long-range plans.

✦ Determine the **timelines** required: the approximate number of weeks the unit will last (review the section on long-range plans), and the time during the day when you plan to address this unit. (See Chapter 2: Timetabling.)

✦ Collect, briefly examine/skim, and organize the available **teacher resources, guidelines, commercial resources, and student materials** related to this topic and strive to see the "big picture."

✦ **Activate your own prior knowledge**. Think about what **you**, the teacher, already know about this topic, theme, issue, or unit, what related experiences you have had, and what questions you have.

✦ **Brainstorm,** with teaching partners if available (*two heads are better than one*), words and phrases associated with this topic, theme, issue, or unit. You might want to record your ideas using a graphic organizer such as a web (see Figure 5.6), or on sticky notes or cards so that you can more easily sort and classify later. Brainstorming will help to activate your prior knowledge as well as encourage you to expand your thinking beyond specific learning expectations.

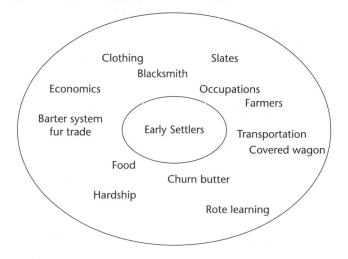

Figure 5.6 *Brainstorming Web*

♦ Using some of the active 'doing' words (Anderson et al.), add to your web of words and phrases by considering possible learning experiences that will incorporate a variety of different cognitive levels of thinking. (See Figure 5.7 below, and Figure 5.8 for a sample web.). (See Chapter 4: Assessment in a Differentiated Curriculum for more information about Bloom's Revised Taxonomy.)

Active 'Doing' Words		
Identifying Labeling Locating Listing Naming Observing **Remembering** Outlining Reciting Recognizing Recording Repeating Retelling Sequencing Visualizing	Adapting Relating Charting Demonstrating Dramatizing Drawing **Applying** Exhibiting Exploring Graphing Implementing Investigating Manipulating Modeling Relating Simulating Transferring Translating Using	Appraising Assessing Critiquing Concluding Deciding Debating Deducing Defending **Evaluating** Inferring Hypothesising Justifying judging Prioritizing Predicting Questioning Problem-solving Recommending Rating Validating Rejecting Respecting
Defining Discussing Describing Explaining Giving main idea Illustrating **Understanding** Paraphrasing Reorganizing Reporting Restating Summarizing Reviewing	Classifying Comparing Contrasting Distinguishing Deconstructing Examining Experimenting Integrating **Analyzing** Investigating Organizing Researching Making Surveying Connections	Acting Composing Constructing Designing Developing Devising Formulating Generating **Creating** Imagining Inventing Originating Planning Proposing Producing Wondering Supposing

Figure 5.7 *Active "Doing" Words*

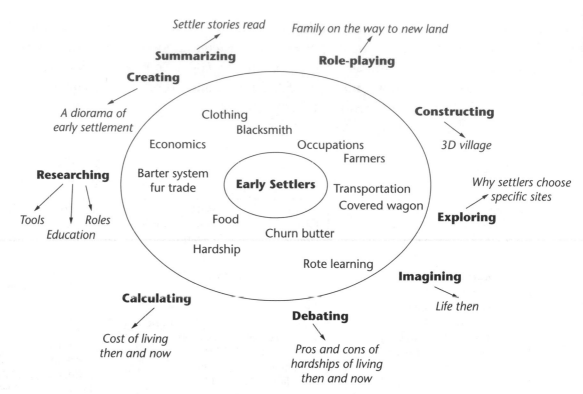

Figure 5.8 *Possible Learning Experiences Web*

✦ Consider the **integration** possibilities. Colour-code the learning experiences on your web into different curriculum areas. For example, circle all the language experiences in red, all the arts experiences in blue, all the science experiences in black, etc. This will make it easier for you to identify the natural integration possibilities without forcing integration. You can then plan accordingly, turning to the appropriate curriculum documents to determine the learning expectations you should address. (See Figure 5.9.)

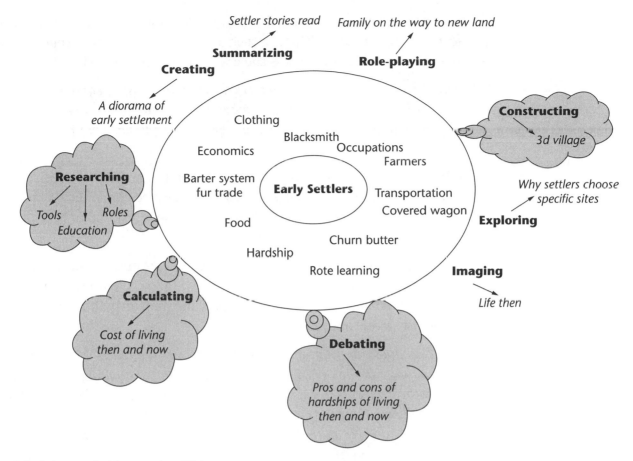

Figure 5.9 *Colour-coded Integration Web*

2. Designing the Unit

✦ Examine the **curriculum document** you will need for this theme, topic, issue, or unit of study and select the student learning expectations to be addressed. Think about what you want your students to know, be able to do, and feel or value at the end of this theme, topic, issue, or unit of study.

✦ Look at other curriculum documents for **integration** possibilities based on the ideas you have generated in your brainstormed web, and select the relevant student learning expectations to be addressed.

✦ Consider the possibilities for broadening your theme, topic, issue, or unit of study to incorporate elements of **equity, diversity, and social justice**, where students are examining critical issues in their lives and in the global community. Here is an example: Clean water is a necessity of life. More than a billion people in the world do not have access to safe, clean drinking water. Consider what your students can do to help create an environment that includes clean, safe drinking water for all global communities. This topic of water, sanitation, and health could be integrated into a grade 2 science unit on water in the environment, or in a more sophisticated way for grade 8 students who might be required to study water systems in their science and technology curriculum. Through such a study, you are helping your students raise their social consciousness and engage in issues of social justice.

NOTE: As you become more comfortable with addressing equity, diversity, and social justice, you might even begin your planning process with these critical issues in mind, and then integrate these issues with the topics required by your school or district.

✦ **Cluster** these expectations by looking for commonalities between and among expectations and ones that can naturally be combined so that you are not attempting to teach to individual expectations, but rather to a number of expectations that represent a "big idea."

✦ **Prioritize those clusters** of expectations to determine the most important one(s). These become your priorities, the "big ideas," or the lasting or enduring understandings that you hope your students will learn, be able to do, and/or value above all else.

NOTE: This does not mean that your students will not learn other elements of this unit, but the "big ideas" or enduring understandings are the most important concepts, themes, or issues that you hope your students will come away with at the end. These concepts, themes, or issues may often be represented by more abstract thoughts, such as points of view, theories, assumptions, questions, or principles. Big ideas will have lasting meaning and represent concepts that are essential to your students' lives. It is here that you can integrate concepts of equity, diversity, and social justice. Often district or ministry curriculum documents will identify the big ideas for you when they outline the learning expectations or goals for your grade.

✦ Decide on the **assessment** *for* **learning** (**diagnostic assessment**) strategies and tools you will use to find out what your students already know or think they know, what experiences they have had, and what they want to know or what questions they have in relation to the topic, theme, issue, or unit of study. The information you collect will help you to program more effectively to meet your students' needs, interests, and abilities. (See Chapter 4: Assessment in a Differentiated Curriculum.)

NOTE: Assessment for learning or diagnostic assessment strategies (the actions you will take to find out about your learners) and the tools (forms, charts, templates, graphic organizers, etc. you will use to help you to assess) guide your program and will serve as your baseline. In order to plan appropriate and effective learning experiences based on your assessment for learning, you should consider collecting baseline data well in advance of the implementation of your unit as it will inform the planning process. Your diagnostic assessment could also serve as part of your introduction to the overall unit. Referring to this baseline information at a later date during and at the end of the unit will allow you to see what your students have learned over time.

✦ Think about what you would like your students to know, be able to do, and value or feel at the *end* of the unit, and decide on the **assessment** *of* **learning** (**summative assessment**) you will use. These might include unit tests, speeches, oral and written reports, project displays and presentations, including audiotapes, videotapes, drama, songs, visual presentations, and multimedia presentations. (See Chapter 4: Assessment in a Differentiated Curriculum.)

✦ Decide on the **culminating task(s)** for this unit that will allow your students to demonstrate their understanding of the most important aspects or concepts. The previous work in which they have engaged and the formative assessment you have completed all build the foundation for these culminating tasks. Even though a culminating task is considered an assessment *of* learning and summative assessment, it usually does not assess everything that the students have learned in the unit, but rather the most important, the "big ideas," or the enduring understandings. (See Chapter 4: Assessment in a Differentiated Curriculum.)

✦ Identify the **success criteria** to be used to determine your students' learning achievement during this unit of study. You could create a **checklist** and/ or **rubric** to clearly identify the success criteria by which the students will be assessed in relation to the expectations you have chosen to address. (See Chapter 4: Assessment in a Differentiated Curriculum.)

✦ Decide on the **assessment** *for* **and** *as* **learning** (**formative assessment**) you will use throughout the unit. This assessment involves *ongoing* tracking of your students' progress over time, allows you to check whether your students are learning what you are teaching, and helps you to make decisions about next steps to take. These might include ongoing observation, anecdotal note-taking, work samples, tests or quizzes, checklists, interviews, conferences, self-assessments, goal-setting, portfolio reflections, peer assessment, and descriptive feedback. (See Chapter 4: Assessment in a Differentiated Curriculum.)

✦ Decide on the methods and tools you will use to **track** student completion of tasks and expectations, assignments, etc. These tracking sheets will be valuable additions to the assessment data collected. (For examples of tracking tools and strategies, see Chapter 6: Effective Learning Stations— Small Group Differentiated Learning.)

✦ Review the **resources and materials** you have already browsed and collected, and make decisions about what you will use during the unit. These will include teacher resources, guidelines, commercial resources, and student materials.

✦ Collect or order any **media resources** (e.g., stories, poetry, or songs on audiotapes, CDs, DVDs, videos, websites) and computer software that would be relevant to the topic, making sure that they are appropriate to your students' maturity level and interests.

✦ Find out what possible **human resources** are available and arrange for these people to visit with your students at specific and convenient times. Communicate with these guests well in advance via email, telephone, or letter.

✦ Decide how you will organize your learning **environment/space**. Consider furniture, meeting spaces, display areas, storage, learning stations, audio-visual and technological requirements. (See Chapter 1: Classroom Design and Organization.)

3. Planning the Learning Experiences

✦ Design the tasks, lessons, or **learning experiences** in which your students will take part. Review your brainstormed webs and integration possibilities, and make connections to the expectations you will address. Focus the learning on the **"big ideas"** or **enduring understandings** that were identified as a result of the clustering activity.

✦ Plan to use a range of **instructional strategies** in your lessons that involve direct instruction, independent activity, and small-group cooperative learning.

✦ As you plan the learning experiences and instructional strategies, think about how you will create an **inclusive classroom atmosphere** and accommodate the learning needs of all students, including English Language Learners and students with exceptionalities, taking into consideration the various learning styles and multiple intelligences represented in your classroom. Consider the possible instructional, environmental, and assessment accommodations that might be required, and for which students you might need to modify the grade level expectations. (See Chapter 4: Assessment in a Differentiated Curriculum, as well as later in this chapter in the Creating Lesson Plans section.)

✦ Plan learning experiences that **differentiate** your instructional approach to better meet the diverse needs of your learners. Students differ in various ways, so in addition to thinking about learning styles and multiple intelligences, you need to consider prior knowledge or skill expertise, learning rate, cognitive ability, motivation, attitude, effort, interest, strengths, or talents. When you differentiate, you are enhancing the match between the learners' characteristics and the components of the curriculum. Therefore, consider the **processes** you are using and the **products** you are asking your students to produce. The following are ways you might differentiate:

- Build on past knowledge and experiences.
- Provide alternative tasks and/or activities for some students.
- Vary your instructional strategies.
- Give students clues as to what they need to do; depending on their multiple intelligences, these clues might be visual or auditory in order to use the strengths that they have and build on ones they need to develop.
- Build in opportunities for those kinesthetic learners to experience some movement.
- Provide a variety of resources, texts, and materials that might appeal to different students.
- Use further manipulatives and visuals.
- Use technology (see Chapter 9: Technology in a Rapidly Changing World).
- Provide a variety of graphic organizers for students to use (see more information about and examples of graphic organizers later in this chapter).
- Allow for choice in the selection and completion of tasks.
- Provide sufficient and/or extra time for some students to complete the tasks assigned, taking into account the different learning styles of students.
- Adjust the timing or pace of your direct instruction.
- Provide opportunities for some students to engage in more independent study.
- Provide opportunities for peer and group support.
- Vary groupings.
- Implement learning stations.
- Vary types of products.
- Plan out-of-classroom excursions.

✦ As part of differentiating your program, plan for a variety and balance of **groupings**, including whole class, small group, heterogeneous, homogeneous, ability, and interest. Creating appropriate groupings helps to make the delivery of your lessons more manageable. If you select instructional strategies that address the learning needs of small groups of students, you are teaching at the point of need while making it more efficient and practical to respond to student needs. Your groupings should be temporary and flexible, and will therefore change as the content changes and the needs, interests, and abilities of your students change.

- Another effective way to differentiate your program is to use **learning stations** where students work in small groups to explore, reinforce, refine, or practise some of the learning expectations to be addressed in the unit. You will need to decide how you will set up your stations, how students will use and move through them, and how you will track and assess students' work. (For an in-depth look at how to implement learning stations, see Chapter 6: Effective Learning Stations—Small Group Differentiated Learning.)

- When differentiating the **types of products** that your students might produce in order to demonstrate their learning, ensure that you provide them with some choice to allow for more motivation and ownership. (Refer to Culminating Tasks in Chapter 4: Assessment in a Differentiated Classroom for some examples of products your students might produce.)

- Consider and plan for an **out-of-classroom excursion** or field trip to address some of the learning expectations in your unit. By doing so, you are exposing your students to a valuable learning experience and providing yet another important opportunity for differentiation. (For more information about including out-of-classroom excursions or field trips as part of your unit, see Chapter 7: Out-of-classroom Excursions—Experiencing the Wider Community.)

- **Prepare a flexible plan**, recording the learning expectations to be addressed and describing the learning experiences that will be used to teach those expectations.

- **Sequence** the learning expectations and experiences in the order that you plan to present them. By doing this, you are creating an overview of the learning experiences that clearly illustrates the sequence of the lessons and the scope of the unit. Figure 5.10 provides an example of a flexible plan.

Learning Expectations	Assessment	Learning Experiences
Compare maps of early civilizations with modern maps of the same era.	*Observation Checklist Work samples - map*	*Group concept map on what is a civilization*
Explain how ancient China shaped and used the environment to meet their physical needs.	*Discussion Checklist Response*	*Jigsaw text with info on food, homes, clothing, and health. Create a table representing information learned.*

Figure 5.10 *A Flexible Plan*

♦ Decide how you will **introduce** your theme, topic, or unit of study. For example, if your class is going to study early settlers, you might decide to dress as an early settler, read a story about life as a settler, show a film or video, do some role playing, conduct a lesson using rote learning and relate it to settler life, or bring in an artifact and have students guess what it is and what its purpose was.

NOTE: Any of the above introductions could provide you with diagnostic assessment data about your students. Keep in mind that other diagnostic assessments that you have planned, such as KWL, could also serve as a viable introduction to your unit. (See Chapter 4: Assessment in a Differentiated Curriculum.)

♦ Decide which lessons will require **detailed lesson plans**. (Refer to Creating Lesson Plans later on in this chapter.)

♦ **Be flexible** in the length of time that some lessons will require, depending on the students in your classroom. Some students may take one day to accomplish a certain task; others may take a week. Also, once you are into the unit, you may find that the order of learning experiences must be changed. Flexibility and a focus on meeting the needs, interests, and abilities of your diverse group of students are key to effective programming.

4. Completing the Process

♦ Decide on the **homework** you will assign to accompany this unit and the learning expectations it will address. (See Chapter 11: Creating Community—Partnerships with Parents).

♦ Decide how you will **communicate with parents** about your program and about individual student progress. (See Chapter 11: Creating Community—Partnerships with Parents).

♦ Decide how you will **celebrate** and share the learning with your students and with others. Possible activities include an open house, invitations to the classroom, sending home newsletters or student-made newspapers, conducting a scavenger hunt through the classroom or school, an authors' festival, a literacy or arts celebration of learning, a mathematics evening, a computer/technology evening, a science fair, a musical concert, a photo display, a slide show, a video, etc. (See Chapter 11: Creating Community—Partnerships with Parents.)

♦ Be sure to **reflect** on your lessons and overall unit. Think about your successes, challenges, changes, and next steps. Be sure to involve your students in helping to plan and provide feedback about your program. Input from your students is invaluable. Be flexible and open to change, based on their feedback.

✦ Now that you have a good idea about how to plan a unit, you may find it useful to experiment with a few different unit planning templates or modify one to meet your needs.

See **LM 5.6** on the Text Enrichment Site for an annotated step-by-step process to guide your unit planning based on the steps outlined in this chapter, and **LM 5.7** for a simplified non-annotated template with headings only.

Figure 5.11 (and **LM 5.8**) is an at-a-glance unit planning template that highlights the important information needed to plan a unit.

Unit Title	Main Curriculum Area	Integration (other curriculum areas)						Grade/Timeframe	
Unit Expectations: [Overall curriculum expectations for the unit]								"Big Ideas"/ Enduring Understandings	
Culminating task								Celebrating the Learning	
Specific Expectations	Assessment				Sequence of Tasks	Teaching/ Learning Strategies	Groupings		Materials/ Resources	Accommodations	Modifications
	Strategies	D	F	S			W	S	I		
		x			**1.** E.g., Introductory Lesson						
					2.						
					3.						
					4.						
					5.						
					6.					Homework	Home Communication
					7.						

* D = Diagnostic, F = Formative, S = Summative, W= whole group, G = Group, I = Individual
Other Notes:

 **LM 5.8** **Figure 5.11** *Sample Unit Overview Plan*

Creating Lesson Plans

Once you have the "big picture," or a sense of where you are going and the expectations you will be addressing in a theme, topic, issue, or unit of study, you are ready to outline the important lessons in the unit. These detailed lesson plans become an integral part of your unit plan design process. If a lesson is part of a unit of study, it is important to think about how it fits into the overall flow of the unit and what your students have already learned before it. If it is an introductory lesson to your unit or a final summary lesson, it could be considered part of your diagnostic or summative assessment for the unit. However, lessons are not always linked to your units of study and **can stand alone** in order to teach specific knowledge, skills, or attitudes/values. Therefore, the information in this section will assist you in designing any lesson. Consider the designing of your lesson plan as a two-step process—the **preparation** and the **delivery** of the actual lesson.

1. Preparing for the Lesson

+ Think about and record the **background information** that your students bring to the lesson in terms of the context and where this lesson fits in your overall planning. If this lesson is part of a unit plan, think about whether it is an introductory, middle, or culminating lesson.

+ Select the **learning expectations** (knowledge, skills, attitudes/values) that your specific lesson will address. Think about what you want your students to learn, be able to do, or feel/value, and identify how these learning expectations relate to any "big ideas" that are part of the unit of study.

+ Consider how this lesson might be used to raise and/or heighten your students' awareness of critical issues of **equity, diversity, and social justice**, either at the local or global level. By doing this, you are raising issues of social consciousness and encouraging your students to go beyond the prescribed curriculum and make significant links to world issues and to their own lives.

+ Decide on the specific **assessment** *for, as*, or *of* **learnings** trategies and tools you will use (**diagnostic, formative, summative**) to determine how well your students will achieve the identified expectations for this particular lesson. If this lesson is part of a sequence of lessons, either from a unit of study or a subject area topic, it is assumed that the diagnostic assessment completed at the beginning of your unit or topic is guiding your lessons. (See earlier in this chapter, as well as Chapter 4: Assessment in a Differentiated Curriculum for more information.)

- ✦ Decide how you will **differentiate** and/or adapt or change the lesson (**accommodations and modifications**) for individual students or groups of students if necessary. (See Chapter 4: Assessment in a Differentiated Curriculum.)

- ✦ Decide on the **student materials, teacher resources, human resources, and equipment** you will need to teach this lesson.

2. Delivering the Lesson

- ✦ When delivering the lesson, think about how you will **actively engage** the students in learning. Decide on the delivery of your lesson by considering the elements of lesson design (Hunter & Russell):
  - introduction, mental set, or "hook" to grab the audience's attention
  - sharing the purpose, learning expectations, and how they will be assessed in student language
  - body of the lesson, including the aspects of:
    - o providing input/sharing information
    - o modelling and demonstrating
    - o practising the learning (guided and/or independent practice)
    - o checking for understanding
  - conclusion/closure, reflecting on what was learned, and wrap-up to the lesson

  NOTE: Designing effective lesson delivery is like designing a dynamic presentation to any audience. Both should include a motivating introduction or beginning; objectives that are openly shared with participants to outline purpose and direction; content where the key concepts are outlined, modelled, practised, and internalize; and a conclusion that inspires thoughtful reflection. These key elements are not meant to be a rigid step-by-step formula or recipe to be applied to each and every lesson. Instead, you are encouraged to carefully and deliberately consider the elements when planning your lessons and make decisions on which elements to use and in which order to use them. Teaching then becomes a conscious decision-making process. The strength of this delivery model lies in the myriad of combinations that are created by the teacher for each lesson (Wolfe; Hunter & Russell).

- ✦ A detailed description of lesson design components appears as Figure 5.12.

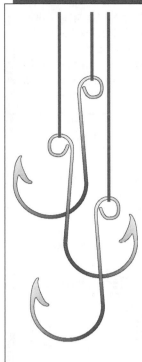

Introduction, mental set, or "hook"

The mental set or "hook," sometimes also referred to as "minds on," is perhaps the most important part of your lesson as it sets the stage for engaging the learner. It should motivate and inspire your students to participate and become immediately involved. It allows you to link the past experiences of your students (through questioning or activities) to the learning objectives and expectations of the lesson. Depending on the type of learning experience used, this introduction to your lesson can range in time from thirty seconds to a full day. Here are some examples of effective mental sets:

- a powerful read-aloud
- a lively song, poem, or chant
- a thought-provoking question or quote
- a photo, picture, movie, or video
- a riddle or puzzle to solve

Sharing the purpose, learning expectations, and assessment criteria (in student language)

For each lesson, you will need to decide how you will share the purpose and learning expectations, and how students will be assessed using vocabulary and language that are appropriate to your students' specific age and maturity level. When you inform your students about the purpose of the lesson, you are answering the questions "What's in it for me?" and "Why are we studying this topic?" Sharing the learning expectations builds ownership and motivation and is key to making the lesson meaningful and relevant. Articulating the success criteria or how students will be assessed, as well as clarifying what exemplary learning looks like, makes explicit what evidence is needed to demonstrate their learning and achievement. (See Chapter 4: Assessment in a Differentiated Curriculum.)

Body of the lesson

Providing input: You do not have to deliver input in a didactic, teacher-directed way. Instead, you could read aloud to students, ask students to read material independently, or have your students sing a song, watch a video, listen to a tape, look at pictures, participate in drama, or go on a field trip, for example. Students also acquire information and input from each other, as in a cooperative learning lesson such as a jigsaw strategy. (Refer to Chapter 3: An Inclusive Classroom Atmosphere.) During the body of the lesson, it is advisable that as many of the learning styles and multiple intelligences as possible be tapped, in order to involve all learners in an auditory, visual, tactile, and kinesthetic way. Knowledge of learning styles and multiple intelligences benefits teachers as they strive to involve all students in an active/interactive way.

Modelling and demonstrating: Doing this for your students provides them with clear examples of what the learning looks like and sounds like. It increases memory by giving students visual and concrete cues. It helps to provide variety to your lessons and it generates interest.

Practising the learning (guided practice and/or independent practice): In this part of the lesson, students are given time to experiment, experience, and apply their understandings. Practice is extremely important and allows students to consolidate the key learnings and to gain confidence and competence. To be effective, it should relate to the learning expectations and the appropriate level of thinking of your students. Practice activities often occur after the input and modelling, when the students are ready to apply what they have learned to a real and meaningful situation. Practice illustrates the transfer of learning to new situations.

- *Guided practice* is when the students follow instructions and practise with support and guidance from the teacher.
- *Independent practice* is when students work on a task by themselves or in a group with minimal teacher support.

Checking for understanding: When checking for understanding, you help to increase your students' success. You can see where you should intervene before students become frustrated and uncertain during

Figure 5.12 *The Components of Lesson Design*

a lesson. When you stop to ensure understanding throughout the lesson, you are better able to adapt and modify to meet the needs, interests, and abilities of your students. With experience, you will become better able to "read" your students to see the learning and understanding that is occurring—this is the "art" of teaching. Ways to check for understanding include asking a few key questions, doing a think-pair-share in partners or a think-pair-square with four students, or making a statement and encouraging a thumbs-up or thumbs-down response to indicate that they agree or disagree with the statement. (See Chapter 3: An Inclusive Classroom Atmosphere.)

Conclusion/closure, reflecting on what was learned, and wrap-up to the lesson:

Every effective lesson should have a conclusion that calls for thoughtful reflection by the students. Encourage the students to tie together the key learnings: to summarize, synthesize, or consolidate them in some way. Teachers tend to leave out closure when they run out of time and/or underestimate the time it takes to complete parts of the lesson. Careful consideration of **timing** will allow you greater opportunities for closure. Ways to close a lesson include sharing in a small or large group, taking a gallery walk where students circulate to look at work accomplished, and asking for an oral or written response before students can exit. This is sometimes called a **"ticket-out-the-door"** strategy, where students are required to articulate an oral response or submit a written response as they exit. A ticket-out-the-door strategy can be modified to become a **ticket-on-the-door** using sticky notes posted on the door as students leave.

Figure 5.12 *The Components of Lesson Design (continued)*

> *NOTE: You may want to include as part of your lesson plan, any personal notes or reminders, or information about homework.*

✦ Examine and reflect on your lesson design and think about whether you have addressed the **learning styles** and **multiple intelligences** of your students (Armstrong). When reflecting on your lesson, ask yourself the following questions:

- How can I use and reinforce the spoken or written word? (*linguistic*)

- How can I include numbers, calculations, logic, classifications, or critical thinking? (*logical-mathematical*)

- How can I use visual aids, visualization, colour, art, metaphor, or visual organizers? (*spatial*)

- How can I include music or environmental sounds, or set key points in a rhythm or melody? (*musical*)

- How can I involve the whole body or hands-on physical experiences? (*bodily-kinesthetic*)

- How can I engage students in peer or cross-age sharing, cooperative group learning, or large group simulations? (*interpersonal*)

- How can I foster personal feelings or memories, or provide students with choices? (*intrapersonal*)
- How can I involve nature and the outdoors in learning? (*naturalistic*)

NOTE: It is not necessary that you plan to include tasks that tap into every intelligence (or learning style) in every single lesson, but you should balance the use of the intelligences across a number of lessons. Thomas Armstrong in his book Multiple Intelligences in the Classroom, 3rd Edition *(ASCD) writes: "You won't always find ways of including every intelligence in your curriculum plans. But if this model helps you reach into one or two intelligences that you might not otherwise have tapped, then it has served its purpose very well indeed!"*

Using Graphic Organizers

✦ Consider using **graphic organizers** as an instructional or assessment tool in any component of your lesson and in all subject areas. Graphic organizers are visual representations that act as a tool to assist students to make sense of their learning, organize their thinking, and express their thoughts and ideas. Graphic organizers also help students better remember important information because the content is presented visually. Connections and complex information can be more easily shared in an organized way. When introducing a new graphic organizer to students, it is advisable to follow the lesson design components outlined above where you will do the following:

  - introduce the graphic organizer (mental set)
  - share the purpose in student language
  - model how to use it
  - provide time to practise with both teacher guidance and independently
  - share the learning that has occurred through a closure activity

✦ You might also want to ask students to create their own graphic organizers (Bennett; McTighe). A graphic organizer can become a vehicle as well as a creative way for students to express their learning across all curriculum areas. See Figure 5.13 for examples of various graphic organizers you may want to use.

NOTE: Other graphic organizers in Chapter 3: An Inclusive Classroom Atmosphere include a mind map, concept map, T-chart, and placemat (Things in Common). A KWL, which is also a graphic organizer, is found in Chapter 4: Assessment in a Differentiated Curriculum.

Webs: are useful in brainstorming as well as in generating ideas, questions, and topics in any subject area.

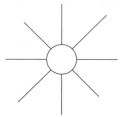

Venn Diagrams: are useful to show similarities and differences by entering information in the different sections of the circles. The overlapping middle is used to highlight similarities. Venn Diagrams are useful to compare and contrast characteristics of characters in a novel or content material in a science unit, etc.

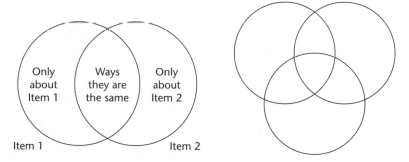

Writing Sandwiches: are useful when teaching students about organizing their writing (stories or essays) into beginning, middle, and end, or introduction, body, and conclusion. The top of the sandwich indicates the beginning or introduction. The middle could include a number of fillings representing different sections or the "meat" of the writing, and the bottom of the sandwich represents the ending or closure.

An Essay

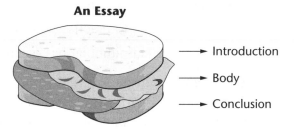

→ Introduction

→ Body

→ Conclusion

You can also create sandwich poetry with a similar structure. *The Important Book* by Margaret Wise Brown (Harper Collins) is a good example of a sandwich poem and could be used to introduce the concept to your students. In this book, the first line (the top of the sandwich), and the last line (the bottom of the sandwich) are the same (for example, *The most important thing about . . . is . . . .* The middle of the sandwich represents the "meat" of the poem.

Figure 5.13 *Graphic Organizers*

Fish Bone Structure: is useful for organizing information to be used in a research project, essay, or report writing.

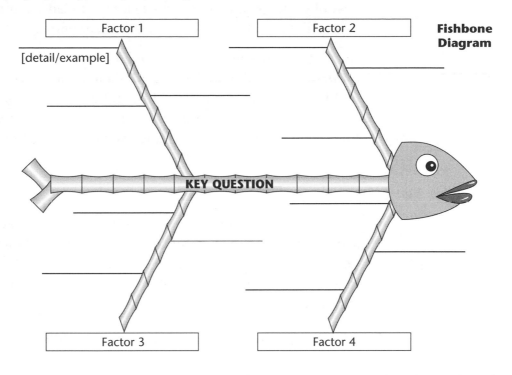

Story Maps: are useful in assisting students in organizing and understanding the components of a story.

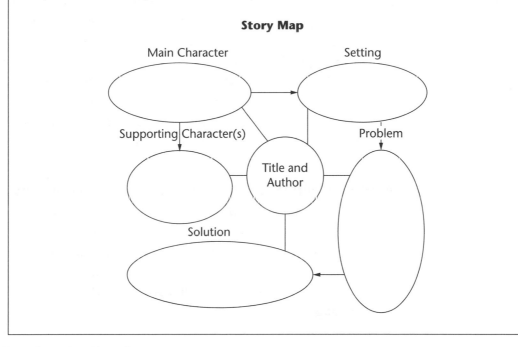

Figure 5.13 *Graphic Organizers (continued)*

** Jay McTighe, in *Graphic Organizers: Collaborative Links to Better Thinking* (Teacher's College Press), discusses the importance and usefulness of using graphic organizers to assist students before, during, and after instruction and also as tools for assessment purposes

** Barrie Bennett's text, *Graphic Intelligence: Playing with Possibilities (Pearson)*, is a comprehensive, illustrated, and practical text that highlights many examples to differentiate instruction and understand multiple intelligences. It clearly illustrates how to apply graphic intelligence with Venn diagrams, web diagrams, flow charts, mindmaps, concept maps, etc.

Lesson Plan Templates

✦ Modify or create **your own template** for a lesson plan. A template should include all the components of Madeline Hunter's lesson design, yet each lesson does not necessarily have to include every component in a step-by-step fashion. Figure 5.14 illustrates a possible lesson plan template you might use.

*NOTE: See **LM 5.10** on the Text Enrichment Site for a similar lesson plan template without boxes.*

✦ If you decide that what needs to be taught requires only a brief lesson, teach a **mini-lesson**, either planned in advance or taught at the point of need, thereby capturing a teachable moment. A mini-lesson can occur at the beginning of an activity, during a lesson to ensure understanding, during a conference with a student or group of students, or even when students are lining up for recess. Modelling, demonstrating, and think-aloud strategies can be seen as types of mini-lessons, where you make the learning explicit by sharing what is happening in your mind. If you decide in advance to include a mini-lesson, you may want to record it on your lesson plan or in your daily plans.

✦ **Read-aloud** experiences provide numerous opportunities to use mini-lessons to teach specific skills. For example, reading a pattern book to young children allows you to point out punctuation, capital letters, rhyming words, plurals, initial consonants, blends, and compound words. Reading a novel provides many opportunities to point out literary elements such as characterization, climax, and epilogue. (See Chapter 8: Literacy and Language Learning.)

PLANNING THE LESSON/SUBTASK: Part 1

Date: _____ Grade: _____ Timeframe (time available): _____

Curriculum Area: _____ Title of Unit (if appropriate): _____

Context: *Where does this lesson fit into your overall unit planning—introductory, middle, culminating? How have you or will you activate your students' prior knowledge?*

Curriculum Expectations:
  Academic:
  Social:

Big Ideas:

Connections to Equity, Diversity, and Social Justice:

Cross Curricular Connections:	**Connections to Students' lives (local/ global):**

Assessment: *How will you know that your students have achieved the expectations? What evidence of learning will you have collected? What will achievement look like?*

☐ Assessment *for* learning (Diagnostic) ☐ Assessment *for/as* learning (Formative) ☐ Assessment *of* learning (Summative)

☐ Observation
☐ KWL
☐ Retelling, relating, refle
☐ Anecdotal notes
☐ Work Samples
☐ Peer-assessment
☐ Interviews/Conferences
☐ Oral reports
☐ Learning logs/Journals
☐ Personal reflection
☐ Self-assessment
☐ Rubric

Differentiated I

Instructional

☐ Provide an alternative task.
☐ Decrease amount/workload.
☐ Increase time.
☐ Provide visual aids, models, calculators, manipulatives, real objects, graphic organizers.
☐ Slow down the rate of delivery.
☐ Provide direct teacher assistance.
☐ Scribe for the student.
☐ Introduce and explain new vocabulary.
☐ Use simplified language.
☐ Adapt teaching materials.
☐ Repeat and reword instructions.
☐ Check for understanding often.
☐ Encourage peer-tutoring.
☐ Use a timer.
☐ Use technology or media.
☐ Extend learning.
☐ Provide a challenge.

Modifications for (names of students):

Materials/Resources:

Teacher Resources	**Stude**

ONLINE MATERIAL

LM 5.9

Figure 5.14 *Sample Lesson Plan*

DELIVERING THE LESSON/SUBTASK: Part 2

Grouping: W = Whole class; S = Small group; I = Independent/Individual

Timing	Grouping W	S	I	Mental Set *(Hook)*:	Materials/Resources
				Sharing the Purpose/Objectives/ Success Criteria *(in student language)*:	
				Body (Input, Modelling, Check for Understanding, Guided Practice, Independent Practice):	**Bloom's Taxonomy:** __Remembering __Understanding __Applying __Analyzing __Evaluating __Creating **Learning Styles:** __Visual __Auditory __Kinesthetic **Multiple Intelligences:** __Verbal/Linguistic __Logical/ Mathematical __Musical/ Rhythmic __Body/ Kinesthetic __Visual/Spatial __Interpersonal __Intrapersonal __Naturalist
				Closure *(Sharing the learning in some way)*:	
				Homework/Reminders:	
				Reflections: *Ask yourself about your successes, challenges, changes, next steps.*	

NOTE: Recording specific plans for major lessons is an important exercise for teachers new to the fundamental structure of lesson design and delivery, such as pre-service and first-year teachers. As you internalize the structures inherent in effective lesson design, it becomes less essential to record the specific details of each of your lessons. The basic components of your lessons can be included in point-form weekly and daily plans. (See next section.)

Creating Weekly and Daily Plans

You may want to create weekly and/or daily plans to outline the lessons, learning experiences, and tasks in which your students will be involved. You may also want to include the corresponding learning expectations, assessment required, and materials needed. For experienced teachers, these can take the place of detailed lesson plans on a day-to-day basis, while essential and detailed lesson plans are incorporated into the unit planned for that period of time.

Weekly and daily plans put your thoughts and ideas into immediate practice. They have much to do with timetabling procedures as you begin to decide when certain learning experiences will occur within your month, week, and day. These plans will depend on the timing of other school requirements, such as physical education, French, and the Arts, especially if other teachers work with your students in such curriculum areas. Weekly and daily planning cannot be separated from timetabling. See Chapter 2: Timetabling for procedures and specific examples of different timetabling possibilities. We invite you to review these possibilities and decide what works best for your class.

✦ As your long-range, unit plans, and lesson plans begin to take shape, design weekly and daily plans for smooth implementation of your program. Weekly and daily plans can also include a record of the specific **routines and procedures** that you will be reinforcing.

✦ **Weekly plans** allow you to see your week at a glance, highlight specific lessons, tasks, and learning experiences taking place over the course of the week, and help you see the direction you are heading. See Figure 5.15 for a weekly plan template over two pages.

See also **LM 5.12** on the Text Enrichment Site for a week-at-a-glance plan on one page.

✦ Create **daily plans** that allow you to focus on each lesson and the routines that accompany your teaching day. Often, daily plans can be easily generated from your weekly timetable in which you enlarge each day of the week, adding more information and detail.

Time	Monday_____	Tuesday_____	Wednesday_____
DAY PLAN for week of:			Grade 1, Rm. 104
9:00 9:10	Circle Time	Circle Time:	Circle Time:
9:10 10:00 10:30	**Language Arts:**	**Language Arts:**	**Language Arts:**
10:30–10:45	Recess	Recess	Recess
10:45 11:05	Science/Social Studies	Science/Social Studies	**Gym Prep—60 minutes**
11:05 11:45			Science/Social Studies
11:45–12:45	Lunch	Lunch	Lunch
12:45 1:25	**Gym Prep**	**Music Prep**	Math:
1:25 2:05	Math:	Math:	
2:05–2:20	Recess	Recess	Recess
2:20 3:00			

Time	Thursday_____	Friday_____	THINGS TO DO!
9:00 9:10	Circle Time:	Circle Time:	Monday:
9:10 10:00 10:30	Language Arts:	Language Arts:	
10:30-10:45	Recess	Recess	Tuesday:
10:45 11:05	Science/Social Studies	Science/Social Studies	
11:05 11:45			
11:45-12:45	Lunch	Lunch	Wednesday:
12:45 1:25	Music Prep	Math:	
1:25 2:05	Math:		Thursday:
2:05-2:20	Recess	Recess	Friday:
3:00 3:30	Finish Work/tidy up/ Read Aloud	DPA Read Aloud	Tidy/Read Aloud
2:20 3:00		**Computers**	
3:00 3:30	DPA Read Aloud	DPA Friday Folders: Read Aloud	

LM 5.11 **Figure 5.15** *Sample Weekly Plan (two pages)*

Source: Used with permission. Florence Guttman, TDSB.

✦ Figure 5.16 illustrates a possible daily plan that you might want to use, and Figure 5.17 illustrates a daily plan for a program that includes rotary subjects.

Daily Plan Date		
Time	Teaching Block	Notes
8:45–9:00	Opening exercises, attendance, bell work	
9:00–9:45	LANGUAGE ARTS	
9:45–10:15	LANGUAGE ARTS	
10:15–10:30	Recess	
10:45–12:00	MATHEMATICS	
12:00	Lunch	
1:00–3:00	SCIENCE	
3:00–3:15	Student Homework Planners time	
3:15	Dismissal	
	After school activities	

LM 5.13 **Figure 5.16** *Sample Daily Plan #1*

Source: Used with permission. Meagan McRae, TDSB.

WEDNESDAY Nov. 19th		
Time	**Subject**	**Activity/Strategy/Interaction**
8:55 – 9:45	MATH 7/8P	First review a bit of math (Test Friday) Laptop Cart Publisher, movie maker
9:45 – 10:35	MATH 8B	Laptop Cart Publisher, movie maker
10:35 – 10:55		Recess
10:55 – 11:45	ART 7/8P	Work period on the line design assignment
11:45 – 12:35	ART 8B	Work period on the line design assignment
12:35 – 1:35	Lunch	
1:35 – 2:25	HISTORY 8B	Collect Louis Riel eulogies. Debate on Louis Riel—provide time to gather arguments and prepare. Have an informal debate.
2:25 – 3:15	LANGUAGE 7/8P	**Reading/Writing** Laptop Cart Publisher, movie maker / **Guided Reading/Writing** Work with novel group.

LM 5.14   **Figure 5.17** *Sample Daily Plan with Rotary Subjects #2*
Source: Used with permission. Kimberly Pollishuke, YRDSB.

> *NOTE: Additional daily plan templates can be found on the Text Enrichment Site, including one that involves the implementation of learning stations (see **LMs 5.15, 5.16, and 5.17**).*

Preparing for the Occasional Teacher

An important part of a teacher's planning process and teacher responsibilities is preparing for absences from the classroom. Preparing plans for the occasional teacher is essential to ensuring that there is consistency and stability for your students when you are not in class.

✦ Ensure that you have prepared a folder (or binder) for the occasional teacher in the event that you are absent. See Figure 5.18 for a checklist that can assist you in preparing the materials that might be included in an Occasional Teacher Folder.

Checklist for an Occasional Teacher Folder

Have you included the following:

- ❏ Your yard duty schedule
- ❏ Class list
- ❏ Student seating plan
- ❏ List of students with special needs (on an Individual Educational Plan, with health issues, who may need medication, are new to English, or are withdrawn from the classroom by resource teachers for specific support)
- ❏ List of resource teachers providing in-class support or withdrawal
- ❏ List of student helpers
- ❏ List of your class rules, routines, behaviour expectations/code of behaviour
- ❏ Procedures for entry, dismissal, fire drills, etc.
- ❏ Procedures for taking attendance and dismissal
- ❏ The name of another teacher or student leader who may be able to answer any questions.
- ❏ Legible and easy to follow plans, including: lesson plans, weekly plan, daily plan, pertinent unit plans in the case of a prolonged absence
- ❏ Other

LM 5.18   **Figure 5.18** *Checklist for an Occasional Teacher Folder*

✦ Some of the items in the checklist can be prepared in advance in a folder or binder and left at the office or in a prominent place on your desk. Detailed lesson plans for specific learning experiences can be added as needed when you know you will be away. See Figure 5.19 for a sample detailed lesson plan for the occasional teacher.

✦ If you are unaware in advance that you will be absent, you can **send your plans** to school in the morning of your absence with a colleague or family member, or email your plans to the school office to be printed for the occasional teacher. You may also want to include in your Occasional Teacher Folder an **emergency day plan** for those unusual situations when you are unable to include current plans.

Daily Plan-TUESDAY June 2nd

Hi there, Thank you for coming in for me today! Please find the attendance form in the office. Please meet the class outside at the 2nd bell. They line up at the intermediate doors, right outside our room. They will go to their lockers and make their way to the room on their own. They should come in and sit quietly. If they are still outside during the National Anthem, they are expected to stand quietly and will simply be marked late in the attendance but do not need to actually get a late slip. If they show up after the attendance has been sent down, please ask them to go and get a late slip from the main office.

NOTE: Please put an "S" in the attendance box beside the following students' names as they are at the area track meet: Andrew, Michelle, Yosi, Rochelle, Ethan, Nofar, Mohammed, Sandra, Melley, Steffano, Nora (11 students in total). Also, check my Occasional Teacher Binder (located on my desk) for important information about the location and procedures for the epipen for Sherrine who has severe allergies. Also, check this binder to familiarize yourself with my classroom routines, etc.

Time	Subject	Activity/Strategy/Interaction
8:55 – 9:45	MATH	**Graphing Ordered Pairs** Please see the lesson plan attached. Remind the students that they have a test tomorrow on Algebra. Although this lesson is important, it will not be on their test. They should review homework questions when studying for the test tomorrow.
9:45 – 10:35	6S SOCIAL STUDIES	**Trading Partners of Canada** Yesterday, we began to examine the United States closely. Students are currently working on a homework assignment that will be taken up next Monday. Please remind them that they should be researching their state at home throughout the week and I will be collecting their work on Monday. **For today**: Ask them how they would respond and why: Would you say that we live independently or are we dependent on other nations? Explain that, as we have discussed in the past, Canada produces items that we sell to other countries (exports) and other countries produce items that we need to buy (imports). These countries are called "trading partners:" Please distribute the atlases from the side of the room, one to two students. Please ensure that they ALL are returned at the end of the period and are put neatly back on the same shelf. Feel free to ask a student to help reorganize the shelf. Hand out the two-sided sheet that lists Canada's trading partners with maps. Hand out the blank world map and have students colour in Canada in one colour and the trading partners in another colour (only two colours needed in total). They need to use the legend in the bottom left corner. If they are unable to find a country, they should move on to the next one. If they do not finish in this period, they should finish it at home using a home atlas, a map on the internet, or the world map in their agenda. Please review mapping colouring skills: • Only water should be blue (they can colour in the water only if they want to) • For this map, there should be no words on the page as the legend takes care of it I have informed the class that I will collect the assignment and mark it according to the rubric we have developed together.
10:35 – 10:55		Recess
10:55 – 11:45	7/8P H/G	**Ontario's Greenbelt (Grade 8's have a work period. They ALL must work silently in the classroom. No one is to go to the pod.)** Have a brief discussion about what the Greenbelt is and ask the students if they have ever seen part of it. *An area of undeveloped land, usually surrounding an urban area, designated to be preserved in its natural state. Restrictions are placed on this region to prevent it from being developed into residential areas or for other urban uses. The land may be used for purposes such as farming, nature preserves, biological research, and recreation.* **Assignment**: They will each receive a set of fact sheets (on my desk) detailing information about the Greenbelt. Ask groups already organized in table groupings to develop a mindmap that contains the important concepts about the Greenbelt. Show them a few models to see what is expected (on my desk—PLEASE collect them all at the end of the period). They will have the rest of the period to take jot notes on the important topics and begin the mindmap. They should create headings to organize their notes to facilitate the mindmap **DUE: Friday**
11:45 12:35	PREP	Please use the student list to check off the students that have completed their homework and map. Enjoy!
12:35 – 1:35	Lunch	
1:35 – 3:15	7/8P LANGUAGE	**READING/WRITING** Students are working on their essay – Meet with small groups to ensure their progress.

LM 5.19 **Figure 5.19** *Sample Lesson Plan for the Occasional Teacher*

Source: Used with permission. Kimberly Pollishuke, YRDSB.

Final Thoughts

Effective planning, whether long term, unit, or lesson planning, helps you to prepare a viable road map to guide your year. The planning procedures outlined in this chapter represent *one* way to plan your program. In no way should they be construed as set directives to be followed in a lockstep fashion. Designing effective curriculum requires that you take into account a multitude of factors, including your students' past experiences, needs, interests, backgrounds, learning styles, multiple intelligences, etc.; your own unique way of organizing and recording your thinking; and the requirements of your school and school district. The more you experiment with the design process, the more expertise you will develop as you chart a course to guide yourself and your students' learning.

6 Effective Learning Stations— Small Group Differentiated Learning

Learning stations provide opportunities for students to **work together in small groups**, interacting, sharing, and cooperating with one another as they reinforce, practise, apply, and refine previous learnings. Students participate in small group differentiated tasks that help them to internalize and consolidate what they learn, often with minimal teacher intervention or support. At learning stations, students also experiment, explore, question, discuss, and reflect; thus participating in discovery learning, the process of learning how to learn. The tasks and learning experiences at learning stations are usually closely tied to curriculum goals, and should be clear, comprehensible, and differentiated to correspond to your students' cognitive, physical, social, and emotional stages of development.

In implementing the use of learning stations, you make decisions in your planning to include one or more learning stations in your program. Using learning stations does not necessarily mean that specific areas in the classroom must be designated as learning stations. Some stations may be permanent, some may be portable or easily moved, and some may be temporary, used for a specific purpose for a short period of time. A learning station is as varied as the imagination.

At learning stations, learning tasks are **differentiated** when students are presented with a choice of learning experiences at various levels of difficulty. They will begin to take greater responsibility for their own learning, becoming better decision makers and problem solvers. Your students will gain a greater willingness to take risks in these small-group situations. As they gain confidence in their own abilities, they will become more self-motivated and independent and will begin to assess themselves more critically.

Learning stations **facilitate peer teaching** and students gain valuable leadership skills and confidence. Little pressure to compete with others develops because this approach to learning emphasizes cooperation, collaboration, and sharing of materials, resources, and ideas.

Collecting and preparing learning materials is easier when learning stations are incorporated into your program. Resources and materials are shared to a great extent, and only a few students need the same materials at any one time. It is not necessary to have class sets of texts or other materials at learning stations. Instead, funds can go towards acquiring class libraries of literature and a variety of manipulatives enough for small groups of students to use, including magnifying glasses, thermometers, measuring instruments, manipulative mathematics materials, and technology. The materials and resources for station tasks should be accessible and readily available.

Using learning stations also facilitates **integration** and **assessment**. Since a number of curriculum areas are interconnected, integration can occur naturally through learning stations. Assessment can become a manageable and meaningful task when students are actively involved in learning station work. As you circulate, observation and anecdotal note-taking are facilitated. Peer- and self-assessments after students complete tasks will promote reflection and goal setting, both for work habits and academic quality of work.

As your learning stations become an increasingly integral part of your overall program and your students develop as independent workers, you will become accustomed to a variety of learning experiences occurring at the same time in different areas of the classroom. You will circulate, encourage, instruct, model and demonstrate, provide guidance, and ultimately promote independence. As well as learning along with your students, you will serve as a **facilitator of learning**, a full partner in the teaching and learning process. The following are some steps to consider when implementing learning stations in your classrooms.

Creating Effective Learning Stations

✦ Examine your classroom environment and decide which **permanent** learning stations you will create and where these will be located. Permanent learning stations may remain all year long. Possibilities include a listening station, a reading corner, an art area (preferably near a sink), a computer station (near electrical outlets), a design and technology station, an interactive display-board area, and a mathematics station housing mathematics texts and manipulatives.

NOTE: *Keep in mind that a station need not be a physical area. If* **space** *is limited, all materials necessary for a station can be stored in labelled bins, buckets, folders, or other containers that can be taken by the students to any area in the room or school or to a designated work space. The school's resource library can also be used as a designated area for small-group or station work.*

✦ Decide which stations will involve **generic learning experiences**. Such experiences are not directly related to a theme or unit being studied. For example, a generic computer station may focus on tasks such as keyboarding, word processing, skill teaching, and graphic design. It is beneficial to keep generic tasks available for students to work on as they complete assigned tasks in a given unit of study.

✦ If you will be using learning stations **as part of an integrated unit**, examine the small-group and individual learning experiences you have planned and decide which ones would be well addressed at either a permanent or new learning station. For example, during the study of weather, student tasks at your computer station may include creating a database that will record the information gathered about the weather in a particular area and creating a spreadsheet to analyze data collected during a field trip to a weather station.

✦ The following types of stations can be created for either generic or unit-related use:

- a mathematics station
- a writing station
- an arts station a music station
- a puppetry station
- a drama/dress-up station
- a nature station
- a science station
- an invention station
- a take-apart station

- a magnets station
- a design and technology station
- a music station
- a sound station
- a mapping station
- a water station
- a sand station
- a blocks or structures station (see Figure 6.1)

✦ For each learning station you plan to implement, decide on, and record the name and tasks, the learning expectations you will be addressing, the materials you will need, the assessment practices you will use, and the method of tracking student work. See Figure 6.2 for a sample planning template.

Figure 6.1 *A Blocks or Structures Station*

Learning Station Name and Tasks	Learning Expectations	Assessment	Materials Needed	Tracking
Reading Station - read/respond (see generic task cards) - record books read - read aloud and record reading	- read a variety of fiction and non-fiction materials for different purposes - express clear responses to written materials	- audio recording of student reading aloud - self-assessment - teacher comments on reading logs	- novels - picture books - student-authored books - poetry - anthologies - reading logs - reading folders - task cards - audio recording - blank cassettes	- reading log to record books read and responses completed

ONLINE MATERIAL

LM 6.1 **Figure 6.2** *Sample Planning Template for Learning Stations*

✦ Examine the tasks at each station carefully to ensure that they represent **meaningful and relevant age-appropriate learning experiences** based on students' needs, interests, and abilities. Students should have opportunities to do the following:

- reinforce, practise, apply, refine, and consolidate their skills and knowledge

- interact, communicate, reflect, investigate, discover, and explore
- choose from tasks at varying levels of ability
- work with open-ended tasks (no right answers)
- make choices, solve problems, make decisions, and take risks
- participate in cooperative learning experiences
- receive ongoing feedback and assessment
- participate in peer- and self-assessment

*NOTE: Since learning stations are intended to target **independent** individual or small-group experiences, it is critical to ensure that students possess the basic skills and knowledge necessary for completion of tasks. For example, if a task at a reading station requires students to identify the main character, they must understand the concept of "main character" from previous learning experiences.*

✦ Ensure that for each station you have signs and labels, clear instructions, concrete manipulatives, materials easily accessible to students, and storage and display areas for materials, resources, and student work.

✦ Collect, sort, and prepare the materials and resources needed for each station. Figures 6.3 and 6.4 may help you with organization.

THINGS TO DO FOR THE *Structures* STATION

Materials to Collect		Things to Prepare
Equipment	**Manipulative Materials**	
☑ paper	☑ straws	☑ signs
☑ pencils	☑ pipe cleaners	☑ task cards
☑ crayons	☑ pins	☑ student worksheets
☑ scissors	☑ Plasticene	☑ games
☑ glue	☑ junk (boxes, tubes)	☑ student folders/ scrapbook
☑ filmstrip projector	☑ wooden stir sticks	
❑	☑ plastic stir sticks	❑
❑	❑	❑
Student Resources		**Other**
☑ Books on Structures		
☑ Filmstrip "Structures in Toronto"		
☑ Picture File "City Structures"		

LM 6.2 **Figure 6.3** *Checklist for Planning a Station*

Name of Station	Learning Experiences	Materials Needed	Assessment
Structures	– Build a bridge structure using the materials	tubes, rolled newspaper, tape, scrapbook, sketch pencils, photos of structures	– Performance task – Collect work sample
	– sketch different structures		

LM 6.3 **Figure 6.4** *Teacher's Chart for Planning a Station*

✦ Once you are comfortable with using learning stations in your classroom, **involve the students** in the collection and preparation of materials.

✦ Involve the students in decisions about **where to store and display their work** after they complete it at the learning station. (See Chapter 1: Classroom Design and Organization.)

✦ Examine your **timetable** and decide *when* and *how often* during the day and week you will have students working at the stations. (See Chapter 2: Timetabling.)

✦ Decide on the maximum **number of students** allowed at each station at any one time. The ideal number of students at a station is four to six.

✦ With your students, take the time to establish rules, routines, and expectations for the stations. Promote the following practices:

  • Work cooperatively with others.

  • Complete work within an acceptable period of time.

  • Use materials appropriately and clean up each work area.

  • Move on to another task (or station) when work is completed.

  • Keep tracking sheets up to date.

*NOTE: Students beginning to work in stations need to learn **routines, expectations, and responsibilities**. They need to strengthen their self-direction and independence, and develop positive attitudes towards learning and working at stations. When learning stations are first introduced, it is important to provide learning experiences that require a minimum of teacher direction and support in order to establish the basic rules, routines, and expectations. Take the time that is needed to ensure that routines are firmly in place.*

◆ Allow for **input sessions** prior to learning station time. In these sessions, either station tasks are introduced and specific skills are taught, or large-group topic or theme-related learning experiences occur. When introducing new learning experiences at various stations, stagger the instructional input over a few days. By doing so, your input sessions will not become overly long and unwieldy. Remember that students cannot sit and listen for long periods of time (a good rule of thumb is approximately one minute for each year of age) and will begin to tune out or disengage if their listening extends to a lengthy period of time.

◆ Allow **time for sharing** after each learning station time. During sharing, student work is highlighted, questions and issues are aired, and learning is articulated. Students could also engage in self-assessing their behaviour and quality of work.

◆ Decide on how you will **begin to use** learning stations. The following options provide you with three possibilities for implementing learning stations in your program:

Option 1:	Option 2:	Option 3:
Begin with one station, and gradually introduce other stations as students become accustomed to the routines. For example, set up a construction station where students can explore and build structures.	Begin with multiple stations in one curriculum area. For example, set up six mathematics stations with different learning experiences intended to reinforce and practise specific concepts.	Begin with multiple stations in a variety of curriculum areas, perhaps on a particular theme, topic, or unit of study. These might be stations in mathematics, writing, spelling, visual arts, drama, and reading.

Managing Learning Stations in Your Classroom

◆ Decide how best to **move your students** to and through stations. There is no one way to organize and manage a learning station approach. Below are some options.

Option 1:	Use learning stations when assigned tasks are completed.
	This approach introduces the concept of learning stations to both teachers and students but with this approach, learning stations may be perceived as an add-on, not as an integral part of your program. As well, when students use stations only after their work is completed, the stations remain unused for large portions of the day.

Option 2:	Use a sign-up system or schedule.
	This approach indicates specific times when students will use the learning station or indicates the order of use by students. (See Figure 6.5.)

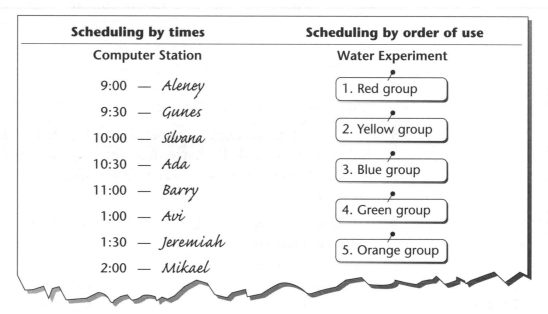

Figure 6.5 *Sign-up System or Schedule*

Option 3:	Use a rotation system whereby students move systematically through stations in set groups.
	This system allows teachers greater control over *when* and *where* students will work. A group rotation method can ensure participation by all students in all stations over a specified period of time. It also allows the teacher and the students to become accustomed to many things occurring simultaneously in the room.

TYPES OF ROTATION SYSTEMS

a. Write group names on cards and post on a chart or board using tape, pins, or magnets. (Magnets may be taped to the back of the cards for easy movement on a magnetic board.) Prepare station name cards and attach them to the board or chart. As the groups rotate through the stations, move all the name cards forward so that the chart reflects the rotation cycle. (See Figure 6.6.)

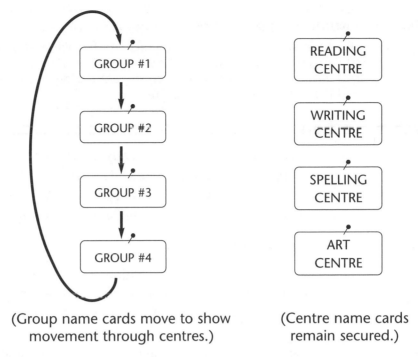

(Group name cards move to show movement through centres.)

(Centre name cards remain secured.)

Figure 6.6 *Group Rotation Chart*

b. The rotation wheel contains group names on the inner circle and station names on the outer circle. These station names can be written on cards and attached to the wheel by paper clips or clothespins to facilitate frequent and easy changes. The two circles are attached in the station by a paper fastener. For each rotation, the inside circle is turned once so that students can see in which station they are to participate next. (See Figure 6.7.)

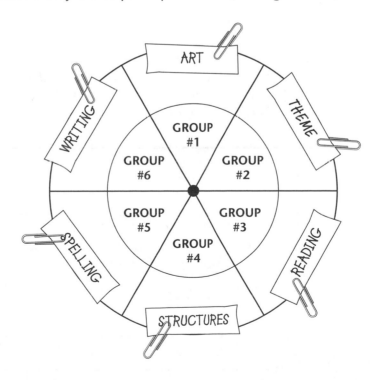

Figure 6.7 *Rotation Wheel*

	Option 4:	Introduce a planning board sign-up.

> Use a planning board to present a menu of learning station opportunities from which students will choose. Students choose to work at specific stations on an individual basis and form self-selected groups. Each student decides the order of learning experiences and the necessary time to complete tasks.

> *NOTE: To avoid the possible chaos of 30 students approaching the planning board at the same time and having to wait to choose, you might want to assign a short, directed task to be completed prior to choosing a station at the planning board. Since students will finish the assigned task at different times, they will approach the planning board a few at a time.*

TYPES OF PLANNING BOARD SIGN-UPS

a. Write the names of the stations on a board or chart. Students either sign up beneath a station name or move their magnetized nametags under the appropriate column heading. (See Figure 6.8.)

Reading	Writing	Math	Puppetry	Structures
Alexey	Sonya	Kerry	Aaron	Mark
Laney	Edison	Matthew	Kaari	Naseeb
Silvano		Hyussein		
Leeor		Ada		
Mike				

Figure 6.8 *Planning Board: Station Sign-up*

b. Write the station names (and/or show pictures) on the pockets. Student name cards (and/or photos) are placed in the pockets of the stations chosen. (See Figure 6.9) Each student may have more than one name card to indicate the day's tasks.

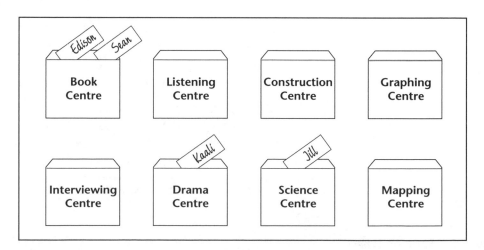

Figure 6.9 *Planning Board: Names on Cards*

c. Write the station names on the cards. Students place the cards for the stations chosen into their own name pockets. The number of station cards available indicates the number of students allowed there at a time. (See Figure 6.10.)

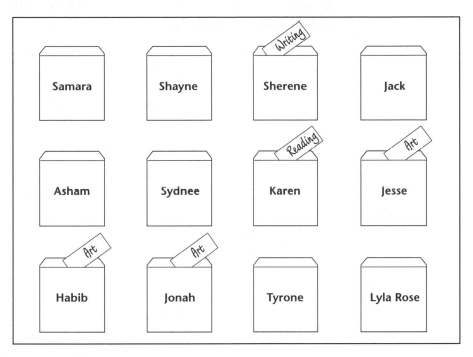

Figure 6.10 *Planning Board: Names on Pockets*

d. Write the station names on cards. The number of pockets beside each station card indicates the number of students permitted at that station at one time. Students place their name cards in the pockets for the station chosen. (See Figure 6.11.)

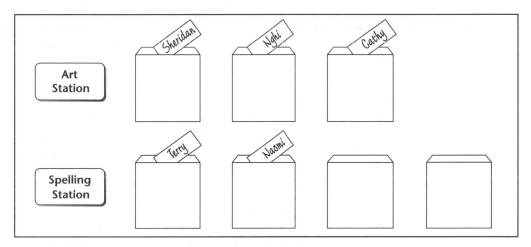

Figure 6.11 *Planning Board Indicating Number of Students at a Time*

e. Write a number on the pocket to indicate how many students are allowed at the station at any one time. Students move their name cards to the appropriate pockets, but also sign on the sheets below the station pockets. They put checks beside their names when the work is completed. (See Figure 6.12.) This type of planning board promotes peer teaching because students who have questions can ask for help from those students who have already completed the task.

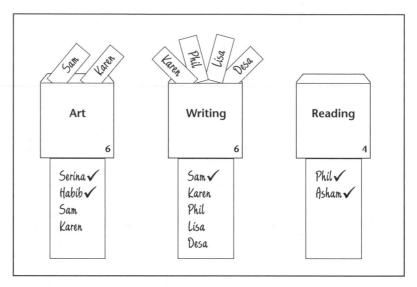

Figure 6.12 *Planning Board Indicating Number of Students and Sign-up*

Option 5:   Use tracking sheets.

Tracking sheets provide a method of monitoring student movement through stations. Students choose a learning task from the tracking sheet and mark the appropriate place when completed. These sheets are kept in desks or personal bins, stored in folders or envelopes, or are glued into scrapbooks or notebooks.

Tracking sheets may also be used in conjunction with group rotations or with planning boards because they serve as important records of student work accomplished. They can include sections for student self-assessments as well as sections for teacher and parent signatures and/or comments. Sending tracking sheets home with students to be signed and commented on by their parents is an effective incentive for those students who need to improve their behaviour, work completion, and/or academics.

a. The tracking sheet in Figure 6.13 can be used in two ways. Very young students can simply choose one task at a time and put a check, sticker, or date stamp in the appropriate box as they begin or complete the task. For slightly older students, some learning experiences on the tracking sheet can be coded, for example, by star or colour. Students are instructed to alternate between coded and non-coded tasks. The coded tasks might represent experiences in which you want all your students to participate. These could be either skill-building or exploratory.

Name: Ashley					
The week of Jan. 9 to Jan. 13					

Activities	Monday	Tuesday	Wednesday	Thursday	Friday
Painting			✓		
Cut and Paste		✓			
Water Table			✓		
Home Station	✓	✓			
Listening Station				✓	
Book Station	✓			✓	

LM 6.4 **Figure 6.13** *Tracking Sheet for Young Students*

b. On the tracking sheet in Figure 6.14, students choose their learning experiences and record the name of the station, the date started, and the date completed.

Stations	Date Started	Date Completed
1. Math	Feb. 9	Feb. 9
2. Structures	Feb. 10	Feb. 11

LM 6.5 **Figure 6.14** *Tracking Sheet: Date Started and Completed*

c. On tracking sheets similar to that shown in Figure 6.15, young students begin to assess their own work and behaviour. They colour in descriptive faces to illustrate how well they think they worked at each station.

MY TRACKING SHEET				Name: _Matthew_
Listening Centre	🙂	😐	☹️	Date Mar. 9
Reading Centre	🙂	😐	☹️	Mar. 6
Writing Centre	🙂	😐	☹️	Mar. 10
Math Centre	🙂	😐	☹️	
Art Centre	🙂	😐	☹️	Mar. 5
Odds 'n' Ends	🙂	😐	☹️	

LM 6.6 **Figure 6.15** *Tracking Sheet: Self-assessment Using Descriptive Faces*

d. Students use the style of tracking sheet shown in Figure 6.16 to comment on how well they did at each learning station.

MY TRACKING SHEET			Name: _Daisleon_
Stations	**Date Started**	**Date Completed**	**Comments (Self-assessment)**
1. Music	Mar. 2	Mar. 4	I think my words are coming out much more clearly now.
2. Spelling	Mar. 5		
3.			

LM 6.7 **Figure 6.16** *Tracking Sheet Including Comments*

e. In Figure 6.17, students use a rating scale of 1, 2, 3, or 4 to indicate their accomplishments. Teachers and students can decide whether to rate behaviour, work habits, or quality of work.

Stations	Date Started	Date Completed	Rate Yourself: 4: Wow! 3: Good! 2: Just okay. 1: Could be better!
Structures	Dec. 8	Dec. 9	4

LM 6.8 **Figure 6.17** *Tracking Sheet and Rating Scale*

f. The tracking sheet in Figure 6.18 illustrates a distinction between teacher-directed learning experiences and student-chosen ones. It clearly indicates which learning experiences must be accomplished and which ones students may choose to do over the course of one or more days.

MY TRACKING SHEET		Name: Roy	Date: April 19			
	Learning Experiences	Monday	Tuesday	Wednesday	Thursday	Friday
THINGS I MUST DO Reading 		✓	✓	✓		
Math		✓	✓	✓		
THINGS I WANT TO DO Spelling		✓	✓	✓		
Writing		✓	✓	✓		
Printing		✓	✓	✓		
Art						
Drama			✓			
Listening		✓				
Games & Puzzles			✓			

LM 6.9 **Figure 6.18** *Tracking Sheet: Musts and Wants—For Younger Students*

g. The tracking sheet in Figure 6.19 also illustrates musts and wants and applies to a weekly period of time.

MY TRACKING SHEET		Name: _Tyrone_
MUSTS		Week of _June 16_
✔	Choose 12 words, 2 activities	
✔	Math: 1 number, 1 measurement, 1 geometry, 1 problem solving	
✔	Read and respond in journal	
	Finish your interview/news articles	
	Create a want ad, commercial, or multi-media presentation	
✔	Create a comic strip	
WANTS		
	Planting activities	
	Write a script	
✔	Keyboarding	

ONLINE MATERIAL

LM 6.10 **Figure 6.19** *Tracking Sheet: Musts and Wants—For Older Students*

h. The format in the tracking sheet in Figure 6.20 permits tracking of tasks over a lengthy period of time. Students must be involved in the top seven tasks, and then can choose from the next five.

Name: _Monique_			Starting Date: _Dec. 8_
MY CHECKLIST OF LEARNING TASKS			
Learning Tasks	**Date**	**My Comment**	**Teacher's Comments**
1. Community Walk	Dec. 8	This was fun.	You set a fine example on our trip—Good Work. MC
2. Alphajobs booklet	Dec. 10	This was hard.	You tried hard to complete this task. MC
3. Interview			
4. Comparative graph	Dec. 11	I learned that graphs give me a lot of information.	Your graphs were detailed and accurate. Bravo!! MC
5. "Roll" model			
6. Earning and spending			
7. When I grow up			

LM 6.11 **Figure 6.20** *Tracking Sheet: Checklist of Learning Tasks*

i. Students can use charts, such as in Figure 6.21 to have a written record of the tasks to be completed.

ANIMAL STUDIES	TRACKING SHEET	Name: Mohammed	
Station	**Tasks**	**Date Completed**	**Comments**
Theme	Which animals live on land, in water, or in air?	Mar. 6	I found that most animals live on land.
	Which animals are vertebrates and which are invertebrates?		
	What do they eat? Choose a card and do research.	Mar. 7	I now know that monkeys are omnivores.
	Complete the food chain and webs.		
Talking	Sort the buttons/animal pictures/models.	Mar. 4	This was fun.
	Tell about your favourite animal.		
Reading	Read an animal fable.	Mar. 12	I didn't like the ending, because it didn't make sense.
	Read and tape an animal poem.		
	Find more animal poems.		

LM 6.12 **Figure 6.21** *Tracking Sheet: Tasks Described*

j. The format shown in Figure 6.22 allows students to record the date, the name of the station, and other pertinent information each time that they begin to work at a station. Teachers can easily see how much time a student spends at a particular task. Some students may take many days to complete work at a station. Others may pass through many stations in one day.

Today's Date	Name of Centre	Description of Each Learning Experience I Worked on or Completed	Comments
Mon. Mar. 6	Diorama Centre	I did Cinderella and the Prince dancing at the ball.	I'm proud of my box.
Mon. Mar. 6	Spelling	I finished my crossword puzzle.	It was fun.
Tues. Mar. 7	Mapping	I started my imaginary map of Hansel and Gretel's trip.	I had trouble starting.
Wed. Mar. 8	Mapping	I'm working on my map.	😐
Thurs. Mar. 9	Mapping	I finished the map.	I worked hard on it.

MY TRACKING SHEET

Name: Lyle

LM 6.13 **Figure 6.22** *Tracking Sheet: Time Spent at Stations*

k. A log or journal such as in Figure 6.23 allows students to plan and organize their day's accomplishments. They write what they plan to do and later reflect upon what they have accomplished. Teachers can also comment and assess daily.

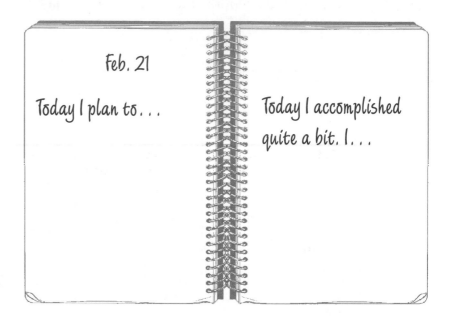

Figure 6.23 *Student Log*

Assessing the Learning at Stations

In order to **assess learning at the stations**, refer back to the assessment strategies and/or tools you outlined in the chart (see Figure 6.2) as you planned your stations. The assessment strategies/tools you have chosen should address the learning expectations you have selected for each station. (See Chapter 4: Assessment in a Differentiated Curriculum.)

✦ **Observe** individuals and small groups of students as they work at learning stations. Record pertinent information as **anecdotal notes**. Assessing students at stations can be quite manageable since you are focusing on a small number of students at any one time.

✦ Use tracking sheets that **include an assessment component** to encourage self-, peer-, and teacher-assessment and descriptive feedback.

✦ Create **checklists or rubrics** that indicate the success criteria for achievement at each learning station, and develop and/or share these success criteria with students before they begin working at learning station tasks. Doing so is essential in providing clear expectations for achievement. Developing the success criteria in collaboration with students builds ownership and commitment. (See Chapter 4: Assessment in a Differentiated Curriculum.)

NOTE: *You might want to include success criteria on your checklists or rubrics that outline necessary* ***social skills*** *as well, to encourage appropriate behaviour and work habits.*

✦ Closely observe, assess, and assist those students who consistently do not complete tasks within an acceptable time frame. A **contract** can be set up between you and such a student. Involving parents in this process can prove beneficial. Figures 6.24 and 6.25 provide examples of student contracts. (See also Figure 3.20 in Chapter 3: An Inclusive Classroom Atmosphere for another example of a student contract.)

My Contract

I, Lolita, agree to finish

my research project

my French story

by Mon. Jan 16

(due date)

Lolita — *Student's Signature*

K. Pollishuke — *Teacher's Signature*

Comments: ______________________

Student's Initials *Teacher's Initials*

ONLINE MATERIAL **LM 6.14** **Figure 6.24** *Student Contract #1*

My Contract

What I *must* do today . . .

Math

Spelling

Finish the pictures for my book

What I *might* do today . . .

cut and paste

_____
Serena
Student's Signature

_____
K. Prantis
Teacher's Signature

LM 6.15   **Figure 6.25** *Student Contract #2*

NOTE: You may want to use a daily plan which incorporates the use of learning stations. See Chapter 5: Designing Your Curriculum and LM 5.19 on the Text Enrichment Site for a sample daily plan template which includes the planning of learning stations. This template can also be incorporated as part of your overall unit planning.

Final Thoughts

Learning stations can prove to be a valuable addition to your classroom program. As you begin to implement learning stations, you will find your students becoming more independent and self-motivated as they make choices and work together cooperatively. It is important to continuously assess and reflect on the learning stations you have designed to ensure that they provide opportunities for students to reinforce, apply, practise, refine, and consolidate their learning, to make choices, solve problems, make decisions, and take risks. Successful implementation of learning stations will engage your students actively and help them to discover and grow as they learn how to learn.

Out-of-classroom Excursions— Experiencing the Wider Community

Taking students out of the regular classroom and school environment into the larger community generates interest and enthusiasm, helps to motivate students, creates positive attitudes towards learning, and provides students with meaningful and relevant experiences. Out-of-classroom excursions or field trips **enhance the classroom program** and encompass all facets of learning. Although field trips can be physically demanding, requiring supplementary funding and extra time for preparation, they should be valued and considered an integral part of your program.

Field trips can be organized to **familiar places** such as the neighbourhood park or local mall, or to **special locations**, such as a space exploration centre, a museum, or an art gallery. As you begin to plan your out-of-classroom excursions, take into consideration the field trips your students have already experienced. Their prior knowledge and experiences play a role in the planning and organization of your out-of-classroom experiences.

Each out-of-classroom excursion should have **curriculum relevance** for the students involved. It should also be **based on clearly defined learning expectations** and should be within the level of understanding and maturity appropriate for your students. Be sure to consider what you will do *before*, *during*, and *after* each excursion. Doing so will help to ensure the success of the field trip and will also enrich the total experience.

Out-of-classroom excursions provide first-hand experiences from which much learning occurs in all areas of the curriculum. Field trips are a genuine form of **integration**. Students learn to appreciate and respect nature and the outdoors, which often stimulates an awareness of and an interest in environmental and global issues. They experience real-life situations, view artifacts from the past, and discover the realm of scientific exploration and experimentation. They see, hear, smell, taste, and touch, using all their senses to make meaning from these relevant excursions.

As a teacher, you need to be aware of all your official responsibilities as you take your students away from the security of the classroom and school environment and into the wider community. Ensure that you have signed parental permission for each and every trip, know your legal obligations, and always provide safe and secure supervision. By doing so, you will make any out-of-classroom excursion a valuable, exciting, productive, and safe addition to your classroom program and to your students' experiences. Field trips allow your students to think, explore, wonder, and investigate people, places, and things in new and exciting ways.

Planning Out-of-classroom Excursions

✦ Investigate all the possible out-of-classroom excursions that correspond with the unit of study you are planning. Some types of appropriate and effective field trips to plan for students of a variety of ages are as follows:

- explorations of the schoolyard, neighbourhood, community, or city
- tours of historical buildings and sites
- visits to a museum, zoo, farm, factory, store, bakery, mall
- trips to plays, musical performances, art galleries, space exploration centre
- travels to new cities and tours of the exciting highlights
- overnight field trips to outdoor education centres or campgrounds

✦ Choose the field trip that is most appropriate in terms of your students' needs and interests and the overall learning expectations for your unit of study.

✦ Ensure that you have some **familiarity with the location** to be visited, especially the itinerary of things to do and see, and knowledge of the facilities, such as washrooms, cafeteria, telephones, and shelter. If at all possible, visit the site ahead of time.

✦ Find out the **cost of the trip** per student and adult, including all taxes and transportation costs, if applicable. Also, think about how this cost will be paid, either from school funds, fundraising, or family contributions.

NOTE: Ensure that no student is excluded from the field trip because of an inability to pay. Usually, the school has procedures in place to accommodate students who are unable to pay the fee. Be especially sensitive to and confidential about these students' situations.

◆ Ensure that you have made all the necessary **arrangements and preparations**.

◆ Book your out-of-classroom excursion well before you begin your unit of study. In some schools, **booking of field trips** needs to be done at the beginning of the year and in consultation with your grade or division group.

◆ Arrange for your **transportation** and confirm details. You may need to review school bus, private vehicle, or public transportation procedures for students.

◆ Decide and record the **learning expectations** for this out-of-classroom excursion. Keep in mind that each out-of-classroom excursion you plan should be within the appropriate level of understanding and maturity for your students.

◆ Plan the learning experiences that the students will do *before, during,* and *after* the trip, and determine the materials needed. Doing so will help to ensure the success of the field trip and will also enrich the total experience.

*NOTE: Any out-of-classroom excursion lends itself to the teaching of **mapping skills**. For example, distribute a map showing the route from the school to the field trip's destination. Encourage the students to observe the route while travelling to and from the site. Consider incorporating **mathematics skills** by asking students to calculate the distance they will travel or the time it will take to arrive.*

◆ Take into consideration the field trips that your students have already experienced and if this is the first time or not that students will be going on this trip. Find out early **what they know** about a potential field trip location, their experiences, and the questions they have so that this information can help you with your planning.

◆ Decide on the **assessment strategies and tools** you will use such as observation, self-assessment, reflection, portfolio entry, etc., and work samples such as sketches, notes taken, tally sheets, or charts.

◆ Consider bringing along a **camera, video camera, or digital audio recorder** to document the field trip experience. The recording could be useful as data for assessment purposes, as well as serve as a form of communication about your trip and as an impetus for discussion and writing. Be sure to decide who will be responsible for the equipment and how you will organize its use.

✦ Prepare for the **inclusion** of students with special needs and second language learners. For example, arrange for someone to act as a translator for students who are new to the language of instruction, arrange for volunteers or teaching assistants to supervise certain students, arrange for a special van to transport a student in a wheelchair, or confirm special funding, if necessary.

✦ Ensure that you have your **principal's approval and signed permission** for all out-of-classroom excursions. When the trip is unusual or potentially risky (e.g., a swimming or boating trip), you may also need to have signed permission and approval from your director of education or a designate, such as a supervisory officer.

✦ Ensure that you are familiar with the **school emergency plan** while on a field trip and all the potential safety issues pertaining to the particular field trip you are planning. You have **a legal duty of care** which involves appropriate and effective supervision, inspection, protection, and instruction. Providing that avoids any charge of **negligence** (e.g., failing to find out about student allergies when providing lunch for students in an outdoor education centre, or not arranging adequate supervision). It is recommended that you take **first aid courses** every few years to be prepared for possible emergency situations.

✦ At least two weeks before the trip, write a **letter to parents**, asking for signed permission and funding if required. In some jurisdictions, a district or board form letter must be used for all out-of-classroom excursions. Specific details such as the following should be outlined in the letter to parents:

- purpose of the field trip
- connection to the program
- intended follow-up
- time and place of departure
- time and place of return to school
- lunch arrangements
- type of transportation to be used and cost if applicable
- suggested clothing to wear
- funds needed

Figure 7.1 shows a sample letter to parents about an upcoming field trip.

Dear Families,

On Monday, March 20, our class will be going on a field trip to the Royal Ontario Museum. We will be travelling by school bus, leaving at 9:00 a.m. and returning by 3:30 p.m. Students are asked to bring a bag lunch and $1.00 on the day of the trip if they wish to purchase a drink. Also, please have your child bring in $4.00 to cover the cost of the entrance fee. It would be appreciated if this money is brought in by March 10.

This field trip reinforces our unit on early civilizations and addresses the learning expectations in the Social Studies curriculum at the Grade 5 level. We plan to visit the Egyptian exhibit to gain a better concrete understanding of the history and life of ancient Egyptians. Students will do research activities in the upcoming weeks to extend their learning in this area.

If you are able to accompany our class on this field trip, we would appreciate your assistance. Please indicate on the form below if you would like to join us.

Please sign the attached form and return it to me by Friday, March 20. Students will not be permitted to go on this trip without the permission form signed and returned.

Thank you for your support and interest.

Sincerely,

Mrs. Pollishuke

Mrs. Pollishuke

PARENT PERMISSION FORM

☐   Yes, I give permission for my child _____ to go on the trip to the Royal Ontario Museum on Monday, March 20.

☐   No, I do not give permission for my child _____ to go on the trip to the Royal Ontario Museum on Monday, March 20.

☐   Yes, count me in as a helper on this field trip.

Please contact me at _____ .

Parent/Guardian Signature: _____   Date: _____

Figure 7.1 *Sample Letter to Parents Re: Upcoming Field Trip*

NOTE: *In most school districts, a blanket permission form signed at the beginning of the year is* not *adequate. Parents need to know what their children are doing and where they are each day.*

✦ Decide where and how you will **collect and store the money** that the students bring in for the field trip. You may want to have a check-off system or enlist the help of one or two students to count the money. Never leave money unattended or in an unlocked desk. It is best if it is kept in an envelope and stored in the office for safekeeping.

✦ Follow up with students for whom you believe the cost will be a concern and make **funding arrangements** on their behalf. Be sensitive to these students' feelings and situations.

*NOTE: Be aware of all your **official responsibilities** as you take your students away from the security of the classroom and school environment and into the wider community. Know your legal obligations, and provide safe and secure supervision.*

** A good resource to refer to for current information about the legal responsibilities of teachers is *Inspiring the Future: The New Teacher's Guide to the Law, 1st Edition,* by Dr. Nick J. Scarfo and Justice Marvin Zuker (Carswell Publishing).

✦ Decide how you will **organize your groups** during the field trip and how many adult volunteers you will need.

✦ If **adult volunteers** accompany you on the field trip, ensure that they have clear guidelines and expectations as to their responsibilities. You may wish to write them a letter outlining their responsibilities on the field trip. Figure 7.2 provides an example.

✦ Before the field trip, **prepare your students** for a successful field trip by reviewing emergency plans, safety rules, appropriate social skills, and code-of-behaviour expectations, as well as academic expectations.

✦ Access to a **cellphone** is advisable on the field trip in case of an emergency. Keep school and emergency numbers handy.

✦ **File the itinerary for the field trip with the school office**, and include a list of your students, the staff, and the adult volunteers accompanying you. Keep a copy of the itinerary for yourself.

✦ **Inform the office** about the whereabouts of the **students who will not be attending the trip**: namely, those who are absent or who will stay with another teacher for the day. Ensure that you leave appropriate work assignments with the students who will stay with another teacher. Make sure that you have prepared them in advance to ensure that they are prepared to work with another class for the duration of the trip.

Dear Volunteer,

Thank you for volunteering to accompany us on our upcoming field trip to the museum. I welcome your offer of assistance. I'm sure that the students will enjoy a richer, more productive day because of it.

Please meet me at 8:30 a.m. on Monday, March 8, in Room 212. I am calling all the volunteers together then to answer questions, clarify expectations, and explain how you can help on this day. In the meantime, here is some information about our school expectations and your role as a volunteer.

RESPONSIBILITIES

- Teachers are responsible for the conduct and manners of the class at all times. Refer any situation requiring discipline to me immediately.
- You will be asked to supervise a small number of students. Please keep a record of their names and use the materials I will provide such as a clipboard, paper, and a pencil.
- While you are on your own with your group of students, please review the rules for taking washroom breaks and water fountain drinks, not running, being respectful, and cooperating with others.
- Please do not purchase treats for your group of students. Other students in the class whose volunteer may decide not to treat them might see this as inequitable. Students have been invited to bring their own money, and will have some time in the gift shop to purchase souvenirs if they wish.
- Please ensure that you are on time to meet the bus at the end of our day.

BUS SAFETY

- The bus driver is responsible for the safety of the bus and its passengers.
- Students must not leave their seats while the bus is in motion.
- Students must sit properly at all times (no leaning in the aisles).
- Students' behaviour shall be the same as in a classroom setting.
- Activities that might distract the driver or other users of the road are not permitted. Singing while the bus is in motion is permitted only with the prior consent of the driver and teacher.
- Windows may be adjusted only with the consent of the driver or adult-in-charge.
- Students must not put their hands, head, or objects out of the window.
- Students' lunch bags, books, parcels, etc. must be placed on the floor or held on laps.
- Eating and drinking are not permitted on the bus unless prior arrangements have been made with the bus driver.
- While the bus is in motion, students and adults must not talk to the driver except in case of an emergency.

SEATING ARRANGEMENTS FOR ADULTS ON THE BUS

1. If there is only one adult, please sit at the back of the bus.
2. If there are two adults present, one should sit at the back and one at the front.
3. If there are three (or more) adults, sit at the back, centre, and front, please.

Buses should be loaded from the rear forward. If there is not a full load, an equal number of front and rear seats should be left vacant with equal distribution on both sides of the bus.

Thank you again for offering your assistance.

Sincerely,

S. Schwartz
Susan Schwartz

LM 7.2 **Figure 7.2** *Sample Letter to Field Trip Volunteers*

+ If some or all students are being transported by **private vehicle**, keep a copy of the list of students in each vehicle and leave a copy with the school office. In your letter to parents, notify them that their children are being transported by private vehicle, and make sure you have signed parental permission. At no time should students be transported by other older students during school trips.

+ For any **overnight** field trip, ensure that at least one adult has a car on-site in case of emergencies.

+ For an overnight field trip or a trip which involves serving a meal, ensure that you have recent **medical information** about each student, as well as parental permission to seek medical attention in case of an emergency.

+ For students with severe allergies, ensure that you know the procedures regarding anaphylactic shock and how to administer **epipens** in crisis situations. You may require a first aid session by a public health nurse or trained professional early in the school year.

+ Ensure that all student information is kept **confidential**, but is easily accessible if needed in an emergency.

*NOTE: Familiarizing yourself with **school emergency plans** and your **students' medical histories** will prepare you for any emergency that may arise so that your students are safe and secure in the wider classroom environment.*

+ Prepare a variety of **follow-up experiences** as part of your classroom program and unit of study. Consider writing thank-you letters to the staff at the site you have visited.

+ Plan to feature highlights of your field trip as part of your ongoing **communication with parents**. You might decide to send home a newsletter, create a class newspaper in which students write articles about different aspects of the trip, create a class scrapbook of photos and writing and send it home with individual students on a sign-out basis over a period of time, or invite parents to an after-school meeting or an Open House evening where related work samples are displayed or a video or multi-media presentation is shown. (Refer to Chapter 11: Creating Community—Partnerships with Parents.)

+ You may want to use an **out-of-classroom excursion planning template** to ensure that you have made all the important preparations for your teaching, as well as for your students' supervision and safety. (See Figure 7.3.)

Out-of-classroom Excursion Plan

Teacher's Name: | Grade:

Location of Field Trip: | Date of Field Trip:

Before the Field Trip

Program Planning:

Curriculum Learning Expectations to be addressed:

Assessment: How will the learning be assessed?

Accommodations & Modifications: How will I meet the needs of specific students who need more support or a challenge?

Where does this field trip fit in the unit of study?
- ☐ Introduction to the unit
- ☐ During the unit
- ☐ At the end of the unit (closure)

Learning Experiences: What lesson(s)/tasks/strategies will I implement to prepare for this trip?

Logistics:
- ☐ Principal permission
- ☐ Trip booked
- ☐ Contact person at location
- ☐ Time and place of departure
- ☐ Time and place of return to school
- ☐ Cost per student
- ☐ Cost per adult
- ☐ Other funding required
- ☐ Transportation – bus, public transport, other, cost?
- ☐ Method of payment
- ☐ Students with special needs re: funding, accessibility (wheelchair), adult support

- ☐ List of students' medical information and special attention (e.g., epipens)
- ☐ Lunch arrangements
- ☐ Suggested clothing to wear if applicable
- ☐ Permission form sent home to parents
- ☐ Emergency/Safety plan
- ☐ List of students to the office before trip (and copy for self)
- ☐ List of students not going on the trip to the office with where they will be and assigned work (and copy for self)
- ☐ Other

Equipment to bring:
- ☐ Cell phone
- ☐ Camera
- ☐ Video camera
- ☐ Digital tape recorders
- ☐ Binoculars

- ☐ Maps
- ☐ Compasses
- ☐ Writing paper
- ☐ Writing tools
- ☐ Other

Supervision:
- ☐ Teachers
- ☐ Volunteer Parents
- ☐ Other

Organization of groups:
- ☐ Number of students
- ☐ Number of groups required
- ☐ Number of adult leaders per group

- ☐ Instructions for group leaders
- ☐ List of students who will need adult or peer support
- ☐ Other

During the trip:
Learning Experiences: What lesson(s)/tasks/strategies will be implemented while en route or on site?

After the trip:
Learning Experiences: What lesson(s)/tasks/strategies will be implemented as follow-up activities?

- ☐ Reflection: What did you learn? Highlights of the trip?
- ☐ Thank you letters
- ☐ Newsletters
- ☐ Class newspaper
- ☐ Class scrapbook of photos and writing

- ☐ Audio
- ☐ Video
- ☐ Multi-media presentations
- ☐ Other

Sharing/Celebrating the learning
- ☐ How will the learning be shared/celebrated with students, parents, others?

- ☐ Other

 LM 7.3 **Figure 7.3** *Sample Plan for Out-of-classroom Excursions*

Final Thoughts

Out-of-classroom excursions are excellent opportunities for students to experience the wider community. Including a field trip in any unit of study will enrich the learning and will provide students with a real-world application. Often, students who may experience difficulties in a classroom will excel in an out-of-classroom environment and become motivated to learn. Adequate preparation and planning, and careful consideration of safety and supervision issues, will ensure the success of your field trips. Check that you have made all the necessary preparations for the field trip and that you have planned appropriate *before*, *during*, and *after* learning experiences for your students. Preparation equals success!

Literacy and Language Learning

Literacy is the cornerstone of all learning and success in school. Before children begin their formal education, they have already learned a tremendous amount about language, the art of communication. The foundations for their future learning, not simply in the language area but in all aspects of the curriculum, are laid during their early years. Literacy cannot be viewed as merely a subject to be learned in school, as it affects all aspects of learning, both in the classroom and in the world beyond. As the learners in your classroom acquire and learn to apply literacy skills, they move towards becoming proficient, independent users of language.

Literacy is multi-faceted and multi-dimensional. No longer can we view literacy as merely the ability to read and write at a proficient level on an everyday basis within our local community. Our "community" now extends well beyond our immediate environment and we are increasingly immersed in international and global issues. The internet and online social interactions have provided us with an evolving environment that brings the world to our doorstep. Our students need to be engaged in all facets of literacy, including print literacy, mathematical literacy, media literacy, technological literacy, musical literacy, information literacy, oral literacy, visual literacy, eco-literacy, multicultural literacy, etc. As students are exposed to these **multiple literacies**, they become more cognizant of global issues and more accepting of diverse perspectives, and this has a significant impact on their own cultural and social identity, leading to social action. Ultimately, students need to understand that to be literate means to have power, to be able to do the things that give us pleasure, satisfaction, and a feeling of commitment and self-worth. Print literacy becomes even more important as students see the need to critically read, write, listen, speak, view, and represent. As children learn to speak, they watch, listen, interact with language, and begin to make meaning from the sights, sounds, and symbols around them. As they begin to read, write, draw, and represent their understandings, they use language in all aspects of their lives. Everything they do revolves around their confidence and ability to read and write, listen and speak, view and represent.

As a teacher, you are responsible for ensuring that you honour and value the **prior experiences** of your students—their language, background, culture, religion, and diversity. You need to provide rich contexts and environments for learning to occur. In your language program, you need to **integrate** reading, listening, and viewing, as well as writing, speaking, and representing, in a supportive and dynamic environment, one that fosters independent and critical thinking. During reading, viewing, and listening experiences, students are immersed in information and make sense of it in light of their prior knowledge, experience, and understandings. They then demonstrate their new learnings in a variety of ways. This demonstration of their meaning-making is evidenced when they write, speak, and represent aspects of their learning. In this environment, where many opportunities for literacy experiences exist, all the components of language are seen to be interconnected.

Children begin to see themselves as **readers** as they look closely at books and notice the print and symbols in their environment. They attach meaning and build relationships between print and the spoken word. They are read to often, learn to listen carefully, and develop a positive attitude towards reading and books. As they develop and grow, they read often and with fluency, in a wide variety of genres, always for meaning, information, and enjoyment. They speak about their reading, listen to others read and speak, and write about what they read in order to share their understandings. They represent their learnings using a variety of mediums and technologies, read what they write, and share what they represent.

Children begin to see themselves as **writers** as they write and represent with clarity, imagination, and in an organized manner. They want to write because they have a purpose and an audience for their writing. They speak to clarify ideas for their writing; they listen to others read and speak; and they read and view the world around them to get ideas for their writing. They respond to questions about their writing, and represent their ideas through the use of line, form, design, media, and technology. Once children see themselves as authors, researchers, and artists, writing becomes a motivational tool for development in all other areas of the curriculum.

With an equal emphasis placed on **oral communication** (listening and speaking), children learn to present their thoughts, ideas, and feelings with confidence. They talk about their writing before, during, and after they compose. They listen to good reading models often and talk about their reading and writing experiences. They have frequent opportunities to communicate with peers and adults in meaningful situations. This emphasis on "talk" provides opportunities for students to develop critical thinking skills. They are better able to organize their thoughts and convey information in both formal and informal situations.

The emergence of **media literacy** as a significant aspect of the language curriculum over the last decade has broadened the area of language arts instruction, and helped to capture students' attention and interests. Teachers increasingly use the media and technology that evolve around students' lives, and integrate that into and across the curriculum.

Critical literacy, another important component of the language arts curriculum, promotes higher level thinking. Students are encouraged to ask questions, examine their own underlying assumptions, values and beliefs, investigate and appreciate diverse perspectives, and evaluate various judgments and conclusions. Critical literacy is essential for students to become proficient at reading, writing, and communicating. They learn to interpret, analyze, and evaluate texts in all forms; make informed decisions; and solve complex problems in a reflective and thoughtful way. Students engaged in these heightened learning experiences are involved in learning about their own thinking and learning (also called **metacognition**).

With so much to consider, it can be a daunting task for teachers to create an effective program that addresses the multiple literacies of today and tomorrow, while at the same time meeting the diverse needs, interests, and abilities of the students in their classrooms. Careful planning and consideration are required to ensure that a **balanced literacy program** is in place. Understanding how children learn to read and write and having a deep understanding of the reading and writing process are the first steps in creating a dynamic balanced literacy program.

As students take in meaning through reading, listening, and viewing, and produce new meaning through writing, speaking, and representing, the components of language are seen to be interwoven, one into the other, in a cyclical pattern, with meaning as the ultimate goal. An effective literacy program has a profound influence on all aspects of the curriculum, and as you develop your philosophy and implement your program, you will see your students become more and more motivated in every way. Therefore, in order to design and implement a balanced literacy program, you first need to have a clear understanding of how children communicate—how they learn to listen and speak, read and write, and interact with media and other literacies in their environment.

The Oral Communication Process

Children have a basic need to communicate with others as they seek to be understood and to understand. They need to be immersed in a language-rich environment where communication is valued and celebrated. They need frequent opportunities to be heard and to use language in whatever format they have at their disposal at that time.

Children begin to use language to communicate from a very early age, almost immediately after birth as they coo and babble. When they first learn to speak, they typically hear good models of speech around them. They begin to experiment at making a variety of sounds as they develop and begin to attach meaning to certain sounds. The sounds they make elicit certain reactions from those around them and as they refine those sounds, they begin to attach meaning to the sounds they can make. As meaning becomes more explicit, they are able to reproduce sounds that convey meaning to others. They mimic. They begin with one-word responses and quickly escalate to using more words in combinations to attempt to have their needs/meanings understood. Their early needs for social interaction and control over people, places and things encourage them to refine and extend their language usage. By the time they are two years old, most children have a fairly basic vocabulary and can express themselves with fluency and understanding.

As children develop their oral language skills and knowledge, they begin to consolidate their understandings in order to better control and have an impact on their environment. As they experiment and approximate their oral language usage, they often over-generalize; for example, they might add "ed" to any verb, whether appropriate or not, such as "comed" instead of "came." They begin to use language to express emotions, explain actions, ask questions, seek clarification, and elicit information.

Their use of grammatically correct language begins to take hold as they emerge as more sophisticated listeners and speakers. Their basic vocabulary expands increasingly as they interact with others, with media, and with the world around them. They begin to see listening, speaking, reading, and writing as integrated processes for learning.

As children mature and continue to interact with people, places, and things, they share their ideas and opinions more readily, react accordingly to the explanations, opinions, and different points of view of others, and evaluate, draw inferences, and make judgments as they arise. They begin to understand that oral language has different "registers" or styles of speaking that are influenced by the situation in which they find themselves, the formality of the occasion, and the medium they are using. For example, you would not use the same vocabulary, grammar, and tone when speaking to your professor as you would with your best friend. Children's use of different "registers" is developed and refined as they become more sophisticated users of language.

Creating Opportunities for Oral Communication

✦ Ensure that you have a good understanding about **how children learn to listen and speak** and the processes inherent in this learning. These processes form the cornerstone of all literacy learning.

✦ **Be a role model** for your students by demonstrating appropriate speech patterns through frequent opportunities for discussion and conversation as well as through a variety of learning experiences.

◆ Provide frequent opportunities **for oral language communication and development** by allowing students to express, clarify, and rehearse their thoughts and ideas verbally, in partners, in small groups, and to the whole class. Be explicit about encouraging them to listen to others, and to speak to clarify their thoughts, ideas, and questions.

◆ Involve your students in opportunities for **informal oral communication** where interactions are more spontaneous and unrehearsed. Informal oral communication might include the following:

- a community circle
- personal recounts
- "show and tell" experiences
- think-pair-shares
- conversations
- large and small group discussion

◆ Involve your students in more **formal oral communication** opportunities where interactions are structured, rehearsed, and often performed for an audience. Formal oral communication might include the following:

- interviews
- debates
- speeches
- presentations
- plays/theatre productions

◆ When speaking in more formal situations, it is important to ensure that students are taught specific skills **for preparing and presenting** in any formal oral communication experience. These skills might involve and/or incorporate:

- topic selection
- focusing the topic
- audience awareness
- researching information and facts
- memorization versus familiarization
- using cue cards or notes
- using artifacts and visuals to complement the presentation
- using multimedia and technology
- projecting voice
- tone, expression, and fluency
- the importance of body language
- the benefits of rehearsal and practice
- adhering to time lines

** An effective resource is *Attention, Please!: Making assignments presentable, enjoyable, and memorable for all,* by Kathleen Gould Lundy (Pembroke).

✦ Ensure that you are demonstrating the use of **different levels of questioning** to encourage more depth of thought and response during large and small group discussions. To ensure varying cognitive levels of thinking, you may want to refer to Figure 4.12 in Chapter 4: Assessment in a Differentiated Curriculum for examples of how to use Bloom's Revised Taxonomy and/or the 3 *R*'s framework to structure your questioning techniques.

✦ When engaging your students in **question and answer** learning experiences, consider the following suggestions to encourage oral language development and to facilitate themanagement of these experiences in both small- and large-group situations. (See Chapter 3: An Inclusive Classroom Atmosphere for more specific information about managing group interactions.)

- Use wait time after asking a question to allow students time to think and formulate a response.

- Avoid repeating questions to encourage students to listen attentively the first time.

- Avoid repeating students' answers, encouraging them to also listen to each other. If you repeat their answers, it can encourage students to only listen to the teacher. If necessary, ask students to repeat their own answers.

- Encourage students to direct their answers to each other and not just to you, in order to promote a more interactive community atmosphere.

- When a student answers a question, ask the members of the group what they think of that student's response. This may open up the thinking behind that answer as well as encourage students to value their own and their peers' contributions.

- Ask your question first before calling on specific students. This encourages all the students to listen and pay attention.

- Encourage students to respond in full sentences to promote oral language development and confidence.

- Look at the errors your students make as diagnostic information for what they know and have yet to learn. Use their errors as guideposts to your planning.

- When students give an inaccurate response to a question, ensure that you show respect for their attempts, which will encourage them to continue to take risks. Analyzing incorrect responses can be useful in drawing out the reasoning behind the response.

- Encourage students to work together in partners and/or small groups to respond to questions or challenges. Rehearsing responses with others is an excellent way to encourage oral language and give even the most reluctant speaker the confidence to speak up. For example, a "think-pair-share" activity is a good one to use to have students rehearse their responses before responding to the whole group.

- If any questions remain unanswered, encourage students individually or in small groups to take up the challenge of researching the answers. This encourages an inquiry approach and provides leadership opportunities.

- Be sure to vary the selection of students who respond to ensure that you are involving a good representation of all the students in your class, considering gender, race, ethnicity, background, etc.

✦ During small and large group situations, encourage students to listen to and share different opinions and points of view. Be explicit about exposing your students to more global issues to ensure that they understand **diverse perspectives** beyond their borders. They need to understand and respect a range of opinions as they develop empathy, tolerance, and greater understanding of others.

✦ Plan how you will **maximize student involvement** and encourage participation by those students who do not respond readily or often. Avoid situations where they may feel singled out or at risk. Here are some strategies you might include:

- Allow all students to "pass" if they do not know the answer.

- Give students opportunities to discuss/rehearse first with a partner or small group, to build confidence when speaking in a larger group situation.

- Ensure that students are aware that after rehearsal opportunities, you might select anyone in the group to respond and not just those with their hands raised.

- After appropriate rehearsal time and prior notice, you might want to write students' names on cards or popsicle sticks and randomly select who will respond.

- Involve your students in collaborative and cooperative learning opportunities, and assign specific roles, including facilitator, encourager, recorder, or reporter. Outline the expectation that all students will assume each role at some point. Students take responsibility for their learning and the learning of others as they engage in solving problems and making decisions throughout the group-learning process. (See Chapter 3: An Inclusive Classroom Atmosphere.)

✦ Engage students in **interactive activities** and **learning stations** (see Chapter 7: Effective Learning Stations—Small Group Differentiated Learning). As young children use manipulatives, blocks, puzzles, games, and toys, and as they explore a variety of learning stations, such as sand, water, and construction, they develop their skills and confidence in listening and speaking in a risk-free environment. The same is true for older students as they interact with their peers and materials in problem-solving and content-based learning activities.

✦ Involve your students in **drama** to encourage and develop their listening and speaking skills, as well as to foster creativity, imagination, positive attitudes and self-confidence. Drama should be a valued part of every program and includes the following:

- storytelling
- role play
- tableaux (freeze frames)
- monologues
- choral reading

- Readers' Theatre
- soundscapes
- improvisation
- mime
- puppetry

** Excellent resources for drama are Larry Swartz's *The New Dramathemes, 3rd Edition* (Pembroke), and Larry Swartz and Debbie Nyman's book *Drama: Schemes, Themes & Dreams* (Pembroke), which provide suggestions and clear outlines on how to use children's literature to invite students and teachers into the world of drama.

✦ Be sure to accommodate for the learning needs of all your exceptional learners, including **second language learners who may experience a silent period** when they are listening and learning but choosing not to speak until they are more confident and competent in the language of instruction. This silent period is typical of the initial stage that second language learners experience when they first arrive in a new environment, and it can last for a significant period of time depending on the student.

✦ Provide specific opportunities to **reinforce good listening skills**. For example, have students listen with headphones to recorded material on a CD or on the computer, listen to adults read aloud frequently, respond to whole-class or small-group presentations, do echo-clapping activities, and follow oral directions.

✦ **Develop criteria for good listening and speaking skills** with your students. Record and post on an anchor chart, and have them refer to it often. You may want to brainstorm with them using a T-chart: "What does it look like and what does it sound like to be a good listener?"; "What does it look like and what does it sound like to be a good speaker?" (See Chapter 3: An Inclusive Classroom Atmosphere for an example of a T-chart.).

✦ **Assess your students' oral language skills and abilities** on a regular basis.
- Observe student contributions in conversations with you and in small- and large-group situations with their peers.

- Record oral language samples for students who might require further in-depth analysis of their oral language development.
- Provide students with opportunities to **reflect orally** on their work. As they mature, they may move from simple retelling or labelling of their work to describing their work in more detail, to explaining the thinking behind their work, and ultimately, to reflecting on the quality of their work.

✦ Keep in mind that oral language does not occur in isolation and is **interconnected** and interwoven with reading, writing, media literacy, and all curriculum areas. Continue to examine your timetable to ensure that you have carefully planned a **balance** of oral communication opportunities throughout your program.

The Reading Process

Think about how *you* first learned to read, and compare learning to read to the process that babies go through when they learn to speak (see Oral Communication). The same is true for reading. Early readers experiment with reading by "**pretend-reading**." They begin to show interest in print and books. They engage in choral reading, echo reading, and reading environmental print. In an ideal world, they are immersed in a print-rich environment. They hear and see good models of reading on a daily basis. As they develop, they **experiment** with familiar text and begin to attach meaning to the print they see and hear.

In the **early** stages of reading, students use their prior experiences to construct meaning, and begin to incorporate some **cueing systems** (see later in this chapter) into their repertoire as they try to make sense of printed material. As they begin to read some unfamiliar text, they usually read word by word. They are also accumulating a store of sight vocabulary that they can readily access.

As readers transition into becoming more efficient and **proficient** readers, they begin to incorporate all four cueing systems and integrate a variety of reading strategies (see below) that allow them to read with comprehension, accuracy, and fluency. As they become more proficient readers, they begin to **read to learn** across various curriculum areas.

✦ Ensure that you have a good understanding about **how children learn to read** and the stages they experience as they become proficient in the reading process.

✦ Understand what **proficient or efficient readers** do. They dialogue with their experiences. The majority of what proficient readers read comes from their heads (prior knowledge and experiences) and not from the printed page. Reading is a constructive process in which readers predict, test their predictions, and fit them into their schema. Proficient readers bring all four cueing systems and multiple reading strategies together and use them to sample the text, predict what it might be about, confirm their predictions, check, reject, search/reread, and continue reading as they strive to make meaning and comprehend what they have read. See Figure 8.1 for a comparison chart of efficient and inefficient readers and the behaviours they exhibit.

Efficient Readers	Inefficient Readers
Focus on meaning	Focus on words
Make errors (miscues) but maintain meaning	Make errors (miscues) but lose meaning
Correct errors that change the meaning	Correct errors based only on sounding out—they might "bark" at the print
Make predictions based on meaning	Make predictions that make little sense
Use knowledge of letter and sounds to confirm or reject predictions	Over-emphasize use of phonics without meaning
Are aware and conscious of what they are doing in the reading process	Have little awareness of what they are doing in the reading process
Demonstrate a love of reading	Demonstrate avoidance behaviour

Figure 8.1 *Efficient and Inefficient Readers*

✦ Gain a clear understanding of the **cueing systems** that proficient readers use to make meaning from text, so that you are able to understand and program effectively. See Figure 8.2 for a description of these cueing systems.

	Semantic	Syntactic	Graphophonemic	Pragmatic
Description	Meaning, system of English, using context and prior knowledge	The structural system of language.	Sound-symbol system or knowledge of words and sounds	Form and function or characteristics of different texts
Questions	Does it make sense?	Does it sound right?	Does it look right?	What text features does it have?
Examples	Uses context clues, synonyms, antonyms, and homonyms.	Includes the grammar of the language, sentence structure, word endings, compound words, prefixes, suffixes, root words, capitalization, punctuation, etc.	Looks at word pronunciation, directionality, spelling, syllables, rhyming words, approximate spelling.	Looks at the purpose of the text, such as menus, phone books, atlases, etc. The format of the text provides a clue to the meaning of the text.

Figure 8.2 *Cueing Systems*

✦ When students read, they incorporate all cueing systems into their repertoire of learning strategies and begin to understand that print conveys a message. When readers are attuned to the cueing systems and use them efficiently, they bring meaning and understanding to what they have read.

• As they use the **semantic** cueing system, they bring all their prior knowledge and experience about print into play.

- As they use the **syntactic** cueing system, they demonstrate that they understand how the grammar of language works.
- As they use the **graphophonemic** cueing system, they make connections between sounds and symbols.
- As they use the **pragmatic** cueing system, or the understanding of how text is laid out or organized, they predict how to go about reading the print. For example, menus, recipes, dictionaries, textbooks, etc. all have specific formats that help the reader make decisions about how to read and comprehend that particular type of text.

✦ Along with the cueing systems, readers use a variety of **reading strategies** to unlock meaning. These reading strategies include using illustrations/ pictures, diagrams, graphs, charts, and other visual cues, reading ahead, guessing, skipping the word, rereading, etc. Ensure that your students know these different reading strategies when they come to a word they do not know how to read. See Figure 8.3 for a list of possible reading strategies. You may also want to create a poster to display as a reference for your students (see **LM 8.1** on the Text Enrichment Site).

Reading Strategies:

When you come to a word you do not know how to read, you can do the following:

- Look at the illustrations/pictures, diagrams, graphs, charts, captions.
- Guess and keep reading.
- Skip it and keep reading.
- Think about what it might be from the context of what went before.
- Read ahead for more information.
- Reread.
- Sound it out.
- Look for word parts.
- Look it up in a dictionary or thesaurus or computer.
- Ask someone.

LM 8.1 **Figure 8.3** *Reading Strategies*

> **NOTE:** *For beginning readers, you should teach/model each reading strategy individually before providing them with a longer list of other possible reading strategies to use. For more proficient readers, find out which reading strategies they already know and supplement their lists by adding/teaching/ modeling any that they have not identified. You may also want to use an interview about reading which taps into the students' sense of how they read and the strategies they are using. (See Figure 4.7 in Chapter 4: Assessment in a Differentiated Classroom for a Reading Q & A (Questions and Answers.)*

◆ Consider creating a **bookmark** for your students to use that outlines the reading strategies listed above so that they can have a quick reference when reading and they come to a word they do not know. You could also have your students create their own bookmarks listing these strategies.

◆ Consider hosting a **literacy evening for your parent community** during which you help them understand the reading process. By highlighting the cueing systems, and by modelling the reading strategies that proficient readers employ, you will be demonstrating how readers make sense of print and what the reading process is all about. (Refer to **LM 8.2** on the TES for specific activities to demonstrate the reading process for an audience.)

Creating Opportunities for Reading

Plan for a wide variety of meaningful reading experiences that incorporate four main reading strategies: **read-aloud, shared reading, guided reading, and independent reading**. As students become more proficient and efficient readers, they begin to take on greater responsibility for their own learning. Figure 8.4 demonstrates a process whereby the responsibility for the learning gradually moves from the teacher to the students. In read-aloud, the teacher has the greatest responsibility for the students' learning as he/she reads *to* the students, modelling and demonstrating the reading process. In shared and guided reading, the teacher reads *with* the students, guiding them through the reading experience. In independent reading, the students take ownership, and become more self-reliant and able to self-regulate their learning.

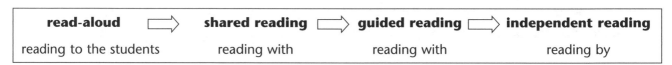

Figure 8.4 *Gradual Release of Responsibility (Pearson & Gallagher)*

Read-aloud: Daily read-aloud immerses students in a wide variety of quality literature, as well as providing them with models of good reading behaviours (intonation of voice, expression, fluency, enjoyment). It encourages discussion and extends thinking while opening students to new worlds and customs. It provides opportunities for students to develop author-illustrator awareness and encourages them to become more critical readers and writers. All teachers, not just those in the primary grades, should value read-aloud as a vital part of their literacy programs. This meaningful reading experience should occur at least three times each day, in different contexts and situations. Beyond a regular read-aloud story time, you can read aloud in all areas of the curriculum. Read-aloud opportunities exist as you read from textbooks, reference books, or other non-fiction material, articles, newsletters, and memos. A good idea is to read poetry or riddles as students line up to go outside for recess or lunch. Any time you model the reading process with students, you are providing them with an excellent opportunity to see reading as a valued, relevant, and meaningful pursuit. The value of the read-aloud experience is in the talk in which children engage *before*, *during*, and *after* the reading.

Plan your read-aloud experiences to complement your program. As you do so, consider carefully what you do *before*, *during*, and *after* you read aloud. For example, before you read aloud, you are setting the context, making connections, activating prior knowledge, and setting purposes for reading, which help you to find out what students already know or think they know and generates interest and motivation. Figure 8.5 provides some direction for the read-aloud experience.

Before, *During*, and *After* a Read-aloud Experience

Before the read-aloud:

Retell	Relate	Reflect
• Set the context. • Note the type of text and how it is organized. • Talk about/discuss/describe the cover, title, pictures, author, illustrator. • Notice the photos, maps, charts, graphs, headings, captions, and discuss the story/text. • Highlight main ideas and key points.	• Make connections. • Activate prior knowledge. • Talk about what this makes you think of . . . what it reminds you of. • Make connections to own experiences, other books, characters, or plot, author's perspectives, issues, world.	• Set purposes for reading. • Think about why you are reading this material (for pleasure, to gain information, to get general meaning, to find particular details). • Predict what this story/text is about. • Ask questions.

During the read-aloud:

Model key reading strategies, including:

• Skip	• Guess
• Read on	• Skim
• Reread	• Look for key words
• Look at the pictures, graphs, charts, maps, etc.	• Stop at intervals to retell, relate, reflect.
• Slow down	

After the read-aloud:

Retell	Relate	Reflect
• Describe the parts you liked or disliked. • Retell ideas or events in sequence. • Identify/name/list key concepts and main ideas. • Note the author's point of view. • Notice details. • Note significant parts. • Determine the importance. • Visualize a picture in your mind. • Summarize.	• Make connections to self, text, issues, world. • Compare. • Contrast. • Analyze. • Share why it is meaning or relevant to you. • Give examples. • Apply learning to other situations.	• Make judgments about the text. • Draw conclusions beyond the text. • State opinions. • Make inferences. • Predict. • Think about suppositions— suppose things were different, what if . . . ? • Synthesize/share insights and new learnings. • Ask and answer relevant questions . . . wonder.

LM 8.3 **Figure 8.5** *Before, During, and after a Read-aloud*

Source: Used with permission of Schwartz, Susan, & Bone, Maxine. (1995). Retelling, Relating, Reflecting: Beyond the 3 R's. Toronto: Nelson.

Shared Reading: In shared reading, students participate *with* the teacher in whole-class or small-group oral reading, choral reading, or chanting of big books, stories, poems, songs, chants, or expository texts. As students read together with the teacher, they are not singled out, but begin to feel more confident in the group. In a risk-free environment, their voices are carried along by the stronger voices in the group, and they begin to recognize familiar and oft-repeated words. Students become more aware of the rhythm and cadence of language, as they read, sing, and chant together. Young students recognize patterns in language as they hear, read, and internalize the patterns in predictable books or poetry. Older students also benefit from shared reading as they engage with more sophisticated language. They are exposed to poetry, raps, song scripts, and more expansive vocabulary that they might not be able to handle in independent situations. These reading experiences can lead to meaningful writing, speaking, and representing extensions. The following are possible teaching points to highlight during a shared reading experience:

✦ print and book conventions

✦ comprehension

✦ sound-symbol relationships

✦ use of syntax

✦ use of semantics

✦ mood

✦ genre (fiction, non-fiction, science fiction, poetry, etc.)

✦ conventions of language, including grammar, punctuation, and sentence structure

✦ descriptive language (adjectives, adverbs, compound sentences)

✦ stylistic devices/figurative language (e.g., similes, metaphor, alliteration, personification, onomatopoeia)

Paired Reading: Reading together in pairs allows students to read and discuss in a risk-free environment. The more fluent readers will often take on leadership roles while the beginning and developing readers gain valuable exposure to higher levels of reading material. Paired reading is an ideal way to promote the reading of novels or chapter books. It is also an excellent opportunity for buddy reading programs. Partnerships are formed with other teachers in the school (or in neighbouring schools) as older students are encouraged to read to, with, and for younger students (refer to Figure 11.15: Paired Reading Guide in Chapter 11: Creating Community— Partnerships with Parents).

Guided Reading: Guided reading provides support for the reader as the teacher guides students through the reading. As children progress in their reading ability, it is essential to help them through the process of understanding and gaining meaning from text. In this small-group learning experience, students are grouped together by instructional reading level to read the same level of text. The groupings, based on assessment data collected on an ongoing basis, should always be flexible and temporary with students moving in and out of groups according to particular needs, interests, and abilities.

Guided reading is a time to talk about a text, predict what might be in that text, and guide students through the initial encounter. You might ask students what they think the story is about after examining the title, cover, and illustrations throughout. You might also talk through the story as students look at the illustrations. A discussion about unfamiliar vocabulary that they might encounter would also be beneficial so as to activate as much prior knowledge and understanding as possible. The more readers know about the text before they read, the more successful they will be in the actual reading.

Most guided reading lessons involve a three-part structure—*before*, *during*, and *after* the read. The teacher's role involves introducing the text, modelling, coaching, questioning, observing, guiding, and directing.

For beginning readers, you might initially flip through the pages and view some of the pictures. In this way, the students are able to gain a sense of where the text is leading in order to predict what the story might be about. You might also rehearse the reading by having the group choral-read the story together before they attempt to read it independently. Older, more proficient readers should also take part in guided reading as they predict, set purposes for their reading, read silently, discuss specific elements, and reflect on the meaning of the text. You might also want to focus more on non-fiction texts as a basis for their instruction. Guiding students through unfamiliar, expository text before asking them to read it independently will ultimately allow them to better understand what they are reading and to be better able to gather the needed information that non-fiction offers.

Figures 8.6 and 8.7 both provide suggestions for Guided Reading lessons. Figure 8.6 is organized by reading proficiency, while Figure 8.7 organizes possible topics into specific categories.

Guided Reading Lessons—Organized by Reading Proficiency	
For Beginning Readers	**For Proficient Readers**
☐ Examine the title, cover, illustrations	☐ Expand their repertoire of texts
☐ Predict what the story might be about	☐ Learn strategies for reading non-fiction texts, such as using headings, subheadings, diagrams, captions, charts, graphs, maps, table of contents, index, chapter summaries, identifying key ideas, making jot notes, etc.
☐ Discuss unfamiliar words	
☐ Learn new vocabulary	
☐ Activate prior knowledge	
☐ Set purpose for reading	☐ Read increasingly challenging texts
☐ Demonstrate the use of the different cueing systems	☐ Adjust reading strategies to suit text and purpose
☐ Demonstrate the use of the different reading strategies	☐ Deepen understanding and extend comprehension skills
	☐ Extend understanding of bias, perspective and point of view
	☐ Develop understanding of stylistic devices
	☐ Expand understanding of figurative language
	☐ Extend understanding of elements of fiction
	☐ Teach strategies for skimming and scanning
	☐ Explicitly teach aspects of Retell, Relate, Reflect (Schwartz & Bone)

LM 8.4 **Figure 8.6** *Guided Reading Lessons—Organized by Reading Proficiency*

Guided Reading Lessons—Categories and Topics

Text-processing Skills and Strategies

☐ Predicting	☐ Skip, read on, reread	☐ Suffixes
☐ Revising predictions	☐ Adjusting reading speed;	☐ Prefixes
☐ Setting purpose	Phonemic awareness	☐ Phrasing
☐ Monitoring comprehension	☐ Chunking text (dividing into	☐ Root words
☐ Look for key words	sections)	☐ Skimming
☐ Concepts about print	☐ Fluency	☐ Scanning
☐ Using context	☐ Intonation	☐ Vocabulary development
☐ Rhyme	☐ Word analysis	
☐ Cloze reading	☐ Using punctuation	

Features and Organizational Patterns of Texts

☐ Headings	☐ Glossary	☐ Graphics
☐ Maps	☐ Diagrams	☐ Italics
☐ Font	☐ Charts	☐ Graphs
☐ Chronological	☐ Cause/effect	☐ Compare/contrast
☐ Index	☐ Captions	☐ Illustrations
☐ Design	☐ Description	☐ Problem/solution

Comprehension Strategies

☐ Main idea	☐ Responding to text	☐ Recognizing bias
☐ Making inferences	☐ Supporting details	☐ Summarizing
☐ Think aloud	☐ Picture events	☐ Retelling
☐ Reflecting	☐ Comparing	☐ Contrasting
☐ Connecting with personal experiences	☐ Interpreting	☐ Evaluating
☐ Drawing conclusions		☐ Finding evidence
☐ Analyzing		

Kinds of Texts

☐ Novel	☐ Poetry	☐ Magazine
☐ Tall tale	☐ Biography	☐ Diary/Journal
☐ Science fiction	☐ Instructions	☐ Fantasy
☐ Article	☐ Folktale & Fairytale	☐ Song
☐ Letter	☐ Short story	☐ Report
☐ Myths & Legend	☐ Information books	☐ Email
☐ Encyclopedia	☐ Picture books	☐ Text messages
☐ Dictionary	☐ Alphabet books	☐ Web sites
☐ Thesaurus	☐ Scripts	☐ Social networks
☐ Editorial	☐ Realistic fiction	
☐ Newspaper	☐ Historical fiction	

Elements of Fiction

☐ Plot	☐ Conflict	☐ Theme
☐ Character	☐ Atmosphere	☐ Imagery
☐ Foreshadowing	☐ Leads	☐ Time
☐ Point of view	☐ Suspense	☐ Flashbacks
☐ Setting	☐ Prelude	☐ Humour
☐ Narration	☐ Epilogue	

LM 8.5 **Figure 8.7** *Guided Reading Lessons—Categories and Topics*

Source: Used with permission. Gillda Leitenberg, Former District-Wide Coordinator, Literacy, TDSB.

When planning your guided reading lessons, the following **lesson plan** template may prove helpful. See Figure 8.8 (and **LM 8.6** on the Text Enrichment Site).

Guided Reading Lesson Plan Template	
Curriculum Expectations:	
Before the Reading	
Teacher	Student
During the Reading	
Teacher	Student
After the Reading	
Teacher	Student

LM 8.6 **Figure 8.8** *Guided Reading Lesson Plan Template*

> *NOTE: **Avoid round-robin reading** where students read a portion of a text orally, one at a time, without rehearsal, in a group situation. This method is not conducive to creating a positive attitude towards reading. Students tend to read at different rates and, if expected to follow along, meaning can be lost. Students are often reading ahead in order to practise their part rather than listening to what is being read aloud, again losing meaning and interest. In round-robin reading situations, students often fail to learn how to monitor themselves by self-correcting when meaning is disrupted because they are often corrected by their peers or the teacher. They can experience anxiety and frustration when they are reading orally in a group without having had time to rehearse beforehand. Read-aloud without prior rehearsal should be used only in a one-on-one situation with the teacher for the purpose of assessing reading progress.*

Independent Reading: Independent reading is when students can master the reading material independently and proficiently. Independent reading can take various formats including many of the following.

Drop Everything and Read (Butler & Turbill): D.E.A.R. time is an extremely important part of every student's day as it provides in-school reading practice and develops the habit of reading for pleasure. This time for self-selected reading can also be called S.Q.U.I.R.T. (Sustained, Quiet, Uninterrupted Reading Time), or U.S.S.R. (Uninterrupted, Sustained, Silent Reading). Often, very young children will role-play reading behaviours as they look at the pictures and talk out the story—and the period is far from quiet. Beginning readers vocalize their reading, but as they become more confident and proficient, they will read silently. Giving students time to read for pleasure helps establish and nurture a love of reading.

The amount of time allotted for D.E.A.R. should correspond to the age and stage of your students. Younger students might spend only 5 to 10 minutes each day reading for pleasure in the classroom, while older, more proficient readers could read self-selected material each day or every other day for as long as 30 or 40 minutes. With older students, it is still necessary to increase time in increments as you establish the routines necessary for D.E.A.R. time. Take your cues from your students as to how long they can sustain independent reading.

You may want to consider scheduling D.E.A.R. as soon as students enter the classroom, either in the morning, after lunch, or after a recess break. In these situations, you might have students put their books out on their desks or tables before they go out for recess/lunch or leave for the day. In this way, they will be able to start reading immediately after they enter the classroom. A good management idea is to ask that your students exchange books within their seating group only, to avoid having them take time to look for another book to read during D.E.A.R. You might also have them choose more than one book. When students are actively engaged in a task as soon as they enter the classroom, it frees you to deal with individual student needs or concerns that might arise, to talk to parents who might come to the door, to collect notes and permission slips, or to take attendance.

Novel Studies: The use of novels or chapter books is most appropriate for readers who are gaining some fluency in reading and can read independently or with some support from a teacher, peer, volunteer, or by using technology. Having students come together to read and respond to a novel helps to foster a love of reading, provides opportunities for sharing and responding in many ways, and introduces a variety of authors, types of novels, and genres of literature. It also allows the reader to interact with a text for a more sustained, intense period of time. There are a number of ways to program for novel studies in a classroom. Possibilities are highlighted below.

Whole-class novel study: The whole-class approach is used to introduce, model, and reinforce the strategies that students will need to use later, when reading novels individually and more independently. It is usually tied to a theme or unit of study being addressed. It provides a model for students and an opportunity to introduce and discuss parts of a novel, such as character, setting, plot, sequence, and climax. In this approach, the teacher usually selects the novel, introduces it in a unique and attention-catching way, and models discussion and follow-up learning experiences. The use of a reading response journal as a follow-up learning experience is a particularly effective strategy, as are creative responses in visual arts, drama, dance, and music. Keep in mind that the 10-questions-to-answer-per-chapter approach has been found to stifle enthusiasm for reading.

Setting the Scene: (Source: Used with permission of Lynda Pogue, author/speaker/artist.) As you engage your students in a whole-class novel study, an excellent idea is to "hook" them into the story by replicating the first scene **using artifacts** that are as real as possible. In this motivating pre-reading "Setting the Scene" activity, the students are encouraged to discover the storyline of a novel (or picture book, short story) through a process of detective work, the steps of which are outlined below:

1. **Setting the Scene:** The teacher creates the scene on a table, floor, or in a section of the classroom before the students enter the classroom. (See Figure 8.9.)

Figure 8.9 *Photo above represents the setting of the scene for the first few pages in the novel* My Name is Maria Isabel *by Alma Flor Ada (Aladdin Paperbacks).*

2. **Detective Clue Search:** As the students enter, they are given a "Clue Search" page to record everything they see and notice about the scene, without talking. They are encouraged to be detectives as they note all details and be as explicit as possible. This note taking task could be used as a precursor to or practice in taking jot notes. (See Figure 8.10 and **LM 8.7** on the Text Enrichment Site.)

3. **Q & A:** After a brief period of time, students are then invited to ask the teacher questions to elicit more of the storyline. A good idea is for the teacher to only provide "yes" or "no" responses, which encourages the students to focus their questions to gain as much information as possible.

4. **W.O.W. Time ("Writing Only Writing" Time):** Individually, using the observations made, and the answers to the questions asked, students are instructed to begin to write the first paragraph for this novel. Students are

only given a short period of time (about 5 minutes) because the main goal is for them to work in groups to create a collaborative story.

```
Name: _____

DETECTIVE CLUE SEARCH

1. Observe the scene.
2. Record your observations. No talking please!
3. Note all details.
```

LM 8.7   **Figure 8.10** *Detective Clue Search*

Source: Used with permission of Lynda Pogue, author/speaker/artist.

5. **Writing Circles:** In small groups of two to four, students are then asked to share their detailed observations and individual paragraphs, and to create a collaborative group paragraph that incorporates ideas and representations from each member's writing.

6. **Sharing:** Each group of students is given the opportunity to share their paragraphs with the whole group in order to experience the variety and diversity of ideas.

7. **Read aloud:** The teacher then reads aloud the first few pages of the actual novel and the students compare the author's version to their own writing.

This **"Setting the Scene" pre-reading strategy** stimulates interest in the novel and activates the students' prior knowledge. It is an effective opportunity to involve your students in discussions about lead sentences, setting, characters, and plot, and clearly demonstrates the reading/writing connection. It is an engaging way to motivate even the most reluctant readers and writers. Using a **picture book** and/or sharing a **short story or visual novel** (story on video or DVD) are also ways to "hook" readers into a story. In either case, the teacher creates the scene that illustrates the beginning of the story to be read.

Consider the following extensions to this strategy:

1. Distribute multiple copies of the novel to each group of students who are instructed to read an assigned chapter or portion of the novel. Their task is to retell/summarize their part of the novel in some way and be prepared to share

with the class. In this way, they can experience the entire novel in a short period of time. Creative retellings such as drawings depicting the story, murals, role play, tableaux, use of music and sound effects, etc. can be encouraged.

2. Have the students create **Literature Museums** as a culminating task to a novel study. Literature Museums are three-dimensional creations depicting important aspects of the novel completed by groups of students or individuals. See Figure 8.11 for some samples.

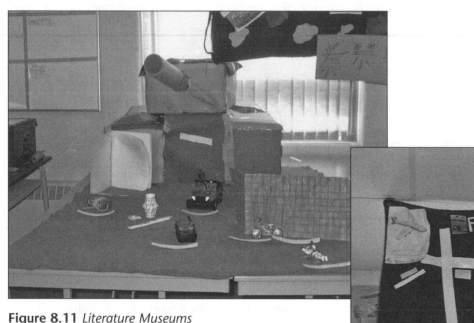

Figure 8.11 *Literature Museums*

Source: Used with permission. Kimberly Pollishuke, YRDSB.

NOTE: Dioramas and trioramas are variations of this idea (see later in this chapter and on the Text Enrichment Site).

Small-group novel studies: With a small-group approach, the teacher is able to tailor the choice of the novel to the students' interests and needs. Each group may be reading the same novel or members of the small group could be reading novels about a similar theme or topic. The groups can be homogeneous in ability so that the teacher can involve the students in guided reading, where specific skills can be taught; or the groups can be heterogeneous, where students might engage in paired reading and help each other through the text. The discussion and follow-up learning experiences are key to small-group novel studies. Small-group novel studies are often organized as literature circles which are outlined below.

Literature Circles (Daniels; Booth): Providing students with the opportunity and time to discuss their thoughts, feelings, and ideas about a text promotes skill and comprehension in reading and enjoyment of the reading process. In literature circles, small groups of students take on specific roles and come together on a regular basis to discuss, make connections, question, and wonder. Usually, these heterogeneous groups are no larger than six to eight students who are either reading the same text, different texts that share a similar theme, or a variety of completely different texts. Whatever they are reading, be sure to provide the groups with guidelines for discussion so that they can derive the maximum benefit from their meetings. Also, the assignment of specific roles encourages individual accountability as students share within their groups.

In launching literature circles in your classroom, it is important to introduce your students to the expectations and structure, and have them clearly understand each role through discussion, modelling, and role-play. You may want to begin with one group at a time. As each group becomes comfortable with and confident in the structure of these booktalks, you can let all groups meet at the same time while you circulate between and among them, acting as a facilitator and guide to the process. With this approach, it is important to structure your groups carefully to ensure that group members are able to work cooperatively and to help each other if needed. Figure 8.12 shows roles that students can assume during literature circles. Figure 8.13 provides a sample procedure for literature circles. A good idea is to plan a culminating task where students create a group mindmap, poster, dramatization, presentation, or multimedia product as a summary of their learning.

Ensure that your students engage in reflection to assess their participation in literature circles. See Figures 8.14 for an assessment tool that students can use to assess their own efforts within the literature circle and the efforts of their group members.

Oral Reading: Oral reading is an effective learning experience when students have time to rehearse and polish their delivery. It enables students to develop the good expression, intonation, and phrasing necessary to present text aloud effectively. Read-aloud, shared reading, and paired reading provide students with the necessary practice to prepare for the oral reading experience. Readers' Theatre is clearly an example of a purposeful oral reading learning experience. Other examples might be choral reading or singing, poetry reading, sharing a favourite part of a book, newspaper, or magazine article, sharing jokes or riddles, presenting commercials or radio shows, sharing their own writing, presenting a speech or project, audio- and/or videotaping stories, recording and reading minutes of class meetings, and beginning an announcer's club where students make class and school announcements over the public address system.

** A good resource to refer to is *Good-bye Round Robin: 25 Effective Oral Reading Strategies, Updated Edition* by Michael F. Opitz and Timothy Rasinsky (Heinemann).

Literature Circles

Procedure:

1. Read and understand the specifics of each role identified below.
2. Choose a different role for each time you meet with your group.
3. Read the assigned reading material in advance, and come prepared to serve in your role for each session.

Session 1: Reading Material: _King of the Castle by Kathy Stinson, Chapters 1-3_

Date: _____   Time: _1:00 p.m._____

_____ Kim _____   E. Illustrator: _Germaine_____
_____ Meda _____   F. Facilitator: _Mike_____
_____ Laureen ____   G Recorder: _Silvan_____
_____richer: _Farhan_____

_____Material: _Chapters 4 -7_____

_____   Time: _1:00 p.m._____

_____eda _____   E. Illustrator: _Mike_____
_____ureen ____   F. Facilitator: _Silvan_____
C. Questioner: _Farhan____   G. Recorder: _Kim_____
D. Vocabulary Enricher: _Germaine____

Session 3: Reading Material: _Chapters 8-12_____

Date: _Jan. 24_____   Time: _1:00 p.m._____

Roles:
A. Summarizer: _Laureen_____   E. Illustrator: _Silvan_____
B. Connector: _Farhan_____   F. Facilitator: _Kim_____
C. Questioner: _Germaine____   G Recorder: _Meda_____
D. Vocabulary Enricher: _Mike_____

Roles for Literature Circles

A. Summarizer: ❏ summarizes the reading for the group (a brief retell of the most important parts and issues).

B. Connector: ❏ relates or finds connections between the ideas in the text and their own lives, other texts, or the real world

C. Questioner: ❏ raises puzzling questions from the text for the group to consider

D. Vocabulary Enricher: ❏ finds new and interesting words from the text and draws the group's attention to them and their meaning

E. Illustrator: ❏ illustrates something of interest in the text to share with the group

F. Facilitator: ❏ makes sure the group stays on task, that everyone participates, and that the group keeps to a time line

G. Recorder: ❏ takes notes of the most important points during the literature circle discussion

ONLINE MATERIAL
LM 8.8 Figure 8.12
Roles for Literature Circles

ONLINE MATERIAL
LM 8.9 Figure 8.13 *Sample Procedure for Literature Circles*

LITERATURE CIRCLES: Self- and Group Assessment	
Date:	
Name:	Group Members:
Title of Book:	Author of Book:

4 = Wow! Participated actively! 3 = Participated well, most of the time.	
2 = Participated some of the time - 3 or more times. 1 = Hardly participated - once or twice.	

What do you think about your participation during Literature Circles?	**What do you think about your group's participation during Literature Circle?**
❑ I was prepared and ready with all my materials.	❑ Group members were prepared and ready with all their materials.
❑ I paid attention and was on topic.	❑ Most group members paid attention and were on topic.
❑ I made suitable and interesting contributions to the group discussion.	❑ Suitable and interesting contributions were made by group members.
❑ I asked relevant questions.	❑ Relevant questions were asked.
❑ I shared aspects of the text that I thought were important for everyone to hear.	❑ Important aspects of the text were shared.
❑ I made predictions about what might happen next.	❑ Predictions were made about what might happen next.
❑ I made connections to my personal experiences.	❑ Connections were made to personal experiences.
❑ I made connections to a text.	❑ Connections were made to different texts.
❑ I made connections to issues.	❑ Connections were made to issues.
❑ I made inferences based on what I know (evidence) and what I thought (opinion).	❑ Evidence from the text was used to support what was said.
❑ I used evidence from the text to support what I said.	❑ Group members listened to each other.
❑ I was a great listener.	❑ Group members encouraged each other.
❑ I encouraged others.	❑ Group members were considerate of other's opinions.
❑ I was considerate of other's opinions.	

One idea I contributed to the group was . . . .

One thing I learned from a group member was . . . .

One thing I learned about participating in a Literature Circle was . . . .

LM 8.10   **Figure 8.14** *Assessment Tool for Literature Circles*

Readers' Theatre: Readers' Theatre allows students to become intimately familiar with the structure and pattern of language in a passage or story. As students take on the roles of narrator and readers, they dramatize the text through words and improve their oral reading fluency through the repeated practice that Readers' Theatre provides. This learning experience can also be an ideal opportunity to demonstrate clearly the interconnected relationship between the processes of writing, speaking, and representing, and reading, listening, and viewing. As students begin to write adaptations to stories used in a Readers' Theatre experience, audiences can read, listen to, and view what they have created.

Reading in the Content Areas: Reading opportunities in the content areas throughout the curriculum are vital components of a balanced literacy program. Students need to know that not only do they learn to read for pleasure, but they also read to learn. They read to obtain facts, knowledge and skills and to learn about people, places, and things. It is important to show students specific strategies to apply when reading **non-fiction texts**. Just as you teach them to reread, skip, sound out, and look for smaller words in fiction, when you teach them to read expository texts such as textbooks or reference books, you must bring their attention to the clues to meaning found in that type of text. Figure 8.15 looks at the reading strategies specific to reading non-fiction texts (Moline). See **LM 8.11** on the Text Enrichment Site for a chart to post.

STRATEGIES TO USE WHEN READING NON-FICTION TEXTS:

- Look at the table of contents, index, glossary, chapter titles and summaries.
- Notice any pictures, diagrams, captions, charts, graphs, maps, tables, figures.
- Note the headings and subheadings.
- Highlight the bold or italicized words.
- Highlight key words and make sure meaning is known.
- Use sticky notes to record questions or new vocabulary.
- Review any sidebar information.
- Slow down.
- Read on and see if it makes sense.
- Recite the words out loud.
- Read and retell in your own words to ensure meaning.
- Reread the first paragraph carefully.
- Reread and/or skim the first line of each paragraph to grasp the main idea.
- Draw sketches, diagrams, labels, to help make sense of the information.
- Make jot notes, lists or webs as a visual record of meaning.
- Look up unfamiliar words in a dictionary, thesaurus, or computer.
- Ask someone to reread the section and discuss.

 LM 8.11   **Figure 8.15** *Strategies To Use When Reading Non-fiction Texts*

By taking jot notes as they read, students are able to refer back to items that might help them make sense of the text. They can read a passage and recite back to themselves what they have just read. They often need to slow down their reading to focus more on the meaning and comprehension to gain a fuller appreciation and understanding of the content. All of these strategies are important to ensure that reading non-fiction is a satisfactory and enlightening pursuit for all readers as they read across the curriculum.

Creating Opportunities for Reading Response

For any reading program to be effective, it is important to provide students with an opportunity to respond in a variety of ways to what they have read. Students need to be able to share their ideas, reactions, and opinions, both in written and graphic formats. They need to respond by expressing their thoughts in writing, answering relevant questions, making inferences, drawing images, reflecting on their learning, and creating representations of any or all aspects of the text they are reading. Whatever the format the response may take, ensure that students understand the nature of the response and what is expected of them. Show students models of exemplary responses, and develop assessment criteria with the students, so that they know what is expected. (See Chapter 4: Assessment in a Differentiated Curriculum.) Below are some different formats for reading response.

Using a reading response journal: Students respond in writing, sharing their thoughts, feelings, opinions, and questions about the plot, characters, setting, issues, problems, information, etc. The use of questions or prompts often helps to provide a structure and support for students as they build confidence and competence in their abilities to respond. The following prompts can prove helpful, especially if they are modelled throughout the program: "I noticed that . . . . I especially liked . . . ." (retell); "This makes me think of . . . . This reminds me of . . . . This makes me feel . . . ." (relate); "I wonder why . . . ." (reflect); I was surprised when . . . . (reflect); "Now I realize . . . . (reflect)." (Schwartz & Bone). Students might also agree or disagree with the author, record supporting ideas, and elaborate on specific points. They might record unusual words, phrases, or details, and discuss these in relation to their own understandings and why the author might have selected them. Teachers and peers can be the audience for reading response journals as different viewpoints are presented, shared, and discussed. Reading response journals are also very effective in the online environment as students engage in discussion on discussion boards, blogs, or class websites, etc. See later in this chapter for more information about journal writing.

Using graphic organizers: These visual models help to organize and represent learnings to facilitate recording of ideas and thinking. For example, you might use a "Story Map" or "Story Summary Sheet" (see **LM 8.12** on the Text Enrichment Site) to summarize the plot. A "Venn Diagram" or a "Web" highlights students' thinking about characterization. A "Writing Sandwich" can be used to illustrate the sequencing of a story or to organize writing. See Chapter 5: Designing Your Curriculum for examples and more ideas about graphic organizers.

Using follow-up questions: Questioning strategies that focus on a variety of levels of thinking help to push students to be critical problem solvers and decision makers and to use language to articulate their ideas. It is important to avoid assigning a list of simple recall questions where students are required only to regurgitate facts and figures found in the text, or to routinely assign a list of chapter summary questions. Both are a sure-fire way to turn students off the reading process. Students need to not only read the words and phrases but read between the lines and beyond the lines, as they infer, analyze, predict, and more. (See the Oral Communication section of this chapter, as well as Tests, Quizzes and Exams in Chapter 4: Assessment in a Differentiated Curriculum, for more information about effective questioning.)

Using a book report format: Book reports can be in oral or written format and usually require that students summarize and/or synthesize, present specific parts, and make recommendations about books they've read. Book reports should be varied to increase motivation (e.g., presented in a booklet format, as a commercial or advertisement, on a poster, or using multi-media or technology) and should be displayed or shared with others. Figure 8.16 shows a **three-fold booklet as a book report** that can be used throughout the time students are reading a book; it incorporates tasks to be completed *before, during,* and *after* the reading.

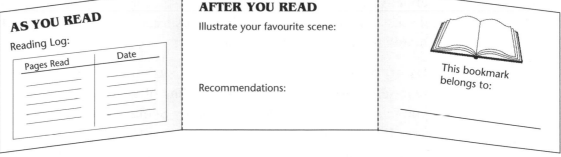

Inside

BEFORE YOU READ
Title:
Author:
Other books by the same author:
Story predictions:

AS YOU READ
New vocabulary:

Questions raised:

AFTER YOU READ
Story summary:

Outside

AS YOU READ
Reading Log:

Pages Read	Date

AFTER YOU READ
Illustrate your favourite scene:

Recommendations:

This bookmark belongs to:

LM 8.13 Figure 8.16 *A Three-Fold Booklet as a Book Report*

Using task cards: Students respond by using task cards which are specific to a text or generic in nature. These tasks need to be geared to the instructional reading and maturity levels of the students. Figures 8.17 and 8.18 show sample task cards.

1. Create a chart in your reading notebook that looks like the following one:

What I already know	What questions I have	What I learned

2. Before you read the book that you have selected, fill in the first column with any facts that you know about _____.

3. Fill in the second column with any questions you have about _____.

4. After you have read the book, record any new information you have learned about _____.

 LM 8.14   **Figure 8.17** *Sample Task Card Re: Non-fiction*

1. Choose a partner with whom to share your buddy journal.
2. Read two chapters of your novel.
3. After you have read two chapters, write an entry in your buddy journal. As you write, describe key ideas, make connections, ask questions, and share insights.
4. Exchange your journal with your partner. (If your partner is in the middle of reading his/her book, continue to read your book until he/she is finished and can exchange journals with you.)
5. Respond to your partner's entry by making encouraging statements, making connections, and asking questions.
6. Return your partner's journal and begin to read the next two chapters.
7. Repeat numbers 1 to 6 until you have completed reading the novel.

LM 8.15   **Figure 8.18** *Sample Task Card Re: A Novel Study*

Using a tic-tac-toe board: Make a tic-tac-toe board to organize generic reading response tasks as follow-up to a text. Figure 8.19 provides a sample tic-tac-toe board, which could be created on a large, laminated piece of poster board. Use tape to attach the cards to the board so that you can change the reading tasks whenever you feel it is necessary. When changing the tasks, make sure that they represent a balance of writing, speaking, and representing experiences. Also, the students should have record sheets to record books read and tasks completed. They write the title of the book and the date completed on their record sheet in the corresponding box that represents the task that they have chosen to complete. The object is to create a tic-tac-toe with the tasks chosen. A tic-tac-toe can be diagonal, straight across, or down. When students have created a tic-tac-toe, they hand in their record sheet and begin a new one. Figure 8.20 provides a sample record sheet.

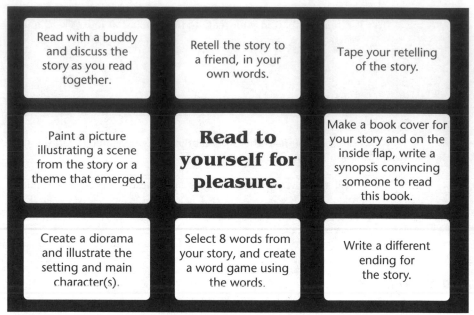

Read with a buddy and discuss the story as you read together.	Retell the story to a friend, in your own words.	Tape your retelling of the story.
Paint a picture illustrating a scene from the story or a theme that emerged.	**Read to yourself for pleasure.**	Make a book cover for your story and on the inside flap, write a synopsis convincing someone to read this book.
Create a diorama and illustrate the setting and main character(s).	Select 8 words from your story, and create a word game using the words.	Write a different ending for the story.

LM 8.16 **Figure 8.19**
Tic-tac-toe Task Cards

TIC-TAC-TOE RECORD SHEET

Name: _Loreen Lee_   Date Started: _Jan 19_

Date Finished:

Title: _Chrysanthemum_ Date: _Jan 20_	Title: _Loreen Lee_ Date:	Title: _____ Date:
Title: _____ Date:	**Read to yourself for pleasure.**	Title: _____ Date:
Title: _____ Date:	Title: _____ Date:	Title: _Whoever You Are_ Date: _Jan 22_

LM 8.17 **Figure 8.20** *Tic-tac-toe Student Record Sheet*

Using art, music, drama, dance, and technology: Students respond to reading material by representing their thoughts, feelings, and ideas through drawing or painting, creating a song, rap, or chant, role-playing, dramatizing, and using technology. Doing so provides students with integrated learning experiences and better allows those students who are less linguistically inclined to express their thoughts, ideas, and feelings. (See Chapter 5: Designing Your Curriculum for more information about multiple intelligences and learning styles.) Options include the following:

- paintings
- drawings
- papier mâché work
- photographs
- scripts
- poetry

- dioramas and trioramas
- literature museums
- computer graphics
- multimedia presentations
- electronic books, videos, movies
- websites/web pages

Figure 8.21 shows possible small-group reading response tasks that are arts-based.

DIORAMA

Materials Needed:
- a shoe box
- scissors, glue, tape
- Plasticine

Visual Arts Concepts:
- three-dimensional art form
- geometric and organic shapes/forms

Task:
Create a scene in a box to illustrate your part of the story. Be prepared to retell what is happening in your scene.

(See the Text Enrichment Site for instructions on how to make a **triorama,** a three-dimensional structure that is a variation of the diorama.)

PAPER SCULPTURE

Materials Needed:
- construction paper and variety of other paper
- glue, scissors, tape

Visual Arts Concepts:
- three-dimensional art form
- geometric and organic shapes

Task:
Recreate the main characters as three-dimensional figures using cut and torn paper. Start with basic geometric forms using construction paper; these can be attached with tabs or glue flaps or masking tape. Add details by scoring, folding, curling, piercing, crumpling, creasing, layering, and weaving the paper. Try adding colour with construction paper or markers. Make certain that these 3-D creations can stand on their own! You might need to make a stand or base.

 LM 8.18 Figure 8.21 *Arts-based Reading Response Tasks*

SOUNDSCAPE

Materials Needed:
- found or class-made instruments
- audiotape and tape recorder

Music Concepts:
- vocal control
- variety, projection, articulation
- pitch, rhythm, timbre

Task:
Think about the different sounds and noises that occur throughout the novel. How does the author help us to hear them? In movies, the soundtrack is the part that you hear — music, noises, voices, singing, and various other sounds that accompany the images. As a group, create sounds and music for your portion of the novel. Use instruments, the keyboard, your own voices, and anything else that you can find to make sounds that will allow others to "hear" a portion of the novel. Tape-record your soundscape so others can hear it.

DRAMATIZE IN COSTUME

Materials Needed:
- a box containing a variety of costumes
- construction paper and cut-and-paste materials

Drama Concepts:
- role-playing
- concentration or focus
- improvisation

Task:
Make the characters and incidents in this section of the novel come alive through playmaking. Use the costumes and props to visually communicate a sense of character or personality. (You may want to make a few simple props out of paper.) Not everyone has to be a living thing, though; some group members can assume the roles of inanimate objects. Try to make your acting as convincing as possible through your imaginative use of movement, voices, gestures, facial expressions, and positioning. Rehearse your scene; add narration for effect.

LM 8.18 **Figure 8.21** *Arts-based Reading Response Tasks (continued)*
** Adapted from ideas shared by Bob Phillips, Ontario Institute for Studies in Education, University of Toronto.

Ways to Organize a Reading Program: There is no one way to organize a reading program. The following ideas represent ways to begin.

✦ As part of your language arts block, **schedule time for reading daily**. Ensure that you include read-aloud, shared reading, guided reading, and independent reading each day. (See Chapter 2: Timetabling for more information about schedules.).

✦ Encourage your students to use **reading folders** to house their reading response work. You might also have them use a **reading record sheet or log** to track their reading process and progress. See Figures 8.22 and 8.23 for samples. Providing them with a notebook to record their responses is a good organizational tool.

✦ Determine your students' reading levels and abilities through the use of **diagnostic assessment**, and then prepare follow-up tasks that correspond with their needs, interests, and abilities. (See Chapter 4: Assessment in a Differentiated Curriculum.)

Name: Rena	MY READING LOG			
Date	What I'm reading	Pages read today	What it's about	Rating 1: Wow! 2: Good 3: Okay 4: Could be better
Jan 15	Elbert's Bad Word	25	It's about a boy who says a bad word that comes out of his mouth and looks like a spider.	1

LM 8.19 **Figure 8.22** *Sample Reading Record Sheet #1*

Name: Marnie		MY READING RECORD			Term: 2
Title	Author	Date started	Date completed	Number of pages	Comments
The Bee Tree	Patricia Polacco	Jan 8	Jan 11	29	I loved the way the grandfather described reading as honey and sweet.
The Girl Who Hated Books	Manjusha Pawagi	Jan 12	Jan 14	23	This book makes me think of the book and movie Jumanji when the animals came to life.

LM 8.20 **Figure 8.23** *Sample Reading Record Sheet #2*

✦ Organize **guided reading groups** once routines are in place and students can work independently. For kindergarten and early grade 1 students, guided reading groups should not be organized until students understand that print conveys a message. At that point, while the rest of the class is involved in other tasks not dependent on an ability to read text, you can then begin guided reading groups for those students who are ready. As more of the students emerge as readers, you can schedule a specific time for guided reading daily during your language arts block. For older students, clear expectations and firmly established routines, where students are able to work well independently and in group situations, are also necessary for successful implementation of guided reading groups.

✦ Teachers often wonder **how to program for the rest of the class** while they are meeting with a guided reading group. For guided reading groups to work successfully at any grade level, it is essential that the rest of the class is able to work independently. The tasks listed below are ways to engage the rest of the class during guided reading lessons. When you conduct guided reading lessons, the other students might be involved in the following literacy tasks:

- using response journals
- working with graphic organizers
- writing summaries
- making notes
- engaging in research
- doing extension activities related to the guided reading lesson
- writing a poem, story, etc. related to reading
- working on word work (vocabulary, spelling) where appropriate
- reading independently
- working on multimedia presentations
- using book bins (see below)

✦ To facilitate planning, organization, and management of independent and guided reading, consider implementing a **Book Bin** time where students read and respond to a variety of materials geared specifically to their levels of reading ability. The premise of Book Bins is to allow your students to **work independently** and on an ongoing, continuous basis so that you, the teacher, gain maximum flexibility to meet the specific needs, interests, and abilities of small groups and individuals. The key to making this method of organization successful is to ensure that the **routines are firmly established** before you begin to meet with small groups or individuals.

✦ Divide your students into instructional reading groups, and **prepare bins** of books that correspond to the instructional reading levels you have identified through your diagnostic assessment. Include in these bins a variety of reading material (picture books, novels, non-fiction, poetry, etc.), ensuring that all groups have experience with a variety of genres throughout the year. That is, one group might be reading a novel while another reads from a bin of picture books or non-fiction texts. Also include in each bin a reading folder, reading record log sheet, and/or a reading notebook for each student to facilitate access and storage.

*NOTE: When students are grouped into instructional levels, it is essential that these groupings be **flexible** and tied to their progress in reading ability. Students should move in and out of different reading groups and bins as their reading abilities and interests change and grow. Remember that all homogeneous groupings should be flexible and temporary—never static. You do not want students to become labelled or have difficulty changing perceptions about that label.*

** A good reference for you to refer to when deciding on levels of texts are *The Fountas & Pinnell Leveled Book List, K–8* (Pearson) by Irene C. Fountas and Gay Su Pinnell.

✦ Ensure that students are **seated heterogeneously** as they work at their Book Bin tasks so that they can cooperate with and help one another in the different reading and follow-up tasks when necessary. It is very important that students sit with peers at varying levels of reading ability so that students do not perceive that all the "good" readers are together and all the "poor" readers are together. When you want to work with one particular group of readers for guided reading or to check Book Bin work, merely call them up from all the work groups situated around the room and have them convene at a meeting area with you. Once the time with you is over, they can return to their original, heterogeneous work groups.

✦ For each reading group, prepare **reading activities** or **follow-up reading response tasks** for the reading materials that are general in nature to any text, or that correspond directly to the texts in the bins. Ensure that tasks, presented on cards, worksheets, chart, board, or computer, are meaningful and purposeful learning experiences that will address the expectations required for your grade level.

✦ Alternative to reading activities and follow-up response tasks in books bins, you could prepare **more generic literacy tasks** where students are engaged in activities, such as independent reading, paired reading, listening to a taped reading, word study activities, and/or writing tasks. You may want to use any of the **reading response opportunities** or other activities suggested earlier in this chapter (for example the **tic-tac-toe** board and record sheet). While the students are engaged in and independently move through these activities using the books in the book bins (or at times, self-selected books), you will have the opportunity to work with individuals or guided reading groups.

✦ Ensure that your routines are firmly in place before you begin to work with small groups or individuals. Achieving this could take a few days or a few weeks. Meet with each group as needed to discuss, track, or assess the work being completed during Book Bin time. Your goal is to check with each Book Bin group at least once per week. You might set specific times for each group to meet with you. These times could be displayed to promote independence and time management.

** A good resource to use to implement routines for your literacy block is *Guiding Readers and Writers (Grades 3 to 6): Teaching Comprehension, Genre, and Content Literacy,* by Fountas and Pinnell (Pearson), which provides guidelines for implementing a literacy block.

** Other very effective resources to help implement a balanced literacy program are *The Daily 5: Fostering Literacy Independence in the Elementary Grades,* and a follow-up text entitled *The CAFE Book: Engaging All Students in Daily Literacy Assessment and Instruction,* by Gail Boushey and Joan Moser (Stenhouse).

◆ Continue to use **diagnostic, formative, and summative assessment strategies and tools** to direct the students' learning in reading. (See Chapter 4: Assessment in a Differentiated Curriculum.) Figure 8.24 highlights some important assessment strategies and tools for reading and the corresponding assessment data that will be collected through the use of these strategies and tools.

Reading Assessment Strategies and Tools and Assessment Data	
Assessment Strategies and Tools	Assessment Data
Running Records	❏ Fluency ❏ Reading strategies ❏ Use of cueing systems ❏ Use of punctuation ❏ Change in text reading level over time
Miscue Analysis	❏ Fluency ❏ Detailed analysis of strategies ❏ Use of cueing systems ❏ Comprehension
Retellings	❏ Ability to sequence information and ideas ❏ Ability to paraphrase and summarize ❏ Use of precise vocabulary ❏ Ability to make connections ❏ Comprehension ❏ Inference skills ❏ Ability to make insights ❏ Critical thinking
Cloze Passages	❏ Comprehension ❏ Use of syntactic and semantic cueing systems
Observation and Anecdotal Records	❏ Attitudes and interests ❏ Fluency ❏ Strategies ❏ Response to text ❏ Comprehension
Conferences & Interviews	❏ Reading strategies ❏ Fluency ❏ Comprehension ❏ Metacognition ❏ Level of confidence
Surveys & Questionnaires	❏ Interests and attitudes ❏ Reading 'history' ❏ Level of experience with genres ❏ Level of confidence
Records of Book Reading Progress (reading logs)	❏ Interests ❏ Amount of independent reading ❏ Genres ❏ Level of confidence
Reading Response Journals	❏ Use of 'retell, relate, reflect' (Schwartz & Bone) ❏ Comprehension ❏ Understanding of story elements ❏ Critical thinking ❏ Understanding of relationships among text, author, and reader
Work Samples	❏ Comprehension ❏ Response to text ❏ Understanding of text features and story elements ❏ Interpretations and world view ❏ Critical thinking
Other?	❏

LM 8.21 **Figure 8.24** *Reading Assessment Strategies and Tools and Assessment Data*

Source: Used with permission. Gillda Leitenberg, Former District-Wide Coordinator, Literacy, TDSB.

** Good resources on reading assessment including running records are *An Observation Survey of Early Literacy Achievement* and *Running Records for Classroom Teachers,* by Marie Clay (Heinemann); a good resource on miscue analysis is *Reading Miscue Inventory: Alternative Procedures, 2nd Edition,* by Yetta Goodman, Dorothy Watson, and Carolyn Burke (Richard C. Owen Publishers).

✦ Keep in mind that reading does not occur in isolation and is interconnected and interwoven with oral communication and writing across all curriculum areas. Continue to examine your timetable to ensure that you have carefully planned a balance of reading opportunities throughout the days and weeks. Doing so will encourage your students to remain committed, enthusiastic, and motivated throughout the year.

The Writing Process

In an ideal world, students are immersed in a print-rich environment. When young children first learn to write, they typically see people around them writing, drawing, and putting lines onto paper. Early writers engage in **"pretend-writing"** or making scribbles on the page to represent writing and their ideas. The use of scribble or approximate spelling allows even young children to believe that they are writers.

They **experiment** with writing, and begin to attach meaning to the print that they see and hear around them. They begin to write some letters and words that they know, recognizing the sound-symbol correspondence, along with left to right progression of print in the English language. They begin to understand that print conveys meaning.

NOTE: Second language learners often arrive with a first language that might have unique symbols or a different organization to it, such as right to left or top to bottom progression. It is important to recognize and value the attributes of a student's first language, making connections to any specific structures that might assist in making sense of the new language being learned.

In the **early** stages of writing, students become more aware that writing is a tool for communication as they begin to develop a sense of authorship. They use a variety of familiar forms of writing and incorporate different sentence structures, and a wider range of vocabulary. They gain some understanding of the writing process, including basic revising and editing skills.

As writers **transition** into becoming more efficient and **proficient** writers, they begin to incorporate all phases of the writing process, including a focus on sharing and presenting their writing in different formats to an intended audience. They recognize that the purpose and the audience determine the specific format their writing will take. They begin to develop a personal style and voice to their writing. They also gain more control over the mechanics and conventions of writing, using spelling, punctuation, and grammar with increasing efficiency. As they become more proficient writers, they begin to use **writing as a tool to learn** across various curriculum areas.

✦ Ensure that you have a good understanding about **how children learn to write** and the stages that they experience as they become proficient writers. Writing incorporates the understanding of and skills in spelling and grammar, but these are not separate subjects to be taught in isolation.

✦ When students are engaged in writing, they should be encouraged to spell the words they need independently, using a process of approximation or coming as close as they can to conventional spelling. When they write independently, they bring together all the knowledge and skills they already possess about sound/symbol relationships. As they communicate their ideas onto paper, they become risk takers, experimenting with sounds, letters, words, and sentences. Their writing and spelling skills develop concurrently as they write and mature. Figure 8.25 illustrates the **stages of spelling** that learners experience as they become proficient writers.

Stages of Spelling	
Scribble stage	*elmem*
Random letter stage	x I t d z d
Consonants stage	t bw d t s
Phonetic spelling stage	the bo wt dn the sttt
Conventional spelling stage	the boy went down the street

Figure 8.25 *Stages of Spelling*

✦ Continue to keep in mind your knowledge and understanding about **the writing process**. As you involve students in the writing process, they work through the same phases of writing as professional authors—pre-writing, drafting, revising, editing, and publishing for an audience.

Pre-writing: During this phase, students search for, contemplate, and choose **ideas** and topics to write about. They experience, discuss, brainstorm, question, rehearse, and clarify their ideas. They talk out, plan, make connections, and think about the **organization** of their ideas. They articulate their **purpose** for writing, choose appropriate vocabulary, and orally revise. They might engage in a variety of storytelling and role-playing experiences. Teachers often provide the impetus for writing as they involve students in a variety of learning experiences across the curriculum. Be sure to allow some **choice of topic** in order to give students ownership over their ideas, topics, and formats for their writing. As students contemplate the **form** that their writing may take, they consider their **audience** or who will be reading their writing, and they tailor their messages to that specific audience.

Drafting: This is the "write-it-down-as-fast-as-you-can" phase, the phase in which thoughts and ideas are recorded onto paper or inputted into the computer. Here, the emphasis is clearly on the **content** and **meaning** of the writing. As students compose their draft, they consider the message they want to convey, the **organization** of the writing, the **vocabulary** they will use, and the variety of **sentence structures** they will include. As they write, their voice begins to emerge.

Revising: During this phase, students are encouraged to "revisit" or take another look at the content and meaning of their writing. As they change, rearrange, add to, omit, and improve their draft, they again consider the ideas, organization, vocabulary, sentence structures, and voice in their writing.

Editing: When students, often in collaboration with the teacher, decide to present and share their writing with an audience, they recognize the need to edit: to proofread and to polish the **mechanics** of their writing. It is at this phase that they concern themselves with the **conventions** of language: spelling, grammar, and punctuation.

Publishing/Sharing: Students present their selected pieces of writing to an **audience** in a variety of presentation styles and formats that correspond to the intended audience.

Conferencing: Throughout the phases of the writing process, students confer with each other and with the teacher on a regular basis. They engage in self, peer-, and teacher-**assessment**, receiving **descriptive feedback** about their work, and gaining **clarification** and valuable **insights** into how best to improve their writing.

For a visual representation of the writing process, see Figure 8.26.

NOTE: Not every piece of writing will go through all phases of the writing process. Beginning writers might participate only in the pre-writing, drafting, and publishing/sharing phases. Older writers may do many pieces of writing, and be involved in pre-writing, drafting, revising, editing, and sharing before moving on to the publishing phase. Also, some writing, such as personal writing and reflection, is not meant to be shared. You need to be aware of each writer's developmental stages, and to help him/her understand the purpose or intention of the writing and the intended audience.

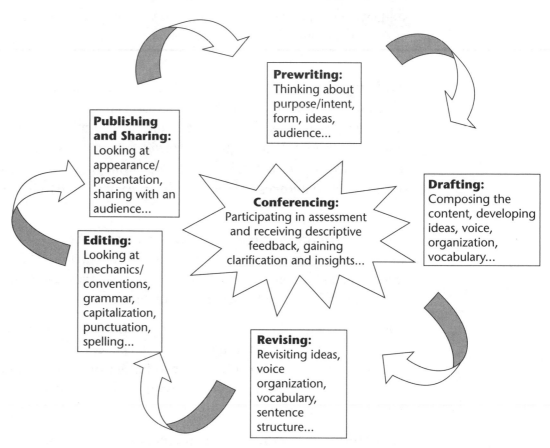

Figure 8.26 *The Writing Process*

Creating Opportunities for Writing

✦ Introduce your students to **different purposes or intentions for writing**. These include the following:

- to entertain, as in a narrative story, a script, poetry, a joke, a riddle, or a puzzle
- to express feelings and thoughts, as in a journal entry, a diary, poetry, or a personal letter
- to obtain information, as in a questionnaire, a survey, or an interview
- to clarify thoughts, as in making notes or explaining

- to inform, as in a poster, an invitation, a program, a report, a speech, a research project, or a presentation

- to describe, as in a description, a story, a characterization, a sequence of events, an advertisement, a label, or a sign

- to explain, as in instructions, directions, recipes, rules, or a science experiment

- to state opinions and/or persuade, as in an editorial, a letter to the editor, a debate, or cartoon

NOTE: Students learn that the intent *of the writing, combined with knowing the* audience *for the writing, determines the* **form** *that the writing will take.*

✦ Provide for a wide variety of meaningful writing experiences. Be sure to include different **writing forms** on a regular basis in your program. See Figure 8.27 for a clarification about narrative, poetry, reports, recounts or retellings, procedures, explanations, exposition or persuasive writing (point of view), and letter-writing.

Narrative/Story writing

Intent: To entertain

Attributes:

- includes characters, setting, plot
- has an introduction, problem, and a resolution to the problem
- includes stylistic devices, descriptive language, imagery

Poetry

Intent: To entertain

Attributes:

- conveys a message or story
- includes rhythm and might include rhyme
- includes stylistic devices, descriptive language, imagery

Procedural Writing

Intent: To provide instructions re: how to do or make something (e.g., recipes, science experiments)

Attributes:

- has an introduction
- includes clear instructions or directions
- is factual
- has a logical sequence—is step by step
- includes a summary statement(s)

Figure 8.27 *Different Forms of Writing*

Reports/Research
Purpose: To describe and classify information
Attributes:
- includes facts, information, description about a topic or issue
- has an introductory statement
- demonstrates some kind of organization
- can include diagrams, illustrations, etc.
- has topic-specific vocabulary
- includes a summary statement(s)

Recounts or Retellings
Purpose: To describe or retell an event or experience
Attributes:
- has an introductory statement
- is in chronological order (e.g., first, second, third, last)
- has a logical sequence
- includes a summary statement(s)

Explanation
Purpose: To explain
Attributes:
- has an introductory statement (e.g., definition, what it is)
- describes something
- illustrates a logical sequence
- is in chronological order
- has a cause and effect
- includes a summary statement(s)

Exposition or Persuasive Writing (Point of view)
Purpose: To persuade, present supported opinions
Attributes:
- is an essay about a topic
- has an introduction
- might present a point of view and/or arguments
- includes a summary statement(s)

Letter Writing
Purpose: To inform, describe, thank, share news, etc.
Attributes:
- includes the address, date, salutation, body, closure, signature
- can be informal (to friends and family) or formal (business, professional language) depending on the audience and language used
- types of informal letters include thank yous, invitations, love letters, letters of condolence, etc.
- types of formal letters include business letters, letter of complaints, apologies, interest, recommendations, resignation, cover letters for employment, formal thank you letters, etc.

Figure 8.27 *Different Forms of Writing (continued)*

- Plan for a wide variety of meaningful writing experiences that incorporate the four main writing strategies of: **modelled writing, shared/interactive writing, guided writing, and independent writing**. As students become more proficient and efficient writers, they begin to take on greater responsibility for their own learning. Figure 8.28 demonstrates a process whereby the responsibility for the learning gradually moves from the teacher to the students. In modelled writing, the teacher has the greatest responsibility for the students' learning as he/she writes *for* the students, modelling and demonstrating the writing process. In shared and guided writing, the teacher writes *with* the students, guiding them through the writing experience. In independent writing, the students take ownership and become more self-reliant and able to self-regulate their learning.

modelled writing ⇒	**shared/interactive writing** ⇒	**guided writing** ⇒	**independent writing**
writing for the students	writing with	writing with	writing by

Figure 8.28 *Gradual Release of Responsibility (Pearson & Gallagher)*

Modelled Writing: As students begin to experiment with or refine their writing skills, it is essential that they see good writing models. Teachers model and demonstrate how ideas are generated, organized, and recorded, and show how these ideas can be formatted, revised, edited, and prepared for an audience. Modelled writing should be both planned and spontaneous. Teachers share models of different formats, structures, and methods as they engage students in direct teaching experiences, and in their own response to students' writing. It is also important that students see teachers writing for their own purposes and needs in order to understand the relevancy of learning conventional writing skills and strategies.

Shared/Interactive Writing: In this learning experience, either a student or the teacher can act as scribe as participants collaborate to record ideas, thoughts, events, reactions, and/or opinions, usually during whole-class or small-group mini-lessons. Often, the teacher will be the sole scribe, but will always take his or her cues from the students as they negotiate the message to be recorded.

Language Experience: This learning experience can also be called shared and interactive writing as you capture students' thoughts and ideas on a chart, board, overhead or interactive display board. The language recorded stems from the students as you scribe their own words to encourage reading and an understanding of phonemic awareness, grammar, and spelling. This is a good opportunity for teachers to find out what students already know about a subject, and can be used as a diagnostic assessment at the beginning of a unit of study. A good idea is to record each student's name beside their contribution on the chart. (See Figure 8.29.)

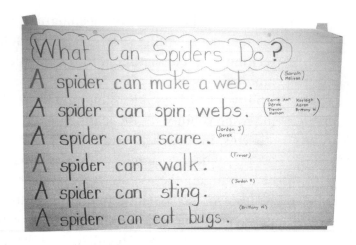

Figure 8.29 *Shared Writing Chart*

Guided Writing: Guided writing provides support for the writer as the teacher guides students through the writing process and/or teaches them about specific writing skills. In these small-group learning experiences, students are grouped and regrouped together who have similar needs and for specific skills. The groupings, based on writing samples and other assessment data collected on an ongoing basis, should always be flexible and temporary, with students moving in and out of them according to their particular needs, interests, and abilities. Guided writing is also a time to conference with students in small groups to give feedback, provide input, and set goals for further development. See Figure 8.30 for possible guided writing lessons.

Independent Writing: During independent writing time, students use the skills and strategies learned during modelled and shared writing to create their own pieces. Independent writing can grow out of both student-selected and teacher-generated topics. It is vital that students be allowed to choose their own topics for writing; it is just as important that teachers involve students in more focused writing, where the topics are negotiated with the students and are relevant and meaningful to their interests, needs, and abilities, as well as to the curriculum. As students become more knowledgeable in and comfortable with the writing process, independent writing will take on even greater significance in their writing progress as they experiment with different ideas, formats, and purposes for their writing. During this time students begin to feel like authors, often making decisions about which pieces of writing to share or take to publication.

Journal Writing: Journals, diaries, or logs provide students with opportunities to express their thoughts, feelings, ideas, insights, and reflections in written format. Journal writing usually remains speech-like or in draft format as it is not intended to be shared with a wider audience. It is important to monitor what students are writing in journals as it can provide insights into their feelings of self-esteem and sometimes reveal difficulties that need to be addressed. Since journal writing can be a very personal experience for students, be sure

Possible Guided Writing Lessons	
CONTENT	**MECHANICS/CONVENTIONS**
Ideas ❑ Beginning/Introduction ❑ Middle/Body of text ❑ End/Summary/Closure ❑ Appropriate features re: the form selected ❑ Sufficient information ❑ Well developed ❑ Unity of thought ❑ Smooth flow of ideas ❑ Stylistic devices	**Grammar and Usage** ❑ Variety of sentence structure ❑ Subject-verb agreement ❑ Conjunctions ❑ Adjectives ❑ Adverbs ❑ Clauses ❑ Adverbial clauses
Voice ❑ Demonstrates passion, excitement, joy, sadness . . . ❑ Awareness of audience ❑ Clear purpose	**Capitalization** ❑ Beginning of sentences ❑ Proper names ❑ Places
Organization ❑ Coherent ❑ Logical ❑ Sequential ❑ Suits the purpose of the writing	**Punctuation** ❑ Periods ❑ Question marks ❑ Exclamation marks ❑ Quotation marks ❑ Commas ❑ Colons ❑ Semi-colons
Vocabulary/Word Choice ❑ Appropriate to the writing ❑ Descriptive words ❑ Conversation/Dialogue ❑ Metaphors ❑ Similes	**Spelling** ❑ Scribble ❑ Random letters ❑ Initial consonants ❑ Phonetic spelling ❑ Conventional spelling with few errors ❑ Plurals ❑ Prefixes ❑ Suffixes/Endings (-ed, -ing, -tion)

ONLINE MATERIAL

LM 8.22 **Figure 8.30** *Possible Guided Writing Lessons*

to respect a student's request for privacy, should that occur. The student could fold back the page and mark "Confidential" on the outside to indicate to you that he/she would prefer a particular entry not be read.

Several different kinds of journals exist:

- **Reading response journals:** Students record their reactions to literature in response to a reading experience, such as read-aloud, literature circles, novel studies, or independent reading. (See the section on reading response earlier in this chapter.)

- **Buddy journals:** In buddy journals, students practise written conversations with their peers within a framework of firmly established routines for the exchange of journals. This strategy can be used to respond to literature and or to follow up on a class event, experience, discussion, or debate.

- **Online buddy journals:** The use of the online environment, such as email, blogging, or wikis, etc. facilitates online buddy journals, where students improve their technology skills at the same time as they are communicating their ideas and improving their writing skills. Communication online eliminates the routines of exchanging journals and facilitates writing at different times during the day. Communicating online also assists teachers in the monitoring of buddy journals. In email communications, students can copy their messages to the teacher who then acts as the reader on the side, commenting on the entry only when the need arises. In blogging or wikis, the teacher can be included as part of the group.

- **Dialogue journals:** In this type of journal, students also practise written conversations, but in this instance, they can do so with their teacher, parents, or other adults, such as an author or illustrator. Adults have a unique opportunity to model grammatically correct and effective writing as they respond to the students' entries. This way of demonstrating correct grammar, spelling, and punctuation to your students is much more meaningful than the use of worksheets. Responses and questions asked need to be genuine and to reveal the adult as an interested participant in the process.

- **Learning logs:** In learning logs students record what they are planning to do and what they have learned, or how they have solved a problem and what strategies they have used to do it. This practice can be used in all areas of the curriculum including mathematics and science where communication is a vital component of the learning process. It allows students to think critically, analyze problems, and communicate or articulate their understandings. Learning logs can also be used to record reflections, self-assessments, and goals.

Word Study, Spelling, and Grammar: Children need to learn about sound/symbol relationships or phonics in order to write, and need to use this knowledge and understanding in order to read. The use of phonics as a beginning writing strategy is essential for young writers, who experiment with letters, sounds, and words. However, always remember that phonics, grammar, and spelling need to be put into the context of real writing opportunities, not handled as external, independent worksheet exercises that do not allow for the transfer of skills learned. The most effective way that students will learn about sound/symbol representation, or develop phonemic awareness, is to approximate spellings during mini-lessons and modelled, shared, and independent writing experiences. As teachers model and share writing, they talk about sounds, letters, and combinations of letters and sounds, how different words are spelled, and why they are spelled that way; they also talk about how language patterns are organized and used. The rules of conventional spelling and grammar need to be modelled, and those rules need to be practised as students attempt to write down their own thoughts and ideas.

Writing in the Content Areas: Just as reading in the content areas is vital to a balanced literacy program, so too is writing in the content areas. Here, students begin to understand that they write to show what they have learned. Most often, writing in the content areas means writing expository or non-fiction material, so students should be taught how to record information collected, how to organize that information, and how to present it for an audience. Teaching students how to take jot notes will provide them with the skills necessary to collect data as they research topics of need or interest. Demonstrating the use of graphic organizers will assist them when they attempt to sort and classify the information they have collected. Providing them with models of how to publish their information will help them see a purpose for the different formats available.

Ways to Organize a Writing Program: There is no one way to organize a writing program. The following ideas represent some ways to begin.

✦ As part of your language arts block, **schedule time for writing daily**.

✦ Encourage students to **write across the curriculum** and in all subject areas.

✦ Do not expect very young writers to write at the same time. Writing opportunities should be provided throughout the day to encourage even the youngest student to write. **Invitations for writing**, such as the ones listed below, need to be provided to help young writers see the purposes and opportunities for writing.

  • Create a writing centre.
  • Have a wide variety of writing materials available including these items:
    o paper of all sizes, shapes, colours, blank paper, construction paper, mural paper, chart paper, graph paper, cards
    o writing materials including markers, crayons, pens, pencils, chalk, pastels, etc.
  • Have ready-made booklets in all shapes, sizes, and colours for drawing and/or writing stories, personal journals, reading responses, experiments, etc.
  • Have postcards, envelopes, and commercially- made, teacher- and/or student-made stationery to encourage letter writing.
  • Provide unusual things on which to write, draw, or paint including newspaper, acetate, leftover laminating film, wallpaper, cloth, wood, etc.
  • Put a message pad at a toy telephone in the house centre.
  • Tape a shopping list to the toy fridge.

- Have a mailbox on a stand or construct a mailbox from a liquor box so that each student has his/her own mail slot.
- Leave "architect" books (shaped like a building or tower) in the blocks centre or have students create their own architect books in the blocks centre to encourage students to draw and/or write about what they have constructed.
- Leave doodle pads at the art centre or encourage students to create their own doodle pads.
- Leave a scientist note pad at the science centre, or have students create their own scientist notepad to record their experiments and observations.
- Encourage students to write in the math centre—e.g., a "Shapes I Made" book.
- Encourage students to write from the themes presented in your classroom—e.g., "What I Know About My Neighbourhood," or "New Words I Have Learned about Snow."
- Make class cooperative books where each student is responsible for illustrating and/or writing one page of the book, either individually, in partners, or in small groups.
- Use environmental print to encourage students to read and also create rebus books based on what print they see in the environment.
- Label everything in your room.
- Highlight the value of literacy during role-playing:
  - o   as children read recipes and cook or bake
  - o   as they go to the corner store with a shopping list
  - o   as they dress up at a clothes store where they write sales tickets and bills of sale
- Have a draft stamp, an author stamp, or a flag sticker to place on their book.
- Have your students begin with a picture as they "draw" a story and then tell their story to a partner.
- Have an Author's Chair where students present and celebrate their writing.

NOTE: Many of the ideas listed above can be adapted for older, more proficient writers to encourage the process of writing daily. Reinforce for all your students that they will be working through the same phases of writing as professional authors do.

✦ Become a **storyteller** for your students and model storytelling skills. Encourage your students to become effective storytellers. Thinking like a storyteller should assist them in the pre-writing phase.

◆ **Become a writer yourself** and serve as a model for your students as you engage in modelled and/or shared/interactive writing:

- Make lists with your students.
- Write messages or letters to your students and parents. (Use school or personalized stationery, or use sticky notes for brief comments and questions about students' work.)
- Write poems, stories, riddles, advertisements, etc., and share your work with your students.

◆ Plan **modelled writing lessons** where you model and demonstrate different aspects of the writing process. For young writers, model how you begin to write and demonstrate scribble, random letters, using a magic line (initial consonant and then a line for the rest of the word), approximate spelling, and conventional spelling, reminding them that everyone begins to learn to write using different methods and at different times. For older, more proficient writers, model and demonstrate the different aspects of the writing process and help them with lessons on how to write more effectively.

◆ During modelled writing lessons, demonstrate and encourage your students to **pattern** language introduced during read-alouds or shared reading. These include the following:

- Pattern the **word structure**, such as in *Brown Bear, Brown Bear, What Do You See?* by Bill Martin Jr. (Henry Holt & Co.). In pattern books, words and specific word structures recur. The familiarity of the literary pattern gives even the most reluctant writer the confidence to make an attempt at writing. Once the pattern is enjoyed and internalized, the students easily create their own versions by extending the pattern and using their own ideas and experiences. Through exposure to many different patterns in literature, students begin to see that everything in life has some kind of interconnective relationship and that patterns exist among everyone.
- Pattern the **storyline**, such as in fractured fairytales, or using a favourite recurring character such as Curious George, or Choose Your Own Adventure formats.
- Pattern the **book format** and reproduce different formats of books. (See Publishing below).
- (See **LM 8.23 on the Text Enrichment Site** for a poem entitled "*A pattern is . . .* " which can be enlarged as a poster and used to reinforce the idea of pattern.)

- Plan **shared/interactive writing lessons** for large or small groups, based on curricular expectations that highlight specific concepts, skills, or strategies, as well as on particular needs that you notice in your students' writing.

- Plan **guided writing lessons** for small groups based on your assessment of your students' writing progress and on curricular expectations. You can discuss, share, revise, edit, and celebrate writing, in addition to addressing specific learning expectations. (See Figure 8.28 earlier in this chapter for a list of possible guided writing lessons.)

- Involve students in specific lessons that demonstrate the **different phases of the writing process**: pre-writing, drafting, revising, editing, and publishing/sharing.

Pre-writing: Lessons might span brainstorming, using artifacts, beginning with a picture, creating word association webs, using story maps, role playing, dramatizing, and working with puppets and/or technology.

Drafting: Develop expectations for draft writing with your students. Here are some pointers to pass on:

- Write down your thoughts and ideas as quickly as you can.

- Cross out any words, phrases, sentences, or paragraphs that need changing. Do not use an eraser during the drafting phase, as this might slow down the flow of your ideas.

- Write on every other line to allow space for your revisions.

- Use only one side of the paper so you can revise, cut and paste, and reorganize your writing.

- Use loose-leaf paper so you can revise large sections of your writing.

- Use a writer's notebook for your ideas and writing attempts.

- Encourage writing with a computer and save drafts on the computer or to a USB stick using "Save As" and a new date to ensure that all drafts are maintained.

Revising: Keep in mind the following while students are revising their work:

- Model good questioning techniques at every opportunity.

- Reinforce the use of *who, what, when, where, why,* and *how* questions.

- Demonstrate the cut-and-paste feature when using the computer for word processing.

- Brainstorm and use word webs to generate alternatives for overused words such as "said," "asked," and "walk."

- Advise students to use the thesaurus, both in hard copy or on the computer, to find alternate words to use.

Editing: Lessons address the use of the dictionary and the use of the spelling/ grammar check on the computer. Quotation marks, appropriate punctuation, avoiding run-on sentences, paragraphing, and combining simple sentences to make compound and complex sentences are other possible lessons on editing skills.

** A good resource to use for teaching writing is *Craft Lessons: Teaching Writing K–8, 2nd Edition*, by Ralph Fletcher and JoAnn Portalupi (Stenhouse).

Publishing ("Going Public") and Sharing: There are several ways in which to help students develop a sense of authorship.

✦ Highlight **authors and illustrators** at every opportunity.

✦ Celebrate an *Author of the Month/Student Author of the Week*.

✦ Share writing using an **Author's Chair**.

✦ Share models of different ways to publish.

✦ Encourage your students to publish their writing in **different formats**. The following may provide ideas for you.

- accompanying audio story with book
- accordion book
- acetate book (created using acetate)
- autobiography
- banner
- biography
- book in a box
- book of bags (paper or plastic bags taped together—stories or artifacts can be included inside each bag)
- book of letters (students write letters which are put together to create a book, e.g., letters to fairytale characters)
- book with bookmarks attached
- characters-on-the-move book— character is created out of cut-and-paste, attached with a ribbon, and is moved from page to page

- chart book
- diorama
- fabric book
- flap book
- flip book
- literature museum (see Independent Reading—Novel Studies in this chapter)
- peek-a-boo book
- photo book
- pop-up book
- puppet book
- shape book
- television or movie box
- touch-me book
- wheel book using paper fasteners
- wordless picture book
- 8-page book
- double 8-page book
- two or more 8-page books together (e.g., Circus Book)

See **LM 8.24** on the Text Enrichment Site for five lesson plans that you might use with your students to introduce and reinforce the phases of the writing process.

** Good resources to use for helping students to "go public" are *The Ultimate Guide to Classroom Publishing* by Judy Green (Pembroke) and *Making Books: Over 30 Practical Book-Making Projects for Children*, by Paul Johnson (A & C Black Publishers).

✦ Involve your students in **word-study lessons** to build vocabulary, and to develop spelling and grammar skills during your shared/interactive and/or guided writing lessons. Word-study, spelling, and grammar lessons should be meaningful, stem from genuine writing samples, and correspond to the expectations of each grade level as well as to the developmental stages and needs of the students in your classroom.

*NOTE: Skill-building shared/interactive and/or guided writing lessons during the **editing phase** of writing provide an alternative to the traditional isolated spelling and grammar lessons, which were customarily followed by fill-in-the-blank worksheet assignments. These "busy work" types of exercises produced little transfer of learning into daily work.*

✦ If your school or district requires you to use a **formal spelling program** calling for the use of commercially produced spelling textbooks, incorporate variety into such a program by adding theme words or words that students need to spell to the list words in the text. Keep in mind that it is not always necessary to follow a spelling textbook program in a lockstep manner. Be creative! Giving students a pre-test of the list words in the speller and seeing what words they need to know how to spell will meet the needs of individual students and can justify to parents and administrators why you are deviating from the text. If appropriate, you may also want to send the speller home as homework.

✦ Plan **independent writing opportunities** for your students during the literacy block and across the curriculum.

✦ Allow students opportunities to **choose their own topics for writing**. Having them make decisions often about their own writing topics builds ownership and fosters greater motivation for writing. You can help students develop their own topics for writing by providing the following:

- stimulating literature, artifacts, pictures, quotes, photos, films, videoclips, books, CDs, DVDs, magazines, newspapers
- storytelling experiences

- opportunities for role-playing
- opportunities for picture making and creative art
- meaningful experiences, including class events, field trips, group activities, presentations, and performances

✦ Encourage students to try to **spell or approximate the words** they need for their writing. (See Figure 8.25 earlier in this chapter for the developmental stages that students go through as they develop their writing and spelling skills.)

✦ If students are reluctant to use approximate spelling, encourage them to write the initial consonant and draw a line for the rest of the word (**'magic line'**). They can later go back and fill in the remaining letters. (See Figure 8.31, a draft letter to the editor showing the use of the magic line.)

> *Dear Edt__,*
> *I am vry con_____ about the p_____ in our prk.*
> *Please help us cleen up re prk.*

Figure 8.31 *Magic Line*

✦ Encourage students to write down all the sounds that they hear and to try to spell the words on a separate spelling notepad or sheet of paper. Figure 8.32 shows an example of a **spelling notepad**.

First Try	Second Try	Third Try
mistree	misteree	mistery
sudnlee	suddenly	

LM 8.25 **Figure 8.32** *A Spelling Notepad*

◆ Teach **strategies that students can use to spell words** that they do not know how to spell. "Look, say, think, print, check" is one example, outlined in Figure 8.33.

Look, Say, Think, Print, Check

Look Look at the word with a partner.

Say Say the word carefully.
Your partner listens carefully.

Think Cover the word and get a picture of the word in your head.

Print Your partner gives you the word.
Repeat the word out loud and print it from memory.

Check With your partner, check to see if you wrote the word correctly.

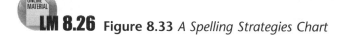

LM 8.26 **Figure 8.33** *A Spelling Strategies Chart*

◆ Consider involving your students in a **home spelling program** so that they can independently practise and reinforce at home the concepts they have learned in class. See Chapter 5: Designing Your Curriculum as well as Chapter 11: Creating Community—Partnerships with Parents for information about homework..

◆ If you decide to introduce a home spelling program, send a **letter home to parents** informing them about the routines. (See Figure 8.34.)

◆ Explain to your students their roles and responsibilities in this home spelling program.

◆ Ensure that your students understand the spelling tasks that they will be completing at home before you begin this program. For example, if one of the tasks asks the students to create an acrostic poem using their spelling words, then you need to have already taught your students what an acrostic poem is. Figure 8.35 outlines several spelling tasks.

Dear Families,

The Grade 6 classes will begin a home spelling program on Monday, September 26, which will run every second week. For this program, students will be learning standard spelling rules and common patterns that are intended to improve their overall writing progress. The program will run as follows:

> Every other Monday, we will be discussing in class one or more spelling rules or patterns. Students will choose 20 spelling words from a list that follows that pattern. At times, this list may include words that are associated with our theme or unit of study, or words that students are using in their personal writing. At all times, students will select words that they need to learn to spell. As a result, each student's list of words may be different.

> For homework, students must write each of the spelling words in a sentence to show its meaning. Using the words, they must also complete three tasks (from a choice of 12) from their spelling task sheet. This sheet is attached to their spelling notebooks.

> On Friday, spelling homework is due and a spelling dictation will be given. Students will work in pairs to administer the Friday dictation to each other.

We are looking forward to starting this home spelling program and request that you encourage your child to complete the requirements.

Sincerely,

J. Hargraves
Ms. J. Hargraves

Please sign below and have your child return this form as soon as possible.

- -

I will check that my child has completed his/her spelling homework regularly.

Parent's Signature:_____

LM 8.27 **Figure 8.34** *Sample Letter To Parents Re: Home Spelling Program*
Source: Based on ideas shared by Joan Hargraves, formerly with the York Region District School Board.

✦ Encourage your students to use a **writing folder** to house their writing. An effectively organized folder can have two or three pockets, which may contain and organize draft writing, edited and polished pieces, topic ideas and lists, ongoing records, titles of books, and lists of most commonly used words.

Spelling Tasks

For every new list of words, you must complete a task from the following. Choose three different tasks each week until you have completed all of the tasks once. These tasks are to be done in your spelling workbooks. Your books will be collected every other Friday.

1. **Syllabication**
   Write your words in one column.
   Write your words in syllables in column two.
   Check the dictionary to see if you are correct.
   In column three, write the dictionary page number where you found each word.

   Example:

Word	Syllable	Page Number
Sister	sis-ter	507
Rotate	ro-tate	319

2. **Smaller Words**
   Choose five of the longest words from your list.
   For each of these words, create as many small words as possible.
   You can scramble the letters to create the words.

   Example:
   environment – men, iron, on, mint, vet

3. **Magazine Search**
   Find and cut out each word from a magazine. Paste these words into your notebook.

4. **Acrostic Poems**
   Create an acrostic poem for five of your words.

   Example:
   Snow

   Soft and fluffy
   Never warm
   Open the door
   Wade into the cold . . .

LM 8.28 **Figure 8.35** *Spelling Tasks*

✦ Have your students use a **writing record sheet** such as the one shown in Figure 8.36.

✦ Ensure that your students see writing as purposeful and for an intended audience. When students understand that the intention of writing is to share thoughts, ideas, information, and feelings with an audience, they see the purpose for what they are doing.

WRITING RECORD SHEET Name: _Sandy_

Date started	Theme/Title of writing	First draft	Revised	Edited	Published: Tell how	Teacher's comments
Jan 12	My trip to California	✓	✓	✓	Pop-up Book	*I especially enjoyed the visuals you used.*
Jan 23	Medieval life					

LM **8.29** **Figure 8.36** *Writing Record Sheet*

✦ Make flexible **writing conferences** an integral part of your writing block. During this time, you will meet with individuals and sometimes with small groups to monitor where they are in the writing process as well as to assess their writing progress. Students are encouraged to reflect on their work and to set goals for improvement.

✦ **Keep records of your writing conferences** to document what was discussed and what was planned for follow-up. This is an important part of your assessment and tracking process for writing. Figure 8.37 provides a model.

Writing Conference Record

Student Name: _Rena_   Date: _Nov. 10_

Form of Writing: _Narrative writing_

Subject/Title of Writing: _Julie on "The Price Is Right"_

Issues Discussed: _use of quotation marks_

Follow-up: _point out books using dialogue and note quotation marks, observe further writing to see if any transfer occurs_

LM **8.30** **Figure 8.37** *Writing Conference Form*

♦ Encourage peer and group interaction by establishing with the **students routines and expectations for peer writing conferences**. You might want to establish a routine where students choose partners during the pre-writing stage: they talk out their writing to their partners and answer any questions they may be asked before they begin their draft. Another practice is to allow students to talk to someone about their writing-in-progress, but at a designated talking area (on the carpet or at a table) where they won't disturb others who are working quietly.

♦ You might want to introduce a **writing board** to help focus and organize your students as they move through the various phases of writing. (See Figure 8.38.) When students complete a phase (for example, finish a draft),

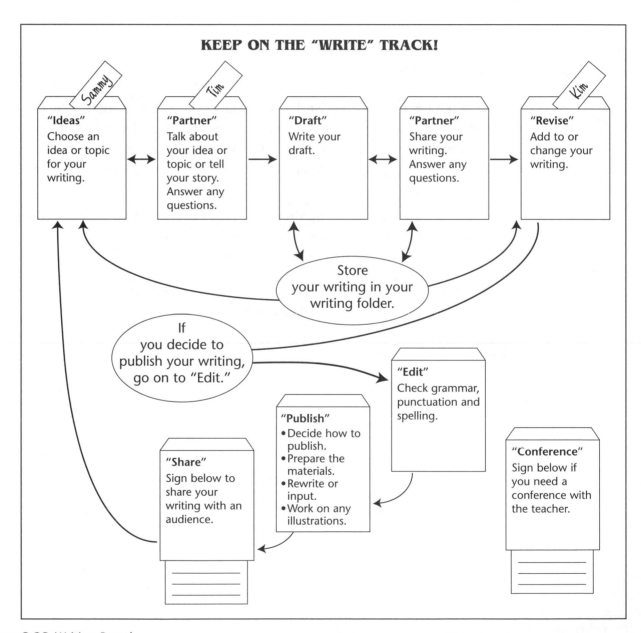

Figure 8.38 *Writing Board*

they move their name cards to the appropriate pocket on the display board (for example, they move to revising). Upon completion of one piece of writing, they begin another. They decide whether or not to publish and share. They meet with the teacher and/or their peers to conference at intervals throughout the process. They write one piece of writing after another, become authors as they present their work to others, and come to understand that writing is a continuous, ongoing process of learning.

NOTE: The arrows on the writing board indicate that the process is not linear. Rather, students move back and forth among all the phases of the process.

✦ Keep in mind that writing does not occur in isolation and **is interconnected and interwoven** with oral communication and reading across all curriculum areas. Continue to examine your timetable to ensure that you have carefully planned a balance of writing opportunities throughout the days and weeks. Doing so will encourage your students to remain committed, enthusiastic, and motivated throughout the year.

Creating a Language-rich Environment

✦ Ensure that your classroom is rich in print and provides many opportunities to stimulate language development.

✦ Collect and have available a wide variety of **print material**. Ensure that your print-rich environment includes resources and materials that reflect the maturity and interests of the students you are teaching. See Figure 8.39 for choices.

✦ Collect and have available a wide variety of **materials, resources, and equipment** that stimulate literacy learning experiences and cross-curricular connections. See Figure 8.40 for possibilities.

✦ When **choosing resources** for your classroom, ensure that they are suitable for your students' level of maturity and appropriate to your program needs. Resources should also be durable and cost efficient, as well as representative of people of varying abilities, lifestyles, backgrounds, ages, races, religions, and cultures.

✦ Ensure that the visual images and resources in your classroom environment **represent the diversity** of your own student population as well as that of the broader, global community. Students need to see many groups represented in order to honour and value those not necessarily in their immediate sphere of life.

✦ When choosing your resources, check to see that these are **free from stereotypical language or images**.

Beginning readers and writers	More proficient readers and writers
• fiction books	• fiction books
• non-fiction books	• non-fiction books
• multi-lingual books	• multi-lingual books
• beginning novel sets	• novel sets
• poetry	• poetry
• picture book	• picture books
• big books	• pattern books
• wordless books	• anthologies
• predictable books	• levelled text sets
• pattern books	• books with accompanying tapes or CDs
• levelled text sets	• author studies (multiple titles by the same author)
• books with accompanying tapes or CDs	• character studies (multiple titles about the same character)
• read-along books on DVD and other software	• recipe books
• author studies (multiple titles by the same author)	• textbooks
• character studies (multiple titles about the same character)	• encyclopedias
• recipe books	• dictionaries
• beginning encyclopedias	• thesauri
• picture dictionaries	• magazines
• crossword puzzle books	• newspapers
• joke and riddle books	• telephone directories
• maps	• television guides
• class-made books	• crossword puzzle books
• student-authored books	• joke and riddle books
	• catalogues
	• atlases
	• maps
	• graphs
	• timelines
	• travel brochures
	• class-made books
	• student-authored books

Figure 8.39 *Print Material*

NOTE: Some resources, including literary classics, can contain negatively biased stereotypical material. If you believe that the material may still have some relevancy and usefulness to your program, it is essential that you address the bias and stereotyping by involving your students in relevant discussions and debates. Be sensitive to the feelings of individual students in your classroom.

✦ Ensure that your **classroom library** is well stocked, and that books and resources are on display and accessible in many areas of the classroom. You may need to borrow books from the school or neighbourhood library in order to have many books in your classroom.

Beginning readers and writers	More proficient readers and writers
• posters	• posters
• charts	• charts
• songs	• songs
• labels	• labels
• lists	• lists
• anchor charts	• anchor charts
• word wall with high frequency words and from reading and writing experiences	• word wall from reading experiences, literature, content areas, and personal writing
• task cards	• task cards
• message boards	• message boards
• magnetic boards	• magnetic boards
• mailboxes	• writing materials
• writing materials	• a student author display (student of the week)
• a student author display (student of the week)	• displays of texts related to content areas, literature
• a library corner	• mathematics materials
• mathematics manipulatives	• visual arts resources and materials
• art supplies	• costumes and props for role play activities
• puppets, materials to make puppets	• audiovisual equipment
• puppet stage	• interactive display boards
• costumes and props for dramatic play	• computers and appropriate software
• blocks and building manipulatives	
• sand and water activities	
• audiovisual equipment	
• interactive display boards	
• computers and appropriate software	

Figure 8.40 *Materials, Resources, and Equipment to Stimulate Literacy*

✦ Make available a wide variety of **non-fiction** reading materials at varying levels of difficulty to correspond to topics, themes, issues, or curriculum units of study for your grade and interest level.

✦ Provide a wide variety of **writing materials**: paper in a range of colours, sizes, and shapes, blank and lined, ready-made into booklets; writing tools, such as pencils, pens, markers, and chalk; sources of writing ideas, including class-generated topics listed on posters or charts, a table displaying artifacts to stimulate discussion, and theme books and materials; and publishing materials, such as cardboard, paper with adhesive backing, wallpaper, staplers, string, wool, dental floss, and needles (to sew books together), and/or desktop publishing software to create hard copy or e-books and multi-media presentations.

✦ Provide your students with both **reading and writing folders**, either commercially produced or student-made, to serve as working files as they engage in the reading and writing process. Depending on your access to computers, you may want to provide each student with a USB key to house their writing files.

✦ Create an area in your classroom where **authors and illustrators** are highlighted and celebrated. Featuring a professional author or illustrator and celebrating an Author/Illustrator of the Month helps to develop a sense of authorship. This focus introduces students to different styles of authorship and illustration, and provides them with models for their own personal writing.

✦ You may want to invite **guest authors/illustrators** to your classroom or school. Seeing real authors and illustrators and hearing their stories and insights are a huge motivator for students' writing.

✦ Devote a section of your classroom environment to **student-authored books**. When your students write and publish their own books, they see firsthand the link between reading and writing. Students bring a new understanding to their own reading and to subsequent writing tasks, because they have inside knowledge about and experience with the development of storylines, characterization, and setting. In working with non-fiction material, they learn about procedural writing, point of view, research, and report writing. Students become motivated when reading and rereading their own and their peers' writing.

Figure 8.41 *A "Hot off the Press" Display of Student-authored Books*

✦ Use **environmental print** in your classroom. The signs, labels, posters, billboards, ads, etc. in your students' environment can represent young children's first opportunity to bring meaning to print. These opportunities help to make necessary links to students' prior experiences. For older students, posting signs and labels in different languages encourages their development in a second language of instruction.

NOTE: For children just beginning to read and write, you might want to set up an area in your classroom that features pictures of traffic signs, fast food restaurant signs, and exit/entrance signs, or bring in samples of cereal boxes, magazine ads, store bags, and more. Students will recognize these signs and symbols from their experiences outside the classroom and begin to associate the reading process with print conveying meaning. This helps them to see themselves as readers.

✦ **Label** all your bins, buckets, storage containers, and stations or centres.

✦ **Create signs** for your walls, doors, and bulletin boards that convey messages for students to read, such as a *We Can Read* bulletin board, a welcome sign in different languages, or students' names on your classroom door. To encourage greater ownership, have students help you create the signs. For young children, ensure that signs and resources are at their eye level.

✦ Create a **word wall**, a large, visual representation of words that students learn and use. These words might be high-frequency words, words that correspond to the themes or units being studied, or words that they use in their everyday life in the classroom or beyond. For older students, a word wall could be arranged around a theme or topic in a content area. For younger students, **word families**, such as "all" words—fall, ball, mall, etc.—are good choices for word lists. The words on a word wall are usually arranged under each letter of the alphabet or under other phonetic representations of the alphabet, and new words are added as students acquire new vocabulary. Students can refer to the word wall during reading and writing. See Figures 8.42 and 8.43 for examples of word walls.

NOTE: A variation of the word wall is called Vocabulary Fridays (based on ideas from Kimberly Pollishuke, YRDSB). On Fridays, students, individually and at the same time, record on a large white or black board any new vocabulary encountered in any of their classes throughout the week. They take a few minutes to review the words and then each select at least three words that will challenge them and that they will "own" as part of their everyday vocabulary. The following week, they begin to use these words in conversations in class and with their friends in order to incorporate the words into their daily use, thus helping to expand their vocabulary. (You can also have students write words on a card or sticky note, display them on the board, and then later reorganize them alphabetically or in a different way.)

Figure 8.42 *Word Wall in a French Immersion Classroom*
Source: Used with permission. Michelle Walk, YRDSB.

Figure 8.43 *Word Wall for Older Students*
Source: Used with permission. Kimberly Pollishuke, YRDSB.

◆ Post **rules and routines** established for and with your students. Chapter 3: An Inclusive Classroom Atmosphere provides guidance in this area.

◆ Use a chart (or the board, overhead, interactive display board, etc.) for a **morning message** which allows students to read for a purpose as they begin their day. As young children approach the morning message individually or, more likely, in partners or groups, they help each other bring meaning to the print. For both young and older students, the morning message can show the outline of events/tasks for the day, thus providing students with a sense of organization and a clear direction for the day's tasks. (See Figure 8.44.) Students in junior/intermediate classrooms might find the morning message as a quote of the day, a poem, a riddle or perplexor, a question or challenge, a song, an issue to discuss, or directions for work to be completed upon entry to the classroom.

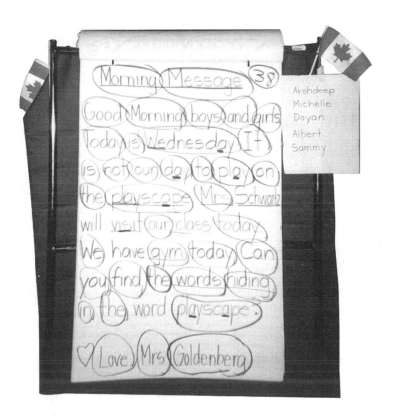

Figure 8.44 *Morning Message*

◆ Work with **students' names,** and put them on display in a variety of ways. Names are usually the first words that young students recognize, read, and write, so they are very important. Older students also enjoy working with names as inclusive team-building activities at the beginning of the year. (See Chapter 3: An Inclusive Classroom Atmosphere.)

- As you introduce poems, chants, or songs, record them on chart paper for **display around the room**. These charts should be left up for a prolonged period of time so that students can continuously refer to them for words, phrases, and ideas. You might also want to give students a smaller, individual copy of each poem, chant, or song for inclusion in their own reading booklets.

- Display around the room the **anchor charts** you create with your students that identify criteria for assessment, and demonstrate models of products and processes so that students can continuously refer to them as they work. (See Chapter 4: Assessment in a Differentiated Curriculum.)

- Display a few **commercial posters** for students to read, ones that highlight poetry, favourite children's books and authors, memorable sayings, and thoughts of the day. Often, publishers, distributors, or bookstores will give away free posters that highlight children's books or events.

NOTE: *For examples of excellent print and language-stimulating resources for students and teachers, see the accompanying Text Enrichment Site for Favourite Children's Literature and Recommended Teacher Resources.*

Media and Other Literacies

Media literacy, the study of communication through various forms of media text, includes different ways to transmit meaning to an audience. Media literacy, using different images, sounds, graphics and/or words, incorporates the creation, analysis, and interrelationships between text and audience. Media literacy is timely, important, multidisciplinary, easily integrated into classroom learning experiences, and promotes critical literacy and critical thinking. Teaching about media encourages students to ask questions about what they view, hear, read, and think. Students critically review, relate, analyze, evaluate, and create messages, in a wide variety of different modes of media, genres, and formats.

In today's 24-hour news, entertainment, and mass media cycle, it is vitally important that our students become critical viewers, listeners, readers, and thinkers, able to analyze the messages or information found in different print and media texts in their environment. The messages these texts convey might be explicit or implicit, and can have a profound impact on students' lives and actions. Consequently, it is essential that students develop awareness and critical thinking skills, are able to determine fact from fiction, assess the reliability of sources, see different points of view, and recognize and react against stereotyping and bias.

Engaging your students in creating various texts in multiple and diverse formats encourages them to understand how media works through their own investigations and creations. As they become more adept at constructing and analyzing media texts, they gain a better understanding of the influence that multimedia has on today's society and the impact it can have on their lives.

Creating Opportunities for Media and Other Literacies

It is important that our students understand that literacy is not confined to the language arts curriculum, but rather crosses all subject areas, incorporating media literacy, technological literacy, mathematical literacy, musical literacy, information literacy, environmental literacy, etc.

✦ Expose your students to **different texts**, including:

- books (fiction, non-fiction, different genres, picture books, novels, atlases, thesauri, dictionaries, etc.)
- textbooks
- maps
- songs
- photographs
- newspapers
- magazines
- television
- radio
- movies
- videoclips
- advertisements
- billboards
- Internet
- websites
- video games
- social networking media

✦ Have your students explore different texts by critically viewing, examining, asking questions, discussing, and debating **issues and concerns** such as these:

- how illustrations, pictures, posters, photos, presentations are formatted, organized, and/or possibly manipulated in a variety of texts
- how the use of videoclips, videos, films, television programs, commercials, and advertisements influence the public
- the positive and negative aspects of specific computer programs, websites, and/or video games
- how the content and messages are presented and perceived in plays, films, television, and webcasts
- how the differing points of view in the news—on radio, television, newspapers, or news websites—are presented, and their impact on the public
- violence in the media
- privacy and confidentiality
- censorship
- cyberbullying and other Internet risks

◆ Explicitly address all forms of **bias, prejudice, and stereotyping** in the texts to which your students are exposed, and ensure that you address race, culture, religion, ethnicity, gender, age, sexual orientation, socio-economic status, differently abled, etc. How you address these issues will depend on the age and maturity of your students, but even very young children should be involved in these important learning experiences.

- Examine the illustrations, photos, and images in different texts, looking for bias, stereotyping, tokenism, and discriminatory practices.

- Help young children examine toys, games, dolls, and play activities that they are exposed to in the classroom and at home.

- Examine a text to identify the author's perspective, point of view, background, and purpose. What perspective is being presented? Whose perspective is it? Whose perspective is missing?

- Check the copyright date to discuss when and why the text was created, and how the author's point of view or perspective represents the era in which the text was created.

- Discuss the storyline of a text in relation to the characters to identify who is the dominant person? Who holds the power and leadership opportunities? Who resolves the issues? Who are the heroes? Who are the villains? Who makes a difference and in what way?

- If the text is a folk tale, legend, or historical fiction, discuss the cultural perspective being portrayed.

- Relate content you view, hear, and read about to current life. Having students make connections to their own lives and situations makes what they are learning more relevant and meaningful and increases their interest and engagement.

- If the text is a classical piece of literature that contains stereotypical content or bias but has content significance, use it as a teaching tool and address the bias or stereotyping to ensure that your students understand what is acceptable and why.

- Ensure that the images you use in your classroom (pictures, posters, photos, books, video, games, materials, etc.) represent a balance of the cultures, races, ethnicities, genders, and differently abled in your classroom.

** An excellent resource to use to encourage critical thinking is David Booth's *It's Critical: Classroom strategies for promoting critical and creative comprehension* (Pembroke).

✦ Encourage your students to closely examine their own **underlying assumptions**, values and beliefs. Have them investigate and appreciate diverse perspectives, and evaluate various judgments and conclusions. Students engaged in these heightened learning experiences are engaged in **metacognition** or learning about their own thinking and learning processes.

✦ Have your students identify **how** different forms of media are created.

✦ Invite students to **create their own media texts**, using a form and design specific to their purpose and audience. For example, younger students might create a audio or video recording, a series of pictures, a sign or poster. Older students might create a multi-media presentation, website, public service announcement, story board, advertisement or commercial, etc.

✦ Begin to incorporate media literacy **across the curriculum** and in all subject areas in an integrated way.

✦ Highlight **multi-literacies** by illustrating for your students that literacy is not limited to reading and writing. Explicitly demonstrate how other symbols and/or notations are different forms of literacy. For example: the notations on a musical staff represent musical literacy; the numbers, symbols, and formulas we use in mathematics represent mathematical literacy; the textures and materials we use in art represent visual literacy, etc.

As students begin to observe, listen, speak, read, write, and think with a new focus and understanding, they become more critical and perceptive in the way they view the world around them. They begin to view things from a variety of perspectives with greater depth and understanding. By developing students' knowledge and skills in media and other literacies, they become more aware and responsible decision makers and problem solvers, engaging with diverse forms of media and technology in all aspects of their lives.

As you strive to create an effective and differentiated **balanced literacy program** that meets the needs, interests, and abilities of all your students, you will integrate meaningful literacy experiences into all areas of the curriculum. Figure 8.45 illustrates the individual components of a balanced literacy program as well as its interconnected nature.

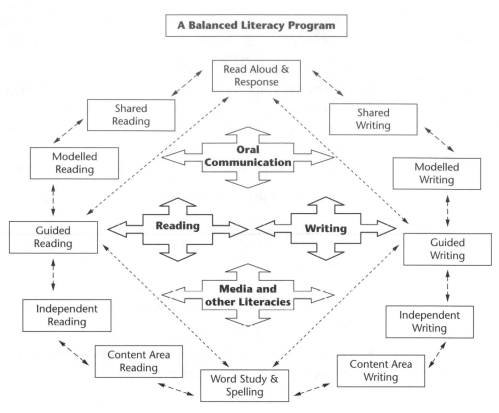

Figure 8.45 *A Balanced Literacy Program*

When oral communication, reading and writing, and a focus on media and multi-literacies are included in all areas of your program in an integrated, interconnected and effective way, you will be . . .

- ✦ *immersing* your students in rich, purposeful literacy opportunities,

- ✦ setting appropriate *expectations* for success,

- ✦ *demonstrating* what language looks like and sounds like,

- ✦ *modelling* appropriate literacy practices,

- ✦ providing *time* for students to *practise* their skills and demonstrate their knowledge,

- ✦ giving them *feedback* on how they are progressing, and

- ✦ *celebrating* what they produce! (Brian Cambourne)

In this way, you will be creating a dynamic classroom that fosters independent, self-motivated, literate, critical thinkers, learners, and "doers."

Technology in a Rapidly Changing World

In a rapidly changing world of advanced technologies, teachers stand on the brink of a new way of teaching and learning. Computers have revolutionized what you do in the classroom and how you do it. The advent of computers into education in the 1970s and early 1980s paved the way for the multitude of technological tools you currently have at your disposal. In addition to cassette recorders, televisions, VCRs, overhead projectors, and cameras, you now have access to laptop computers, "smartphones," digital and video cameras, CD and DVD players, laser printers, computer-generated synthesizers, scanners, interactive display boards (digital interactive whiteboards), document cameras, clickers, the Internet, and more.

Keeping up with the unpredictable and **rapidly changing technological landscape** is an exciting and challenging task for teachers, but it is absolutely essential that you maintain a high degree of proficiency. By the time children are ready to begin kindergarten, many have already been exposed to multimedia and technologies that have kept them entertained, taught them new concepts, and equipped them with valuable technological skills. Little children as old as one or two years are playing with hand-held computerized toys identifying shapes, sounds, letters, colours, etc. As more and more computer-literate students arrive in your classroom, you need to know how to engage them effectively and prepare them adequately for the future. Students need to learn how to collect and analyze information using databases, use spreadsheets to document and calculate data, create electronic books and portfolios, and conduct research using search engines and the Internet. Your students need to develop **digital literacy** as they communicate with others in the online environment; as they read, write, calculate, explore, and create using a variety of technologies as digital tools.

No matter what career your students will eventually have, they are almost certain to require skills that involve the use of a variety of technologies. You must prepare your students to be literate in whatever environment they will eventually face—**print, technological, and/or virtual reality**. Today, so many adults and children seem to have an email address, cellphone, and laptop, and wherever you are, you are bombarded with websites to refer to and services available by "logging on." Additionally, most commercial and financial transactions are conducted using email and the Internet. The prospect of our continuous and rapidly changing technological world can be mind-boggling, but you, as a teacher, must be prepared for it.

The **challenge** for teachers has been the speed at which change has occurred. For experienced teachers, it has been difficult to keep up with the changes while still delivering a full and meaningful curriculum. The answer is not to look at computers as a separate subject, but rather, to see technology as a tool that can make teaching and learning in all subject areas easier, at times more efficient, and usually more interesting and exciting. As technology assists in so many different ways, it will free you up to become a true facilitator of learning.

The first thing you will need to do as a professional is to ensure that your own technology skills are as proficient as possible. The more you **integrate technology into your own lifestyle**, the easier it will be to integrate it into your classroom and your program. Using the computer to record your lesson plans, prepare your report cards, pay your bills by electronic banking, or research information on the Internet, is a clear demonstration of how integral it is to your own life and how important it is to include in all aspects of your program. Electronic communication through the use of **social networking** has exploded over the past decade. Teaching your students about the pros and cons, advantages and dangers of communicating online, is now an essential life skill. Exploring **digital etiquette** or **digital citizenship** is a vital component of your classroom practice. As more and more communication is conducted in an online virtual environment, the need to demonstrate appropriate, respectful, and responsible online conduct is intensified. The use of electronic communication can foster excellent dialogue in your classroom on the issues of Internet best practice. As you teach your students to become critical readers, writers, observers, and thinkers, you can include discussions about respect, cyberbullying, plagiarism, censorship, freedom of speech, and media literacy.

Computer literacy is usually not as pressing an issue for teachers new to the profession since you are the first generation brought up with technology as part of your everyday life. Most university or college students graduating today could not have made it through their courses without the use of a computer. Your task, therefore, is to become proficient at and familiar with what technology can offer a classroom environment, and how you can **maximize the benefits** for your students. As a new teacher or an experienced teacher relatively new to the use of advanced technology, you must possess skills beyond your own comfort with the actual hardware and software. You must know what hardware and software is available and which are appropriate for your students; understand how to teach keyboarding skills to young students; be well versed in Internet capabilities, limitations, and challenges; and have first-hand experience with a number of online communication tools, such as wikis, blogs, discussion boards, chatrooms, websites, etc.

When you become **technologically savvy** and comfortable in today's high-tech classroom, you will have to deal with issues that require reflective thought and critical decisions. From the important decision of how to effectively use the computers in your classroom as well as the computer lab or laptop cart, to the much deeper issue of equity between genders, among students with special needs, and within diverse learning communities, it is clear that issues about technology need to be discussed, debated, and resolved in order for all students to have the best, most current, and relevant education possible. That is a tall order to fill, but one that must be filled in this fast-changing digital world.

Creating a Technology-rich Classroom

✦ Gather any technological equipment you will keep in your classroom **on a continual basis**:

- an overhead projector
- a document camera
- LCD projector and laptop computer
- a digital recorder and/or CD player
- headphones
- computers
- speakers
- microphone

✦ Find out how you can access other technological equipment and materials for **periods of time**, and if there are procedures for loan and use. Such equipment might include these items:

- interactive display board (digital interactive whiteboard—e.g., SMART board or Promethean board)
- television
- DVD player
- webcam
- digital camera
- video camera
- clickers
- portable laptop carts
- "smartphone" hubs

- software programs
- wireless internet
- other

✦ Find out whether you will have access to one or both of **classroom-based computers** or a **computer lab**. An ideal situation is to have both, and also have access to **portable laptop carts** (and/or "smartphones"), which can be transported into your classroom for your students to use at specific times. With these portable computers, each student can have easy access at their fingertips, and will quickly move from computers as a novelty to using technology as a tool for authentic and purposeful learning.

✦ Decide where the **one or more computers** will be situated in your classroom. You will want to put them near ample electrical outlets or use the proper power bars so that you can plug in all the necessary pieces of equipment. Always allow for extra outlets for future expansion of your equipment. Also situate the computers in an area where other students are not attracted to what is happening on the monitors, and away from any sand, water, food, paints, and window glare.

✦ Decide **where other technology**, such as your printer, scanner, overhead projector, etc. will be situated in your classroom.

✦ **Try out any technology** you plan to use. Be sure you know how to use it *before* you need it and before you use it with your students. Having ample opportunities (for you and your students) to experiment with the technology adds to confidence and competence, and allows the technology to be used in more creative ways.

✦ Discuss **routines for use of the computer**, and decide what other students can and cannot do when someone else is on the computer.

✦ Decide how you will **organize** who works on the computer(s), at what time, and for how long. Your decision may depend on how you have integrated the computer into your units of study.

- **Scheduled Time**: If your students need access to the Internet to research a topic, you may want to schedule specific times for each student.

- **Sign-in System**: If your students are expected to use the computer for writing or another literacy activity, you may want to introduce a sign-in system for students to have access to the computer for an extended period of time, as needed.

- **Computer Learning Station:** A good way to use one or more computers in your classroom is as a computer learning station (as one station among many others). You may want to use a rotation and or tracking system (see Chapter 6: Effective Learning Stations—A Small Group Differentiated Approach).

NOTE: You will want to make sure that the one or more computers that you have in your classroom will be used to their full potential and that they are not sitting idle during the day. At the same time, you should ensure that the use of computers is equitable among your students and that one or two students do not monopolize the computer. Regularly using the computer lab, or the laptop cart in your classroom if available, will provide all students with easy and ongoing access.

✦ Find out who the **technology lead teacher** is in your school. Most schools designate a staff member to support others in their use of technology.

✦ Get to know your **school librarian**, who is often up to date on current information technology and web-based resources and has usually thought about curriculum integration.

✦ Work together with other teachers in your school in **small learning groups** to explore how technology can be meaningfully integrated into your teaching. Working in teams can take some of the fear out of learning to use the technology and can encourage you to think about how it might add value to your classroom teaching.

✦ Train a few students to act as **peer tutors** who will teach other students in your class. You might want to set up a **peer tutor list** so that students know whom to go to for help depending on the problem. Never assume that all students have the basic technological skills necessary to work with the tools you have available in your classroom. You can use your peer tutors to help provide basic skills to students who need it.

✦ For each student in your classroom, obtain a **USB key** (also called a USB flash drive or data storage device). Students need to be able to save, organize, and manage their own work as files. Encourage them to always save their work with a clear title and current date for easy retrieval.

✦ Before they are distributed, demonstrate for your students how to **safely insert and eject** a CD or USB key, as well as how to handle CDs and equipment. Remind them to check that they have clean hands before handling any technology or working on a keyboard.

✦ Consider how computers can be used to assist your **students who are new to the country and/or language**:
   • Use software programs that highlight specific language patterns, which allow students to repeat words and phrases, and record their attempts at speaking the new language.
   • Use software programs that show visuals to generate oral and written language.
   • Have students work in pairs to stimulate second language development as they discuss what they are doing at the computer.

✦ Consider how using computer technology hardware and/or adaptive technology software can assist your **students who have special needs**. **Adaptive technology** is a term that refers to specific hardware and/or software that can help people who have learning and/or physical disabilities—for example, challenges with learning, vision, hearing, and mobility—in performing tasks that they might not have been able to accomplish without the technology. The following are some examples:

Example 1:	Students with **small-muscle coordination difficulties** can find handwriting a challenge and often find a keyboard easier to manipulate than a pen or pencil.

Example 2:	For students with a **learning disability** (i.e., who have difficulty learning), you can use **scan and read software** (such as Kurzweil 3000 or E-Text Reader),which helps students with reading disabilities to see the text on the computer screen as it "reads" aloud and highlights the word/sentence as it moves along. **Speech recognition software** (such as Dragon Naturally Speaking) can be used to help students compose on the computer without typing or writing because it records the speaker's words as heard. A number of hours of training are needed for this computer program to learn to recognize the speech patterns of the user.

Example 3:	For students with a **visual impairment** (who have difficulty seeing or who cannot see at all), aids include computers with enlarged screens and print, talking watches, calculators, computers, scales, compasses, and thermometers. Specific software has the computer read aloud stories or information: the student speaks and it types the words; and/or the student types the first few letters and the program offers suggestions for the spelling of the remainder of the word. Speech recognition software is also helpful here as it can change a student's speech to text. Other products focus on using Braille to read, such as Braille writing tools and Braille watches.

Example 4:	For students with a hearing impairment (who have difficulty hearing or cannot hear at all), you can use closed captions on television and telephones, blinking lights and vibration tools, and text-messaging on cellular phones and email.

Example 5:	For students with a **speech impairment** (who have difficulty speaking and/or having others understand what they want to say), you can use computer programs which provide text to speech capabilities as above, and text-messaging on computers and mobile phones.

Example 6:	For students with a **coordination or mobility impairment** (who have difficulty moving or using hands, arms, or legs), you can use a computerized program (e.g., a "sip and puff" tool) that enables the student to make choices by inhaling and exhaling. There are also eye-driven keyboarding or speech-recognition programs, as well as the use of robotic arms.

✦ Examine **available resources, documents, and guidelines** to determine what you expect your students to be able to know, do, and value in technology. Make sure that these learning expectations are appropriate to the age and stage of development of your students. (Refer to Chapter 5: Designing Your Curriculum.)

*NOTE: Many school districts have developed detailed technology standards that can be used as a reference. These standards may be based on an international set of technology standards from the **International Society for Technology in Education (ISTE)** for students and teachers, accessed at http://www.iste.org/standards.aspx.*

✦ Take time to assess **new software and/or websites** before you use them with your students. Most districts have policies, procedures, and/or priorities for the selection, evaluation, and use of computer software and educational websites.

✦ Make limited use of the type of **skill-and-drill software** and/or **games** that require little depth of understanding or critical thinking on the part of the student.

✦ Ensure that **word processing** is a vital aspect of your program and is integrated into all subject areas, especially in the revision and editing stages of the writing process. The cut-and-paste features of word processing programs allow students to move and rearrange text with ease. The "Search" and "Find" features allow students to substitute words and look for inconsistencies. Spell checks encourage students to use their knowledge of how words are spelled to choose the correct one from a list. Grammar checks require students to know how to recognize and understand appropriate structures. Using word-processing programs encourages students to create and save multiple drafts without having to rewrite, and helps them feel like real authors as they revise, edit, and publish their work.

✦ Provide training in **keyboarding** to any students, even kindergarten or grade 1 students, who may not already have these skills. If most of your students need training in keyboarding, you may want to use a computer lab or a portable laptop cart for this purpose.

✦ Integrate other computer **software programs** into your program, such as graphic arts, desktop publishing, databases, spreadsheets, presentation software, multimedia, and simulations.

✦ If you have access to an **interactive display board (digital interactive whiteboard)**, find out how to use it as a tool to support various lessons. An interactive display board immediately engages students as they manipulate text, graphics, and images in a hands-on active/interactive way. As you increasingly use this type of technology to record and archive your students' contributions, they will see that you value their work, their words, and their creative ideas. In some schools, you may have to book a specific time to use this technology (which is usually on wheels and can be transported to your classroom), whereas in other schools, these have been purchased in multiple quantities to provide frequent classroom access.

✦ You may have access to a document camera or projector (e.g., an Elmo) that will project the image that is placed beneath it, and can also capture the teacher or student writing or drawing on it, much like an overhead projector with acetate and pen. A document camera often works in conjunction with an interactive display board and is an extremely useful tool in the classroom.

✦ If you have access to a class or group set of **clickers**, students can respond actively during a lesson. Responses can be graphed to illustrate data management and probability.

✦ Consider using **podcasts** (videofiles or videoclips) as part of your lessons to facilitate and/or motivate learning. Students can use digital cameras to videotape events or dramatizations and can create their own podcasts to share with audiences.

✦ Involve your students in **electronic communication using a variety of digital tools**, including the following:

- **Email:** Students can engage in online buddy journaling with you as the "reader on the side" as they copy journal entries to you.

- **Wikis:** Teachers create a document using a wiki tool, where students can post their work, collaborate in revising and editing the product, and/or engage in shared writing such as a collaborative narrative, report, or class newsletter. **Wikis** allow students to work together in the online environment to build their knowledge, conduct research, write stories or reports, and present their creativity in final projects.

- **Blogs:** Students engage in online discussion by posting their ideas, opinions, and questions, while others can comment. **Blogs** provide students with an authentic audience, and foster thinking and learning, teacher and peer modelling, and feedback in an online environment.

- **Discussion Board:** Students enter a forum where they can share news items or experiences and engage in discussions by posting their ideas and responding to others, and/or respond to questions or readings.

- **Chatrooms:** Students enter an online environment and communicate in "real time" about their experiences, their responses to readings or questions, their thinking process in solving a problem in mathematics or science, etc. Sometimes there might be more than one "chat" happening at once.

- **Online Learning Environments:** Teachers can use online learning environments to create websites where course or subject information, assignments, resources, or student work can be easily shared, and where students can communicate in a variety of ways, including using a discussion board, email "blasts" to all affiliates of the website, chatrooms, etc. Teachers can include links to articles, research, or educational websites for students to access. In this way, it is a controlled environment, and teachers can usually also track the participation and progress of students who use it. This type of online environment is convenient in that everything is housed in one online location and is available as a reference.

✦ Consider creating a **class website** for your students and parents to access. You might want to post information about yourself, your school, classroom events, student work, homework and upcoming projects, and/or interactive activities based on your classroom units of study. Encouraging parents to regularly access the class website provides you with another format for keeping your parents informed and involved. (For a sample class website, refer to Chapter 11: Creating Community—Partnerships with Parents.)

✦ Find out the types of **social networking sites**, such as Facebook, MySpace, Twitter, blogs, etc., that your students are using, and explore how you can capitalize on their interests by *carefully* using some of these in the classroom. For example, set up a class Facebook site for students to work together on specific assignments, and/or establish a homework site for peer support and to answer any questions that might arise.

*NOTE: Although the use of **social networking** is very current, be very careful about how you use social media with your students. Some schools, school districts, and educational institutions are recommending that teachers NOT use Facebook or Twitter. They are recommending that teachers should avoid the following: texting with students using informal language; engaging in inappropriate topics; communicating online using a personal email account; and/or sharing personal information with students. Teachers are being cautioned to only contact students using protected educational platforms, and to only communicate at times that they might be telephoning home (e.g., not late in the evening). Teachers also need to be very aware of previous or current postings of their photos and stories on Facebook that might be seen by their students, parents, community, colleagues and/ or administrators (some which may be perceived as inappropriate or unprofessional). Teachers' conduct can and has come into question in recent times as they become involved in social networking.*

** The Council of the Ontario College of Teachers' *Professional Advisory: Use of Electronic Communication and Social Media,* issued in February, 2011, is an example document highlighting the cautions for educators in the use of social networking.

◆ Talk with your students about the **pros and cons** of the use of the Internet. Discuss the misuse of the Internet and the existence of inappropriate websites, and ensure that you have a system in place that will block access to these inappropriate sites.

◆ Engage in discussions with your students about **safety, responsibility, and respect** in using any type of online communication. Teach them how to safeguard their privacy by always using "pen names" or pseudonyms and never sharing confidential information. Discuss their roles as **digital citizens** in a technological world, and educate them about the issues of Internet best practice, professionalism, respect, cyberbullying, plagiarism, censorship, freedom of speech, and media literacy.

◆ Examine your curriculum areas and themes, topics, issues, or units of study to see where technology can integrate well. The following examples will give you some ideas of how you might integrate technology into your curriculum.

Example 1: *Social Studies*

◆ When engaging in research on specific topics and issues, students can explore educational websites, learn how to use different search engines, develop skills for exploring and evaluating credible sources, and can learn how to cite websites.

◆ For a study on Native Peoples, Early Settlers, or Medieval Times, students can create a podcast from the perspective of an aboriginal, a pioneer, or a medieval nobleman, etc.

◆ Students can create multimedia presentations on their research or present different points of view about their topics.

◆ They can participate in online debates using a chatroom or classroom/ group blog.

◆ They can create mindmaps or concept maps about a topic using specific software programs.

◆ They can create a public service announcement or videotaped advertisement to raise awareness about global issues or world events.

Example 2: *Health Education*

◆ For a study of drug awareness, students can use the Internet to research information on the uses and misuses of drugs, and find the statistics on drug use and their implications.

◆ They can present their information using technology as a tool, in the form of a computer slide show presentation, overhead presentation, multimedia presentation, or video.

◆ Using a video camera and film editing software (Windows Movie Maker, iMovie, Audacity, Garage Band, etc.), students could create public service announcements on anti-bullying or substance abuse or harassment.

Example 3: *Mathematics*

✦ Divide your class into groups and assign each group a mathematics question. Each group could videotape the solution to their question from start to finish and be assessed on their ability to clearly communicate the process. (Rather than filming themselves, they could use a tripod and position the camera on the whiteboard.) Each video could then be posted on a classroom website (with permission) and act as review or input for the rest of the class.

✦ Students can use Excel to create a spreadsheet for a budget.

✦ Students can use a class set of clickers to record their responses to questions asked and then examine the created graphs and charts.

✦ Young students can sort objects displayed on an interactive white board and manipulate the objects on the board. They can then classify the groups and graph the results. See Figure 9.1 for an example.

Figure 9.1 *Sorting Chart*

Example 4: *Language*

✦ To encourage students to write, have them use a word-processing program that includes graphic arts to create the accompanying illustrations.

✦ Invite students to create cooperative stories, one page per student, for a class big book complete with photos or images.

✦ Involve students in creating PowerPoint or Prezi presentations and/or write poems, letters, cards, or invitations, complete with sound effects and/or videoclips.

✦ Have students use a virtual learning environment utilizing digital tools such as wikis, blogs, chatrooms, and/or discussion boards to respond to texts rather than journaling by hand.

- Invite students to use handheld digital audio recorders that can be plugged into a computer to record brainstorming sessions prior to writing.

- Have your students communicate with online pen pals in a different school or a different part of the world to encourage discussion and greater understanding about different communities and/or global issues.

- Use Skype to have a conversation/debate between two different classrooms in two different schools in two different countries.

- Record literature circle discussions using a variety of programs (Windows Movie Maker, iMovie, Audacity, Garage Band, etc.). This will dramatically increase student accountability and make it much easier for you to assess each student's participation and reading comprehension.

- Use a video conferencing tool (such as Adobe Connect) to broadcast a literature circle over the Internet. Parents and other classes can be invited to watch from other locations as guest users.

Example 5: *The Arts*

- Have your students create photo essays and then edit the pictures using a photo editing program.

- Synthesizers and digital music software allows students to create their own sound tracks or musical compositions to accompany presentations, podcasts, public service announcements, or dramatizations.

- Use software such as Comic Life and Bitstrips to encourage your students' creativity and writing skills as they create their own comic strips for a subject.

Example 6: *Science*

- For a study of weather, have your students create a graph or table detailing the weather for a prolonged period of time. They might be required to use a database or spreadsheet to gather and organize the data as they collect it, and the computer could create a pie chart from the information received through the database.

- For a unit on simple machines, you may want to create a simple machines or take-it-apart learning station where students are engaged in looking at different aspects of kitchen gadgets, simple machines, (screwdriver, bicycle, etc.), and other technologies (computer, calculator, telephone) to find out how they work. (See Chapter 6: Learning Stations—Small Group Differentiated Learning.)

** A must-read text filled with many practical strategies for using technology in the classroom is Lisa Donahue's text *Keepin' It Real: Integrating new literacies with effective classroom practice* (Pembroke).

- You may want to communicate with your parents about your technology initiatives and guidelines for technology use in the classroom. See Figure 9.2 for a sample letter to parents.

Dear Parents,

The use of technology in schools today is a vital part of the curriculum and a very important life skill for all students to learn. The computer and other technologies are integrated into all aspects of our program. Students will write using word processing, create databases and spreadsheets, collect, sort, and calculate data, and collect information using the Internet, videotape and audiotape their work, and create multimedia presentations that might involve a number of different technologies. We will use the Internet for a variety of purposes, including searching for and collecting information, as well as a variety of digital tools in an online environment.

We also have a **class website** that we invite you to use to check school events, homework, and student expectations. Ask your child to show you how to access the class website and please visit on a regular basis. Your feedback is always welcomed in the Comments section of the website or via the school telephone.

Additionally, a special initiative this year is the students' work with **electronic portfolios or e-portfolios**. These are mini-websites created by each student where students will upload important pieces of work and their reflections to demonstrate their growth and learning. The students will share these e-portfolios with you during our upcoming **student-led conferences** in March. We will take every precaution to ensure that each e-portfolio is password protected and that students know that sharing of e-portfolios and its contents is confidential.

In our classroom, school, and district, we have strict guidelines for the use of the Internet with students and we would like to make you aware of these guidelines. Students will:

- access the Internet only with prior approval by the teacher
- visit only those sites that have been predetermined by the teacher
- never give out their names or any other distinguishing information to anyone else while using the Internet
- adhere to clear guidelines for sharing their work online
- properly reference all material taken from the Internet (plagiarism remains a serious offence whether from print materials or from the Internet).

Please discuss the above guidelines with your child, sign the attached form, and return it to the school as soon as possible.

Thank you for your support.

Sincerely,

S. Schwartz

- -

I have discussed the guidelines above with my child and give permission for him/her to use the Internet in class.	I have read and agree to abide by the guidelines outlined in the letter above.
Kate Sangelle	*Linda Sangelle*
Parent's signature	Student's signature

LM 9.1   **Figure 9.2** *Letter to Parents Re: Use of the Internet*

- Invite your students' parents to take part in **information sessions** about the use of technology in your program. You might want to offer a series of **family technology evenings** (similar to Literacy or Math Family Nights) where parents and students attend sessions together. (Refer to Chapter 11: Creating Community—Partnerships with Parents.)

It is important to ensure that you are as technologically literate as possible. Keep abreast of new resources, including guidelines, software programs, and appropriate educational websites. Consider taking courses and/or workshops that will expand your horizons and build on the expertise you are developing. Since technology is rapidly changing each day, digital literacy will always be an important focus for your ongoing professional learning. As you increase your expertise in the use and integration of technology into all aspects of your program, you will be more confident in saying that your students will achieve the necessary skills for today and tomorrow's technological environment. Incorporating technology and digital literacy into all aspects of your classroom program will ensure that your students are well prepared for the present and for the future that awaits them.

10 Evaluating and Reporting Student Progress

The final stages in the **planning, design, and assessment processes** are **evaluation and reporting student progress**. During these processes, we demonstrate that we are accountable for the curriculum design and assessment practices that we have implemented, and we ensure that we carefully examine our collected evidence of student learning. Teachers engage in evaluative practices *after* the learning has occurred and this becomes the foundation for reporting to parents, administration, and other professionals what the students have achieved in relationship to the curriculum expectations for that grade.

Evaluation is the application of a value or judgment about student performance and ability at certain end points during the learning process. It puts a value on the sum total of all that students have demonstrated through the assessment strategies used. Evaluation forms the basis for reporting student progress and achievement, and can be expressed in a variety of formats ranging from anecdotal comments to the assignment of specific numerical or letter grades.

It is important to note that the terms "assessment" and "evaluation" are often used synonymously, but there are distinct differences (Davies). Assessment occurs *during* the learning process and provides feedback and direction for learning to continue. As outlined in Chapter 4: Assessment in a Differentiated Curriculum, assessment *for, as,* and *of* learning (Earl) is the gathering and analysis of data (diagnostic, formative, and summative) collected about each student. However, the goal of both assessment and evaluation is to support student learning. As we evaluate student achievement, we provide opportunities for students to reflect on their achievements and set new learning goals and next steps for future growth and progress.

Since we live in times of accountability and open communication, it is expected that you will **report student progress**, build upon students' strengths and successes, and help them address or deal with needs and areas of weakness. These expectations require that you have recorded evidence about how you work with your students and what outcomes ensue. They can also serve as an impetus to your own self-assessment and reflection, when you track student progress, monitor achievement, and modify your program to meet the needs, interests, and abilities of your students.

Assigning marks or **grades** is an essential component of the evaluation process. Marks or grades refer to the numerical or letter representation assigned to a student task or performance according to the level that they have achieved in relation to the curriculum expectations. Marks or grades can be assigned to many different summative assessment tasks over the course of the term or year. **Grading** is the overall *process* of assigning a final **letter grade** or **numerical mark** to student achievement over a period of time, and is often accompanied by anecdotal comments that clarify meaning and cite specific examples of achievement.

Evaluation provides students with the knowledge and understanding of where they are in their learning process. With that knowledge and in collaboration with their teachers and parents, they can self-assess, begin to set their own learning goals, and participate in the decision-making process about their learning pathways. As they assume more ownership for their growth and achievement, they can become more motivated and engaged in learning.

Reporting to parents is an integral aspect of the evaluation process and requires a great deal of thoughtful preparation. As you prepare to write detailed **report cards** that will include grades or marks, and often anecdotal comments, you will need to have ample evidence or data to support the grades/marks you assign and the statements you include.

Reporting is a two-step process that involves the preparation of the actual report card and the opportunities to share achievement information with parents. Most often, the **sharing** of this information involves a face-to-face conference, but could also entail telephone conversations or email communication when face-to-face interactions prove challenging.

Often, report cards include a section for students to complete where they reflect on their achievement and set future learning goals. This **student involvement** in report card preparation reinforces ownership as they become actively involved in the evaluation process. Students can also be included in the reporting process by attending conferences with parents and sharing their learning. When you incorporate **student-led conferences** into your reporting process, you are again helping your students to set their own learning pathways and become involved in making decisions about their learning.

Another important purpose of evaluation is to make **appropriate placement decisions** when deciding the class or grade level for each student. Involving all partners in this process—teachers, administrators, parents, and students—will ensure that decisions are made in the best interests of each student and that clear and open communication is maintained.

One of the most challenging times for you as teachers is when you have to **make those judgments** and put a value on student achievement. There is no easy or exact way to do this, meaning you must use your professional knowledge, experience, and judgment to arrive at the most objective evaluation you can make. This can be a difficult process, but you will find that the more evidence you collect, the more summative assessment data you have at your fingertips, the easier the process will become, and the more confident you will be when you engage in reporting and inform parents and the students themselves where they stand in relationship to their growth and learning.

Determining Student Achievement

+ Examine all the relevant data that you have collected about each student. Look for patterns of behaviour and evidence of growth.

+ Look at all the **assessment of learning** or **summative evidence** you have collected—your student products (e.g., work samples, performances, projects, test results, reflections, rubrics, marks, and grades assigned), as well as the conferences and interviews that have occurred.

+ **Make inferences and judgments** based on a student's progress and behaviour patterns. Ensure that you have ample evidence to support the judgments that you will make. Think about what the student now knows, is able to do, and feels or values, and the areas in which they have demonstrated growth.

+ When deciding on appropriate **grades or marks**, ensure that you are only evaluating students' achievement in terms of their knowledge and skills and not factoring in their attitudes, work habits, and/or efforts. Learning skills, such as time on task, submission of assignments, attendance, completion of homework, etc. are often commented on in a separate section of the report card.

*NOTE: There has been much discussion as to whether **learning skills** or work habits, such as organizational skills, time on task, task completion, working collaboratively, showing initiative, etc., should or should not be factored* *into the determination of grades or marks. When effort, attitude, and/or work habits are included as a component of their mark or grade, students often place more value on the work that is being assessed and become more responsible in meeting deadlines and producing their best work. However, including learning skills as a component of a grade or mark can confuse* how *a student learns with* what *they are learning. Effort is often challenging to quantify because it is such a subjective aspect of learning.*

✦ If your school or district requires you to give each student a numerical mark or letter grade, be sure to use a full range of assessment data to generate the grade. Do not rely on a few or an individual assignment or performance task to form the basis of the grade.

✦ When assigning grades, you could attach a numerical mark or letter grade to each level of achievement identified on a rubric. For example, a level 4 on a rubric could represent a grade of A to A+ or a numerical range of 90 to 100 per cent.

✦ As you examine the data you have collected, assign **levels of achievement** to the data collected in order to arrive at a final decision about a mark or grade. For example, Figure 10.1 shows one student's literacy assessment *of* learning data.

DATE	ASSESSMENT DATA	LEVEL	COMMENTS
Sept. 15	Diagnostic reading assessment	2	
Sept. 30	Reading conference	2	
Oct. 25	Novel study	2	
Nov. 1	Readers' Theatre presentation	4	group assignment
Nov. 30	Reading conference	2	
Ongoing	Reading response journal	3	

Figure 10.1 *One Student's Literacy Assessment* of *Learning Data*

✦ When you are determining the grades or marks for your students, ensure that you consider the **consistency** of their performance in relation to summative tasks, the relative **importance** of each assignment, and the **point in time** of each summative assessment. In other words, consider data that is:

• **THE MOST CONSISTENT**
• **THE MOST IMPORTANT**
• **THE MOST RECENT**

+ Your summative assessment data also needs to take into account your **knowledge of the whole child**, what you know about their cognitive, emotional, social, and physical needs.

+ To make the final decisions on assigning grades or marks, you will ultimately need to use your **professional judgment**, which is based on your understanding of child development, and your experience working with children at this age and stage of development.

+ Marks or grades should **not be an average** of the collected levels of achievement for each summative task. Rather, you need to take a holistic view of the levels of achievement for each assessment task and, considering **the most consistent, the most important, and the most recent**, come to an overall level of achievement. In the literacy example outlined in Figure 10.1, the final mark might be a **level 2 in reading** for this student, based on the following criteria:

  • The **most consistent** assessment is level 2 for four out of the six assessments

  • The **most recent** assessment is a level 2

  • The **most important** assessment is the ongoing reading response journal of level 3.

+ You will then need to **convert the final level to a letter grade or numerical mark**. For example, level 2 usually translates to a letter grade of C or a numerical mark of a range of 60 to 69 per cent. Then consider whether this C is a *high* C or a *low* C in relation to your understanding of what a level C achievement represents (based on your knowledge of child development and the expected levels of achievement for students at this age and stage). Again, in the above example, since the student had a level 3 for the most important ongoing reading response journal assignment, in your professional judgment and knowledge of that child, you could decide that the mark will be a high level 2 or C+.

+ You might want to use the following description of **criteria for levels, grades, and marks** as a guide for your final evaluation decisions. (See Figure 10.2.)

NOTE: *Grades should never come as a surprise to students. Students should be well aware of how they are doing so they are able to take ownership to improve their performance. It is important to know your students well in order to avoid issues with grading. The assignment of grades can have a negative impact on some students with low self-esteem, and may result in a lowering of their self-confidence, which can prove counterproductive to their progress and attitude towards learning. Grades should be reserved for knowledge and skill and not for effort. You do not want students to think that they can even fail at trying.*

Level of Achievement	4	3	2	1	Failing Grade
Letter Grade	A + A A −	B + B B −	C + C C −	D + D D −	F
Numerical Mark	90–100 85–89 80–84	77–79 73–76 70–72	67–69 63–66 60–62	57–59 53–56 50–52	Below 50
Assessment Criteria	Demonstrated **excellent** understanding and performance. Exhibited **outstanding** ability to synthesize, evaluate, and create. Displayed **exceptional** evidence of in-depth knowledge of subject content.	Demonstrated **very good** understanding and performance. Exhibited **very good** ability to synthesize, evaluate, and create. Displayed **solid** evidence of knowledge of subject content.	Demonstrated **adequate** understanding and performance. Exhibited **sufficient** ability to synthesize and evaluate. Displayed **some** evidence of knowledge of subject content.	Demonstrated **little** understanding and performance. Exhibited **minimal** abilities. Displayed **minimal** evidence of knowledge of subject content.	Demonstrated **superficial** or **confused** understanding and minimal to no performance.

Figure 10.2 *Criteria for Levels, Grades, and Marks*

** Ken O'Connor's work, including *How to Grade for Learning, K–12* (Corwin Press), shares practical ideas about evaluation and grading, and is well worth pursuing.

Preparing Report Cards

✦ Using the collected assessment *of* learning data, write clear, concise comments describing each student's achievement and progress in the different subject areas for which you are responsible. In writing these comments, emphasize what students have learned and focus on their specific strengths. It is important to personalize the comments that you make to ensure that they relate directly to the specific student and are not seen as merely a selection of generic comments from a bank of prepared comments. Parents should be able to clearly identify their child through the comments you make. For some sample comment stems which may assist you in personalizing your report card comments, refer to **LM 10.1** on the Text Enrichment Site.

◆ As an important part of report card comments, you should include **next steps** in each section, so that students can clearly see what they need to do to further meet with success.

◆ If your report card includes a section for students to complete in order to reflect on their achievement, make sure that you provide your students with ample time to consider what they have learned and where they need to go in their growth, and provide the support necessary to clearly express their thoughts and feelings on this section of the report card. Some report cards may also include a section for parents to complete in order to comment on their child's achievement.

◆ If at all possible, have the report cards **translated** for parents whose first language is not English. For reporting purposes, a **translator** could be a relative or an educator, such as another teacher, a bilingual assistant, or a multicultural consultant. For confidentiality reasons, you should avoid asking another parent in the school or an older student to act as a translator.

Reporting Student Progress

◆ **Create a schedule** for your conferences with parents, allowing adequate time for each conference. Ensure that you begin and finish on time. Try to arrange siblings' conferences on the same day or evening. Be flexible when arranging time for some working parents to meet with you. Arrange for translators if necessary for some parent meetings.

◆ Ensure that you are **well prepared** for your parent conferences by thinking through all aspects of the conference from beginning to end, and having all your assessment of learning data collected and accessible. Being prepared will add to your own confidence.

◆ Prior to the beginning of your conference time, **prepare the environment** into which parents will be welcomed.

- Set up chairs outside your classroom door for parents who are waiting for their appointment.

- Consider leaving some materials accessible for parents to read while they are waiting, such as handouts for home learning activities, articles about discipline or curriculum, children's magazines, and other relevant materials.

- Post a schedule of the conference times on your door.
- If possible, sit *beside* the parent at an adult level table rather than opposite them at your desk to present a collaborative and a team approach.
- Have dated work samples for each student accessible to show concrete examples of what that student has accomplished.
- Consider posting a sign on your door to ask each parent to knock when it is time for his/her appointment. The parent in the classroom knows that the time is up and if more time is needed, you can schedule another meeting to discuss further. This encourages you to stay on schedule and shows that you value each person's time.

✦ Begin and end a conference with positive statements about the student's **strengths and interests**.

✦ During conferences with parents, do the following:
- Discuss the child's progress.
- Examine and discuss your assessment *of* learning, such as dated work samples, informal and formal test results, observations, and your interpretations.
- Answer questions about your report card comments, grading system used, and your program.
- Be positive and encouraging while also being straightforward.
- Avoid jargon and always use language that parents can understand.
- Always maintain a professional stance.
- Be an active and empathetic listener and a team player.
- Allow parents time to share their issues, concerns, etc.
- Repeat back or paraphrase so that parents feel validated.
- Reinforce the idea of a **team effort** between home and school.

✦ When discussing a student's areas of **challenge**, always note how you plan to assist the student in improving his/her performance, and outline next steps for your focus of instruction. Invite parents to also suggest next steps that they can take. Consider developing an **action plan** with parents and the student, which might include a list of next steps, responsibilities, and timelines.

✦ During parent–teacher conferences, provide parents with concrete examples of **how they can help their children at home**. (Refer to Chapter 11: Creating Community—Partnerships with Parents.)

✦ After the meeting, **document the meeting** and file your notes accordingly.

Student-led Conferences

✦ Consider **including students** in conferences with you and their parents. Prepare them for what to expect and advise them on how they can participate actively.

✦ Consider initiating **student-led conferences**, which place the students at the centre and give them the responsibility of presenting to their parents what they have learned, the goals they have set, and the actions they plan to take. Such conferences allow parents and students alike to become more relaxed and confident as they engage in a dialogue about progress and achievement. Portfolios can easily be presented by each student to his/her parents during this time.

✦ Introduce the idea of student-led conferences **early in the year** so students and parents will be fully prepared for the process and know what to expect. You can do this at the same time as you introduce your portfolio process.

✦ **Model a conference** with your students, walking them through every step of the process, from greeting their parents until they say goodbye.

✦ Ensure that your students have had significant **rehearsal time** to practise articulating their learnings and identifying their goals. Having them rehearse in pairs or groups of four prepares them for the big day and alleviates any anxiety.

✦ Provide students with a **structure** or steps to follow to help them organize their time during the conference. Figure 10.3 may prove helpful.

Checklist for Your Student-led Conference

☐ Introduce your parents to your teacher.

☐ Take your parents on a tour of your classroom.

☐ Highlight the work you see on display.

☐ Demonstrate for your parents something you enjoy doing in the classroom, for example, how to do a spreadsheet or construct a model.

☐ Share your work with your parents. Do one or more of the following:

    ☐ Walk your parents through your portfolio, folder, or collection of work.

    ☐ Highlight your best work and explain why it is your best.

    ☐ Highlight your most significant learning.

    ☐ Show your parents something that was difficult for you to do, and explain why you think so and what you did about it.

    ☐ Share a sample of your favourite writing.

☐ Discuss with your parents the goals you have set for next term.

☐ Thank your parents for coming and looking at your work.

☐ Say goodbye to your teacher.

LM 10.2 **Figure 10.3** *Checklist Re: Student-led Conferences*

*NOTE: Once you, your students, and their parents become comfortable with this process, you might want to schedule **multiple conferences at the same time**. While you are circulating as a facilitator and are available to answer questions and offer support, four conferences might be taking place at the same time at four different tables in the room. Students and parents are usually so focused on what they are doing that they are not distracted by the numbers of people talking at the same time.*

✦ Reassure parents that they can schedule a **traditional parent conference** if needed. However, usually parents' questions are answered and their concerns alleviated during a student-led conference.

✦ Prior to using student-led conferencing, ensure that you have the **support of your administrators**. They may receive questions about the process from concerned parents, and you will want your administrators to be well informed and supportive. Invite them to join you in facilitating a practice session with the students or the actual student-led conferences with parents.

✦ Reflect on the process with your students, parents, and administrators by **asking for feedback** either orally or in writing. For example, you might have conversations about student-led conferences or ask for an open-ended evaluation form, such as Figure 10.4, to be completed after the student-led conference.

Reflections on Student-led Conferences

Student Name: *Kimberly*

Parent Name: *Jennifer Craighton*

Date of Conference: *Nov. 10*

Highlights of Conference: *My daughter has done so much work this term*

Next Steps: *Kimberly needs to read more at home*

Other Reflections: *I was so impressed with Kimberly's confidence and the way she talked talked about her work. Wow!*

Signature of Parent: *Jennifer Craighton*

LM 10.3   **Figure 10.4** *Parent Reflections on Student-led Conferences*

** For more information about student-led conferences, see *Student-Led Conferences* by Janet Millar Grant, (Pembroke Publishers) and *Implementing Student-led Conferences*, by Guskey and Bailey (Corwin Press).

Final Thoughts

When you begin the process of evaluation, you are forming the judgments and making decisions about student achievement and progress based on the assessment data that you have collected throughout the term, semester, or year. These judgments will then be shared with your students to encourage them to reflect on their own progress and set learning goals for continued improvement. Sharing with parents to keep them abreast of how their children are progressing is one of the most important aspects of the evaluative process. Successful and collaborative interactions with parents in which a team approach is developed help to pave the way for positive partnerships between the home, school, and community.

As you engage in the evaluative process of forming judgments, creating report cards, and reporting student progress, you will also be better able to determine the effectiveness of the curriculum you have designed and the instructional processes that you have implemented. By doing this, you will be engaged in continuous critical analysis and will become a more dynamic reflective practitioner.

11 Creating Community— Partnerships with Parents

$\mathcal{C}$reating community and establishing strong partnerships with parents* ensures that parents are consistently and positively involved in their children's progress at school and at home and will reap many rewards. As parents become an integral part of your classroom and school community, they will become more knowledgeable about and supportive of your program and school. Helping your parent community to understand how children learn and how to help their children at home is an essential component of creating strong partnerships. In today's political climate, many parents are critically attuned to the education of their children and many participate actively. In some communities, however, it continues to be a challenge to involve parents in the school experience. Nonetheless, it is essential that you continue to reach out to all families.

* As previously stated, the term "parent" represents parents, guardians, and appropriate caregivers.

Regular communication with parents is an essential part of creating community and building strong partnerships. Everyone wins when teachers and parents work together to help a child. There are many ways to communicate with parents to keep them informed about your classroom program. Sending home classroom and school newsletters, notes, or communication outlines, and inviting parents to attend curriculum nights and information sessions will keep parents up to date.

Parent–teacher interviews or conferences, reporting procedures, the use of daily agenda or homework planners, and regular homework assignments help parents to keep abreast of how their children are progressing. Regular telephone calls and, in some cases, email communication, (good news calls, as well as messages to discuss concerns and questions) help to keep parents informed about their children's progress and school events. When parents are well informed about their children's educational program and progress, they become better able to assist their children at home. They can participate to a much greater extent in their children's physical, social, emotional, and cognitive development.

Inviting parents to school and classroom events, such as assemblies, musical or drama presentations, open-house evenings, or curriculum fairs, encourages them to take part in the celebrations and successes of your students and classroom program. When children accompany their families to these events, they all share in the pride and ownership of these successes.

There are many ways to help your parent community become knowledgeable about child development, how children learn, and the school environment. **Sharing the learning** with your parents to help them better comprehend and appreciate the nuances of the educational realm will assist them in understanding how established theories of child development influence your classroom practice, and how active/interactive learning and engaging curriculum influence their children's progress. The more knowledgeable parents become, the more supportive they will be, and a stronger partnership can evolve. Conversely, we as educators have much to learn from parents and need to welcome their participation and input.

When parents become actively **involved in your program as volunteers** in the classroom, school, or on field trips, not only do they serve as a beneficial support to students and teachers, they gain a better understanding of what school is all about and how children learn. With the many budget cuts today, teachers and administrators need to take a serious look at how volunteers can contribute to the learning process. Volunteer programs can be initiated as a school project where educators, parents, and community members work together to make it successful.

Homework can be seen as a window into the classroom as it acquaints parents with their children's in-school learning experiences. When your students do their homework, parents see concrete examples of your classroom program. It is important that parents realize the significance and relevance of homework assignments to their children's overall educational experience. Homework has the potential of involving parents as partners in the teaching/learning process. It is a shared commitment among teachers, students, and parents, who all have an important role to play in making the experience positive and productive. Homework is a powerful tool to use to connect and communicate with parents. It can also be a vehicle to assist parents in helping their children at home.

Homework supplements and supports in-school experiences as students are provided with opportunities to practise, integrate, and apply their learning. Regular and meaningful homework experiences encourage students' development of responsibility, self-discipline, time management, and work habits, and can help to develop positive and enthusiastic attitudes towards independent study and lifelong learning. With careful planning and thought, and when all partners are involved and valued, homework can contribute positively to educational growth.

As an educator, you need to **know your community** and understand the socioeconomic, religious, cultural, and linguistic backgrounds of your students, parents, and community members in order to better appreciate and support their needs. Parents from diverse cultures need to be consciously considered, and programs should be put into place to ease them into the school environment. When providing programming information, newsletters, reports, and invitations to classroom and school meetings and events, you should offer translations, translators, and materials in various languages to meet the needs of the whole community. You need to continuously plan how to involve all parents in positive ways in order to create community and to develop strong partnerships.

** A good resource about parental involvement is *Types of Parent Involvement* by Joyce L. Epstein, Ph.D., et. al., (Partnership Center for the Social Organization of Schools). Epstein's work describes six important types of family involvement and provides practical information about involving parents as partners.

Communicating with Parents

The following are concrete actions you can take to communicate regularly and effectively with your parents.

Making Initial Contact

✦ Make an **initial contact** with all parents early in the school year by telephoning or writing a letter or postcard. Making early contact creates a positive impression, immediately establishes the relationship, and can decrease parents' apprehensions. (See Figure 11.1.)

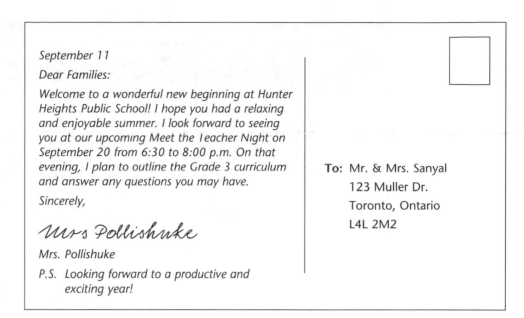

Figure 11.1 *September Postcard to Families*

NOTE: You might want to send postcards or letters to your new students before September. Students love receiving mail addressed to them and a postcard or letter is a great way to introduce yourself and welcome them to your class.

✦ Early in the school year, send home information about your program, rules, routines, expectations, timetable, and special events, such as a Curriculum Night or Open House, so parents are well informed about their children's program. You may decide to use a newsletter or letter format. Figures 11.2 and 11.3 provide examples.

NEWS FROM ROOM 203!

WELCOME TO OUR ROOM!

I would like to welcome you to Room 203. This is going to be an exciting and productive year for all of us. We are all looking forward to learning new things, trying out new ideas and celebrating our successes in Grade 5 this year. If you have any questions or concerns, please do not hesitate to call me at 905-974-6661.

Sincerely,

Mrs M. Pollishuke

GYM SCHEDULE

Our class is scheduled for the use of the **gym** every Monday and Wednesday morning. It is essential that all children wear appropriate clothes in order to participate fully in the gym program. Please ensure that your children bring shorts and running shoes to school on gym day or if you wish, they may leave a gym bag at school. It is important that all clothing and materials from home be clearly marked with your children's names.

LUNCH PROGRAM

As you may be aware, Hunter Heights does have a **school lunch program** for those children who cannot go home for lunch. Please make sure that you have returned the forms to allow your children to remain in school for lunch and that they are aware that they may not leave school property if they are part of the program.

AGENDAS

We will be using the **homework agendas** to plan our days and reflect on our achievements. These agendas will be coming home each night and will provide you with a good idea of what your children have done for each day. Please discuss the homework agenda with your children, highlighting what they have accomplished and in what areas they may need to spend more time.

TRIPS

We hope to be able to offer our students many **out-of-classroom excursions** throughout the year in order to broaden the scope of our program. Please ensure that all permission forms are returned promptly to the school so that your children do not miss out on these important learning opportunities.

If you would like to volunteer to help on any of these trips, please fill out the request for volunteers form when it is sent home.

INFORMATION SHEET

I will be sending home a **student information sheet** in the next few days and hope that you will fill out all the pertinent information and return it promptly to the school. The more information I have on your children, the better able I will be to program for their specific needs.

Figure 11.2 *Class Newsletter*

Dear Families,

Please join us at our Curriculum Night on Wednesday, September 20, to find out what we have planned for this year. At that time, I will give you an overview of the upcoming program and answer any questions you may have.

As the year progresses, I plan to be in constant communication with all the homes of the students in my class. I want to keep you well informed about what we are doing and learning throughout the year. In the meantime, I would like to outline some initial routines that you need to be aware of immediately.

- We will be using **homework planners** to plan our days and reflect on our achievements. These planners will be coming home with your children each night and will provide you with a good idea of what they have done each day. Please discuss the homework planners with your children, highlighting what they have accomplished and what areas may need more time and attention.

- Our class is scheduled for the use of the **gym** every Monday and Wednesday morning. It is essential that all children wear appropriate clothes in order to participate fully in the gym program. Please ensure that your children bring shorts, t-shirts, and running shoes to school on gym days, or, if you wish, they may leave gym bags at school. It is important that all clothing and materials from your home be clearly marked with your children's names.

- Hunter Heights has a **school lunch program** for those children who are unable to go home for lunch. Please make sure that you have returned the forms to allow your children to remain in school for lunch and that they know that it is inappropriate to leave school property if registered in the lunch program.

- Please complete the **student information form** attached and return it promptly to the school. The more information I have about each child, the better able I will be to program for students' specific needs.

Welcome to our classroom. I look forward to getting to know both you and your children throughout this school year. Please do not hesitate to contact me if you have any questions or concerns.

Sincerely,

M. Pollishuke

Mrs. M. Pollishuke

LM 11.2   **Figure 11.3** *Sample Letter to Parents Re: Beginning of the Year*

Collecting Background Information

✦ At the beginning of the year, **collect background information** about your students and parents including the family structure, languages spoken at home, medical history, the way the child travels to and from school, and any other information pertinent to the child's time in school. If your school does not already have a set procedure, you might consider sending home a form such as in Figure 11.4.

Student Information Form

Please complete this form and return it promptly. Thank you for your cooperation.

Child's Name: _____   Birthday: _____

Address: _____   Home Phone #: _____

Mother's
Name: _____   Mother's
Work Phone #: _____

Father's
Name: _____   Father's
Work Phone #: _____

When is the best time to reach you? _____   Emergency Name: _____

Phone #: _____

Names of Brothers and Sisters: School   Grade

_____

_____

_____

Languages Spoken at Home: _____

Allergies: _____

Medication: _____

My child will not eat lunch at school. _____

OR

My child will eat lunch in the lunch program on

　　　　MONDAY　　TUESDAY　　WEDNESDAY　　THURSDAY　　FRIDAY　(Circle the days.)

My child walks to and from school. _____

OR

My child will be picked up by _____

OR

My child goes home on the school bus _____ on public transit _____ (Check one.)

If you have any other pertinent information you wish to share with the school, please note below.

_____
　　　Parent's Signature

LM 11.3   **Figure 11.4** *Student Information Form*

Regular Communication with Parents

✦ On a regular basis, **greet your parents** at the door or in the schoolyard as they drop off or pick up their children. This is a good opportunity to learn about what is happening in your students' lives. This is especially important during the first few days of school as you begin to develop a strong relationship between home and school.

✦ Throughout the year, **communicate with your parents on a regular basis** via telephone, email, websites, newsletters, letters, or in face-to-face meetings to keep them informed and aware.

- Call the parents of each student in your class early in the school year to lay the groundwork for positive relationships with parents.

- Make good news calls to every parent in addition to any calls you may need to make to discuss progress or difficulties.

- Calling a parent immediately after you notice a student concern is good practice and helps to avoid surprises.

- Think about the timing of your call. Choose a time and place when you will not be interrupted. It is often good to find out in one of your information forms that you send home early in the year what time is the best time for you to call.

- Be prepared for your conversation. Create some jot notes before you call to stay focused. Include your purpose for the call, possible actions to be suggested, and how you will elicit further information from the parent.

- When you receive a parent phone call, return it promptly, usually within 24 hours. However, consider returning parent phone calls at the end of the day so as not to disrupt your positive attitude for that day, especially if there are challenging issues to be discussed.

- Take notes as you engage in your telephone conversation. Always document each telephone conversation you have with a parent for future referral if necessary.

- If a topic of conversation becomes sensitive during a phone call, or if a parent becomes angry or upset, arrange for a face-to-face meeting where you and the parent can discuss issues in more detail. Always be respectful, polite, and an empathetic listener.

- Ensure that you use a school phone to conduct telephone conversations. If you decide to call from your home, make use of different phone companies' blocking procedures to ensure that parents do not have your home phone number. Although most parents would be respectful of your personal privacy, you do not want to take the chance of having your personal access information out there for all to see and use.

- In some schools, **email communication with parents** is becoming common practice. Email is effective for quick distribution of clear-cut information. Since not all parents will have computers at home or will be competent in the use of computers, it is always necessary to offer options.

- Remember that emails are never private conversations, but can be saved, printed, or forwarded and distributed to others as a written record. Be discreet and professional. Always save copies of all email communication you send and receive for future referral if necessary.

- To ensure your own privacy, do not use your own private email address, but rather one that is provided by your board or district. Think about email communication as similar to phone conversations—you do not want parents to have access to your personal email address any more than you would want them to have access to your home phone number. It is important to ensure that these boundaries remain intact.

- Consider creating a **classroom and/or school website**, and post important information about your program for your students' parents to access. (See Chapter 9: Technology in a Rapidly Changing World.) See Figure 11.5 for a sample class website.

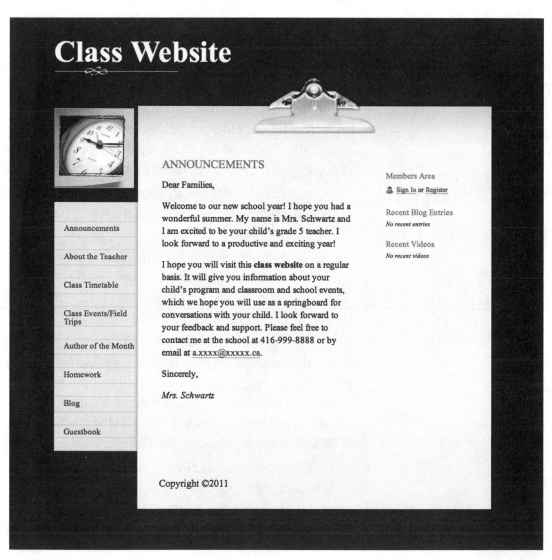

Figure 11.5 *Class Website*

◆ When **documenting your communication** with your parents, you can do the following:

- Keep a file or binder with the notes and messages, etc. that you have sent home.

- Keep a list of the telephone conversations you made, including decisions or timelines established.

- Keep a print copy of important email communications you sent and received.

- Record issues and concerns that are shared, and consider including an action plan that would outline recommendations and next steps. See **Figure 11.6** for an example of a **parent–teacher communication form** you might want to use.

- Be objective and non-judgmental in any notes you make.

Parent–teacher Communication Form

Student's Name:

Parent's Name:

Date:
- ☐ Phone Call
- ☐ Meeting

Topics discussed:

Teacher's Issues, Concerns, Questions:

Parent's Issues, Concerns, Questions:

Action Plan:

Recommendations/goals—what will be done at school, what will be done at home:

Next steps:

Follow-up contact date:

LM 11.4 **Figure 11.6** *Parent–teacher Communication Form*

◆ To share information about your classroom program or school events, you may decide to use **a newsletter format** (see Figure 11.2), **a calendar format** (see Figure 11.7), **"Ask Me About" newsletters** (see Figures 11.8 and 11.9), or a **Friday File** (see Figure 11.10).

SEPTEMBER

Sunday	Monday	Tuesday	Wednesday	Thursday	Friday	Saturday
	Welcome Back to School				1	2
3	Labour Day 4	First Day of School 5	6	Gym Day Bring your shorts 7	8	Happy Birthday Jennifer 9
10	11	12	Library Day Pick a great book! 13	14	15	16
17	18	Computer Lab 19	20	Curriculum Night Bring your parents! 21	22	23
24	25	26	27	28	29	Rosh Hashanah 30

LM 11.5   **Figure 11.7** *Class Calendar*

Dear Families,

This **Ask Me About** newsletter is intended to let you know about some of the things we are doing in class. When you ask your children "What did you do in school today?" they often answer "nothing" even though much learning has occurred. The format of this newsletter encourages you to ask the questions that will spark your child to talk about his/her day and the learning that took place. These prompts can help to focus your conversations about school happenings. They are built on the premise that if parents ask the right questions based on a bit of knowledge, the children will carry the rest and a flood of talk can result. We hope you will find this newsletter informative and useful.

Please take the time to ask your child about some of the things listed below.

Sincerely,

S. Smith

Mrs. Smith

ASK ME ABOUT

❑ one math activity I did this week.
❑ one of the books my teacher read to us.
❑ the book I am reading for my novel study.
❑ what I am writing.
❑ my art project.
❑ the new song I learned this week in choir.
❑ the visitor that came to our school this week.
❑ the trip we went on today.

LM 11.6   **Figure 11.8** *"Ask Me About" Newsletter*

Ask Me About...

Kindergarten Newsletter
Park View Heights Public School

Friday, June 12

On Monday, our Painted Lady butterflies emerged. One emerged in the morning before we came to class. The other emerged in the afternoon when we went to the library. Ask me to tell you about the Painted Lady butterfly. They were in a terrarium. We kept them for four days. We released them yesterday. I'll tell you how we did that. Ask me to tell you why we let them go.

We read more books about butterflies and moths. Ask me to tell you what I found interesting.

We have other objects about insects. We have a paper wasp home, a dead Monarch butterfly, the empty chrysalides of Painted Lady butterflies and some models of insects. Ask me to tell you about them.

Mrs. Hartman has read many stories this week. I'll tell you what I liked about one of them.

Ask me to tell you what I have been writing in my writing book.

On Monday, Mrs. Garden, a volunteer, showed us how to drip paint on paper to make butterflies. I'll tell you about my butterfly.

I have been making letters in a new printing book. Ask me to tell you what letters I have been practising. I am also printing words.

Ask me to tell you what mathematics activities I have been doing this week. We can do a shape activity at the paint centre.

LM 11.7 **Figure 11.9** *"Ask Me About" Newsletter for Kindergarten*

Source: Used with permission. Elizabeth Hartman, TDSB.

Dear Families,

Every Friday, your child will be bringing home a file folder containing work accomplished during the week and/or letters or notes for you to see. The purpose of this **Friday File** is to inform you about our classroom program and the progress that your child is making. Please review with your child the work in this folder and ask him/her questions about specific items. Your child should be able to tell you about the things that he/she has learned.

Please sign the front of the folder and send it and the work to school with your child each Monday morning.

Thank you for your cooperation.

Sincerely,

M. Pollishuke

Mrs. M. Pollishuke

LM 11.8 **Figure 11.10** *Sample Parent Letter Re: Friday File*

> *NOTE: You may want to identify one or two learning expectations that you have addressed during that week on the back of your "Ask Me About" newsletter. Doing this will give your parents insights into the curriculum expectations*

for the grade. You will want to review the "Ask Me About" newsletter with the students before sending it home, so that students are well aware of what they might be asked by their parents. This is a type of in-class rehearsal for the talk that might occur at home. You may also want to generate the content of this newsletter by brainstorming with the students each week for the points they think should be included. This may provide even more ownership.

✦ Ensure that any written communication sent home has been **proofread for spelling, grammar, and content**. It is often advisable or required to show your administrator any written communication before sending it home. You may want to use a colleague or mentor to proofread your writing.

✦ If some of your families are new to the country and do not speak English, ensure that you send home **translations** of your important letters in the appropriate languages.

✦ **Arrange translators** for your families whose first language is not English. A translator might be a bilingual assistant or district employee, another teacher, a parent in the school who speaks the same language, or an older student. Keep in mind the issue of confidentiality when involving other parents or students.

✦ If you are concerned about a particular student and you know his/her family's first language is not English, connect with a **multicultural consultant or other resource personnel** who may be affiliated with your school or district or with an appropriate community agency.

Curriculum Nights and Information Meetings

✦ At a scheduled **curriculum night or information meeting**, introduce yourself and outline clear program objectives and expectations as well as information about your routines, timetable, special events, and so on.

✦ During a **Curriculum Night** or initial information meeting with parents, you may want to do the following:

- Share your philosophy of teaching and learning in a creative way (e.g., posters, artifacts, using a picture book, presentation, etc.).

- Create posters or charts that clearly outline connections between your program topics and the district expectations.

- Prepare relevant handouts for parents to take home as reference.

- Have student materials, texts, sample activities, etc. on display for parents to peruse.

- Display examples of completed student work that demonstrates some aspects of your program.

- Display professional resources (e.g., articles, books) for parents to borrow to help them better understand your classroom and aspects of education today.

✦ During a **curriculum event where students accompany their parents to the school** (or during an Open House), plan a **scavenger hunt** through your classroom or school, ensuring that families visit all important areas. In this scenario, the child is put into a leadership role as he/she becomes a guide and provides a walking tour, talking to family members about the learning that is taking place in the classroom and school. Figure 11.11 is an example of a scavenger hunt page, which you may want to modify for your own classroom and school.

Let's go on a Harbour Woods HUNT...

Please check after you visit each one.

OUR CLASSROOM:
_____ The table where I sit
_____ Timetable (on board)
_____ Computer centre
_____ Book corner
_____ Mathematics area
_____ Science corner
_____ Social Studies area
_____ Painting centre
_____ Current events
_____ Word wall
_____ Parent news bulletin board
_____ Homework folders (on round table)
_____ Information about homework (Please pick up.)

LIBRARY RESOURCE CENTRE:
_____ Say hello to Mr. Sturnick, our teacher-librarian.
_____ Say hello to Mrs. Brown, our Special Education resource teacher.
_____ See the new books on display.
_____ View the new computers.
_____ See how fast you can type using the "All the Right Type" keyboarding program.

MUSIC:
_____ Meet Ms. Taylor, our new music teacher, in Room 5.
_____ Name and play some of the instruments we've used.

COMMUNITY CHILD CARE:
_____ Meet some of our child-care staff.

SCHOOL ADVISORY COUNCIL:
_____ Meet some of the members of our School Council.
_____ Enjoy some refreshments (provided by the Council).

Figure 11.11 *Sample Scavenger Hunt*

Meeting the Needs of a Variety of Family Situations and Parental Concerns

✦ In all communications with your students' parents, consider the various family situations and develop strategies for positive interactions. Examples include the following:

To ensure parents do not feel intimidated in the school environment:

- Keep them regularly informed about their child's successes.
- Provide extra personal contact.
- Provide translations and translators, if required.

To ensure parents do not feel discouraged when their child is not meeting with success:

- Encourage the positive and highlight even small successes and accomplishments.
- Together set small, realistic goals.
- Monitor homework.
- Encourage extracurricular involvement.
- Graph the student's progress.
- Suggest family support programs.

To support single parent families:

- Be knowledgeable about custody issues.
- Communicate with both parents if appropriate.

To work with parents who are overly involved in their child's school life:

- Welcome their questions and concerns and avoid defensive responses.
- Provide prompt responses to questions.
- Be proactive and provide information about your program early and often.
- Involve them whenever possible and appropriate.
- Find ways for them to act as a resource.

To deal with challenging parents:

- Listen without being defensive and stay calm at all times.
- Acknowledge other issues that may be influencing behaviours.
- Determine the issues, ask questions, and take notes if appropriate.
- Use "I" statements to share your feelings and thoughts.
- Encourage working together towards a solution.
- Arrange additional meetings if necessary with your administrator present.

- Keep in mind that in any confrontational situation with a parent you are not alone, and if you face significant issues with parents, seek advice and support from your mentor or administrator.

Sharing the Learning with Parents

- Provide interested parents with **professional reading material**, such as educational documents and resources, to promote a better understanding of current philosophy and practices. Set up a lending library for parents to borrow your resource books and educational videos, and recommend appropriate websites for parents to visit.

- Provide parents with ideas and concrete examples of **how they can help their children at home**. You may find the following three letters helpful, shown as Figures 11.12, 11.13, and 11.14.

Dear Families,

Keep in mind that your interest, involvement, and support will help to improve your child's achievement and success. The following are suggestions of activities that you and your child can do at home.

- Have your child see you read and write.

- Relate reading to everyday life, for example, billboards, traffic signs, store signs, menus, TV guides, catalogues, magazines, comics, labels, maps, and crossword puzzles.

- Share experiences, work samples, and anecdotes.

- Take your child on outings — to shopping malls, museums, planetariums, art displays, concerts, sporting events, airports, farms, zoos, amusement parks, family vacations. Enjoy spending time together!

- Leave notes for your child, for example, in a lunchbox, under a pillow, on the refrigerator door, and encourage writing back.

- Write letters, shopping lists, invitations, things-to-do lists, and more together.

- Help your child find a penpal.

- Keep a diary, journal, or log and share with your child. Think about having everyone write and draw in a family journal when on a holiday together or at the cottage.

LM 11.10 **Figure 11.12** *Sample Letter to Parents Re: Home-initiated Activities*

Dear Families,

Here are some tips for helping your young child with reading. I hope you find them useful.

• Read to your child as often as you can.

• Talk about the cover, title, author, and illustrator. Predict what the story might be about.

• Draw attention to the illustrations when reading to your child.

• Make connections, telling your child what you are reminded of. Ask a few *why* questions as you read.

• Encourage your child to choose the books you read together and help your child to tell the story from the pictures in the book.

Figure 11.13 *Sample Letter To Parents Re: Helping Young Children with Reading*

Dear Families,

Here are some helpful hints on how you can help your child with reading. I hope you find them useful.

• Continue to read to your child every day. Vary the type of books read, for example, humorous stories, jokes/riddles, short stories, poems, chapter books, newspapers, magazines, recipes, and puzzle books.

• Encourage your child to go to the local library regularly, continue to visit bookstores together, and use the Internet to find information.

• Emphasize with your child the importance of *making sense* when they read. Encourage them to take risks and "have-a-go" at a word.

• De-emphasize the need to get 100 percent accuracy and try strategies such as reading ahead, rereading, looking at the word parts, and sounding out the word.

• Accept your child's efforts with praise and concentrate on all the things he/she does right, not on any errors.

• If your child makes a mistake when he/she is reading aloud, allow time for self-correction. If the mistake makes sense, ignore it.

Figure 11.14 *Sample Letter to Parents Re: Helping Older Children with Reading*

✦ Provide some information sessions for your parents about different areas of the curriculum or classroom program. Common today are **family literacy, numeracy, or technology nights**. Parents come *with* their children to a school evening program where they become engaged in learning together.

✦ The following **paired reading guide** can be introduced at an information meeting with parents and may prove helpful as a tool and process for parent and child reading together. This guide can also used as a tool for volunteers, including older students or seniors, who can be taught to work one-on-one with students in the classroom to help them read. (See Figure 11.15.)

PAIRED READING GUIDE

The following procedure will provide you with a guide to follow when reading one-on-one with a student. The focus of this interaction is for you and the student to have an enjoyable experience reading together. We hope that the student will develop a positive attitude towards reading, as well as reinforce and extend comprehension and oral language skills. We encourage you to have as natural a conversation as possible about the text. Please refrain from correcting the student if it seems that he/she understands the meaning of the passage.

BEFORE YOU READ

Retell   • Talk about the title, author, illustrator, picture, diagrams, characters, setting...

Relate   • Make connections: "This reminds me of...;" "This makes me think of...."

Reflect   • Predict what will happen.

          • Ask questions: "I wonder why...?"

STRATEGIES TO USE WHILE READING TOGETHER

• Listen and stop to make comments about the content of the reading.

Retell   • "I notice that..."

Relate   • "This reminds me of..."; "This makes me think of..."

Reflect   • "I wonder why..."; "What will happen next?"

• Encourage the child to talk about the reading.

• Point and follow along (or encourage the child to follow along with his/her finger).

• When the student cannot read a word, encourage him/her to use a variety of reading strategies:

- skip the word
- look at the pictures or diagrams
- think about what went before and what might happen next
- read ahead
- reread
- sound out using phonics
- look at the root words or word parts
- guess

• When the student is still unable to read the word, then give the word.

• If you have given the word a number of times, this material may be too difficult. Try the following:

- read together with the student
- read and the student reads the last word of each sentence
- read one line and the student reads the next
- read the first paragraph, poem, or line, and the student reads the same again: "Repeat after me."

DURING/AFTER THE READING

RETELL:	**RELATE:**	**REFLECT:**
This is about...	This reminds me of...	I wonder if...?
I notice that...	This makes me think of...	I wonder why...?
I especially like...	This makes me feel...	Now I understand...

LM 11.13   **Figure 11.15** *Paired Reading Guide*

Source: Used with permission of Schwartz, Susan, & Bone, Maxine. (1995). *Retelling, Relating, Reflecting: Beyond the 3 R's*. Toronto: Nelson.

♦ Invite parents to information sessions where they will learn more about how children learn and the school program. You may want to include information about the developmental characteristics of children, multiple intelligences, and theories about how children learn. See Figures 11.16, 11.17, 11.18, and 11.19 for sample handouts you might distribute to parents during an information session or interactive workshop.

DEVELOPMENTAL CHARACTERISTICS OF CHILDREN

As a volunteer, you will find that a knowledge of the developmental characteristics of children can provide you with greater understandings as you interact with students of different ages.

CHILDREN AGES 5–7
(SK to Grade 2)

- starting to develop small muscle and eye-hand coordination (cutting and pasting)
- possess a high energy level (unable to sit still for long)
- learning physical skills that will let them play games (tossing a ball)
- learning to recognize words
- memory is developing
- enjoy telling stories
- beginning to make judgments and decisions
- beginning to accept that rules apply, but do not yet understand the underlying principles
- subject to extreme expressions of emotions

CHILDREN AGES 8–10
(Grades 3 to 5)

- possess high energy level (need lots of physical activity)
- able to look after personal hygiene
- show great variety in reading levels
- like to talk and discuss
- understand money and how to make change
- developing logical thinking (rules and consequences)
- experimenting with abstract words (slang common)
- becoming independent
- wanting to belong or be with others
- sensitive to criticism and ridicule

CHILDREN AGES 11–14
(Grades 6 to 9)

- subject to growth spurts (awkward times, clumsiness)
- increasing in strength
- developing refined physical skills (sports)
- beginning puberty
- capable of thinking independently and critically
- beginning to question rules and authority
- showing some understanding of ethics (honesty, justice)
- prone to a lack of self-confidence
- finding peer acceptance important
- prone to loud, boisterous behaviour

ONLINE MATERIAL

LM 11.14 **Figure 11.16** *Information for Parents Re: Developmental Characteristics of Children*

INFORMATION FOR PARENTS RE: LEARNING STYLES

Children learn in different ways but usually have a dominant style or method of learning.

The Visual Learner

- learns best by seeing
- prefers to read, watch, observe
- likes to watch videos, work on the computer
- likes to use note-taking techniques as a study aid

The Auditory Learner

- learns best by hearing
- prefers lecture, discussion, interaction, audio-tapes, talking out loud
- likes to audio-tape lectures

The Kinesthetic Learner

- learns best by doing, hands-on
- likes to experiment
- usually likes to draw, write, move

LM 11.15   **Figure 11.17** *Information for Parents Re: Learning Styles*

✦ Involve your parents in **interactive workshops** that put them in the role of learners to demonstrate how students learn and why teachers do what they do in the classroom. During these workshops, involve your parents in activities that invite participants to observe, manipulate, explore, think, talk and write about real objects and experiences. Activities such as these will show how you scaffold learning to create a bridge between learners' previous experience and new and more abstract knowledge. These activities can also demonstrate the value of talk, interaction, and the shared roles of all partners in the learning process.

AN INTRODUCTION TO MULTIPLE INTELLIGENCES

Harvard psychologist Howard Gardner, in his book *Frames of Mind* (Harper & Row), concludes that all individuals possess distinct intelligences, though one or more may be stronger than others. This tendency towards greater strengths in certain types of intelligences over others can make a difference in many areas of our lives: from preferred learning styles, to the things that interest us both in school and out, to our career choices later in life. Here's how to recognize the characteristics of each form of intelligence.

1. THE LINGUISTIC LEARNER:
"The Word Player"

- loves to read books, write, and tell stories

- is good at memorizing names, places, dates, and trivia information

- learns best by saying, hearing, and seeing words

2. THE LOGICAL-MATHEMATICAL LEARNER: "The Questioner"

- likes to do experiments, figure things out, work with numbers, ask questions, and explore patterns and relationships

- is good at math, reasoning, logic, and problem solving

- learns best by categorizing, classifying, and working with abstract patterns/ relationships

3. THE SPATIAL LEARNER:
"The Visualizer"

- likes to draw, build, design, and create things, look at pictures/slides, watch movies, play with machines

- is good at imagining things, sensing changes, doing mazes/puzzles, and reading maps and charts

- learns best by visualizing, dreaming, using the mind's eye, working with colours/ pictures

4. THE MUSICAL LEARNER:
"The Music Lover"

- likes to sing, hum tunes, listen to music, play an instrument, respond to music

- is good at picking up sounds, remembering melodies, noticing pitches/rhythms, keeping time

- learns best by rhythm, melody, music

5. THE BODILY/KINESTHETIC LEARNER:
"The Mover"

- likes to move around, touch, and use body language

- is good at physical activities (sports, dance, acting), and crafts

- learns best by touching, moving, interacting with space, processing knowledge through body sensations

6. THE INTERPERSONAL LEARNER:
"The Socializer"

- likes to have lots of friends, talk to people, join groups

- is good at understanding people, leading others, organizing, communicating, manipulating, and mediating conflicts

- learns best by sharing, comparing, relating, cooperating, and interviewing

7. THE INTRAPERSONAL LEARNER:
"The Individual"

- likes to work alone, pursue own interests

- is good at understanding self, focusing inward on feelings/dreams, following instincts, pursuing interests/goals, being original

- learns best by working alone, doing individualized projects, self-pacing instruction, having own space

8. THE NATURALIST LEARNER:
"The Nature Lover"

- likes to be outdoors, shows an interest in nature (plants and animals)

- is good at scientific exploration in the outdoors

- learns best by being outdoors, exploring, and experimenting

LM 11.16 **Figure 11.18** *Information for Parents Re: Multiple Intelligences*

HOW CHILDREN LEARN

Dr. Brian Cambourne, in *The Whole Story* (Scholastic), outlines seven conditions that must be evident in order for children to learn.

Immersion: to be immersed in a wide variety and number of resources, concrete materials, books, and experiences

Demonstrations: to be exposed to direct teaching, seeing concrete examples, instructing, modelling

Expectations: to be provided with clear, appropriate expectations and messages; to have consistency

Responsibility: to be able to make choices, have ownership, show responsibility

Approximations: to experiment, guess, become risk takers

Practice: to use, reinforce, and have adequate time on task

Feedback: to receive constructive support and feedback from others

Keeping in mind the above conditions of learning, how can you, as a volunteer, reinforce students' learning? Here are some of the ways:

- *Immerse* the students in a book or experience.

- Provide *demonstrations* and model enthusiasm.

- Have clear *expectations* and be consistent.

- Allow the students to make choices and be *responsible*.

- Encourage the students to *approximate*, guess, become risk takers. Reinforce the idea that "it's okay to make a mistake — we learn from and through our mistakes."

- Help the students *practise* and encourage them to stay on task.

- Provide positive *feedback* in any one-on-one situation and celebrate the learning that occurs.

LM 11.17 **Figure 11.19** *Information for Parents Re: How Children Learn*

Involving Parents in Your Program

✦ Provide opportunities for parents to become involved in your program by taking part in **classroom/school events or out-of-classroom excursions.** For example, parents may be invited to:
- help supervise class trips
- listen to students read

- type student stories
- help with the editing and publishing of students' writing
- present topics about which they know a lot
- answer interview questions about their occupations, experiences, and interests
- organize fun fairs, fundraising events, and conferences for young authors
- arrange pizza or hot dog lunches or regular lunch programs for students
- offer lunchtime and/or after-school enrichment activities, or help to organize such activities
- participate in the work of the School Council or parent–teacher association
- act as parent volunteers in the classroom and library.

(See Chapter 5: Designing Your Curriculum, and Chapter 7: Out-of-Classroom Excursions—Experiencing the Wider Community. Also refer to Chapter 8: Literacy and Language Learning for more information about reading and writing.)

Working with Volunteers

✦ Actively enlist the help of your parents to work in your classroom or school as regular **volunteers**. At a curriculum night, community event, or Open House, post on a chart, board, or door specific ways parents can help in your classroom. Invite them to sign up and, at the same time, ask them to indicate the times they are available, or send home a letter inviting parents to work as volunteers in your classroom.
(See Figure 11.20.)

Dear Families,

Would you be interested in volunteering in my classroom? If yes, please indicate the days you may be available and the time of day that would best suit you. Also, be sure to let me know the types of activities you might be interested in doing. Please note that you may need to participate in some training sessions to prepare you for this role. If you are interested, I encourage you to complete the form below and return it to me at your earliest convenience.

Sincerely,

Mrs. Schwartz

Mrs. Schwartz

- -

Yes, I am interested in volunteering in the classroom.

Name: _____

Phone Number: _____

Days Available: _____

Time of Day: _____

Type of Activities: _____

LM 11.18   **Figure 11.20** *Sample Letter to Parents Re: Asking for Volunteers*

✦ Follow up later with another letter or phone call finalizing the times, list of responsibilities, and expectations.

✦ Ensure that you provide your volunteers with a **timeline for their involvement**, perhaps a month, and check with them at intervals to see how they are enjoying their work. Give them options and, if you can, rotate the tasks to create interest.

✦ Ensure that you **plan ahead** so volunteers always have something to do in your classroom. Volunteers need to feel useful and valued when they give their time.

*NOTE: Before volunteers begin working in your classroom or school, **hold an input session** to encourage them to share their strengths, interests, and talents and to allow you to clarify expectations and provide training in specific areas, such as computers and reading.*

✦ Encourage your volunteers to ask questions if they are unsure about what you are asking them to do.

✦ Ensure that your volunteers are aware that what they do and learn about other students and teachers in the school and in your classroom is strictly **confidential**. A letter such as the following would be useful in clarifying expectations and the seriousness of the confidentiality issue. It is often best if the letter is signed by the principal and seen as part of school policy. See Figure 11.21.

Dear Volunteer,

Once you begin to work in a school setting, you will have access to knowledge about children's behaviour patterns, academic ability, emotional maturity, and relationships with others. In some cases, information of this nature is imparted in order that you might work more effectively with an individual child. In other cases, it is simply acquired in the course of frequent contact in the school. You, as a school volunteer, are also in a position to know more about staff members than most parents. However, it is essential that you recognize the confidential nature of any such information. Under no circumstances should such knowledge or opinions be shared in the community or with anyone who has no legitimate need to know. Similarly, care must be taken to refrain from expressing comments harmful to the reputation of a pupil or professional. If any questions or concerns develop, first approach the staff member involved, and then, if necessary, go to the principal. A volunteer has every right to expect that his or her participation will be treated with the same confidentiality and respect.

Thank you for your time, interest, and participation as a volunteer in our school.

Sincerely,

Susan Schwartz

Susan Schwartz

LM 11.19   **Figure 11.21** *Sample Letter to Volunteers Re: Confidentiality*

✦ Ensure that your volunteers are aware of the **school code of behaviour, consequences for inappropriate behaviour,** and **expectations for their role**. The following letter, Figure 11.22, is useful as clarification. You may also need to make sure that your volunteers have a copy of the school or district code of behaviour.

See **LM 11.21** for information for volunteers re: **fire drills and emergency procedures**.

✦ Give your volunteers specific information **about how children learn** (see previous section) as well as a greater understanding of what they will see while in your classroom in terms of groupings and learning stations. The following information sheet **about classroom groupings**, Figure 11.23, may prove helpful.

Dear Volunteer,

Classroom teachers are responsible for establishing and maintaining classroom routines. If, in your role as a volunteer, you encounter any situation requiring discipline, please refer it to one of us.

When dealing with inappropriate behaviour by students in our classroom and school, the focus is always on providing logical consequences (versus punishments), encouraging students to take responsibility for their own actions, and creating opportunities for growth and learning.

As a volunteer, you need to be aware of our Student Code of Behaviour and the consequences for any inappropriate behaviour.

We hope that, with a better understanding of our goals for student discipline, you will find working in our classroom a positive experience.

Sincerely,

Mrs. Schwartz   *Mrs. Pollishuke*

Mrs. Schwartz and Mrs. Pollishuke

Figure 11.22 *Sample Letter to Volunteers Re: Discipline*

CLASSROOM GROUPINGS

As a volunteer, you may find that an understanding of classroom groupings will serve you well as you see students and teachers engaged in a variety of activities and experiences in the classroom or school.

- *Large-group experiences with a teacher*
  Students may participate in read-aloud experiences, discussions, input sessions, direct instruction, chanting, choral reading, dramatic reading, and singing.

- *Small-group experiences with a teacher, volunteer, or other students*
  In these learning experiences, students practise cooperating, working together in active/interactive ways. They are encouraged to become problem solvers, decision makers, and independent workers. The teacher may work with one group or an individual, or may be seen circulating among the many groups, asking questions, encouraging, and facilitating the learning.

  Students may say they are doing "centres," "stations," or "tubs". These usually include a variety of small-group tasks about a specific theme or unit of study (e.g., fairy tales, the environment, place value). Students may use tracking sheets which show when and what they have accomplished and help them move from one task to another. These tracking sheets often include self-assessments where students think about how well they have done or how well they have worked with others on a certain task.

- *Individual students*
  Students may be seen working one-on-one with a teacher or volunteer, or working independently without assistance.

A balance of large-group, small-group, and individual learning experiences is important in every program across the grade levels.

Figure 11.23 *Information for Volunteers Re: Classroom Groupings*

- You may want to encourage **others in your school community** to become involved as volunteers in your classroom or school.
  - Involve **caregivers** in the school as volunteers. They often walk children to and from school, and might be willing to give up a morning or afternoon to volunteer in different ways.
  - Establish a program where **older students from a neighbouring school** will buddy up with younger students. Both sets of students will benefit from this enrichment experience.
  - Establish a program where **seniors** read with students in a particular class or in the library.
  - Consider involving **community members and outside agencies** into your classroom or school. Guests may be invited to share their expertise with classes or groups of students, or as a special school event.

- Encourage your parents to participate in **School Council meetings** to help make decisions for the school. Positive and enthusiastic parent leaders can be developed through their involvement in these meetings and events.

- Ensure that you show your parents and other volunteers that they are appreciated. Thank them for their contributions to your program or school. Organize **appreciation events** such as these:
  - special breakfasts, lunches, after-school barbecues
  - thank-you gatherings involving singing, reciting poems, sharing pictures or cards made by your students for the volunteers
  - the presentation of a book for the library with volunteers' names in a plaque at the front of the book in their honour

Homework: A Window into Your Classroom

Homework is often seen as a window into the classroom as it acquaints parents with their children's in-school learning experiences. When your students do their homework, parents see concrete examples of your classroom program. It is important that parents realize the significance and relevance of homework assignments to their children's overall educational experience. Homework has the potential of involving parents as partners in the teaching/learning process. It is a shared commitment among teachers, students, and parents, who all have an important role to play in making the experience positive and productive. (See Figure 11.24.) Homework is a powerful tool to use to connect and communicate with parents. It can also be used as a vehicle to educate parents on how to help their children at home. Homework should never take the place of remedial teaching, and under no circumstances should it be assigned as a punishment for misbehaviour or for failure to perform as expected.

Homework supplements and supports the in-school experiences as students are provided with opportunities to practice, integrate, and apply their learning. Regular and meaningful homework experiences encourage students' development of responsibility, self-discipline, time management, and work habits, and can help to develop positive and enthusiastic attitudes towards independent study and lifelong learning. With careful planning and thought, and when all partners are involved and valued, homework can contribute positively to your students' educational growth.

Responsibilities Re: Homework Process

Students
- ❑ complete assignments on time and in an acceptable form
- ❑ manage their time and work
- ❑ ask teachers for help if they do not understand something

Teachers
- ❑ ensure homework is meaningful, relevant, and geared to each student's needs, intellectual abilities, and interests
- ❑ clearly communicate homework expectations, purpose, method, and requirements to students and parents
- ❑ ensure that students understand how to do assignments
- ❑ notice any learning concerns
- ❑ communicate with parents regularly
- ❑ provide follow-up, and identify areas that require further work
- ❑ check and assess homework regularly and in a timely fashion
- ❑ provide appropriate feedback to students and to parents
- ❑ include comments on report cards about each student's success with homework

Parents
- ❑ ensure that children carry out their responsibilities re: homework
- ❑ create a suitable environment at home for children to work
- ❑ set aside time and oversee that work is completed
- ❑ monitor children's stress levels in relation to homework assignments and report to the teacher if there is a concern
- ❑ take children to the library, answer questions, show support of homework, and help relate homework to their children's world
- ❑ read to children and talk about homework and school events

---

LM 11.23 **Figure 11.24** *Responsibilities Re: Homework*

✦ Find out if your school or district has a **formal homework policy**, and if so, refer to it as you plan homework experiences for your students. It should provide you with homework goals and objectives, address the amount, frequency, and scheduling of assignments, and articulate the responsibilities of all partners.

- Ensure that your parents are aware of your classroom homework expectations and requirements through your **communication** with them through notes sent home, weekly newsletters, or monthly calendars that highlight school and classroom events. (See Communicating with Parents section above.) If district or school homework policies stipulate specific amounts of time to be spent on homework, emphasize to parents that these are to be used as a guide only and will vary depending on the program as well as on the developmental levels, learning styles, and individual needs and interests of the students.

- Ask your students to record their **after-school activities and commitments** for your information and planning and for the fostering of their own planning and time-management skills. This can be included in the Student Information Form that can be sent home early in September for parents to complete. (See Figure 11.4 earlier in this chapter.)

- When you assign homework, pay due consideration to **student involvement in after-school co-curricular activities** and to overall **student workload** in the assignments that may be due for other teachers.

- Include information about your homework expectations **at curriculum nights and parent–teacher conferences**. Indicate clearly when and how you wish parents to be involved.

- Every time you assign homework, determine and **be able to articulate the purpose** of the homework and its type, as well as the specific learning expectations that it is addressing. Homework needs to be relevant, meaningful, appropriate to the needs, interests, and abilities of each student, and closely connected to your program.

- Homework assignments should reflect **a variety of tasks** that are appropriate to the age, academic needs, learning styles, multiple intelligences, and maturity of individual students.

- Be sure that homework tasks are **varied and clearly focused**.

- **Involve students** in the planning and organizing of their homework assignments when appropriate and within their ability range.
This is an effective way to build ownership and provide meaningful experiences.

- To avoid student frustration, always ensure that students **have the prerequisite skills** to complete the homework assignment independently. If you wish to involve parents, communicate this clearly to the parents and students and be flexible with the results in case some parents cannot participate fully.

✦ Provide **appropriate and timely feedback** for homework. Providing positive and constructive comments validates the homework and reinforces work habits and work completion.

✦ To emphasize the relevancy and importance of homework, **make comments on report cards** about each student's success with homework completion, accuracy, and quality of work.

✦ For major homework assignments or projects, identify in advance the **criteria for assessment**. You may wish to share and/or develop a checklist or rubric that outlines the criteria and levels of achievement with the students. (See Chapter 4: Assessment in a Differentiated Curriculum.)

✦ **Track** students' work completion and accuracy of homework assignments, and **monitor** carefully those students who may be struggling.

✦ Monitor **students with special needs**, including those **new to the country**, who may require a change in the homework expectations.

✦ Work together with **resource staff** to monitor certain students re: their homework and in-class work completion.

Homework Planners

✦ Have your students use a **student homework planner** to regularly record assignments, commitments, and events. These weekly agendas, or day timers, are most appropriate for students in grade 2 and up, but younger students may benefit too from a modified approach.

✦ **Communicate with parents** about the importance of student planners. Ensure that your students and parents understand their responsibilities regarding the homework planner. Figure 11.25 provides a sample letter to parents about their use.

✦ Include a **time for students to write in their planners** each day, for example, the last ten minutes before dismissal from school.

Dear Families,

This year, the students in our school will be using student planners designed to help them develop the important life skills of responsibility, organization, and time management. These planners encourage students to become more reflective about their learning process and progress, and at the same time, invite sharing and positive interaction with family members. We highly recommend the use of these planners as a continuing link between home and school and as part of our school's homework initiatives.

In these planners, the following expectations will be reinforced:

- Students will bring their planners back and forth to school and home daily.
- Students will use the allotted class time daily to record homework assignments, responsibilities, and events.
- Teachers will monitor the planners on a regular basis and provide support as needed.
- Parents will ask to see the child's planner, will review progress, and will sign the planner each day or week (to be determined in consultation with the teacher).
- Parents are invited to ask questions, express concerns, and make positive comments in the planner.
- Growth in skills developed through the use of the planner will be reflected on each child's report card.

Please sign the commitment contract found below and have your child return it to the school as soon as possible. We welcome your input, and if you have any questions, concerns, or ideas to share, please call the school.

Sincerely,

S. Schwartz

Susan Schwartz

- -

Please complete this part of the form and return it to the school at your earliest convenience.

We agree to commit to the use of the student planner for the academic year.
We also agree to contribute towards the replacement cost of any lost planner.

_____

Student

_____   _____

Parent   Date

LM 11.24   **Figure 11.25** *Sample Letter to Parents Re: Student Planners*

✦ Check to ensure that students are recording their homework assignments in their planners each day and initial the planners before they go home. Doing this is especially important at the beginning of the year when you are establishing routines. Later on, you may wish to initial only the planners of certain students each night, or choose a student monitor or a classroom volunteer to initial planners.

✦ Communicate your expectations to parents regarding when they should sign the student planners (every day, week, or month, depending on the student).

◆ Contact parents immediately when you have a concern about homework. Involve resource staff or inform your principal if you anticipate problems. Be proactive. (See Chapter 3: An Inclusive Classroom Atmosphere.)

◆ Consider brainstorming with students, and sometimes with parents, about appropriate **consequences** for not completing homework. These could include the following:

  • Insist that students complete the assignment even after the due date.

  • Negotiate a new due date with students.

  • Arrange for students to finish their homework during class time.

  • Involve parents by sending a note home, talking on the telephone, or meeting with all partners.

◆ For students who have difficulty in using the homework planner consistently, consider taking any of the following measures:

  • Acknowledge students who remember their planners each day and provide positive recognition.

  • Give out group points or use a reward system, such as entering tickets for a weekly draw, when planners are brought back and forth.

  • Brainstorm with the specific student or with the whole class possible consequences when planners are forgotten or lost.

Home Reading Program

◆ Include a **home reading program** as part of your homework expectations. Use the following suggestions:

  • Have a wide variety of reading materials available in your classroom.

  • Create a quick-and-easy-to-use sign-out system. For example, write students' names on library book pockets and display on a poster. Students place their book-borrowing cards in their name pockets each night and return them to their books the next morning.

  • Have book bags available for students to take their books home.

  • Provide support to students when they select books to read independently at school and at home. Figure 11.26 provides tips for students on selecting books to read.

◆ Work with the librarian to teach library skills so students will know in which section of the library they will find specific books.

◆ Use interest inventories and surveys to assist children and their parents in choosing books.

◆ Provide information about authors and illustrators. Highlight an Author/ Illustrator of the Month.

Tips for Selecting Books to Read

- Listen to what other people say about this book.

- Look at the cover, title, and illustrations and predict what the story might be about.

- Look at the table of contents, index, pictures, and captions for information about the book.

- Read the outline on the book jacket to find out what the book might be about.

- Read the first page of the book, and then flip through the book to see if it interests you.

- If you become "stuck" on five words on one page, you may want to consider looking for another book that might be easier to read.

- Look for familiar authors and illustrators.

 **Figure 11.26** *Tips for Students Re: Selecting Books to Read*

◆ Keep a list of all the books read by the class on display so that others can refer to it. Create a "We recommend . . ." bulletin board and include the titles of favourite books and names of authors and illustrators.

◆ Have students track the books read at home by recording the author's name and/or number of pages read each night. (See Chapter 8: Literacy and Language Learning, for sample reading records.)

◆ Schedule time in class for students to informally talk about the books they have read or are reading at home.

◆ Ask for book reports in a variety of interesting formats. (Refer to Chapter 8: Literacy and Language Learning, for ideas about book reports.) Provide opportunities for students to share or present what they have done.

◆ Send home audio recordings of stories or information for students to listen to and follow along. Adopting this practice is especially beneficial for students new to the English language. Consider loaning digital recorders to students who may not have these at home.

◆ Inform your parents early in the year about your expectations regarding reading at home. Encourage parents to read *to* and *with* their children often, even after children are able to read for themselves. Once children are reading on their own, advise parents to talk with their children about their reading. Also, parents should be encouraged to read to and talk with their children in their first language if it is other than English. If they do so, families will continue to value and share their language, culture, background, and experiences. Figure 11.27 shows a sample letter to parents of young children about reading at home.

Dear Families,

Welcome to our **Home Reading Program.**

Research has shown that children will become better readers if they are read to regularly. By reading *to* and *with* your children, you help them to see the importance that you place on reading; you allow them to hear good literature which they may not yet be able to read on their own; and you show them in a concrete way that you care about their learning.

For our home reading program, your child will be bringing books home on a regular basis. Please read the books to him/her and discuss the stories. If the book is easy enough for your child to read, you might take turns reading the pages. Your child may ask for the same book many times — this is a part of the learning-to-read process and should be encouraged.

Happy reading together!

Sincerely,

S. Schwartz

Susan Schwartz

LM 11.26 **Figure 11.27** *Sample Letter to Parents Re: Home Reading Program*

✦ Consider extending your home reading program to other areas of the curriculum, such as mathematics, science, and social studies. These theme-based homework activities can become part of a **Homework in a Bag** program (Schwartz & Bone). The program advocates these strategies:

- Regularly (e.g., once a week) send home with a number of students, each time, a variety of fiction and/or non-fiction books centred around different themes in a bag or backpack.

- Each homework bag can include an ongoing writing journal in which students and parents together read and write responses to the resources provided.

- Materials to write on and to write with, samples of previous students' work, and directions should be included in the bag.

- This program works well if you value the work done for the Homework in a Bag by setting aside class time each week for the students to talk about and show what they have learned, written, and created at home.

Different Types of Homework

✦ Along with your home-reading program (and possibly a Homework in a Bag program), ensure that you vary the types of homework you assign. Below are some examples of different types of homework:

Example 1: Practice-and-review Homework

Such homework reinforces skills previously taught in class and assists in improving speed of recall and accuracy of skills and concepts. With this type of homework, you need to guard against overuse of worksheets. Vary the tasks or provide an active component such as a game or an activity to reinforce skills and concepts. Examples of practice-and-review homework include the following:

- Learn the spelling of new vocabulary by doing activities with a list of words.
- Study for an upcoming test.
- Learn the lines for a play, poem, riddle, or song.
- Play a game to reinforce a skill or concept.
- Choose five questions on this page and complete.
- Complete the odd numbered questions, from question 1 to the end.
- Ask someone to time you for one minute, and see how many questions you can answer.
- Make up five questions of your own, using two dice. Roll and multiply two numbers together. Write the number story (e.g., 5+4=? or 6x4=?) and answer.
- Answer the questions and check your answers with a calculator.

Example 2: Finish-up Homework

When students do not finish their work in class, they are often asked to complete it for homework. The expectation that class work is to be completed helps students develop personal responsibility, time-management skills, and self motivation. However, if a student has finish-up homework every night, it may indicate that the classroom program is not meeting his or her needs and abilities. An overwhelming amount of finish-up homework can cause a decrease in students' self-concept. They may feel inundated with the workload and resent having to finish up at home when they see others who complete work easily and quickly. Thus, it is important to monitor the amount of finish-up homework your students are doing and their rate of accuracy and completion. If a student is spending an inordinate amount of time on homework each night, you may need to modify the homework, and possibly the classroom program, for that child.

Parents can provide the input necessary to highlight that a student is experiencing difficulty with homework or with your classroom program. Encourage parents, through letters, newsletters, homework planners, phone calls, or conferences, to let you know if students are experiencing stress or concerns. You may want to ask the parents of students with a great deal of finish-up homework to record the amount of time spent on homework each night. Work with parents to monitor the time spent at home and establish an appropriate schedule for homework. Set up a system where the student is checked regularly, reinforced, or praised when classroom work is completed in class.

Example 3: Preparation Homework

This type of homework helps students to prepare for an upcoming assignment or to contribute during the next day's lesson. It is usually followed by related lessons in class and can serve to stimulate interest in a new theme or topic. You can assign this type of homework through a letter to parents which can describe the homework as well as provide information about your upcoming theme or topic. Here are some examples:

- Interview someone at home on what they know about . . . .
- Ask three people to explain their understanding of . . . .
- Find an article about . . . in the newspaper or magazine and be prepared to share.
- Watch the program on TV and be prepared to discuss.
- Read this article/chapter/poem and be prepared to discuss . . . .

Example 4: Extension or Application Homework

This type of homework helps students to extend and apply the concepts and skills they have learned in class. Here are some sample homework suggestions:

- Measure your bedroom, and calculate the area in square metres.
- Develop a food budget for a week for your family by collecting newspaper ads to verify prices.
- Complete a problem using the problem-solving strategies we have practised.

Example 5: Projects as Homework

Projects are examples of the extension and application type of homework, but are completed over a longer time period. In projects, students integrate, extend, or apply a variety of skills or concepts learned in class to new situations. Projects can be as varied as the imagination, and need to be meaningful and tied to the learning expectations of your program. Completing projects at home usually calls for much independence, critical thinking, planning, and problem solving. It involves organization, time management, and responsibility in meeting due dates. Projects can also permit an expansion of personal interests and creativity. For example, students could be asked to paraphrase, summarize, and organize information; to interview, take notes, and do research; or to employ creative and artistic skills. A project can be the culminating task for a unit of study, as well as an example of performance-based assessment where students demonstrate their learning in authentic ways. (Refer to Chapter 4: Assessment in a Differentiated Curriculum.) Some examples of project types are as follows: research assignments, reports, presentations, speeches, commercials, plays, dioramas, trioramas, structures, artistic creations, slide shows, multimedia presentations, and video. Projects requiring technology are becoming more common as technology becomes increasingly integrated with and important in classroom programs. (Refer to Chapter 9: Technology in a Rapidly Changing World.)

♦ For any project or major assignment, **establish realistic timelines and due dates**. Keep in mind that students need to practise and learn how to budget their time. Assignments with a short due date (e.g., two weeks) help to teach time management, while lengthy assignments with due dates scheduled sometime in the future create frustration. Throughout the year, all students should do many mini-assignments or mini-projects which involve teaching and application of specific skills, such as labelling, taking jot notes, summarizing, recording footnotes, or creating a table of contents.

NOTE: Major projects of considerable length should be assigned only after students have done many mini-projects and should be monitored at intervals to ensure success, with checkpoints and feedback along the way. You may want to divide the assignment or project into parts and ask to see proposals, plans, and on-going work. Doing this safeguards the student with few time-management skills and helps all students be more successful in meeting the appropriate expectations. Keep in mind too that it is sometimes difficult to determine whether a project completed at home, was accomplished independently or with significant support from the home. Therefore, requiring some aspects of the project to be completed in the classroom is a helpful idea.

♦ For projects or major homework assignments, send home a letter to parents outlining expectations, criteria for assessment, the purpose, timelines, due dates, and so on. Suggest how parents can be involved in positive ways. (See Figure 11.28.)

Dear Families,

April will be an exciting month as we will be working on a new integrated unit, Inventions, which covers expectations in Science, Social Studies, Language Arts, and Mathematics. During this time, we will be researching many different inventions.

For homework, your child is expected to choose a piece of technology in the home, such as a lightbulb, refrigerator, television, or computer, and to research how it was invented and how it has changed people's lives. A project outline, noting timelines for your child's work completion, is due on April 14. The first part of the project, which includes research jot notes, any illustrations, and a bibliography of references used, is due on April 20. The completed written project, including all drafts, as well as the completed invention, is due on April 29.

The students have a chart which outlines how the project will be assessed. This chart has been developed in consultation with the students in the class so your child should be well aware of the criteria.

We would appreciate your support in these ways:

• Talk with your child about his/her topic.

• Discuss the chart with your child to ensure that he/she is aware of the criteria.

• Help your child by taking him/her to the library to find supplementary books about the topic.

• If you have access to a computer and the Internet, help your child search for appropriate sites that might elicit information.

If you have any questions, please call me at (416) 777-8888.

Sincerely,

S. Schwartz

Susan Schwartz

Figure 11.28 *Sample Letter to Parents Re: Upcoming Project*

Homework as a Holiday Follow-up

✦ When students go on a holiday and parents ask for homework, give the following suggestions:

- Keep a journal or log about the people you see, the places you go, and the activities you do. Encourage other members of your family to make journal entries.

- Take photographs and write captions describing what is happening in the photos. Present this as a report of your trip.

- Take video recordings, and be prepared to talk or write about exciting parts.

- Collect souvenirs (menus, plane tickets, artifacts, postcards) and organize them in some way to be shared with classmates on your return.

- Collect bags on your trip and tape them together as a bag book, which serves as a recount or story about your trip. Souvenirs or stories can be inserted into the bags and also shared.

Assessing Your Homework Program

✦ Survey your students and parents to learn about your students' homework habits as well as to find out about the effectiveness of your homework program. The following questionnaire, Figure 11.29, may prove helpful.

✦ Brainstorm with your colleagues, students, and parents for other ideas about homework, the use of the homework planner, and ways to involve all partners in the process.

✦ Reflect on your homework program and consider carefully whether it is meeting the needs, interests, and abilities of each of your students. Act to ensure that homework is always relevant and meaningful as your students practise, review, reinforce, extend, and apply their learning in their home environments.

Homework Questionnaire

Home Reading

- How much time do you usually spend reading at home each night? _____

- When do you usually read at home? _____

- Where do you usually read at home? _____

- How many books did you read this month? _____

- How many books did you read last month? _____

- How many books did you read the first month of school? _____

- Comparing your reading this month with that of the first month of school, what can you say about your reading progress? _____

- What book did you enjoy reading the most this year? Why? _____

Homework Assignments

- Where do you usually do your homework? Why? _____

- What time do you usually do your homework? _____

- How much time do you usually spend doing homework each night? _____

- Who helps you most often with your homework? _____

- What was your favourite homework assignment this month? _____

- What was your hardest homework assignment this month? _____

- What was your easiest homework assignment this month? _____

Homework Planner

- Do you remember to take your planner home at the end of each day? _____

- Do you remember to bring it back to school every morning? _____

- If you answered no to one or both of the above questions, what strategies can you think of to help you improve? _____

- When do you look at and use the planner? _____

- How does using this planner help you with organization and time management? _____

- How has feedback from your teacher helped you to improve? _____

- How have comments from your parents helped you to improve? _____

- Other comments? _____

_____

LM 11.28   **Figure 11.29** *Homework Questionnaire*

Final Thoughts

A sincere commitment to creating community and developing strong partnerships with parents can only benefit you and your students. Ongoing and open communication with parents, a commitment to sharing important information about school processes and how children learn, regularly involving parents and volunteers in your program, and a focus on the homework program as a window into your classroom, will help to establish and maintain strong partnerships. Parents will feel valued and involved in their children's educational life and knowledgeable about the school environment, your program, and their children's progress.

12 "Your Mountain Is Waiting" — Your Career in Education

Teaching is one of the most noble and rewarding professions. It allows you to make a significant impact on the lives of others as you contribute to the future generation by sharing your skill and knowledge. When you interact with students daily, you are giving of yourself in innumerable ways. Your enthusiasm, your positive attitude, and your passion for learning will influence each and every student with whom you come into contact. As you share yourself with the learners in your care, they, too, will experience that exhilaration, that optimism, and that love of learning. Nothing quite compares to seeing a small child's face light up upon first realizing that the squiggles on the page have meaning or when a student cries out, "Aha, now I understand!" When this happens, you will know for sure that you are making a difference in the lives of children!

As a beginning or experienced teacher, you need to maintain a **positive attitude** because teaching can be exhausting and at times stressful. You will have so many things to consider, so many plans to make, and so many processes to master that you may feel overwhelmed. Careful and thorough planning will set your mind at ease and ensure that you have everything you need to be successful and effective. It will allow you to gracefully begin or continue that wonderful professional journey.

Often, teachers new to the profession, as well as experienced teachers new to a school, ask, *"What do I do first? Where should I begin?"* These can be daunting questions, but ones that require clear and concise answers. Each chapter in this book is intended to assist you in answering those questions.

As you set up your classroom, we hope you will use the ideas in many of the chapters to establish the learning environment and inclusive classroom atmosphere, to design a stimulating curriculum, and to assess and differentiate accordingly and effectively to meet the needs, interests, and abilities of all your students. We believe that the concepts noted in the various chapters of this book will work together to help you create your very own dynamic classroom. However, those two brief questions may still remain: *"What do I do first?"* and *"Where should I begin?"* We hope that the content of this chapter will help you address these particular concerns. Successful teachers grow in their effectiveness throughout their careers.

Just as planning a program for your students helps you to chart their course, considering your own needs helps you to succeed in a seemingly challenging situation. We encourage you to strive for **balance** in your life as you juggle the needs of your students, parents, and community with the requirements of your school and school district and your desire for fulfillment in your personal life. Our best advice is to look to others for support. Teaching is a continuous pathway of collaboration and learning as you move from your teacher education program, through the induction process, to effective mentoring and coaching relationships, and to ongoing professional growth as an experienced, knowledgeable, and reflective practitioner.

Whether you are entering the teaching profession for the first time, reflecting on your practice as an experienced teacher, changing teaching assignments, schools, or districts, assuming a new role, or pursuing a leadership opportunity, there are steps to follow, preparations to make, and advice to be sought. All of these pursuits involve an application package and an interview process. In addition, once the position is secured, support, guidance, and collaboration are essential components for a successful career.

Preparing Your Application Package

When you finish your teacher training, change teaching assignments, schools, or roles, return to teaching after a time away, or think about pursuing a leadership role, you will need to face the employment process and that ultimate goal of landing that specific teaching or leadership position. In order to prepare yourself for employment, you will need to prepare an application package to help you stand out as a potential candidate for a specific position.

Your Resume: The first thing to do to prepare for employment is to update your resume.

✦ Your **personal information** is usually at the top—front and centre—including the following:

- name
- address

- telephone number
- email address
- professional website and/or e-portfolio website address if applicable

✦ Consider including these sections or **headings**:

- Education
- Additional Education/Qualifications and Certification
- Professional Development
- Teaching and Related Experience
- Leadership Experience
- Volunteer and Membership Activities
- Scholarships and Awards
- Skills and Interests
- References

✦ As you organize your data on your resume under specific headings, organize it in chronological order with the **most recent first**. Most resumes include the dates for each entry on the left-hand side of the page.

✦ When describing your experiences, consistently use **verbs**. Be consistent in the tenses you use, and use the present tense if you are currently in that position. Some verbs to use include:

- created
- designed
- guided
- implemented
- managed

- organized
- shared
- supervised
- utilized

✦ It is advantageous to include **three references**. Remember to ask permission before including anyone on your resume. Make sure these references give you up-to-date contact information. When selecting possible references, ensure that they will present you in the most positive and enthusiastic light. A "lukewarm" reference can make or break your chances to securing a position. You may want to include references who have different roles—e.g., someone who knows you on a more personal or professional level, a professor who knows you as a student, presenter, team player, leader, and may also have seen you teach in the classroom setting, an educator whom you have worked with in a leadership role or who has observed you teaching or working with other teachers in a school environment.

- Be sure that all your educational experiences are presented on your resume in a **visual** and **organized** way.
  - Leave enough space between words, entries, headings, sections, margins, etc. so that it is easy to read and does not appear to be solid text.
  - Some bolding of headings or certain words make them stand out and add to the visual appeal.
  - Point form is the most common way to list ideas under each heading.
  - Ensure that your text is not too small to read easily, or too large so that you look like you are padding your resume. A good rule is to have your font size at *Times* 11 or 12 or something similar depending on the font you use.
- For the **length** of your resume, consult the district requirements. Often, a two-page resume is preferable for new applicants, whereas someone applying for a leadership position might have multiple pages.
- Ensure that you carefully **proofread** your work before submission. Having a "typo," spelling, or grammar error is not a good message for the interview team.

Your Cover Letter: A **cover letter** accompanies your resume and provides that first impression to the employment team. It should be a one-page synopsis highlighting the strengths and accomplishments that you bring to the position. Remember it is not a duplication of your resume, but rather a snapshot that encourages prospective employers to want to examine your full employment package.

- Begin the body of your cover letter by **identifying the specific position** to which you are applying.
- Ensure that you include a paragraph that outlines your **philosophy** or some of your strong **beliefs** about teaching and learning.
- Highlight **specific skills** that you will bring to the position, such as expertise with technology, extracurricular activities, leadership, personal characteristics and strengths, etc.
- Ensure that you have a **final paragraph**, which usually includes a succinct summary statement, a request for an interview, contact information (phone number and email address), and a thank you for the hiring team's consideration.
- You may want to **create variations** of your cover letter that correspond to, and directly target each position for which you are applying. For example,

you should check the school and/or district's websites to read their mission statement and find out about their areas of focus. You should find out and include the name of the human resources person or school principal for each school district or school for which you are applying and personalize each letter accordingly. Adding this personal touch goes a long way in making a good impression.

✦ Many districts now require an **online application** which can influence what you can submit. Therefore, if you are considering including additional support documents, such as reference letters, testimonials, etc., make sure you check the district's requirements first.

Employment Brochure or Business Card

✦ Consider creating an employment **brochure or business card** to include in your application package and/or leave with prospective employers. This item will showcase your creativity and might provide that extra information about you that might be the tipping point for you in landing a position. This addition to your package helps to make your application come alive and highlights the key points from your resume and cover letter. To create an effective employment brochure or business card, you may want to do the following:

- Include a statement of your philosophy of teaching and learning.
- Make sure you have provided your important information.
- Outline your experiences, education, etc.
- Highlight any other skills and expertise you bring to the classroom.

See Figure 12.1 (and **LM 12.1** on the Text Enrichment Site) for a sample application brochure you might want to prepare.

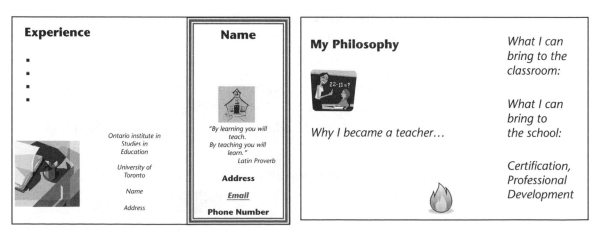

Figure 12.1 *Sample Application Brochure*

Source: Used with permission. Laura Tenenbaum, TDSB.

Employment Package or Career Portfolio

✦ You may consider creating an **employment package**—also called an employment dossier or career portfolio—to leave with prospective employers or to use during the employment process to showcase your strengths and accomplishments as an educator. It should be succinct and organized, usually contained in a thin binder or two-flap folder.

NOTE: A career portfolio should not be confused with an academic portfolio, which usually contains numerous reflections based on academic studies and course work. (See Chapter 4: Assessment in a Differentiated Curriculum.) Each entry in a career portfolio should emphasize who you are as a professional and leader, and target the specific position for which you are applying.

✦ A career portfolio might include some of the following:

- your updated resume
- cover letter
- a quote, poem, image, and/or one or two paragraphs to showcase your philosophy
- reference letters
- lists or evidence of professional development
- an engaging unit plan
- a copy (or first page) of an article or curriculum document you have written or co-written, an abstract of a research study or other educational writing in which you have been involved
- an employment brochure or business card (see Figure 12.1)
- summative reports or evaluations from your principals, colleagues, parents or students
- a "Teaching Reviews" page or selected quotes taken from your teaching reports and evaluations (Siegrist)
- the website address with an invitation to visit your career e-portfolio or website

NOTE: Consider creating a career e-portfolio (see Figure 12.2 and Figure 12.3) where the pages match your hard copy employment package.

Career E-Portfolio

✦ You may also consider creating a **career e-portfolio**, designed electronically as a multi-media presentation or as a personal website. It needs to be equally succinct, organized, and visual, and also should be particularly engaging in order to capture the attention of the viewer. Sharing your e-portfolio will present you as a technologically savvy educator and serves the purpose of showcasing your strengths and accomplishments more visually in the online environment. It has the advantage of being easily accessible to others (e.g., on a CD, USB stick, website, presentation), and can be quickly scrolled and skimmed, especially if the criteria or categories are clearly outlined in the menu which can be seen across the top or along the side of the e-portfolio.

✦ Figure 12.2 illustrates one page of a career e-portfolio. It includes the menu across the top, a photo, a quote, and a "welcome" message.

Welcome   **Cover Letter**   **Resume**   **Reference Letters**   **About Me**   **Beliefs**
Standards of Practice   **Evaluations**   **References**

Welcome to Leslie Siegrist's Professional e-Portfolio

"Our task (as educators) . . . is to help children climb their own mountains, as high as possible. No one can do more."

–Loris Malaguzzi

Thank you for visiting my e-Portfolio. I recently graduated from the Master of Teaching Program at the Ontario Institute for Studies in Education, University of Toronto. I completed a Major Research Paper entitled *A Narrative Journey Through the Landscape of Reggio Emilia*. I am pleased to share that I have been invited to present at two international conferences and a section of my paper will be published in the proceedings.

I am currently looking to join a collaborative, progressive and dynamic educational community. I believe that my relevant experiences and education will enable me to make immediate contributions to the educational experience of your students.

Please feel free to look through this site to gain a better understanding of what I can bring to your school community.

I look forward to meeting with you. Please feel free to email me.

Figure 12.2 *Welcome Page of a Career E-Portfolio*
Source: Used with permission. Leslie Siegrist, teacher.

✦ Figure 12.3 illustrates another e-portfolio which includes the menu across the side, a photo, student work samples, and a centre area which highlights selected quotes from her teaching reports as a "Reviews" page.

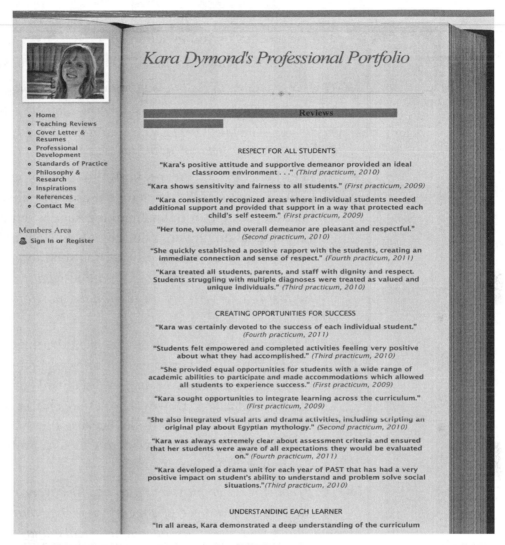

Figure 12.3 *Reviews Page of a Career E-Portfolio*
Source: Used with permission. Kara Dymond, Toronto Catholic District School Board.

✦ A career e-portfolio has the added benefit of allowing you to include **technologically appealing items**, such as these:
  • words that move or flash across the page
  • inspiring and colourful images

- music to capture attention and set the mood
- student work, bulletin boards
- links to files of the work that you did
- links to PowerPoint, Prezi, or other media presentations
- connections to other websites or videos
- videoclips of you in action
- photos or photo albums of you in different situations

NOTE: It is advisable to avoid the use of student or adult photos in your portfolio/e-portfolio unless you include a statement that permission has been granted by parents or adult participants in the photo. This is an important confidentiality and legal issue, especially in the online environment.

✦ Another **benefit** of a career e-portfolio is that you can put it on a USB stick, burn it onto a CD, or include it as a website address in your application package or in an email message when communicating online with a potential employer. You might also want to include a sentence at the end of any email messages that you send to potential employers, such as: *To gain a better understanding about what I can bring to your school, please feel free to visit my professional e-portfolio at* www.xxxxx@iweb.com.

✦ With any portfolio or e-portfolio, its **organization** is extremely important. In a career portfolio/e-portfolio, it is often a good idea to organize according to the province or district's standards of practice or competencies for teachers or leaders. However, you may choose to use other criteria for organizing your specific portfolio, because how you organize it says a lot to potential employers about who you are as a professional and leader and what is important to you.

NOTE: Preparing an employment package or career portfolio/e-portfolio provides that extra piece of concrete evidence that adds further information about your strengths, accomplishments, and who you are as a reflective teacher/leader and professional. This can be especially advantageous when the interview team is deliberating over a short-list of candidates for a position.

Preparing for the Interview Process

It is essential that you thoroughly prepare for the interview process. The more prepared you are, the more information you have about the position for which you are applying, the less anxiety you will experience and the more self-assured, confident, and knowledgeable you will be during the interview.

In preparing for the interview, it is essential to **become as knowledgeable as possible** about the position for which you are applying. You may find that certain school districts have a two-tiered interview process where you might first be interviewed at a district level before being considered for a specific school position. In some districts, you must first be hired to their occasional teacher roster before being considered for a long-term or contract position.

✦ To prepare for a **district level interview**, gather information about their procedures for hiring, areas of focus, mission statement, etc.

✦ To prepare for **a school position**, find out about the specific school's areas of focus, goals, and/or mission statement.

✦ To prepare for **the occasional teacher roster**, do all of the above and also be prepared for questions about the occasional teaching role. (See later in this chapter for more information about occasional teaching.)

✦ If possible, find out who the **members of your interview team** will be in order to determine their areas of expertise and anticipate the types of questions they might ask.

Using the 3 R's Framework for the Interview Process

✦ In preparation for your interview, consider using **the 3 R's framework of "retelling, relating, and reflecting"** (Schwartz & Bone) to organize your thinking and assist you in articulating your responses. Once practised and internalized, this framework can support you in carrying out a coherent, in-depth, connected, polished, and dynamic interview. As you anticipate possible questions that you might be asked, consider how you can retell, relate, and reflect during your responses. (See Figure 12.4.)

Interview Questions: There are different **types of questions** that may be asked during an interview. Four of the most common types are described below, along with suggestions about how to incorporate the 3 R's into your responses.

1. The first type of question poses a scenario for you to consider and can begin with:
   - What would you do . . . ?
   - What would you do if . . . ?
   - How would you deal with . . . ?

Using the 3 R's for the Interview Process

To incorporate the 3 R's as a structure for your responses:

Retell, or describe your knowledge, understandings, and/or beliefs. Therefore, when you retell in your response to a question, you should think about these questions:

- What is the issue, concept, main idea, or area that I need to address in this response?
- What do I know about it?
- What do believe about it?
- What is my philosophy?

Relate, or share your experiences and expertise, as well as make important connections to situations or events in your life. Relating your experiences allows the interview team to see the *breadth* of your experiences and expertise. Providing examples to illustrate that you fully understand each of the points you make adds to the *depth* of your responses and is an important part of relating during the interview. Therefore, when you relate in your response to a question, think about the following:

- What experience have I had in this area?
- What connections can I make?
- What examples can I share to illustrate what I am saying?

Reflect, or project and put yourself into the role or position for which you are applying, and tell how you will accomplish what is being asked about in the question. Speaking from the point of view of someone in the position for which you are applying is an important part of convincing the interview team that you are capable of doing the job, and sharing insights from this role provides a confident and in-depth response. Therefore, when you reflect in your responses, think about these questions:

- What would I do if I were in this situation and role?
- What strategies would I use to respond to this question?
- What actions would I take?
- What insights can I share?

Figure 12.4 *Using the 3 R's for the Interview Process*

Source: Used with permission. Schwartz, Susan, & Maxine Bone.Beyond the 3 R's: Retelling, relating, reflecting, 2nd Edition. Toronto, ON. (pre-publication).

- What strategies would you use to . . . ?
- How would you program for . . . ?
- How will you meet the needs of . . . ?

Example: A student in your class continually interrupts your teaching. *What would you do? or What would you do if* a student in your class is continuously misbehaving and disrupting your class?

The first thing you should think about is, "What is the issue and what do I know and believe about it?" In this case, the issue is classroom management. (See Chapter 3: An Inclusive Classroom Atmosphere.)

Your response could incorporate the 3 R's as below:

Retell: *I believe that it is important to . . .*

- establish a positive, inclusive atmosphere
- be proactive and preventative
- respond to misbehaviours

Relate: *In my teaching experience, I have had . . .*

- students in my class who have interrupted me constantly and I have dealt with them respectfully, without engaging in power struggles, and without embarrassing them in front of their classmates.

Reflect: *In my own classroom, I would . . .*

- use many classroom management strategies, such as proximity in which I would (example), eye contact in which I would (example)

- address the student privately, try to find out what the problem was, reinforce some of the rules and routines established, e.g., mutual respect, set goals together

- examine my program to see if perhaps I was not meeting this child's needs (was he/she struggling with the work, bored, preferred different learning styles, etc.)

- differentiate the program to meet the student's needs, interests, abilities

- consult with the parent because I believe that parents are partners with us in respect to each student

- if the behaviour continued, I would consult with resource staff, the OSR, administrator, school support team, enlist additional support if necessary

2. The second type of question asks you to articulate your understandings about a concept, initiative, or specific content area.

   Example: What are the components of a balanced literacy program? (See Chapter 8: Literacy and Language Learning.)

   Your response could include a **retell** of your knowledge and understandings, but also **relate**/share your experiences and give examples, as well as **reflect**/projecting into the role and talk about your specific actions, strategies, and insights.

3. The third type of question (often called a "behavioural" question because it focuses on experiences and actions) asks you to **relate**/share an experience you have had and comment on your understandings in this area.

   Examples include the following:

   - *Tell us about an experience you have had with* team planning and what influence you had with this group.

   - Give us an example of an incident in which you felt challenged by a student.

   Your response requires you to search your previous experiences and select an appropriate one to address the question (**relate**). To add to the breadth and depth of your response, you should also describe your knowledge, understandings, and philosophy (**retell**), as well as articulate how you handled yourself in the role and how you influenced others in a positive way (**reflect**).

4. The fourth type of question asks you to highlight the characteristics you possess that would make you the best candidate for the position.

   Your response might be: *"In my experience, my colleagues have found me to be . . ."* (**retell**), and then give specific reasons why (**relate** and **reflect**). This response gives you the opportunity to share qualities about you as you relate your experiences with others and through the eyes of others. You come across sounding modest, without the use of a lot of "I" statements (e.g., I did this . . . I am . . . I have . . .).

   ✦ In order to prepare for your interview in a systematic way, brainstorm with friends or colleagues different questions **under broad categories**, such as these:
     • knowledge of child development and how children learn
     • diversity, equity, social action, anti-racist education
     • curriculum and program development
     • assessment, evaluation, reporting
     • instructional skills and strategies
     • technology as a tool for learning
     • parent and community partnerships
     • collaboration/team player
     • contribution to the whole school environment/extra curricular activities
     • professional development and life-long learning

   ✦ To apply for **a leadership position**, the categories might encompass any of the above, as well as some additional ones, including the following:
     • knowledge of adult learners
     • your qualities as a leader (vision, beliefs, insights, skills)
     • conflict management skills, decision making, problem solving
     • coaching, mentoring, staff evaluation
     • team building, staff morale, staff development
     • knowledge of regulations, policies, procedures
     • change, change initiatives, implementation

   ✦ Also, **generate possible questions based on your cover letter and resume**. Be able to talk about each point you have included. Usually the first question asked during an interview is related to your cover letter or resume and is intended to relax you as you talk about something on your resume or cover letter with which you are very comfortable and knowledgeable.

✦ You may benefit by **practising** responding to possible interview questions using the 3 *R*'s framework with a friend or in front of a mirror. You may want to audio or video record yourself to be able to see and hear your responses and reflect on how you can improve. To help structure your thinking while practising, record point-form notes on a chart divided into four columns with the question column at the left, and then Retell, Relate, and Reflect columns respectively (see Figure 12.5). Under these columns, record the points you will say and highlight key ideas. (See Figure 12.5, and LM 12.2 on the Text Enrichment Site for the template.)

Interview Question	Retell	Relate	Reflect
	What is the issue, concept, main idea, or area that I need to address in my response? What do I know about it? What do I believe about it? What is my philosophy?	What experiences have I had in this area? What connections can I make? What examples can I share?	What would I do if I were in this situation and role? What strategies would I use to respond to this question? What actions would I take? What insights can I share?
What would you do if parents were upset about their child's mark on the report card?	*Parents as partners Evaluation/reporting Accountability*		
Tell us about a situation in which you solved a problem with a colleague and how you dealt with it.	*Conflict — difference of opinion, point of view Importance of listening, empathizing, collaborating*		

Figure 12.5 *Practising the Use of the 3 R's for a Dynamic Interview*

Source: Used with permission. Schwartz, Susan, & Maxine Bone. Beyond the 3 R's: Retelling, relating, reflecting, 2nd Edition. Toronto, ON. (pre-publication)

The Interview Process

The interview process can be a stressful time and experience, but if you are prepared and ready, your confidence will increase. Some strategies to keep in mind include the following.

Before the Interview

✦ **On the day of the interview,** dress for success and comfort. Professional attire will make a good first impression.

- **Arrive early**. Having time to relax before the interview is important in presenting a calm demeanour.

- Remember that your **interview begins at the door**. Resist any temptation to "babble" or confide in anyone about your possible state of nervousness.

- Remember a smile, friendly greeting, and a firm handshake.

NOTE: Be aware that not all interviewees and interviewers are comfortable shaking hands for various reasons, such as cultural sensitivity, illness prevention, and general comfort level with physical contact. Therefore, you may want to wait until someone offers their hand first before extending your hand.

During the Interview

- **During the interview** listen to each question carefully, pause before responding, and maintain eye contact. Be aware of your body language.

- Respond by providing a full answer (as outlined by the 3 *R*'s framework).

- **Budget your time** for each question based on the time frame provided for the entire interview. For example, for a 30-minute interview, you will probably be asked five to six questions and need to budget two to three minutes per question. However, a 60-minute interview might have more questions or allow for a longer response time for each question.

- Always speak positively, never criticizing or complaining about a situation.

- Avoid using tentative terms such as: "I might . . . ," "I guess . . . ," "I hope . . . ," "I feel . . . ," and always avoid putting yourself down.

- Ask for clarification if necessary.

- Be enthusiastic, sincere, and positive, and above all, be yourself.

- If you have prepared an employment package or career portfolio for use during the interview, it is a good idea to ask the interview team prior to the start of the interview whether it is permissible to refer to some of your entries during the interview. If this is not doable, you might ask if you can leave a copy with the interview team for their perusal after the interview.

- **When using a career portfolio during the interview**, be sure that it is succinct and visual, with few pages. (A huge binder with lengthy reflections such as what you might have created during a course is not appropriate to be brought to an interview.) Share aspects of your portfolio to support specific questions you are asked, rather than showing each page from beginning to end. Organize it for easy access so that during the interview, you can easily locate and share entries in a natural way. Consider leaving a copy of it with the interview team for them to peruse after the interview.

NOTE: It is usually not advisable to use a career e-portfolio during an interview, but it is impressive if you refer to it and leave a copy of it with the interview team, either on a CD, USB stick, or as a website address on your resume, application brochure, or in an email message.

✦ Towards the end of the interview, you may be asked if you have **any questions or have something you would like to add**. Be selective in the question(s) you might ask so as not to appear as if you have not done your homework about the position, school, or district. Instead, come prepared with a response that will add something that you have not yet had an opportunity to discuss during the interview.

✦ At the end of the interview, thank the interview team for their time and consideration, shake hands (if appropriate), and say goodbye.

After the Interview

✦ **Write down the questions** you remember to help you prepare for future interview situations.

✦ **Reflect on your performance** during the interview. An honest self-assessment helps to improve your interviewing techniques.

✦ At a later date, **ask for feedback** if available.

✦ You might want to write a **letter to the interviewers** thanking them for their consideration.

✦ Continue to be proactive, positive, and patient as you await the decision.

Landing that Position—You have been hired!

After you accept a position offered to you, congratulate yourself and find out more about the position, school, community, and your responsibilities.

Once you are hired . . .

✦ **Celebrate**! Call all the people you care about!

✦ Check out the **district or school website** if available.

✦ Find out about your new school, the neighbouring schools, the neighbourhood, and its clientele.

✦ Obtain a **map** of the school and surrounding area.

✦ Drive or walk through the **neighbourhood** and note the housing, stores, restaurants, post office, bank, malls, community centre, parks, etc.

♦ **Visit the school**, and have someone take you on a guided tour, if possible. Note the following during your tour or at a later time:

- office
- washrooms
- staff room
- lunchroom/fridge
- library
- gymnasium and available gym equipment

- meeting rooms
- storage areas
- stockrooms
- photocopier(s)
- telephone for confidential phone calls
- classrooms

♦ Meet with the **principal** and find out about your expectations, upcoming meetings, grade partners, mentoring program, and possibilities for volunteering before you begin.

♦ Meet all the **staff** in your school:

- the teachers in your grade/ division/team
- administrative staff
- secretaries
- custodial staff
- librarian

- Special Education teacher
- ESL teacher
- guidance teacher
- classroom assistants
- child-care staff, if applicable.

♦ Find out about the **resource staff** in the school district and how you can access them.

♦ Collect **resource documents and materials** you will need:
- ministry or provincial curriculum documents and guidelines
- district policy statements and documents
- commercial resources, guidelines, texts, and student materials available in the school

♦ **Obtain a copy** of the following and review them:
- school handbook (which may include many of the items here)
- school and district mission statement
- fire drill and emergency procedures

- occasional teacher procedures
- district and/or school code of behaviour (discipline, procedures for office support)
- district and/or school homework policy
- schedules for yard duty, gym, music, French, Spanish, or other languages, library, computer lab, preparation time
- list of school committees
- list of co-curricular responsibilities
- confidential staff phone number list
- useful district phone numbers
- parent-teacher groups or School Council information

✦ Find out the **policy and procedures** for your school (some of which may also be included in the School Handbook):

- school hours
- significant dates such as holidays, reporting, and professional development days
- opening day procedures
- school entry and dismissal routines
- bussing procedures
- early dismissal and late arrivals
- recess and yard duty schedule and procedures
- lunch schedule and procedures
- staff meeting schedule and procedures
- assembly procedures
- students staying after school
- student movement in the halls
- assistance from the office for emergencies, illness, or discipline concerns
- Special Education and remedial or support procedures
- safety patrol
- audio-visual and technology equipment distribution and procedures
- teacher and student dress code
- day care information if applicable

- **Research and record the list of acronyms** that are used in your district or school or in education generally. For example: IPRC (Identification Placement Review Committee), LD (Learning Disabilities), SO (Supervisory Officer), etc.

- Find out your **legal responsibilities and the rules, regulations, and procedures** for the following:
  - supervision
  - Special Education
  - second language learners
  - student records and official files
  - student attendance registers
  - report cards
  - reporting to parents

- Find out the **procedures for out-of-classroom excursions or field trips** and if there are any **required field trips** for your specific grade level. (Refer to Chapter 7: Out-of-classroom Excursions—Experiencing the Wider Community and Chapter 5: Designing Your Curriculum.) Consider the following:
  - permission forms
  - ordering busses or other forms of transportation
  - supervision

- Find out about the **budgeting procedures** for your school:
  - Do you have a specific amount to spend for your classroom budget?
  - How much can you allocate for consumables, texts, petty cash?
  - Does the cost of photocopying and paper come out of your total classroom budget?
  - Do you order materials as part of a grade team, division, or school?
  - Do you store your own stock, or is there a general school stockroom?
  - How do you order books and other resources?
  - Is it a good idea to maintain a prioritized "wish list"?

- Find out how to arrange for **films, videos, and software**, and how to gain access to an interactive display board, digital or video camera, and other **technological equipment**.

- Find out if there is an audio-visual or computer **technician** available for assistance in your school or district. (Refer to Chapter 9: Technology in a Rapidly Changing World.)

Once you know your teaching assignment . . .

✦ Clarify what **subjects** you are required to teach and if there are any rotary requirements.

✦ Find out what **preparation time** you might have, and if you are required to provide preparation time for others.

✦ Meet with grade/division partners if available and gather ideas, resources, and sample long-range and unit plans for that grade level. You may also want to call other teachers you know who teach or have taught this grade level.

Once you have access to your classroom . . .

✦ Obtain **keys** to your classroom, and any other keys for cupboards, desks, or other rooms to which you may need access.

✦ **Survey your classroom** and note the entrances, windows, chalk/white boards, bulletin boards, electrical outlets, sink, and security measures in place.

✦ **Determine what you will need** in terms of materials, resources, and equipment.

✦ **Plan your classroom physical environment**—furniture, student desks, storage areas, bulletin boards, etc. (Refer to Chapter 1: Classroom Design and Organization.)

✦ Decide on a tentative initial **seating arrangement** for your students.

✦ Gather any **technological equipment** you will keep in your classroom **on a continual basis**. (Refer to Chapter 9: Technology in a Rapidly Changing World.)

✦ Find out how you can access other **technological equipment and** materials **for periods of time**, and if there are procedures for loan and use. (Refer to Chapter 9: Technology in a Rapidly Changing World.)

✦ Collect and organize some **materials and resources** you will need to begin. (Refer to Chapter 8: Literacy and Language Learning for more information.) Include the following:

• picture books, novels, non-fiction, magazines

• books for a classroom library

• textbooks at your grade level

• dictionaries, atlases, thesauruses

• globes, maps, atlases

• mathematics manipulatives, science and technology equipment

• consumables, such as paper, pencils, markers, notebooks, and art supplies

• technological materials (as above)

- Order any other **consumable supplies or print material** you will need as early as possible. You might need to meet with other teachers at your grade or division level to put in a group order.

- Begin to collect **"found" materials** for classroom use. Visit garage sales.

- Create a **prioritized wish list**. Peruse company catalogues for wish-list materials and keep all ordering information. It is always a good idea to have a wish list available in case you are asked what you need but given a short timeline for ordering materials.

- Decide on **routines and procedures** for your class, including some of the ones below: (Refer to Chapter 3: An Inclusive Classroom Atmosphere, Figure 3.2 (and **LM 3.2** on the Text Enrichment Site) for the Questionnaire for Establishing Classroom Procedures and Routines).

  - washroom
  - entry and dismissal
  - pencil sharpening
  - lost supplies
  - toys and personal items (cards, games) brought to school
  - library visits, book exchange

  - dress for gym class
  - learning stations
  - computers
  - monitors (door, pencil sharpening, boards, distribution of materials)

- Cover your **bulletin boards**, and decide how you will highlight your door and display areas. (Refer to Chapter 1: Classroom Design and Organization.)

- Set up your own **filing system**.

Once you have your class list . . .

- **Find out about your students**:
  - examine student records
  - look at previous work files if available
  - talk to previous teachers
  - talk to administrators and resource teachers

- Note **important information** about your students:
  - total numbers
  - the gender balance in your class
  - names of students and how to pronounce them accurately

- English language learners
- languages spoken in the home
- special needs
- medical information
- custody concerns
- how your students travel to and from school
- if they stay at school during the lunch hour or go home for lunch (you will probably need a signed parent permission form to clarify this)

✦ Find out the procedures used in your school for recording **attendance**.

✦ Think about preparing a welcome letter introducing yourself to parents and students, and/or a student questionnaire for parents to complete during the first week of school (see Chapter 11: Creating Community—Partnerships with Parents).

Once you begin designing your curriculum . . .

✦ Find out the dates of any **significant school events**, including the following:
- curriculum nights
- open houses
- concerts or other special events
- track and field days

✦ Establish a **long-range plan** for the year in collaboration with teaching partners if possible. (Refer to Chapter 5: Designing Your Curriculum.)

✦ Set up an **initial timetable** for the first few weeks. (Refer to Chapter 2: Timetabling.)

✦ Take time to **plan** carefully. Plan your **first day** of school in detail.
- Be sure to include time for students to get to know each other, and begin to engage your students in the process of establishing procedures and routines for your classroom. (Refer to Chapter 3: An Inclusive Classroom Atmosphere.)
- Take your students on a tour of your classroom to highlight the distinct areas in your room.
- Have your students complete a written component appropriate to their ages and stages of development.
- Read aloud and do a response or other literacy activity.
- Ensure that your plans for your first day of school engage your students in activities that are motivating and enjoyable so that they will be looking forward to their year with you.

- Plan your **first week** of school in detail, incorporating more "getting-to-know-you" activities, as well as explicitly teaching social skills, and introducing cooperative learning to build a collaborative, safe, and inclusive learning community. (Refer to Chapter 3: An Inclusive Classroom Atmosphere.)

  - Include opportunities for **diagnostic assessment** to begin to create a baseline of assessment data for each student from which you will develop your differentiated instruction.

  - Equally important during this first week is to firmly establish the **procedures and routines** that you will develop with the students that will allow your classroom to run smoothly for the rest of the year. (Refer to Chapter 3: An Inclusive Classroom Atmosphere, Figure 3.2 and **LM 3.2** on the Text Enrichment Site for the Questionnaire for Establishing Classroom Procedures and Routines.)

- Plan your **first unit** in detail. Meet with the librarian, division colleagues,and outside resource staff to gain additional ideas and resources for your unit. (Refer to Chapter 5: Designing Your Curriculum for support in planning a unit.)

- Plan how you will **assess, evaluate, monitor, and track student work**. (Refer to Chapter 4: Assessment in a Differentiated Curriculum, and Chapter 5: Designing Your Curriculum.)

- Find out about the potential for working with **volunteers** (parents, older students, seniors), the procedures in your school for inviting them into your classroom, and the tasks you might want them to do. (Refer to Chapter 11: Creating Community—Partnerships with Parents.)

- Find out the expectations for an **occasional teacher package or binder** for your school and prepare it in advance so that it is ready to forward to the office when you are absent. (See Chapter 5: Designing Your Curriculum for some possible things to include.)

- **Set priorities**, create a "to-do" or "must-do" list, and check off tasks as they are completed.

Tips for Occasional Teaching

If you are hired into a **long-term occasional position** (in the same class and school for one month or more) or into a **contract position**, you will find the above ideas helpful.

If you are hired onto an **occasional teaching roster**, you will need to be on call each day and ready to teach in different schools, grades, and classes. You may also be eligible to apply for long-term occasional teaching or contract positions. The following are intended to be helpful to you in the role of occasional teacher.

◆ As an occasional teacher working on a day-by-day basis, you will want to be well prepared for any grade, school, or situation. In order to easily find the schools to which you are assigned, be sure to have **access to a map or a GPS navigation system** for directions to different school locations, and have a **cellphone** handy to call for directions if needed.

◆ Be sure to **leave your home early** in order to reach the school in advance to prepare yourself for the school, classroom, routines, program, and plans for the day.

◆ In most situations, the classroom teacher will leave plans for you to follow, either in the office or on the teacher's desk. This provides continuity for the students and the program. Therefore, it is important to **adhere to the plans** as much as possible. However, there may be times when plans will not be available, and you will need to be prepared for that possibility.

◆ Create your own **"bag of tricks"** filled with materials and activities in case you need to quickly plan an activity for students who have finished their required work early, or in case the teacher does not leave plans for you to follow. This "bag of tricks" might include the following:

- a few of your favourite picture books to read aloud
- manipulatives, such as blocks, puzzles, games
- crossword puzzles, games, trivia cards, puppets
- interesting math problems, engaging worksheets, riddles
- "What would you do if . . . ?" scenarios to think/talk/write about
- music, songs, CDs, a musical instrument if you play one
- incentives, such as stickers, certificates, pencils, etc. (Avoid giving out candy or chocolate in case there is a school rule about this and to safeguard against allergies.)

◆ Check day plans for information about students who will need **accommodations and modifications**. Be prepared to work with resource teachers or classroom assistants who may be supporting these students and to adhere to any unique strategies and schedules for these students.

◆ Be proactive and strive to **establish rapport** with all students immediately. Meet them at the door, be friendly, welcoming, respectful, and smile. Remember that you are a role model and the way you treat students is the way you are asking to be treated.

◆ Try to connect with helpful students early in the day to ask about routines and expectations. Take attendance and ask these students to assist, if necessary. Since students are sensitive about their names, try to pronounce names correctly and ask students to self-identify if you think you might say a name incorrectly.

✦ State your expectations clearly, circulate, and give positive feedback often.

✦ Be aware of students who do not engage in their work, finish early, or are frustrated or bored. Here is where your "bag of tricks" might come in handy. Also, using the classroom management strategies outlined in Chapter 3: An Inclusive Classroom Atmosphere, such as proximity, the look, the pause, etc., may prove helpful. In addition, some of the team-building and cooperative learning strategies outlined in Chapter 3 could be useful to get to know the students and to build rapport.

✦ **Write a note to the teacher** at the end of the day indicating how your day went. Let the students know at the beginning of the day that you will be doing this so they will want to be on their best behaviour and be included in your note for positive reasons. This recognition and knowing that there will be some follow-up from their teacher might be incentive for them to cooperate. Here is a list of possible things to include in the note to the classroom teacher:

  - your name and the date

  - comments about how the day went

  - what was completed and what was not accomplished

  - what was marked

  - what newsletters or notes from the office were sent home if applicable

  - any unexpected disruptions to the schedule

  - names of absent students

  - names of helpful students

  - names of students who might have had challenges with work or behaviour and what was done

  - a positive message to end the note

✦ Be sure to visit the office at the end of the day to find out if the classroom teacher is returning or if you are needed the following day.

** A useful resource to use is: *Head of the Class: Making it Work,* Part 3 of "The Occasion to Lead: A Guide for Occasional Teachers," from the Elementary Teacher's Federation of Ontario—see http://www.etfo.ca/resources/foroccasionalteachers/pages/default.aspx.

A Continuum of Professional Growth

When you accept any teaching position, you are entering a profession that highly values continuous lifelong learning. Whether you have taught for many years or have recently completed a pre-service program, your learning will continue and hopefully never end as you continuously reflect on your practice, review what you are doing, and strive to always be the best that you can be.

When you accept a leadership position, you will be continuing your journey as a lifelong learner as you prepare for a new role. Leadership opportunities could include becoming a mentor, assuming the role of an associate teacher for pre-service students, becoming an in-school leader, or taking on the role of a consultant or administrator. You might even consider pursuing master's or doctoral studies and/or teaching in a university faculty program. A career in education affords you many diverse opportunities for growth as you explore different roles and leadership opportunities.

Induction: As you begin your teaching career, whether as an occasional teacher or in a full or part time contract position, or when you change roles and accept a leadership position, you will need support to become the best educator that you possibly can be. Your induction into the teaching or leadership role, whether formal or informal, should provide such support. Investigate whether your district offers an **induction program** which acts as an introduction to the teaching or leadership role, and offers support and guidance in your first few years in the role. The components of an induction program include: (1) an orientation to the system/district/role;(2) a mentoring process; and (3) ongoing professional development.

1. Orientation

Most districts offer some type of *orientation* to their system. This can be a large group initiative or smaller, more intimate gatherings. At an orientation, you should learn about the district in which you will be working, and/or learn about the new role that you will be assuming.

2. Mentoring

When beginning your new position, whether as a new teacher or in a new leadership role, find out what *formal and informal supports* are available to you, including:

- formal mentoring programs

- consultants that have expertise in certain areas

- professional development activities that are geared specifically to your new role

- professional learning communities where you can dialogue, plan, and reflect with more experienced teachers or leaders on an ongoing basis

*NOTE: Mentoring refers to a relationship between two or more educators, where the **mentor** has more experience in the specific role and is there to support the **mentee** in establishing him/herself in the new role. The term "mentee" can refer to a new teacher, or a teacher new to a role or leadership position.*

** A good resource on this topic is *Mentoring Matters: A Practical Guide To Learning Focused Relationships, 2nd Edition,* by Laura Lipton, Bruce Wellman and Carrlette Humbard (MiraVia, LLC).

✦ If your district or school does not have a formal mentoring program, find your own mentor. An **effective mentor** should be:

- supportive
- a colleague with the same or a similar teaching assignment
- someone who has a classroom or office in close proximity to you
- genuinely interested in helping others
- an effective communicator with excellent interpersonal skills
- willing to answer your questions no matter how small
- willing to support you when the going gets rough

✦ When looking for a mentor, or deciding whether you would like to mentor someone, consider the following **characteristics** as important indicators of effective mentors. Effective mentors should be:

• sensitive	• approachable
• patient	• flexible
• sincere	• tactful
• confident	• trustworthy
• encouraging	• confidential
• empathetic	• professional

✦ Ensure that your mentoring relationship is built on the key components of **trust and rapport**. The ability to create a sense of openness and safety allows the relationship to grow and flourish. Four keys to building trust and rapport are as follows:

- the ability to have open and supportive communication
- the assurance that the expectations of both partners are clear and established
- trustworthiness, confidentiality, and professionalism in the mentor
- ownership felt by both partners in the relationship

✦ When establishing a **strong mentor/mentee relationship**, the mentor should consider the following tips:

- Have regular formal and informal contact.
- Build trust and rapport by having open communication and being non-judgmental.
- Provide materials and resources relevant to the mentee's needs.
- Ensure that confidentiality is always maintained.
- Be accessible, positive, and always be available to listen and provide support.

✦ Your mentor can assume a number of roles—that of colleague, advocate, advisor, and coach.

- As a **colleague**, your mentor can help you with the routine tasks of being a teacher, from ordering materials to planning to taking attendance and using the photocopier machine.
- As an **advocate**, your mentor can support you by helping you access resources and materials, and can also intervene on your behalf in different situations with other staff, parents, or administrators.
- As an **advisor**, your mentor can help you with planning your program, or advise you about the nuances of the school (e.g., "Always be on time for yard duty.").
- As a **coach**, your mentor will usually focus on your planning, instructional strategies, and assessment practices. He/she can observe you as you teach and provide you with constructive feedback.

*NOTE: Be aware that there are different mentoring relationships that could be established. Not all are on a one-to-one basis, but could involve a **mentoring team** where a number of experienced staff with specific areas of expertise collaborate to support one mentee. Additionally, an individual mentor could act as a "**broker**", pointing the mentee to other resources or colleagues with expertise in areas in which the mentee may benefit from support.*

✦ Along with a formal mentoring program, **administrators** often act as informal mentors who will provide you with ongoing feedback and guide you in your professional growth. Establish a strong relationship with the principal and vice-principal of your school. Your administrators set the tone and "culture" for the school and will strive to work collaboratively with you. Have a welcoming and open-door policy and invite your administrators to see special events or lessons in your classroom. Ask for and be open to feedback so that you are accustomed to this practice and will be ready for your formal classroom observations for evaluation purposes.

3. Ongoing Professional Development

There are many ongoing professional development opportunities for both teachers new to the profession and experienced teachers looking for change, growth, and leadership. If you inform your mentor, principal/vice-principal, or superintendent about your areas of interest for possible professional development opportunities, they may be able to steer you into appropriate areas of professional growth.

✦ Develop a **professional growth plan**, which might include your career goals and the necessary steps to achieve them. Some schools or school districts may have specific forms to use and processes to follow.

✦ Consider other **professional growth activities** in which you can engage to continue your journey of learning as an educator.

  • Join professional organizations related to your teaching assignments or interests.

  • Read professionally and dialogue with others. Find out if your school has professional resources available for you to read. (Refer to Recommended Resources on the Text Enrichment Site.)

  • Attend workshops, conferences, or seminars, and view webcasts or visit educational websites.

  • Take Additional Qualification or graduate courses, either face-to-face or online, to further your professional growth.

  • Form relationships with teachers outside your school. Build a professional network through involvement with courses, professional organizations, online educational forums, etc.

  • Observe other educators (colleagues, teacher leaders, consultants, mentors, administrators, etc.) in action and debrief with them.

  • Ask other teachers to observe you, and ask for their feedback and insights about your practice.

✦ You may want to maintain a **professional growth journal** to record your professional growth activities and reflect on what you have learned on an ongoing basis. (See Figure 12.6 and **LM 12.3** on the Text Enrichment Site for a sample.)

✦ A **professional portfolio/e-portfolio** can also be used as a reflective tool to document and highlight growth and learning during a teaching and leadership career. This type of portfolio/e-portfolio depends on your purpose and audience, and therefore will look different than a career e-portfolio in format, organization, and content. A professional growth portfolio/e-portfolio can be modified to become an evaluation tool when you use it in the performance-appraisal process with your principal or superior. By using a portfolio and/or e-portfolio in different ways and for different purposes, you will gain an understanding of how useful it can be for you, as well as for your students as a performance assessment tool. (Refer to Chapter 4: Assessment in a Differentiated Curriculum.)

PROFESSIONAL GROWTH JOURNAL

_____
Name

MENTORS AND MENTEES GROWING TOGETHER

TRACKING MY GROWTH

Date(s):_____

Activity/Event:
_____

- Workshop
- Conference
- Professional Reading
- Course
- Visitation
- Observation
- Professional Dialogue
- Other

Highlights:
_____

REFLECTING ON MY GROWTH

LM 12.3 **Figure 12.6** *Professional Growth Journal*

✦ To encourage ongoing **professional dialogue,** you might consider using the content of this book as a basis for discussion during **Professional Learning Communities (PLC)**. (See **LM 12.4** on the Text Enrichment Site for sample questions that teachers and/or administrators may find useful. University faculty may also find these questions of interest when addressing specific aspects of teaching and learning.)

NOTE: Professional Learning Communities (Barth; Dufour; Marzano) promote a collaborative culture as teachers and administrators work together to discuss, analyze, and evaluate what they are doing and how they can improve. The focus is primarily on student achievement and success. In these PLCs, educators are encouraged to read, discuss, and interpret the most up-to-date educational resources and ideas. They often set goals for improvement by closely examining their classroom and/or school-assessment data to plan what they will do, and then later, to see how effective their efforts have been. As teachers and administrators work together in these PLCs and ultimately make changes to their practice, they hold themselves accountable and are able to see concrete examples of positive change.

- ✦ Consider how you might **contribute to the total school or district environment**. Be sure to set realistic expectations for your time and energy in each year and as you engage in new roles.

- ✦ Build in social and family time, and continue to work at **balancing** your personal and professional life. Learn to leave your problems at school at the end of each day, but take your successes and accomplishments home with you.

We hope that the contents of this book and what is included on the accompanying Text Enrichment Site will encourage you to foster that stimulating teaching and learning environment and create your own version of the dynamic classroom. We invite you to read the chapters as you see the need and try out and adapt the strategies and tools to make them your own. Our hope is that we have demonstrated how theory and practice can come together in meaningful, productive, and exciting ways.

Whether you are entering the teaching profession for the first time, reflecting on your practice as an experienced teacher, changing teaching assignments, schools, or districts, or assuming a new role or leadership opportunity, the first time you experience something new can be an exciting and stressful experience, filled with apprehension, exhilaration, and wonderment. We encourage you to take a deep breath, gather all the energy and reserve you have, and jump in.

As Dr. Seuss wrote in his picture book *Oh, the Places You'll Go!* (Random House):

> *You're off to great places!*
> *Today is your day!*
> *Your mountain is waiting.*
> *So . . . get on your way!*

Wishing you all the best in your exciting career as an educator!

References

**We have provided references throughout this text. We apologize in advance if a reference was inaccurately referenced or inadvertently omitted and will do our best to revise any errors or omissions in future editions.

Ada, Alma Flor. 1995. *My name is Maria Isabel*. Bel Air, CA: Alladin Paperbacks. In Chapter 8 and Favourite Children's Literature (on the Text Enrichment Site).

Andrini, Beth. 1989. *Cooperative learning and mathematics: Grades K–8*. Kagan Cooperative Learning. In Chapter 3.

Anderson, Lorin, Krathwohl, David, Airasian, Peter, Cruikshank, Kathleen, Mayer, Richard, Pintrich, Paul, Raths, James, & Wittrock, Merlin. 2001. *A taxonomy for learning, teaching, and assessing: A revision of Bloom's taxonomy of educational objectives, Complete Edition*, New York: NY: Pearson. In Chapters 4 and 5.

Andrade, Heidi. 2000. "Self-assessment through rubrics." *Educational Leadership, 57 (5)*, (13–18). In Chapter 4.

Armstrong, Thomas. 2009. *Multiple intelligences in the classroom, 3rd Edition*. Baltimore, MD: Association for Supervision & Curriculum Development. In Chapters 4, 5, and 11.

Aronson, E., Blaney, N., Stephin, C., Sikes, J., & Snapp, M. 1978. *The jigsaw classroom*. Beverly Hills, CA: Sage Publishing Company. In Chapter 3.

Barth, Robert. 1991. "Restructuring schools: Some questions for teachers and principals." *Phi Delta Kappan, 73*(2), 123–28. In Chapter 12.

Bennett, Barrie. 2009. *Graphic intelligence*: *playing with possibilities*. Toronto, ON: Pearson. In Chapters 3 and 5.

Bennett, Barrie, & Carol Rolheiser. 2008. *Beyond Monet: The artful science of instructional integration* Ajax, ON: Bookation. In Chapter 3.

Bennett, Barrie, Carol Rolheiser & Laurie Stevahn. 1991. *Cooperative learning: Where heart meets mind*. Toronto, ON: Educational Connections. In Chapter 3.

Bennett, Barrie, & Smilanich, Peter. 2012. *Power struggles in the classroom: From start to finish*. Toronto, ON: Pearson. In Chapter 3.

Bennett, B., & Smilanich, P. 1994. *Classroom management: A thinking and caring approach.* Ajax, ON: Bookation or Visutronx Publications. In Chapter 3.

Bezan, Tony. 1974. *Use both sides of the brain.* New York, NY: E.P. Dutton. In Chapter 3.

Black, Paul. & Wiliam, Dylan. 1998. "Inside the black box: Raising standards through classroom assessment." *Phi Delta Kappan, 80,* 139–48. Retrieved on February 20, 2011 from www.pdkintl.org/kappan/kbla9810.htm In Chapter 4.

Bloom, Benjamin S. 1956. *Taxonomy of educational objectives: Handbook 1: The cognitive domain.* New York: David McKay Co. Inc. In Chapters 3, 4, and 5.

Booth, David. 2008. *It's critical: Classroom strategies for promoting critical and creative comprehension.* Markham, ON: Pembroke. In Chapter 8.

Booth, David. 2003. *Even hockey players read: Boys literacy and learning.* Markham, ON: Pembroke. In Chapter 8.

Booth, David. 1998. *Guiding the reading process.* Markham, ON: Pembroke. In Chapter 8.

Boushey, Gail & Moset, Joan. 2006. *The daily 5: Fostering literacy independence in the elementary grades.* Portland, ME: Stenhouse. In Chapter 8.

Boushey, Gail & Moser, Joan. 2009. *The CAFE book: Engaging all students in daily literary assessment and instruction.* Portland, ME: Stenhouse. In Chapter 8.

Brown, Margaret Wise. 1977. *The important book.* New York, NY: Harper Collins Books. (picture book). In Chapter 5 and Favourite Children's Literature (on the Text Enrichment Site).

Butler, Andrea & Turbill, Jan. 1984. *Towards a reading-writing classroom.* Australia: Primary English Teaching Association. In Chapter 8.

Cambourne, Brian. 1993. *The whole story: Natural learning and the acquisition of literacy in the classroom.* Toronto, ON: Scholastic. In Chapters 4, 8, and 11.

Carroll, Lewis. 1865. *Alice's adventures in wonderland.* London, England: Macmillan Company of London. In Chapter 5.

Chappius, Jan. 2010. *The seven strategies of assessment FOR learning.* Needham Heights, MA: Allyn & Bacon/Pearson Assessment Training Institute. In Chapter 4.

Chappius, J., Stiggins, R., Chappius, S., & Arter, J., 2012. *Classroom assessment for student learning: Doing it right, Using it well, Second Edition.* Portland, OR: Pearson, Pearson Assessment Training Institute. In Chapter 4.

Clay, Marie. 2006. *An observation survey of early literacy achievement.* Portsmouth, NH: Heinemann. In Chapters 4 and 8.

Clay, Marie. 2000. *Running records for classroom teachers.* Portsmouth, NH: Heinemann. In Chapters 4 and 8.

Coloroso, Barbara. 2010. *Kids are worth it!* Toronto, ON: Penguin Books Canada. In Chapter 3.

Coloroso, Barbara. 2003. *The bully, the bullied, and the bystander: From pre-school to high school—How parents and teachers can help break the cycle of violence.* Toronto, ON: Penguin Books Canada. In Chapter 3.

Craig, Wendy, & Pepler, Debra. 2007. "Understanding bullying: From research to policy." *Canadian Psychology, 48.* In Chapter 3.

Cummins, Jim. 2000. *Language, power, and pedagogy: Bilingual children in the crossfire.* Clevedon, England: Multilingual Matters. In Chapter 3.

Daniels, Harvey. 2002. *Literature Circles, Voice and choice in book clubs and reading groups, 2nd Edition.* Markham, ON: Pembroke Publishers. In Chapter 8.

Davies, Anne. 2007. *Making classroom assessment work, 2nd Edition.* Courtenay, BC: Classroom Connections. In Chapters 4, 5, and 10.

Davies, Anne. 2008. *Leading the way to making classroom assessment work.* Courtenay, BC: Connections Publishing. In Chapters 4, 5, and 10.

Dewey, John. 1938; 1997. *Experience and education,* New York, NY: Touchstone Publishing. In Chapter 4.

Donahue, Lisa. 2010. *Keeping it real: Integrating new literacies with effective classroom practice.* Toronto, ON: Pembroke. In Chapter 9.

Dufour, Richard. 2004. "Schools as learning communities." *Educational Leadership, 61(8).* Retrieved on February 20, 2011 from http://pdonline.ascd.org/pd_online/secondary_reading/el200405_dufour.html In Chapter 12.

Duprey Stehlik, Tania. 2010. *Violet.* Toronto, ON: Second Story Press. (picture book). In Chapter 3 and Favourite Children's Literature (on the Text Enrichment Site).

Earl, Lorna. 2003. *Assessment as learning: Using classroom assessment to maximize student learning.* Thousand Oaks, CA: Corwin Press. In Chapters 4, 5, and 10.

Education Department of Western Australia. 1995. *Parents as partners: Helping your child's literacy and language development*, part of the *First Steps* series. Toronto, ON: Pearson Education Canada Inc. In Chapter 11.

Education Department of Western Australia. 1997. *First Steps: Writing Resource Book*. Toronto, ON: Pearson. In Chapter 8.

Elementary Teacher's Federation of Ontario. 2011. *Head of the class: Making it work, a supplement to The occasion to lead: A guide for occasional teachers*. Retrieved on February 20, 2011 from http://www.etfo.ca/resources/foroccasionalteachers/pages/default.aspx. In Chapter 12.

Epstein, Joyce L., Ph.D., et. al., *Framework of six types of involvement*. Baltimore, MD: Partnership Center for the Social Organization of Schools. Retrieved on September 3, 2011 from www.unicef.org/lac/Joyce_L._Epstein_s_Framework_of_Six_Types_of_Involvement(2).pdf. In Chapter 11.

Flavell, J. H. 1976. "Metacognitive aspects of problem solving." In L. B. Resnick (Ed.), *The nature of intelligence*. Hillsdale, NJ: Erlbaum. In Chapter 4.

Fletcher, Ralph, & Portalupi, JoAnn. 2007. *Craft lessons: Teaching writing K–8, 2nd Edition*. Portland, ME: Stenhouse. In Chapter 8.

Fountas, Irene, & Pinnell, Gay Su. 2009. *The Fountas & Pinnell levelled book list, K–8*. Toronto, ON: Pearson. In Chapter 8.

Fountas, Irene C., & Gay Su Pinnell. 2001. *Guiding readers and writers, grades 3–6: Teaching comprehension, genre, and content literacy*. Toronto, ON: Pearson. In Chapter 8.

Gardner, Howard. 1983. *Frames of mind: The theory of multiple intelligences*. New York, NY: Harper & Row. In Chapters 4, 5, and 11.

Gibbs, Jeanne. 2006. *Reaching all by creating Tribes Learning Communities*. Windsor, California, CA: CenterSource Systems. In Chapters 3, 5, 8, and 11.

Goodman, Kenneth, & Burke, Carolyn. 1973. "The Language Process: Systems or Systematic?" In Hodges, R.E. & Rudorf, E. H. (Eds.), *Language and Learning to Read, 29–31*. Boston, MA: Houghton Mifflin. In Chapter 8.

Goodman, Yetta, M., Dorothy Watson, Carolyn Burke. 1996. *Reading strategies: Focus on comprehension, 2nd Edition*, Katonha, NY: Richard C. Owen. In Chapter 8.

Gould Lundy, Kathleen. 2009. *Attention, please!: Making assignments presentable, enjoyable, and memorable for all*, Toronto: ON: Pembroke. In Chapter 8.

Grant, Janet Millar. 1995. *Student-led conferences*. Toronto, ON: Pembroke Publishers. In Chapter 10.

Green, Judy. 1999. *The ultimate guide to classroom publishing*. Toronto, ON: Pembroke Publishers. In Chapter 8.

Guskey, Thomas, R. & Bailey, Jane M., J. 2002 *Implementing student-led conferences*. Thousand Oaks, CA: Corwin Press. In Chapter 10.

Hunter, M. & Russell, D. 1976. *Planning for effective instruction: Lesson design*. Los Angeles, CA: Seeds Elementary School. In Chapter 5.

International Society for Technology in Education (ISTE). Retrieved on December 10, 2011 from http://www.iste.org/standards.aspx. In Chapter 9.

Johnson, Paul. 2000. *Making books: Over 30 practical book-making projects for children*. London, England: A & C Black Publishers. In Chapter 8.

Johnson, David W., Roger T. Johnson, & E. J. Holubec. 1990. *Circles of learning: Cooperation in the classroom*. Edina, MN: Interaction Book Co. In Chapter 3.

Kagan, S. 1990. *Cooperative learning resources for teachers*. San Juan Capistrano, CA: Resources for Teachers. In Chapter 3.

Lazear, David. 1991. *Seven ways of teaching: The artistry of teaching with multiple intelligences*. Palatine, IL: Skylight. In Chapter 4.

Lee, Enid. 1985. *Letters to Marcia: A teacher's guide to anti-racist education*. Toronto, ON: Cross Cultural Communication Centre. In Chapter 3.

Lipton, Laura, & Wellman, Bruce. 2004. *Pathways to understanding: Patterns and practices in the learning focused classroom, 3rd Edition*. Sherman, CT: MiraVia, LLC. In Chapter 3.

Lipton, Laura, Wellman, Bruce, & Humbard, Carrlette. 2003. *Mentoring matters: A practical guide to learning- focused relationships,* 2nd Edition. Arlington, MA: MiraVia, LLC. In Chapter 12.

Martin Jr., Bill. 1996. *Brown Bear, Brown Bear, What Do You See?* New York, NY: Henry Holt & Co. In Chapter 8.

Marzano, Robert. 2003. *What works in schools: Translating research into action*. Alexandria, VA: ASCD. In Chapter 12.

McTighe, Jay. 1992. "Graphic organizers: Collaborative links to better thinking." In *Enhancing Thinking Through Collaborative Learning*. New York, NY: Teacher's College Press. In Chapter 5.

Moats, Louisa. 1999. *Teaching Reading IS Rocket Science: What Expert Teachers of Reading Should Know and Be Able to Do.* A Union of Professionals, American Federation of Teachers. Retrieved on September 10, 2011 from http://www.aft.org/pdfs/teachers/rocketscience 0304.pdf. In Chapter 5.

Moline, Steve. 1995. *I see what you mean: Children at work with visual information*, Portland ME/Toronto, ON: Stenhouse/Pembroke. In Chapter 8.

Munsch, Robert. 1987. *Moira's birthday.* 1987. Toronto, ON: Annick Press. In Chapter 4.

Novak, J. D., & Musonda, D. 1991. A Twelve-Year Longitudinal Study of Science Concept Learning. *American Educational Research Journal, 28(1), 117–153.* In Chapter 5.

O'Connor, Ken. 2009. *How to grade for learning, K–12* Thousand Oaks, CA: Corwin Publishing. In Chapter 10.

Ogle, D. 1986. "K-W-L: A teaching model that develops active reading of expository text." *The Reading Teacher, 39,* In Chapter 4.

Opitz, Michael F., & Timothy Rasinsky. 2008. *Round round robin: 25 effective oral reading strategies, Updated Edition.* Portsmouth, NH: Heinemann. In Chapter 8.

Orenstein, Peggy. 2011. *Cinderella ate my daughter.* New York, NY: HarperCollins. In Chapter 3.

Paterson, J. & Rolheiser, C. 2009. *13 Parameters: A literacy leadership toolkit.* Toronto, ON: Pearson Education Canada. In Chapter 3.

Pearson, P.D., & Gallagher, M.C. (1983). *The Instruction of reading comprehension.* Contemporary Educational Psychology, 8, 317–344. In Chapter 8.

Pepler, Debra & Craig, Wendy. 2007. *Binoculars on bullying: A new solution to protect and connect children.* In Chapter 3.

Piaget, John. 1952, 1936. *The origins of intelligence in children.* New York, NY: International University Press. In Chapter 4.

Pohl, M. 2000. *Learning to think, thinking to learn: Models and strategies to develop a classroom culture of thinking.* Cheltenham, Vic.: Hawker Brownlow. In Chapters 4 and 5.

Randall, Kaye, & Bowen, Allyson. 2007. *Mean girls: Creative strategies and activities for working with relational aggression.* Chapin, SC: YouthLight Inc. In Chapter 3.

Rolheiser, Carol, Bower, Barbara, & Stevahn, Laurie. 2000. *The portfolio organizer: Succeeding with portfolios in your classroom.* Alexandria, VA:ASCD. In Chapters 4 and 12.

Scarfo, Nick, J. & Zuker, Justice Marvin, 2011. *Inspiring the future: The new teachers' guide to the law, 1st Edition.* Toronto, ON: Carswell Publishers. In Chapter 7.

Schwartz, Susan, & Bone, Maxine. 1995. *Retelling, relating, reflecting: Beyond the 3R's.* Toronto, ON: Nelson Publishing. In Chapters 3, 4, 5, 11.

Schwartz, Susan, & Maxine Bone. In press. *Beyond the 3R's: Retelling, relating, reflecting, 2nd Edition.* Toronto, ON. In Chapters 3, 4, 5, 11, and 12.

Seskin, Steve, & Shamblin, Allen. 2002. *Don't laugh at me.* Berkeley, CA: First Tricycle Press. In Chapter 3 and Favourite Children's Literature (on the Text Enrichment Site).

Stiggins, R. 2004. *Student-involved assessment FOR learning, 4th Edition.* Columbus, OH: Merrill Prentice Hall. In Chapter 4.

Stiggins, R. & Chappius, J. 2005. "Using student-involved classroom assessment to close achievement gaps." *Theory Into Practice, 44 (1),* In Chapter 4.

Strickland, Kathleen, & Strickland, James. 2000. *Making assessment elementary.* Portsmouth, NH: Heinemann. In Chapter 4.

Seuss, Dr. 1990. *Oh, the places you'll go!* New York, NY: Random House. In Chapter 12 and Favourite Children's Literature (on the Text Enrichment Site).

Swartz, Larry. 2002. *The new dramathemes: A practical guide for classroom teachers, 3rd Edition.* Markham, ON: Pembroke. In Chapters 3, and 8.

Swartz, Larry & Nyman, Debbie. 2010. *Drama schemes and dreams.* Toronto, ON: Pembroke. In Chapter 8.

The Council of the Ontario College of Teachers, 2011. *Professional advisory: Use of electronic communication and social media.* Retrieved on December 10, 2011 from http://www.oct.ca/publications/PDF/Prof_Adv_Soc_Media_EN.pdf. In Chapter 9.

Tomlinson, Carol Ann, & McTighe, Jay. 2006. *Integrating differentiated instruction and Understanding by design: Connecting content and kids, 2nd Edition.* Alexandria, VA: Association for Supervision & Curriculum Development. In Chapter 5.

Wiggins, Grant. 1990. "The case for authentic assessment." *Practical Assessment, Research & Evaluation, 2(2).* Retrieved February 24, 2011 from http://PAREonline.net/getvn.asp?v=2&n=2. In Chapter 4.

Wiggins, Grant, & McTighe, Jay. 2005. *Understanding by design, Expanded 2nd Edition*. Alexandria, VA: Association for Supervision & Curriculum Development. In Chapter 5.

Wolfe, Patricia. 1987. "What the 'Seven-step Lesson Plan' isn't." *Educational Leadership* (February). In Chapter 5.

Yopp, Ruth Helen, & Yopp, Hallie Kay. 1992. *Literature-based reading activities*. Needham Heights, MA: Allyn and Bacon. In Chapter 4.